The Rough **W9-BXX-607**

Mallorca and Menorca

written and researched by

Phil Lee

with additional contributions from
**Suzanne Morton-Taylor, Gareth Rees,
Jan Ogden and Yvonne McFarlane**

ROUGH
GUIDES

www.roughguides.com

Contents

Great places to stay
colour section
following p.112

Island hiking colour
section following p.208

◀◀ Palma Cathedral ◀ Coastal lane with sea view, Mallorca

Introduction to

Mallorca and Menorca

"Nothing could be more beautiful than the views of sea and land. The island rounded in a succession of curves and bays. One headland after another opened out magnificently" wrote the British traveller Charles Wood as he approached Mallorca in 1888. Precious few English-speaking travellers ventured over to Mallorca and Menorca in the late nineteenth century, but those who did were suitably impressed by the beauty of the landscape if not by the islanders themselves, who were generally disparaged as disagreeable peasants. The same conflicting attitudes survive today: for literally millions of tourists Menorca and Mallorca are their favourite holiday destinations, but surprisingly few visitors know anything much about the islanders and neither do they show much interest, which is a real shame. In fact, this easterly section of the Balearic archipelago – which itself includes Ibiza and Formentera – has a rich cultural history and many of its inhabitants still live in the most charming of country towns – Petra, Sineu and Ciutadella to name but three – well away from the teeming resorts of the coast.

It's a dichotmomy nowhere more apparent than on Mallorca, the largest of the Balearic islands, with an unenviable reputation for tacky tourism built on sun, sex, booze and high-rise hotels. This negative image was spawned by the helter-skelter development of the 1960s, which submerged tracts of the

coastline beneath hotels, villas and apartment blocks. In reality, however, the concrete sprawl is largely confined to the Bay of Palma and a handful of mega-resorts notching the east coast, and for the most part Mallorca remains – to the surprise of many first-time visitors – often handsome and frequently fascinating, from the craggy mountains and medieval monasteries of its north coast through to the antique towns of the central plain.

Straddling the sailing routes between the east and west Mediterranean, **Mallorca** was an important and prosperous trading station throughout the medieval period, but it was left behind in the Spanish dash to exploit the Americas from the early sixteenth century onwards. Neglected, Mallorca turned in on itself, becoming a deeply hierarchical

Catalan and Castilian

A Romance language, stemming from Latin via medieval Provençal, Catalan (Català) is spoken by over six million people spread across the Balearics, parts of eastern Spain, Andorra and the French Pyrenees. Franco did his best to suppress Catalan, excluding it from the media and the schools, but, since his death in 1975, the Balearic islanders have reasserted the primacy of Catalan as their language of choice, the most obvious sign of this linguistic renaissance being the replacement of Castilian street names by their Catalan equivalents. Despite the resurgence of Catalan, however, the emigration of thousands of mainland Spaniards to the islands means that Castilian (Spanish) is now the dominant language in around forty percent of Balearic households.

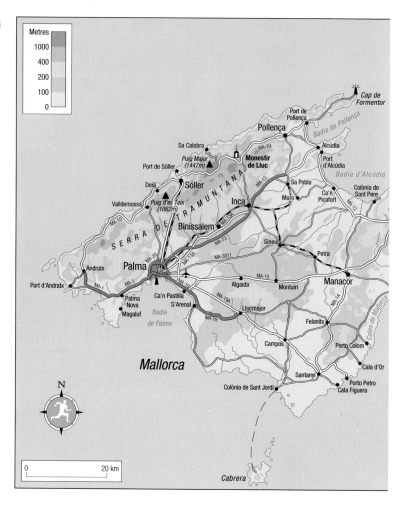

and profoundly Catholic backwater dominated by a conservative landed gentry, who ruled the economic and political roost from their large estates on the fertile central plain, Es Pla. Since the 1960s, however, **mass tourism** has literally stood things on its head. Agriculture, once the mainstay of the local economy, faded into the background and the island's former poverty was all but washed away: **Mallorca's population** of 700,000 now enjoy the highest per capita level of disposable income in Spain.

To the east of Mallorca lies **Menorca**, the second largest and most agricultural island in the Balearic archipelago, with a **population** of just 67,000. Menorca's rolling fields, wooded ravines and humpy hills fill out

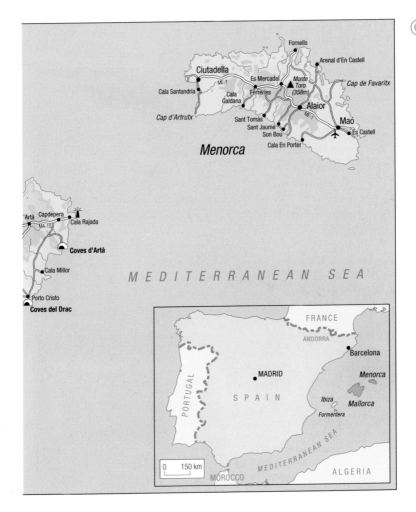

the interior in between its two main – but still small – towns of Maó, the island's capital, and **Ciutadella**. Much of Menorca's landscape looks pretty much as it did at the turn of the twentieth century, though many of the fields are no longer cultivated, and only on the edge of the island (and then only in parts) have its rocky coves been colonized by sprawling villa complexes. Nor is the development likely to spread: the resorts have been kept at a discreet distance from the two main towns and the Menorcans seem to like it that way. Indeed, the islanders seem mustard keen to avoid over-development, pushing ahead with the creation of a chain of conservation areas that will eventually protect about half of the island, including the pristine coves that are one of its real delights.

Where to go

I n **Mallorca**, the obvious place to begin a visit is **Palma**, the island capital, which arches around the shores of its bay just a few kilometres from Mallorca's busy international airport. Palma is the Balearics' one real city, a bustling, historic place whose grandee mansions and magnificent Gothic cathedral serve as a fine backdrop to an excellent café and restaurant scene. Add to this lots of good hotels and you've got a city that deserves at least a couple of days. Indeed, many visitors spend their entire holiday here, day-tripping out into the rest of the island as the mood (and weather) takes them – an easy proposition given that it's only a couple of hours drive from one end of Mallorca to the other. To the east of Palma stretches **Es Pla**, an agricultural plain that fills out the centre of the island, sprinkled with ancient and seldom-visited country towns, the most interesting of which are **Binissalem**, **Sineu** and **Petra**. On either side of the plain are coastal mountains. To the north, the wild and wonderful **Serra de Tramuntana** rolls along the entire coastline, punctuated by deep sheltered valleys and beautiful cove **beaches**, notably Cala Deià and Platja de Formentor. Tucked away here also

Beach life

For all their diverse charms, the main Balearic activity – or lack of it – is **sunbathing on the beach**. At some resorts, like S'Arenal, this is a serious business with acres of roasting, glistening pecs and abs; at others, like Port de Pollença, it's a family affair, involving a bit of sandcastle-building here and a bit of swimming and pedalo-pedalling there.

On Mallorca, the finest sandy beaches are in the north fringing **Port d'Alcúdia**, at **Cala Millor** on the east coast, and, most fashionably – or, in terms of costume, most skimpily – on the **Platja de Palma**, just to the east of Palma. All three of these beaches are flanked by a veritable army of hotels, whereas **Es Trenc**, another long sandy strand on the south coast, is comparatively undeveloped. The rockier northern coast, stretching from Port d'Alcúdia to Port d'Andratx, can't really compete, but it is home to a string of cove beaches, almost invariably made up of shingle and pebble – two of the most scenic being **Cala Deià** and **Cala Estellencs**. On Menorca, there are wide sandy beaches on the south coast at **Sant Jaume** and **Son Bou** and a battery of lovely sandy cove beaches, like those at **Cala Turqueta** and the **Platja de Cavalleria**.

is **Sóller**, a delightful market town of old stone merchant houses that is best reached from Palma on the antique **railway**, an extraordinarily scenic journey. The mountains also hide a string of picturesque villages, most memorably **Banyalbufar**, **Deià**, the longtime haunt of Robert Graves, and **Fornalutx**, as well as a pair of intriguing monasteries at **Valldemossa**, where Chopin and George Sand famously wintered, and **Lluc**, home to a much-venerated statue of the Madonna. The range is also criss-crossed with footpaths and makes for ideal **hiking**, particularly in the cooler spring and autumn. Beyond Lluc, the mountains roll down to a coastal plain that holds the lovely little town of **Pollença** and one of the island's most appealing medium-sized resorts, **Port de Pollença**, which is itself just along the bay from the sprawling but well-kept resort of **Port d'Alcúdia**. In the north, Mallorca finishes with a final scenic flourish in the rearing cliffs of the **Península de Formentor**.

Serra de Tramuntana

Mallorca's second mountain range, the gentler, greener **Serres de Llevant** shadows the coves of the east coast and culminates in the pine-clad headlands and medieval hill towns of the island's northeast corner. Many of the east-coast resorts are overblown, but the pick are **Cala Rajada**, close to several fine beaches, and **Porto Petro**. There are also a couple of easily visited cave systems – the most diverting is the **Coves del Drac** – and the comely hilltop town of **Artà**, close to the substantial prehistoric remains of **Ses Paisses**.

Smaller, flatter **Menorca**, the most easterly of the Balearics, boasts two attractive towns, the island capital of **Maó**, just 5km from the airport, and **Ciutadella**, 45km away to the west. Both towns have preserved much of their eighteenth- and early nineteenth-century appearance, though Ciutadella has the aesthetic edge, the mazy lanes and alleys of its antique centre shadowed by fine old mansions and monasteries, plus a set of charming Gothic churches. Linking the two is the island's one and only main road, the **Me-1**, which slips across the rural interior, passing by the pleasant market towns of **Es Mercadal** and **Ferreries**. A series of side roads connects the Me-1 with the island's **resorts**, the best appointed of which are **Cala Galdana** and the one-time fishing village of **Fornells**, as well as a string of wind-battered headlands and remote **cove beaches**, where there's not a concrete block in sight. The highway also squeezes past **Monte Toro**, Menorca's highest peak and the site of a quaint little convent, from where there are superlative island-wide views. Menorca's other claim to fame is its liberal smattering of prehistoric remains – two of the most important being **Talatí de Dalt**, outside Maó, and the **Naveta d'es Tudons**, near Ciutadella.

When to go

There's little difference between the **climates** of Mallorca and Menorca. Spring and autumn are the ideal times for a visit, when the weather is comfortably warm, with none of the oven-like temperatures that bake the islands in July and August. It's well worth considering a winter break too: even in January temperatures are usually high enough to sit out at a café in shirtsleeves. Both islands see occasional rain in winter, however, and the Serra de Tramuntana mountains, which protect the rest of Mallorca from inclement weather and the prevailing northerly winds, are often buffeted by storms, while Menorca, where there's no mountain barrier, can be irritatingly windy. Reflecting their agricultural past, the islanders have names for the four main winds that blow across their land – Tramuntana, Ponent, Migjorn and Llevant, respectively northerly, westerly, southerly and easterly.

Palma climate

	Jan	Feb	Mar	Apr	May	Jun	Jul	Aug	Sep	Oct	Nov	Dec
Average daily max/min temp (°C)												
	14/6	15/6	17/8	19/10	22/13	26/17	29/20	29/20	27/18	23/14	18/10	15/8
Average daily max/min temp (°F)												
	57/43	59/43	63/46	66/50	72/55	79/63	84/68	84/68	81/64	73/57	64/50	69/46
Average hours of sunshine per day												
	5	6	6	7	9	10	11	11	8	6	5	4
Average number of days with rain												
	8	6	8	6	5	3	1	3	5	9	8	9

20

things not to miss

ACTIVITIES I CONSUME I EVENTS I NATURE I SIGHTS I

It's not possible to see everything that Mallorca & Menorca have to offer in one trip – and we don't suggest you try. What follows is a selective taste of the islands' highlights: gorgeous beaches and magnificent scenery, quaint towns and great places to eat and drink. They're arranged in five colour-coded categories, in no particular order, which you can browse through to find the very best things to see and experience. All highlights have a page reference to take you straight into the Guide, where you can find out more.

www.roughguides.com

01 **Cala Turqueta** Page **266** • Perhaps the finest of Menorca's many unspoilt cove beaches, this *cala* boasts a band of fine white sand set between wooded limestone cliffs and crystal-clear waters.

03 The Mallorcan Primitives
Pages **65**, **67** & **71** • This medieval school of painters produced strikingly naive devotional works – Joan Desi being one of its most talented practitioners.

02 Valldemossa Page **125** • Sitting
pretty in the hills, the ancient town of Valldemossa is home to a fascinating monastery whose echoing cloisters and shadowy cells once accommodated Chopin and George Sand.

04 Cabrera island Page **210** • This austere, scrub-covered islet is home to a
fourteenth-century castle, plentiful birdlife and the rare Lilford's wall lizard.

05 **Cap de Favaritx** Page **241** • This windswept cape, with its bare, lunar-like rocks, is a scenic highlight of Menorca's north coast.

06 **Talatí de Dalt** Page **230** • In an attractive rural setting close to Maó, this extensive site is one of the most satisfying of Menorca's many prehistoric remains.

08 **Jardins d'Alfábia** Page **112** • The lush, oasis-like Jardins d'Alfábia are the finest gardens on Mallorca, their watered trellises and terraces dating back to the Moors.

07 **Península de Formentor** Page **161** • The knobbly peaks and sheer cliffs of this spectacular peninsula backdrop one of Mallorca's best beaches and ritziest hotels.

09 **The Palau March, Palma** Page **68** • The courtyard of this imposing mansion holds one of Mallorca's most treasured collections of modern art.

10 **Hiking in the Serra de Tramuntana** Pages **101** & **143** • Rolling along the west coast, this rugged mountain range holds scores of exhilarating hiking trails.

11 **Monestir de Lluc** Page **147** • This rambling monastery holds the Balearics' most venerated icon, La Moreneta, and is also a great base for mountain hikes.

12 **Ciutadella** Page **256** • The prettiest town on Menorca, with an antique centre full of mazy lanes shadowed by fine old mansions and monasteries, plus a charming set of Gothic churches.

13 Palma Cathedral Page **60** • Dominating the waterfront, the monumental bulk of Palma's magnificent cathedral offers one of Spain's finest examples of the Gothic style, its interior flooded with kaleidoscopic shafts of light.

14 Fornells Page **243** • The attractive mini-resort of Fornells is famous for its gourmet *caldereta de llagosta* – lobster stew – which is on the menu at a string of enticing seafood restaurants.

15 Artà Page **188** • The sun-bleached roofs of small-town Artà clamber up the steepest of hills to one of Mallorca's most important shrines, with the prehistoric village of Ses Païsses close at hand.

16 Palma-Sóller train Page **104** • The antique train that wends its way over the mountains from Palma to Sóller provides wonderful views and serves as a fine introduction to Mallorca's dramatic landscapes.

17 Deià Page **116** ● The coastal village of Deià is an enchanting huddle of old stone buildings set against a handsome mountain backdrop – no wonder Robert Graves made his home here.

18 Maó Page **219** ● Menorca's modest capital has an amiable small-town feel, its tiny centre graced by old stone houses which accommodate laid-back cafés and old-fashioned shops.

19 Eating in Palma Pages **84** ● Palma has the liveliest café and restaurant scene in the Balearics, with a hatful of excellent cafés and tapas bars, where you should be sure to try the islanders' favourite nibble, the spiralled flaky pastry known as an *ensaimada*.

20 Sóller Page **103** ● In a handsome mountain setting, Sóller is an eminently appealing country town of old stone mansions that is just a quick tram ride from the seashore.

Basics

Basics

Getting there

Literally hundreds of flights shuttle back and forth between Britain and Ireland and Mallorca and Menorca during the summer season, and although the pace slackens in winter, there is still a wide choice of flights to Mallorca, if somewhat less to Menorca. Visitors from North America, Australasia and South Africa will need to fly to London, Madrid or Barcelona – or another European hub – before catching an onward flight to the islands. It's also possible to reach Mallorca and Menorca by driving from the UK to Spain's east coast, from where there are ferries and catamarans over to the islands, but this takes two or three days in total.

Flights from the UK and Ireland

From the UK, Mallorca and Menorca are readily reached from London and a veritable raft of regional airports. **Flying times** from London to either island are a little over two hours (2hr 45min from Manchester). Fierce competition tends to keep **fares** way down on flights from London to Palma, but from regional airports the price picture is much more variable. If you strike lucky, a return fare can cost as little as £50, though £150 is more normal, whereas a standard, fully-flexible return can cost up to £400.

From Ireland, there is a good range of flights to both islands during the summer, but out of season you may have to travel via London, Madrid or Barcelona. The **flying time** from Dublin direct to either island is just under three hours. **Prices** are highest during August – reckon on around £200 return from Belfast, €400 from Dublin – but drop a little in the months either side.

Flights from the USA and Canada

There are currently no direct, nonstop flights **from the US** to Mallorca or Menorca, but there are direct nonstop flights from several US cities to Madrid and Barcelona, from where it's a short and easy hop to either island. Often, you'll find it cheaper to travel to London (or an alternative hub city) and pick up an onward flight from there. As sample **fares**, a return, nonstop flight from New York to Barcelona with Delta costs upwards of US$1400, US$1600 from Atlanta to Madrid. The **flying time** on a direct, nonstop service from New York to Madrid is just over seven hours.

There are no nonstop, direct flights **from Canada** to Mallorca and Menorca. However, you should be able to find a fairly convenient routing using a combination of airlines – most likely via another European capital – from any of Canada's major cities. **Fares** from Toronto to a European hub city go for around Can$1100, Can$1400 from Vancouver. The **flying time** from Toronto direct to Madrid is 7hr 30min.

Flights from Australia, New Zealand and South Africa

There are no direct flights to Spain **from Australia and New Zealand**, and you'll need to change planes once or twice to reach Madrid or Barcelona, from where there are regular flights on to Mallorca and Menorca. For **flying times**, count on 24 hours via Asia or 30 hours via the USA, not including time spent on stopovers. **Fares** from Sydney or

roughguides.com

Find everything you need to plan your next trip at ⓦwww.roughguides.com. Read in-depth information on destinations worldwide, make use of our unique trip-planner, book transport and accommodation, check out other travellers' recommendations and share your own experiences.

Melbourne to Madrid or Barcelona are around A$1800–2000, NZ$3000 from Christchurch or Wellington. Another option is to pick up a cheap ticket to London, and then continue your journey to Mallorca or Menorca with a no-frills budget airline (see p.22).

There are no direct flights to Spain **from South Africa**;you have to fly to a European hub to catch an onward plane to Mallorca or Menorca. As for **fares**, flights from Cape Town to a European hub cost around R8600; from Johannesburg, R7300. The **flying time** on a direct, nonstop flight from South Africa to London is just over eleven hours.

Flights from mainland Spain

Menorca and more especially Mallorca are easily reached **by plane from mainland Spain** with regular scheduled flights departing for the islands from a good number of Spanish cities, including Valencia, Barcelona and Madrid. Journey times are minimal (Barcelona to Palma takes just forty minutes) and **ticket prices** characteristically modest, starting out at just €80 for the one-way flight from either Barcelona or Madrid to Palma.

Flights between the Balearic Islands

Three of the **Balearic islands** have international airports – Ibiza, Mallorca and Menorca – and there are frequent inter-island **flights** between Ibiza and Mallorca and Menorca; flights from Ibiza to Menorca are usually routed via Mallorca. There's usually no problem with seat availability, but you need to book ahead during the height of the season and on public holidays. The main carrier is Iberia, which operates between six and eight inter-island flights daily. With Iberia, one-way **fares** between Menorca and Mallorca begin at €50, €60 from Ibiza to Mallorca. The **flying time** between Ibiza and Mallorca as well as Mallorca and Menorca is forty minutes.

By train from the UK

Travelling **by train from London**, it can take as little as thirteen hours to reach Barcelona, from where there are regular ferries to Palma and Maó (see below). The first leg of the journey involves taking a **Eurostar** (@www .eurostar.com) train from London St Pancras

to Paris Gare du Nord. The easiest option on the second leg is the overnight train from Paris Gare d'Austerlitz to Barcelona's Estació Sants. A standard Paris-to-Barcelona return costs £100 and up per person in a reclining seat. For through ticketing, contact **Rail Europe** (@www.raileurope.co.uk).

By car and ferry from the UK

If you intend to travel to either Mallorca or Menorca **by car and ferry from the UK**, you'll need lots of time – a couple of days, maybe more. The quickest way for you and your vehicle to cross the Channel is on the **Eurotunnel** (@www.eurotunnel.com) shuttle service via the Channel Tunnel. Thereafter, it's a long drive across France and Spain to one of the ferry ports that serve the Balearic islands (see below). To save driving time – if not overall journey time – you could also take a car ferry direct from the UK to Spain. There are two main options: Plymouth and Portsmouth to Santander with **Brittany Ferries** (@www.brittany-ferries.co.uk) and Portsmouth to Bilbao with **P&O Ferries** (@www.poferries.com).

Ferries and catamarans from mainland Spain

Three companies – Acciona Trasmediterranea, Iscomar and Balearia (see p.22 for contact details) – operate a dense network of **car ferry and catamaran services from three main ports** on the Spanish mainland (Valencia, Denia and Barcelona) to four ports on Mallorca and Menorca (Palma, Port d'Alcúdia, Maó and Ciutadella). All three ferry companies apply a complex fare structure that takes into account the time of year, your length of stay, your accommodation on board and any accompanying vehicle. That said, all things being equal, the cost of a car ferry or catamaran ticket is roughly the same no matter which mainland ferry port you depart from and which island you sail to. Setting aside special deals and packages, a return ticket is about twice as much as a single. As a **sample fare**, the price of a passenger ticket (without a cabin) from Barcelona to Maó or Palma with Balearia costs €70–100 on a car ferry and €90–150 on a catamaran; cars cost €160 and up. As regards **sailing times**,

Six steps to a better kind of travel

At Rough Guides we are passionately committed to travel. We feel strongly that only through travelling do we truly come to understand the world we live in and the people we share it with – plus tourism has brought a great deal of **benefit** to developing economies around the world over the last few decades. But the extraordinary growth in tourism has also damaged some places irreparably, and of course **climate change** is exacerbated by most forms of transport, especially flying. This means that now more than ever it's important to **travel thoughtfully** and **responsibly**, with respect for the cultures you're visiting – not only to derive the most benefit from your trip but also to preserve the best bits of the planet for everyone to enjoy. At Rough Guides we feel there are six main areas in which you can make a difference:

- Consider what you're contributing to the **local economy**, and how much the services you use do the same, whether it's through employing local workers and guides or sourcing locally grown produce and local services.
- Consider the **environment** on holiday as well as at home. Water is scarce in many developing destinations, and the biodiversity of local flora and fauna can be adversely affected by tourism. Try to patronize businesses that take account of this.
- Travel with a purpose, not just to tick off experiences. Consider **spending longer** in a place, and getting to know it and its people.
- Give thought to how often you **fly**. Try to avoid short hops by air and more harmful night flights.
- Consider **alternatives to flying**, travelling instead by bus, train, boat and even by bike or on foot where possible.
- Make your trips "**climate neutral**" via a reputable carbon offset scheme. All Rough Guide flights are offset, and every year we donate money to a variety of charities devoted to combating the effects of climate change.

a regular car ferry takes eight hours to get from Barcelona to Palma, just over half that on a catamaran; take away thirty minutes or so for Maó. Most services run all year, others have a winter break (usually Jan–March).

In all cases, **advance booking** is recommended and is well-nigh essential if you're taking a vehicle or need a cabin. **Tickets** can be purchased at the port of embarkation or in advance by phone and online.

Ferries and catamarans between the Balearic Islands

The same three companies – Acciona Trasmediterranea, Iscomar and Balearia (see p.22 for contact details) – also operate **inter-island car ferries and catamarans**. There are frequent sailings between Mallorca and Menorca and Mallorca and Ibiza, but vessels linking Menorca and Ibiza are usually routed via Mallorca; Formentera, the fourth and smallest of the inhabited Balearic islands, is only linked by ferry to its neighbour, Ibiza, and the mainland port of Denia. Once again, costings are complicated, but as a **sample fare**, a one-way passenger ticket on a car ferry from Port d'Alcúdia to Ciutadella with Iscomar costs around €40, with cars up to 6m in length costing a further €40–50; note also that car hire companies never let you take their cars from one island to another. **Journey times** are manageable: Ibiza to Palma is four hours by car ferry, half that by catamaran; Maó to Palma six hours, three hours thirty minutes by catamaran; and Port d'Alcúdia to Ciutadella just one hour by catamaran. Most services run all year, others have a winter break (usually Jan–March).

Airlines, agents and tour operators

Agents and operators

ebookers UK ☎0800/082 3000, Republic of Ireland ☎01/431 1311, ⓦwww.ebookers.com.

Low fares on an extensive selection of scheduled flights and package deals.

Mallorcan Walking Tours (MWT) Port de Pollença, Mallorca ☎609 70 08 26, ⓦwww .mallorcanwalkingtours.puertopollensa.com. Small, island-based company operating an outstanding range of hikes. For more details, see p.158.

North South Travel UK ☎01245/608 291, ⓦwww.northsouthtravel.co.uk. Friendly, competitive travel agency, offering discounted fares worldwide. Profits are used to support projects in the developing world, especially the promotion of sustainable tourism.

STA Travel UK ☎0871/2300 040, US ☎1-800/781-4040, Australia ☎134 STA, New Zealand ☎0800/474 400, South Africa ☎0861/781 781, ⓦwww.statravel .com. Worldwide specialists in independent travel; also student IDs, travel insurance, car rental, rail passes and more. Good discounts for students and under-26s.

Trailfinders UK ☎0845/058 5858, Republic of Ireland ☎01/677 7888, Australia ☎1300/780 212, ⓦwww.trailfinders.com. One of the best-informed and most efficient agents for independent travellers.

Tramuntana Tours c/Sa Lluna 72, Sóller ☎971 63 24 23, ⓦwww.tramuntanatours.com. Small but very recommendable company offering guided walks and an extensive programme of adventurous activities. See p.106 for more details.

Airlines

Aer Lingus ⓦwww.aerlingus.com
Air Berlin ⓦwww.airberlin

Air Canada ⓦwww.aircanada.com
Air France ⓦwww.airfrance.com
Air New Zealand ⓦwww.airnz.co.nz
American Airlines ⓦwww.aa.com
bmi ⓦwww.flybmi.com
bmibaby ⓦwww.bmibaby.com
British Airways ⓦwww.ba.com
Cathay Pacific ⓦwww.cathaypacific.com
Continental Airlines ⓦwww.continental.com
Delta ⓦwww.delta.com
easyJet ⓦwww.easyjet.com
Iberia ⓦwww.iberia.com.
KLM (Royal Dutch Airlines) ⓦwww.klm.com
Lufthansa ⓦwww.lufthansa.com
Malaysia Airlines ⓦwww.malaysiaairlines.com
My Travel Airways ⓦwww.mytravel.com.
Northwest ⓦwww.nwa.com
Qantas Airways ⓦwww.qantas.com
Ryanair ⓦwww.ryanair.com
Singapore Airlines ⓦwww.singaporeair.com
South African Airways ⓦwww.flysaa.com
Thai Airways ⓦwww.thaiair.com
Thomas Cook Airlines ⓦwww.thomascook.com
Thomsonfly ⓦwww.thomsonfly.co.uk
United Airlines ⓦwww.united.com
Virgin Atlantic ⓦwww.virgin-atlantic.com

Balearic ferry and catamaran contacts

Acciona Trasmediterranea ☎902 45 46 45, ⓦwww.trasmediterranea.es.
Balearia ☎902 16 01 80, ⓦwww.balearia.com.
Iscomar ☎902 11 91 28, ⓦwww.iscomar.com.

Getting around

On both Menorca and Mallorca you're spoiled for choice when it comes to transport. There's a reliable bus network between all the major settlements, a multitude of taxis, a plethora of car rental firms, plenty of bicycles to rent, plus a couple of very useful train lines on Mallorca. Distances are small and consequently the costs of travel low, whether in terms of petrol or the price of a ticket. On Mallorca, it's only 110km from Andratx in the west to Cala Rajada in the east, and from Palma on the south coast to Alcúdia on the north shore is a mere 60km. Menorca has only one major road, which traverses the island from Ciutadella in the west to Maó in the east, a distance of just 45km.

Hopping from one island to the other is easy and economical too, as there are regular and inexpensive **inter-island flights and** **ferries** (see p.20 and p.21) – though it's advisable to book ahead in July and August. Note also that car hire companies will not

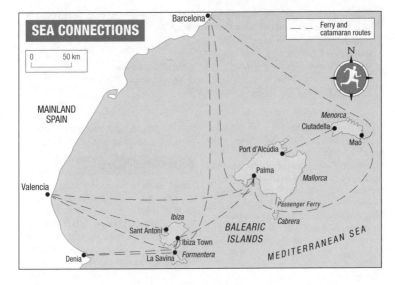

allow you to take their vehicles from one island to another.

By bus

Both Menorca and Mallorca have an extensive network of reliable **bus services** linking the main towns – Palma, Maó and Ciutadella – with most of the villages and resorts of the coast and interior, though in the wintertime (Nov–March) buses to most resorts are scaled back and in Menorca some resorts have no bus services at all. These main bus routes are supplemented by more intermittent local services between smaller towns and between neighbouring resorts. **Ticket prices** are very reasonable: the one-way fare from Palma to Port de Sóller, for instance, is just €3, from Maó to Ciutadella €5. In addition, Palma has its own public transport system, with a multiplicity of bus services linking the centre with the suburbs and surrounding beach resorts (see p.55) – and so do most of the larger resorts, with either bus or electric mini-train.

On all island bus services, **destinations** are marked on the front of the bus. Passengers enter the bus at the front and buy tickets from the driver; alternatively, tickets can be bought in advance at a bus station. Most **bus stops** are now clearly marked in bright yellow and red colours, but a few of the old (and hard to find) green bus stops have yet to be replaced. A confusing variety of **bus companies** operate the various routes on Mallorca, but their efforts are coordinated by **Transports de les Illes Balears** (Ⓦ tib.caib .es/); on Menorca, there are three main bus companies and they fall within the remit of **Transportes Menorca** (TMSA; Ⓦ www.tmsa.es). Island-wide **timetables** are readily available at major bus stations and most tourist offices carry local timetables. Remember that bus services are drastically reduced on Sundays and holidays; for bus company contact details, see box, p.24.

By train

Mallorca has its own, narrow-gauge **train network**. One line, which has old rolling stock and is especially popular with tourists, travels through magnificent mountain scenery on its way from Palma to Sóller (see p.104); the second, a modern line geared up for local use, shuttles across the flatlands of the interior, travelling from Palma to Binissalem and Inca, where the line forks, with one branch nudging south to Sineu, Petra and Manacor, the other pushing on to Muro and Sa Pobla. At the time of writing, work is

Bus and rail contacts in the Balearics

Palma buses: ☎900 70 07 10, ⊛www.emtpalma.es
Mallorca buses: ☎971 17 77 77, ⊛http://tib.caib.es/
Mallorca trains (Inca line): ☎971 17 77 77, ⊛http://tib.caib.es/
Mallorcan trains (Sóller line): ☎902 36 47 11, ⊛www.trendesoller.com
Menorca buses: ☎971 36 04 75, ⊛www.tmsa.es

also underway to extend the line from Sa Pobla to Alcúdia. Both lines have their terminus train stations adjoining Plaça Espanya in Palma (see p.55). The standard **return fare** from Palma to Sóller is €17, €10 one-way, whereas fares on the more modern line are trifling – it's just €3, for instance, from Palma to Inca. The stations on the modern line also serve as starting points for buses to the surrounding towns and villages.

By car

Getting around on public transport is easy enough, but you'll obviously have more freedom if you have **your own vehicle** – most of the more secluded beaches are, for example, only accessible under your own steam. Major and minor roads are very good on both islands, but country byroads are variable, ranging from middling dirt and gravel tracks to the most precarious of dirt trails, which are particularly lethal after rain. Traffic is generally well-behaved, but noisy, especially in Palma, where the horn is used as a recreational tool as well as an instrument of warning. **Fuel** (*gasolina*) comes in three main grades. Different companies use different brand names, but generally *Super Plus* is 98-octane fuel, selling at about €0.90 per litre, and *Super* is 95-octane, selling at about €0.85 per litre; both are without lead (*sense plom/sin plomo*). Diesel (*gasoleo* or *gasoil*) costs about €0.91 per litre. Both Menorca and Mallorca are well supplied with petrol stations; a few are open 24 hours a day, seven days a week, though most close around 9pm or 10pm and on public holidays.

Most foreign **driving licences** are honoured in Spain, including all EU, US, Australasian and Canadian ones. If you're bringing **your own car**, you must have adequate insurance, preferably including coverage for legal costs, and it's advisable to have an appropriate **breakdown policy** from your home motoring organization too.

Some rules of the road

Speed limits are posted throughout the Balearics: the maximum on main urban roads is 50kph, on other roads 90kph or 100kph, on motorways 120kph. Speed traps are fairly frequent on the main highways and if you're stopped for any violation, the Spanish police can (and usually will) levy a stiff on-the-spot fine of up to €1500 before letting you go on your way. Most **driving rules and regulations** are pretty standard: seat belts are compulsory; "Stop" signs mean exactly that; and drink-driving will land you in big trouble. A single, unbroken white line in the middle of the road means no overtaking, even if the rule is frequently ignored; note also that drivers often sound their horns when overtaking. You yield to traffic coming from the right at all junctions, whether or not there's a give way sign; and be prepared for road signs that give very little, if any, warning of the turning you might require. On major trunk roads, turnings that take vehicles across oncoming traffic are being phased out and replaced by semicircular minor exits that lead round to traffic lights on the near side of the major road.

Finally, drivers do not have to stop (and often don't) at **zebra crossings**, which merely indicate a suitable pedestrian crossing place: if you come to an abrupt stop at a crossing, as you might do in Britain, the pedestrians will be amazed and someone may well crash into your rear end.

Car rental

On both islands, there are literally scores of companies offering **car rental** (still rendered in Castilian as *coches de alquiler*) and their offices throng the islands' resorts, larger towns and airports. All of the major international players have outlets, and there are also dozens of small companies. We have provided a small selection in the "Listings" sections for Palma, Maó and Ciutadella, but comprehensive lists of car rental companies are available from the islands' tourist offices. To rent a car, you'll have to be 21 or over (and have been driving for at least a year), and you'll probably need a credit card – though some places will accept a hefty deposit in cash and some smaller companies simply ignore all the normal regulations altogether. However, no car rental firm will allow you to transport their vehicles from one Balearic island to another. If you're planning to spend much time driving on rougher tracks, you'll probably be better off with a **four-wheel drive** (about thirty percent more expensive than the average car and available from larger rental agencies).

Rental charges vary enormously: out-of-season costs for a standard car can fall to as little as €25 per day with unlimited mileage; in July and August, by comparison, the same basic vehicle could set you back €80 a day, though weekly prices are slightly better value and special rates usually apply at the weekend. The big companies all offer competitive rates, but you can often get a better deal through a local rental firm; in this case, however, you should proceed with care. In particular, check the policy for the excess applied to claims, and ensure that it includes CDW (collision damage waiver), applicable if an accident is your fault, and, in general, adequate levels of financial cover. Finally – and this is really annoying – most car rental companies in Mallorca (but not Menorca) now charge you for the full tank of petrol that is in your car when you collect it – whether it is used or not.

Car rental companies

Avis ⓦ www.avis.com
Budget ⓦ www.budget.com
Europcar ⓦ www.europcar.com
Hertz ⓦ www.hertz.com
Holiday Autos ⓦ www.holidayautos.co.uk (part of the LastMinute.com group)
National ⓦ www.nationalcar.com
SIXT ⓦ www.sixt.com
Skycars ⓦ www.skycars.com
Thrifty ⓦ www.thrifty.com

Taxis

The excellence of the islands' bus and train services means it's rarely necessary to take a **taxi**, though they are a particularly convenient way of getting back to your hotel after a day's hiking, in which case you should fix a collection point before you set out – there's no point wandering round a tiny village hoping a taxi will show up. Throughout the Balearics, the taxis of each town and resort area have their own livery: Palma taxis, for example, are black with a cream-coloured roof and bonnet (hood). Local journeys are all metered, though there are supplementary charges for each piece of luggage and for travel at night and on Sundays. For longer journeys there are official prices, which should be displayed at the islands' airport and at some taxi stands. Naturally, you're well advised to check the price with the driver *before* you get going. **Fares** are reasonable, but not inexpensive: the journey from the airport to downtown Palma, a distance of around 11km, will cost you in the region of €20, while the fare from Palma airport to Pollença is about €70.

Addresses are usually abbreviated to a standard format. For example, "c/Bellver 7" translates as Bellver Street (*carrer*) no. 7 and Plaça means square. "Plaça Rosari 5, 2è" means the second floor at no. 5. "Passeig d'es Born 15, 1–C" means suite C, first floor, at no. 15; "s/n" (*sense número*) indicates a building without a street number. In Franco's day, most avenues and boulevards were named after Fascist heroes and, although the vast majority were rechristened years ago, there's still some confusion in remoter spots. Another source of bafflement can be house numbers: some houses carry more than one number (the by-product of half-hearted reorganizations), and on many streets the sequence is absolutely impossible to fathom.

Cycling

Cycling can be an enjoyable way of exploring the islands, though the quiet(er) roads of Menorca are much more suitable for easy family outings than the busy roads of Mallorca. Menorca is also a good deal flatter than its neighbour, which means the going is much easier if less scenically dramatic, but there again ardent cyclists prefer the mountain challenges of Mallorca, where many of the roads are signed for cyclists even though bicycle lanes per se are rare. The Spanish are keen cycling fans, but unfortunately this doesn't mean they will necessarily be obliging on the roads and neither is information readily forthcoming: local tourist offices may be able to provide route information and a handful issue the

Guia del Ciclista, a free leaflet which details key routes. Bear in mind also that cyclists are not permitted into the Sóller tunnel at the end of the Palma-Sóller road. Bicycles are transported free on the Palma-Inca train line and either free or at minimal cost on ferries from the mainland (and between the Balearic islands); you can't, however, take bikes on the Palma-Sóller train and, although some buses allow cycles, most do not.

Renting a bike costs anywhere between about €8 and €14 a day for an ordinary bike, about thirty percent more for a mountain bike. Renting is straightforward: there are dozens of suppliers (there are usually several at every resort) and tourist offices can provide a list or advise you of the nearest outlet; we've also listed a handful in the Guide.

Accommodation

Package-tour operators, both large and small, have a virtual stranglehold on thousands of hotel and *hostal* rooms, villas and apartments in both Mallorca and Menorca. Nevertheless, there is sufficient slack in the system to allow independent travellers a good selection of vacant accommodation for most of the year in most of the islands' villages, towns and resorts, though things can get tight in high season – essentially late June to August – when advance reservations are strongly advised. Outside of peak season – and especially at the large deluxe hotels – it's often worth bargaining over room prices as the posted tariff doesn't necessarily mean too much. Most hoteliers speak or read at least a modicum of English, so visitors who don't speak Catalan or Spanish can usually book over the internet or by phone, but in either case a confirmatory email is always a good idea.

Many hotels and *hostales* have rooms at different prices, and tend to offer the more expensive ones first. Many places also have rooms with three or four beds at not a great deal more than the price of a double room, which represents a real saving for small groups. On the other hand, people travelling alone invariably end up paying over the odds. We've given a **price range** for each of the hotels and *hostales* described in this Guide (see box, p.27) and we've also indicated where an establishment closes

over the winter – a common occurrence in Menorca and frequent in Mallorca.

In **Mallorca** the easiest place to get a last-minute room is Palma, with Sóller and Pollença lagging not far behind, though you might also consider staying at one of the island's former monasteries (see p.28), where there's nearly always a vacancy and prices are very low. In **Menorca**, accommodation is much thinner on the ground, with only Maó, Ciutadella and maybe Fornells likely to have high-season vacancies.

Accommodation price codes

All the **accommodation** detailed in this guide has been graded according to the nine price categories listed below. These represent how much you can expect to pay in each establishment for the **least expensive double room in high season** excluding special deals and discounts; for a single room, expect to pay around two-thirds the price of a double. Our categories are simply a guide to prices and do not give an indication of the facilities you might expect; as such they differ from the star-system applied by the tourist authorities. Note that in the more upmarket *hostales* and in anything calling itself a hotel, you'll pay a **tax** (IVA) of seven percent on top of the room price.

❶ €70 and under	❹ €111–130	❼ €171–190
❷ €71–90	❺ €131–150	❽ €191–220
❸ €91–110	❻ €151–170	❾ €221 and over

Fondas, casas de huéspedes, pensions, hostales and hotels

The one thing all travellers to the Balearics need to grasp is the diversity of types of places to stay – though in practice the various categories often overlap. The least expensive places are **fondas, casas de huéspedes** and **pensions** (*pensiones* in Castilian), further categorized with either one or two stars. Establishments in these three categories are few and far between in the Balearics, and the distinctions between them blurred, but in general you'll find food served at *fondas* and *pensions* (some rent rooms on a meals-inclusive basis only), while *casas de huéspedes* – literally "guest houses" – are often used as long-term lodgings. Confusingly, the name of many *pensions* does not follow their designation: lots of *pensions* call themselves *hostales* and vice versa. As a result, the name isn't always a reliable guide to the establishment's price, though the sign outside usually is (see box below). Slightly more expensive are **hostales** and **hostal-residencias**, categorized from one to three stars. Many *hostales* offer good, functional

rooms, often with a private shower. The *residencia* designation means that no meals other than breakfast are served. No matter the category, **prices** at this end of the market start at around €60 a double room.

Moving up the scale, **hotels** are also graded by stars, ranging from no stars to five stars. One- and no-star hotels cost no more than three-star *hostales* (sometimes less), but three-star hotels cost a lot more, and at four or five stars you're in the luxury class with prices to match. There are also a handful of **hotel-residencias**, where the only meal provided is breakfast, and an increasing number of (un-starred) **hotels d'interior**, mostly bijou family-run hotels away from the coast (hence "interior"). As an average **price**, a double room in a two-star hotel should cost in the region of €80–90.

It's safe to assume that bedrooms will be adequately clean and furnished in all the higher categories of accommodation, but down amongst the budget rooms you'd be well advised to ask to see where you'll be sleeping before you part with any money: standards vary greatly (even between rooms in the same place) and it does no harm to check that there's hot water if there's

Accommodation signage

In theory at least, every place offering accommodation in the Balearics has to carry a **square blue sign** on the outside, inscribed with its category and number of stars. These are as follows:

F	CH	P	H̊	H̊R	H
fonda	*casa de huéspedes*	*pensió*	*hostal*	*hostal-residencia*	*hotel*

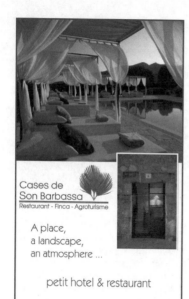

Cases de
Son Barbassa
Restaurant - Finca - Agroturisme

A place,
a landscape,
an atmosphere ...

petit hotel & restaurant

Ctra. Cala Mesquida - Capdepera
Tel. +34 971 565 776 - www. sonbarbassa.com

supposed to be, or that you're not being stuck at the back in an airless box. Note that bathrooms in many *pensions* and *hostales* (some hotels too) will have only showers, not bathtubs.

By law, each establishment must **display its room rates**, and there should be a card on the room door showing the prices for the various seasons. If you think you're being overcharged, complain there and then.

Monasteries

Mallorca's monasteries have run out of monks, so five of them have given up the monastic ghost and now let out empty cells to visitors of both sexes. All occupy delightful settings in the hills or on hilltops, and the majority are dotted across the interior of the island. The **five are**: the Santuari de Sant Salvador near Felanitx (see p.202); the Ermita de Nostra Senyora de Bonany near Petra (see p.184); the Ermita de Nostra Senyora del Puig outside Pollença (see p.152); the Monestir de Lluc (see p.149); and the Santuari de Nostra Senyora de Cura, on Puig Randa near Algaida (see p.187). At all five, it's possible just to turn up and ask for a room, but it's still a good idea to either phone ahead or, if your Spanish isn't fluent enough, get the local tourist office to make a reservation on your behalf. As regards **prices**, a double room at the more rough-and-ready monasteries costs around €22 per night, rising to about €40 at Lluc and €60–70 at Sant Salvador and Cura. The last three have been remodelled and refitted and easily the most popular of the five is Lluc. Reasonably priced food is usually available at these monasteries, but check arrangements when you book. In the same vein, the former **monastic lodgings** above the Ermita de la Victòria (see p.167) have been turned into a small hotel with doubles at €66, making another excellent budget choice.

Mountain refuges in Mallorca

Mallorca's principal long-distance hiking route is the **Ruta de Pedra en Sec** (Dry-stone Route), the **GR221**, which threads its way across the Serra de Tramuntana mountains. It begins in Sant Elm and passes through Sóller before continuing onto Pollença – or at least it will do when everything is sorted out: at the time of writing, access disputes with local landowners mean that a section of the GR221 west of Sóller in between Banyalbufar and Estellencs is inaccessible. To assist hikers, Mallorca's governing council is in the process of constructing **six refugis** (hikers' hostels) on the GR221. Five are finished – *Can Boi* at Deià (see p.118); *Muleta*, near the lighthouse at Port de Sóller (see p.110); *Tossals Verds* (see p.146), in the mountains east of the Embassament de Cúber; *Son Amer*, near Lluc (see p.150); and *Pont Roma* in Pollença (see p.152) – and one is still being built at La Trapa, near Sant Elm (see p.137). Each of these hikers' hostels offers simple but perfectly adequate lodgings in dormitory-style rooms with bunk beds and shared bathrooms. The **charge** is just €11 per person per night with additional charges for breakfast (€4.50), lunch (€10.50) and dinner (€8); picnic lunches are also available (€6.50). Advance reservations are required a minimum of five days and a maximum of two months beforehand either direct with the hostel concerned or on the website ⓦwww .conselldemallorca.net.

Agrotourism – fincas

Many of the islands' **old stone fincas** (farmhouses) have been snaffled up for use as holiday homes and lots are now leased out to package-tour operators for the whole or part of the season. Others, however, can be booked direct or through the government agency responsible for developing rural tourism, the **Associació Agroturisme Balear** (☏971 72 15 08, ⊛www.agroturismo -balear.com). Some of these *fincas* are modest affairs and still a part of working farms, but the majority are comparatively luxurious and many are situated in remote and beautiful spots. They are not, however, cheap: prices range from €80 to €200 per person per night, and a minimum length of stay of anything between two nights and two weeks is often stipulated.

Camping

Menorca possesses **two official campsites**: the well-appointed Son Bou (see p.249), just outside the south-coast resort of Son Bou, and the plainer but very pleasant S'Atalaia (see p.254), near the resort of Cala Galdana. The Son Bou can accommodate about four hundred campers, the S'Atalaia just one hundred – and both take tents, trailer caravans and motor caravans. Although neither has a seashore location, they're both very popular, and in the summer it's best to make a reservation well ahead of time. Prices and specific details of each site are given in the relevant chapters. There are currently no recommendable campsites on **Mallorca**.

Camping rough is legal, but not encouraged, and has various restrictions attached: you're not allowed to camp in urban areas, military zones, parks and tourist resorts. Neither are you allowed to camp on beaches – though there is some latitude if you're discreet – and if you want to camp out in the countryside you'll need to ask locally and/or get permission from the landowner.

Food and drink

Traditional Balearic food, which has much in common with Catalan food, is far from delicate, but its hearty soups and stews, seafood dishes and spiced meats can be delicious. In common with other areas of Spain, this regional cuisine has, after many years of neglect, experienced something of a renaissance, and nowadays restaurants offering Cuina Mallorquína (and to a lesser extent Cuina Menorquína) are comparatively commonplace and should not be missed. Neither should a visit to one of the islands' many pastry shops (*pastisserias* or *pastelerias*), where you'll find the sweetest of confections and the Balearics' gastronomic pride and joy – the *ensaimada* (a spiralled flaky pastry).

While scores of touristy restaurants dish up bland and overpriced pizza, burgers and pasta, or sanitized versions of local favourites, such as omelettes and grilled meats, there are still plenty of places where the food is more distinctive and flavoursome. **Fresh fish and seafood** can be excellent, though it's almost always expensive, partly because much of it is imported – despite the best efforts of the local fishing industry. Nevertheless, you're able to get hake, cod (often salted) and squid at very reasonable prices, while fish stews and soups are often truly memorable, as is the lobster stew – *caldereta de llagosta* – that turns up in many restaurants in Menorca. **Meat** can be outstanding too, usually either grilled and served with a few fried potatoes or salad,

For a **menu reader** and a list of popular **Balearic dishes**, see pp.312–317.

or – like ham – cured or dried and served as a starter or in sandwiches. Veal is common, served in large stews, while poultry is often mixed with seafood (chicken and prawns) or fruit (chicken/duck with prunes/pears).

Vegetables rarely amount to more than a few chips or boiled potatoes with the main dish, though there are some splendid vegetable concoctions to watch out for, such as *tumbet*, a pepper, potato, pumpkin and aubergine (eggplant) stew with tomato purée. It's usual to start your meal with a salad, either a standard green or mixed affair, or one of the islands' own salad mixtures, which come garnished with various vegetables, meats and cheeses. Dessert in the cheaper places is nearly always fresh fruit or *flam*, the local version of *crème caramel*; look out also for *crema catalana*, with a caramelized sugar coating (the Catalan version of *crème brûlée*), and *músic*, dried fruit-and-nut cake.

Opening hours vary considerably. As a general rule cafés open from around 9am until at least early in the evening, and many remain open till late at night. Restaurants open from around noon until sometime between 2pm and 4pm, before reopening in the evening from around 6/7/8pm until 10/11pm. Those restaurants with their eye on the tourist trade often stay open all day and can be relied upon on Sundays, when many local spots close. There are lots of **websites** recommending island restaurants, but the pick of the lot is Ⓦ www.mallorca-restaurants-121.com.

Breakfast, snacks and sandwiches

For **breakfast** you're best off in a café or café-bar. Some *hostales* and most hotels will serve a basic continental breakfast, but it's generally less expensive and more enjoyable to go out. A traditional Balearic breakfast (or lunch) dish is *pa amb tomàquet* (*pan con tomate* in Castilian) – a massive slice of bread rubbed with tomato, olive oil and garlic, which you can also have topped with ham – washed down with a flagon of wine. *Pa amb*

oli (bread rubbed with olive oil) arrives in similar style, but dispenses with the tomato. If that sounds like gastronomic madness, other breakfast standbys include *torradas* (*tostadas*; toasted rolls) with oil or butter and jam, and *xocolata amb xurros* (*chocolate con churros*) – long, fried tubular doughnuts that you dip into thick drinking chocolate. Most places also serve *ou ferrat* (*huevo frito*; fried egg) and cold *truita* (*tortilla*; omelette), both of which make a fortifying breakfast.

Coffee (see p.33) and **pastries** (*pastas*), particularly croissants and doughnuts, are available at some bars and cafés; for a wider selection of cakes, head for a *pastisseria* (pastry shop) or *forn* (bakery). These often sell a wide array of appetizing baked goods besides the obvious bread, croissants and *ensaimadas*. Some bars specialize in **sandwiches** (*bocadillos*), usually outsize affairs in French bread served either hot or cold, or you can get them prepared – or buy the materials to do so – at grocery shops. Menorcan cheese (*formatge*), commonly known as *queso Mahón,* is a popular filling – the best is hard and has a rind.

Tapas and racions

Tapas are small snacks of three or four chunks of fish, meat or vegetables, cooked in a sauce or served with a dollop of salad. Traditionally, they were provided free to accompany a drink, but these days you have to pay for anything more than a few olives, though a single helping rarely costs more than €8 unless you're somewhere very flashy. **Racions** (*raciones* in Castilian) are bigger portions of the same, served with bread and usually enough in themselves to make a light meal; they cost around €10. The more people you're with, of course, the better: half-a-dozen or so different dishes can make a varied and filling meal for three or four people.

One of the advantages of eating tapas in bars is that you are able to experiment. Most places have food laid out on the counter, so you can see what's available and order by pointing without necessarily knowing the names; others have blackboards.

Full meals

Meals are usually eaten in a **café or restaurant**, though the distinction between the two, particularly at the cheaper end of the market, is often very blurred. In similar fashion, cafés blend seamlessly into café-bars and bars, almost all of which serve at least some food. That said, the average price of an average meal in an average establishment does slide down the scale from restaurant to café to bar. At a café, something like egg and steak, chicken and chips, or *calamars* and salad will generally cost in the region of €8, excluding drink, whereas the price of a main course at a good-quality restaurant averages about €17. Restaurants run from simple affairs with formica tables to expense-account palaces. Many have a daily set menu – the lunchtime **menú del día** – which consists of two, three or four courses, including bread, wine and service, and usually costs €10–20.

In all but the most rock-bottom establishments it's customary to leave a small **tip**; ten to fifteen percent is generally regarded as sufficient. The other thing to take account of is **IVA**, a sales tax of seven percent, which is either included in the prices (in which case it should say so on the menu) or added to your bill at the end.

Vegetarian and vegan

Palma has a couple of **vegetarian** restaurants and most of the resorts are accustomed to having vegetarian guests, but elsewhere the choice isn't so great and is essentially confined to large salads, fried eggs and chips or omelettes. If you eat fish, however, you'll find seafood almost everywhere.

If you're a **vegan**, you'll no doubt come prepared to cook your own food at least some of the time. That said, some restaurant salads and vegetable dishes are vegan – like *espinacs a la Catalana* (spinach, pine nuts

---

If you're a **vegetarian**, try in Catalan "Sóc vegetarià/ana – es pot menjar alguna cosa sense carn?" (I'm a vegetarian – is there anything without meat?). In Castilian, that's "Soy vegetariano/a – hay algo sin carne?" Alternatively, you may be better understood if you simply resort to the Catalan "No puc menjar carn" (I can't eat meat).

---

and raisins) and *escalivada* (aubergine/eggplant and peppers) – but they're few and far between. Fruit and nuts are widely available, and most pizza restaurants will serve you a vegetarian pizza without cheese: ask for *vegetal sense formatge* (in Castilian, *vegetal sin queso*).

For vegetarian and vegan **shopping**, use the markets – where you can buy ready-cooked lentils and beans, and pasta – or look out for shops marked *Aliments regim* (*dietética* in Castilian), which sell wholefoods, soya milk and desserts, and so on.

Drinking and drinks

You'll do most of your everyday **drinking** – from morning coffee to a nightcap – in a **bar or café**. Bars situated in old wine cellars are sometimes called *cellers* or *tavernas*; a *bodega* traditionally specializes in wine. **Opening hours** are difficult to pin down, but you should have little trouble in getting a drink somewhere in Palma between noon and 2am or even 3am. Elsewhere you're OK until at least 11pm, sometimes midnight. The islands' night-clubs tend to close by 3am or 4am. Some bars close on Sundays, and don't expect much to be happening in the resorts out of season.

Wine

Wine (*vi* in Catalan, *vino* in Castilian) is the invariable accompaniment to every meal and is, as a general rule, inexpensive whether it be red (*negre/tinto*), white (*blanc/blanco*) or rosé (*rosada/rosado*). What's more, if you're having the *menú del día*, house wine will be included in the price – you'll get a third- to a half-litre per person.

On both Mallorca and Menorca, all the more expensive restaurants, supermarkets, and some of the cheaper cafés and restaurants carry a good selection of **Spanish wines**. The thing to check for is the appellation **Denominació d'Origen (DO)**, which indicates the wine has been passed as being of sufficiently high quality by the industry's watchdog, the Instíluto Nacional de Denominaciónes d'Origen (INDO). Over forty regions of Spain currently carry DO status, including the north central region that

Mallorcan wine

The Balearics became a major **wine producer** in classical times, but it was the Moors who finessed the sweet "Malvasia" wine – akin to Madeira – that was long one of the islands' main exports. This all ended in the late nineteenth century when the islands' vineyards were devastated by **phylloxera**, whose root-eating activities changed the course of Spanish wine history. The small yellow phylloxera aphid, about 1mm long, was indigenous to eastern North America. It first appeared in Spain in 1878, carried either in soil or on agricultural tools and footwear, and in the space of twenty years it destroyed Spain's existing vine stock and made thousands bankrupt. Indeed, vine cultivation has never re-established itself on Ibiza or Menorca, and Mallorcan wines, produced from newly imported vines, were long regarded as being of only average quality.

During the late 1980s, however, a concerted effort was made to raise the standard of Mallorcan wine-making, driven on one side by the tourist industry and on the other by local producers who realized that they could prosper by producing wine of international quality. This meant new methods and new equipment, and the investment began in earnest, especially in and around **Binissalem**, a small town northeast of Palma (see p.179). The results were encouraging and, following vigorous local campaigning, Binissalem was justifiably awarded its Denominació d'Origen credentials in 1991. Binissalem remains Mallorca's leading wine, but its success has inspired others and in 2000 a second Denominació d'Origen was granted, **Pla i Llevant**, covering the central and eastern part of the island from Algaida to Felanitx.

Widely available throughout Mallorca, **red Binissalem** is a robust and aromatic wine made predominantly of the local mantonegro grape. It is not unlike Rioja, but it has a distinctly local character, suggesting cocoa and strawberries. The best producer of the wine is **Franja Roja**, who make the **José Ferrer** brand – well worth looking out for, with prices starting at around €7 per bottle, or €15 for the superior varieties; you can also visit their Binissalem winery (see p.180). White and rosé **Binissalem** struggle to reach the same standard as the red, but the **Binissalem Blanco** made by **Herederos de Ribas** is a lively and fruity white that goes well with fish. Names to look out for with the **Pla i Llevant** designation include the white wines of **Miquel Oliver**, whose Petra winery is open to the public (see p.183), and the whites and reds of **Miquel Gelabert** and **Toni Gelabert** from Manacor. Also around the island are various country wineries making inexpensive and unpretentious wine predominantly for local consumption. The best places to sample these local, coarser wines is in the *cellers* and bars of the country towns of the interior – and the best of them carry the label **Vin de la Terra**.

produces Spain's most famous and widely distributed **red wine**, **Rioja**, which is hard to match for reliability and finesse. The names to look for in red Rioja include Martínez-Bujanda, Tondonia and Monte Real. The **region of Navarra** also produces excellent wine using similar techniques and grape varieties at a fraction of the price of Rioja. The labels to watch for here are Chivite and Señorío de Sarría.

Spain's **white wines** have not enjoyed the same reputation as the reds, but the country's **sparkling wines** are big sellers, their popularity built on the performance of two producers, Freixenet and Codorniú, which hail from a small area west of Barcelona. Local grape varieties are used and the best examples, known as **cava**, are made by the same double-fermentation process as is used in the production of champagne.

For a comprehensive introduction to the wines of Spain with precise definitions of all the various Denominaciónes d'Origen (DOs), including Mallorca's two DOs, Pla i Llevant and Binissalem, check out Ⓦwww.winesfromspain.com.

Sherry, brandy, gin and beer

Fortified wines and spirits in the Balearics are the same as those found throughout Spain. The classic Andalucian wine, **sherry** – *vino de Jerez* – is served chilled or at room temperature, a perfect drink to wash down tapas. The main distinctions are between *fino* or *jerez seco* (dry sherry), *amontillado* (medium), and *oloroso* or *jerez dulce* (sweet); these are the terms you should use to order. In mid-afternoon – or even at breakfast – many islanders take a *copa* of **liqueur** with their coffee. The best – certainly to put *in* your coffee – is **coñac**, excellent Spanish brandy, mostly from the south and often deceptively smooth. If you want a brandy from Mallorca, try the mellow but hard-hitting Suau, or look for Torres, from Catalunya. Most other spirits are ordered by brand name, too, since there are generally cheaper Spanish equivalents for standard imports. Larios **gin** from Málaga, for instance, is about half the price of Gordons, but around two-thirds the strength and a good deal rougher. The Menorcans, who learnt the art of gin-making from the British, still produce their own versions, in particular the waspish Xoriguer. Always specify *nacional* to avoid getting an expensive foreign brand.

Almost any **mixed drink** seems to be collectively known as a *Cuba libre* or *cubata*, though strictly speaking this should refer only to rum and Coke. For mixers, ask for orange juice (*suc de taronja* in Catalan), lemon (*llimona*) or tonic (*tònica*).

Pilsner-type beer, **cervesa** (more usually seen in Castilian as *cerveza*), is generally pretty good, though more expensive than wine. The two main brands you'll see everywhere are San Miguel and Estrella. Beer generally comes in 300ml bottles or, for a little bit less, on tap: a small glass of draught beer is a *cana*, a larger glass a *cana gran*. Equally refreshing, though often deceptively strong, is **sangría**, a wine-and-fruit punch, which you'll come across at *festas* and in tourist resorts.

Soft drinks

Soft drinks are much the same as anywhere in the world, but one local favourite to try is *orxata* (*horchata* in Castilian) – a cold milky drink made from tiger nuts. Also, be sure to try a *granissat*, or iced fruit-squash; popular flavours are *granissat de llimona* or *granissat de café*. You can get these drinks from **orxaterias and gelaterias** (ice cream parlours; *heladerías* in Castilian).

Although you can drink the **water** almost everywhere, bottled water – *aigua mineral* – is ubiquitous, either sparkling (*amb gas*) or still (*sense gas*).

Coffee and tea

Coffee is invariably espresso, slightly bitter and, unless you specify otherwise, served black (*café sol*). A slightly weaker large black coffee is called a *café americano*. If you want it white ask for *café cortado* (small cup with a drop of milk) or *café amb llet* (*café con leche* in Castilian) made with hot milk. For a large cup ask for a *gran*. Black coffee is also frequently mixed with brandy, cognac or whisky, all such concoctions termed *carajillo*; a liqueur mixed with white coffee is a *trifásico*. **Decaffeinated coffee** (*descafeinat*) is increasingly available, though in fairly undistinguished sachet form.

Tea (*te*) comes without milk unless you ask for it, and is often weak and insipid. If you do ask for milk, chances are it'll be hot and UHT, so your tea isn't going to taste much like the real thing. Better are the infusions that you can get in most bars, such as mint (*menta*), camomile (*camamilla*) and lime (*tiller*).

The media

English-language newspapers and magazines are widely available in both Mallorca and Menorca, and most hotel (if not *hostal*) rooms have satellite TV.

Newspapers and magazines

British and other European **newspapers**, as well as *USA Today* and the *International Herald Tribune*, are all widely available in the resort areas and larger towns of Mallorca and Menorca. These are supplemented by a hotchpotch of locally produced English papers and journals, easily the most informative of which is the enjoyably chatty *Majorca Daily Bulletin*. The online edition is available at ⓦ www.majorcadailybulletin.es.

Spain is awash with glossy **magazines**, both native to the country and Spanish versions of international periodicals. And, of course, Spain is the home of *Hola* – the original of *Hello*, heaven help us.

Television and radio

Spaniards love their **television**, and consequently you'll catch more of it than you might expect sitting in bars and cafés. On the whole it's hardly riveting stuff, the bulk being a mildly entertaining mixture of kitsch game shows and foreign-language films and TV series dubbed into Spanish. **Soaps** are a particular speciality, either South American *culebrones* ("serpents" – they go on and on), which take up most of the daytime programming, or well-travelled British or Australian exports, like *EastEnders* (*Gent del Barri*). **Sports fans** are well catered for, with regular live coverage of football (soccer) and basketball matches; in the football season, you can watch one or two live matches a week in many bars. The number of TV stations is increasing all the time, but the two main national channels are TVE1 and TVE2, and you'll probably also spot the Catalan TVE3 and Canal 33. Most Balearic hotel rooms have satellite TV, which gives access to some or all of the international channels – CNN and so forth.

The *Majorca Daily Bulletin* and other local English-language newspapers detail the **BBC World Service** radio's frequencies and broadcasting schedules; alternatively, consult ⓦ www.bbc.co.uk/worldservice. For **Radio Canada** go to ⓦ www.rcinet.ca; for **Voice of America**, ⓦ www.voa.gov.

Festivals

Everywhere in Mallorca and Menorca takes at least one day off a year to devote to a festival. Usually it's the local saint's day, but there are also celebrations for the harvest, deliverance from the Moors, of safe return from the sea – any excuse will do. Each festival is different, with a particular local emphasis, but there is always music, dancing, traditional costume and an immense spirit of enjoyment. The main event of most *festas* is a parade, either behind a revered holy image or a more celebratory affair with fancy costumes and *gigantones*, giant carnival figures that rumble down the streets to the delight, or terror, of children.

Although these *festas* take place throughout the year – and it's often the obscure and unexpected event which proves to be most fun – Easter Holy Week (*Setmana Santa*) stands out, its passing celebrated in many places with magnificent processions.

January

Revetla de Sant Antoni Abat (Eve of St Antony's Day) 16 Jan. This is celebrated by the lighting of bonfires *(foguerons)* in Palma and several of Mallorca's villages, especially Sa Pobla and Muro. In these two villages, the inhabitants move from fire to fire, dancing round in fancy dress and eating *espinagades*, traditional eel and vegetable patties. Also takes place in Sant Lluís on Menorca.
Beneïdes de Sant Antoni (Blessing of St Antony) 17 Jan. St Antony's feast day is marked by processions in many of Mallorca's country towns, notably Sa Pobla and Artà, with farmyard animals herded through the streets to receive the saint's blessing and protection against disease.
Processó d'els Tres Knocks (Procession of the Three Knocks) 17 Jan. Held in Ciutadella, Menorca, this procession commemorates the victory of Alfonso III over the Muslims here on January 17, 1287. There's a mass in the cathedral first and then three horsemen lead the way to the old city walls, where the eldest of the trio knocks three times with his flagstaff at the exact spot the Catalans first breached the walls.
Revetla de Sant Sebastià (Eve of St Sebastian's Day) 19 Jan. Palma has bonfires, singing and dancing for St Sebastian.
Festa de Sant Sebastià 20 Jan. This feast day is celebrated in Pollença with a procession led by a holy banner (*estenard*) picturing the saint. It's accompanied by **cavallets** (literally "merry-go-rounds"), two young dancers each wearing a cardboard horse and imitating the animal's walk.

You'll see *cavallets*, which are of medieval origin, at many of the island's festivals.

February

Carnaval Towns and villages throughout the islands live it up during the week before Lent with marches and fancy dress parades. The biggest and liveliest is in Palma, where the shindig is known as *Sa Rua* (the Cavalcade).

March/April

Setmana Santa (Holy Week). Easter is as keenly observed in the Balearics as it is everywhere else in Spain. On **Maundy Thursday** in Palma, a much venerated icon of the crucified Christ, La Sang, is taken from the eponymous church on the Plaça del Hospital (off Passeig de la Rambla) and paraded through the city streets. There are also solemn **Good Friday** (*Divendres Sant*) processions in many towns and villages, with the more important taking place in Palma and Sineu. Most holy of all, however, is the Good Friday **Davallament (The Lowering), the** culmination of Holy Week in Pollença. Here, in total silence and by torchlight, the inhabitants lower a figure of Christ down from the hilltop Oratori to the church of Nostra Senyora dels Àngels.

During Holy Week there are also many **romerias** (pilgrimages) to the island's holy places, with one of the most popular being the climb up to the Ermita Santa Magdalena, near Inca. The Monestir de Lluc, which possesses Mallorca's most venerated shrine, is another religious focus during this time, with the penitential trudging round its Camí dels Misteris del Rosari (The Way of the Mysteries of the Rosary).

In Menorca's Ciutadella, there's also the **Matança dels bruixots** (the Slaughter of the Wizards), in which puppets representing well-known personalities are hung in the streets.

May

Festa de la Verge del Toro (The Festival of the Virgin of the Bull) 8 May. The day of the patron saint of Menorca begins with a special mass at the hilltop shrine of Monte Toro and continues with a shindig down in the little town of Es Mercadal.

Sa Fira i Es Firó Mid-May. In Port de Sóller and Sóller. This knees-up features mock battles between Christians and infidels in commemoration of the thrashing of a band of Arab pirates in 1561. Lots of booze and firing of antique rifles (into the air).

June

Corpus Christi Early to mid-June. At noon in the main square of Pollença an ancient and curious dance of uncertain provenance takes place – the *Ball de les Àguiles* (Dance of the Eagles) – followed by a religious procession.

Festa de Sant Joan 23–25 June. This midsummer festival has been celebrated in Ciutadella since the fourteenth century. There are jousting competitions, folk music, dancing and processions following a special mass held in the cathedral on the 24th. Another highlight is on the Sunday before the 24th, when the *S'Homo d'es Bé* (the Man of the Lamb) leads a party of horsemen through the town. Clad in animal skins and carrying a lamb in honour of St John the Baptist, he invites everyone to the forthcoming knees-up.

July

Día de Virgen de Carmen 15–16 July. The day of the patron saint of seafarers and fishermen is celebrated in many coastal settlements – principally Palma, Maó, Port de Sóller, Colònia de Sant Pere, Porto Colom and Cala Rajada – with parades and the blessing of boats.

Festa de Sant Martí Third Sun. The feast day of St Martin is celebrated in Es Mercadal, Menorca, with a popular religious procession followed by dancing and all sorts of fun and games.

Festa de Sant Jaume Last Sunday. This festival in Alcúdia and Menorca's Es Castell celebrates the feast day of St James with a popular religious procession followed by folk dances, fireworks and the like.

August

Mare de Déu dels Àngels 2 Aug. Moors and Christians battle it out again, this time in Pollença.

Festa de Sant Llorenç Second weekend. High jinks on horseback through the streets of Alaior, Menorca.

Cavallet 20 Aug. (see p.35) Dances in Felanitx.

Festa de Sant Bartomeu Last week. Three days of festivities in Ferreries, Menorca.

September

Festa de la Mare de Déu de Gràcia 7–9 Sept. This three-day festival in Maó celebrates the Virgin of Grace, the city's patron saint, and begins with a pilgrimage to the chapel of the Virgin. Thereafter, there are processions and parades along with horseback games.

Nativitat de Nostra Senyora (Nativity of the Virgin) Second week. In Alaró, honouring the Virgin with a pilgrimage to a hilltop shrine near the Castell d'Alaró.

October

Festa d'es Butifarra (Sausage Festival) Third Sun. Of recent origins, this festival follows on from tractor and automobile contests held in the village of Sant Joan. It features folk dancing and traditional music as well as the eating of specially prepared vegetable pies (*coca amb trampó*) and sausages (*berenada de butifarra*).

December

Nadal (Christmas). Christmas is especially picturesque in Palma and Ciutadella, where there are Nativity plays in the days leading up to the 25th.

Sports and outdoor activities

During the day at least, tourist life on Mallorca and Menorca is centred on the beach. There are long and generous strands at several of the major resorts – for instance Port d'Alcúdia, Port de Pollença, S'Arenal and Son Bou – and several dozen smaller cove beaches. At all the larger resorts, a veritable army of companies offer equipment for hire for a wide range of beach sports and activities, from sailing and pedalo pedalling through to jet skiing, water boarding, windsurfing and scuba diving, not to mention sandcastle-building competitions.

Away from the coast, **cycling** (see p.26) is a popular pastime as is **horse and pony riding** with a clutch of stables and many kilometres of bridle path. The most popular riding areas on Mallorca are the low hills of the Serres de Llevant in the east and the foothills of the Serra de Tramuntana, whilst Menorca's stables are mostly inland close to the (one) main road. For a list of outlets in Mallorca, see ⑭www.mallorcaonline.com /sport/equitau.htm; for Menorca, begin with ⑭www.menorcaacavall.com.

A wide range of **adventure sports** are offered by Mallorca's Tramuntana Tours (see p.106), including **canyoning**, which has recently experienced a dramatic increase in popularity.

Hiking

Hiking is a popular activity on both islands, with hundreds of hikers arriving here in the spring and autumn, necessarily away from the heat of the summer sun. On Mallorca, the prime hiking area is the Serra de Tramuntana mountain range that bands the northern coast, whereas Menorca is

sufficiently rural to offer pleasing walks almost everywhere, though it's the island's northern coast that offers the most dramatic scenery. It is also encouraging to note that the islands' **hiking trails**, which were once notorious for their poor signage, are in the process of being re-signed. We have described a number of **day-long hikes** on both Mallorca and Menorca (see p.122, p.132, p.158, p.168, p.232, p.240 & p.252) and recommended two Mallorcan companies that organize **guided hikes** – Mallorcan Walking Tours (see p.158) and Tramuntana Tours (see p.106). For more on hiking, see *Island hiking* colour section.

Windsurfing

Windsurfing is common to lots of resorts on both islands, but the prime spot – or at least one of the prime spots – is the windswept coast and wide, wave-less bay of Fornells, on Menorca (see p.243). Fornells is home to one of the best windsurfing companies in the Balearics, **Wind Fornells** (☎971 18 81 50, ⑭www .windfornells.com).

Parks – regional and national

There are over thirty protected areas in Mallorca, mainly concentrated in the north of the island, and four **Parcs Natural** (Natural Parks) – Mondragó on the east coast (see p.204); Sa Dragonera (see p.137); S'Albufera (see p.172); and the Península de Llevant just north of Artà and including the Ermita de Betlem (see p.191). Menorca has one, S'Albufera des Grau (see p.239), but most of the rest of the island is protected to some extent or another, hence its UNESCO designation as a "Reserva de la Biosfera" (Biosphere Reserve). Finally, Cabrera island (see p.210) and its surrounding waters are a **Parc Nacional** (national park).

Three scuba diving contacts

Diving Center Fornells Fornells, Menorca ☎971 37 64 31, ⓦwww.divingfornells
.com
Diving Centre Poseidon Cala Santandria, Menorca ☎971 38 26 44, ⓦwww
.bahia-poseidon.de
Scuba Activa Sant Elm, Mallorca ☎971 23 91 02, ⓦwww.scuba-activa.de

Scuba diving

By and large, **scuba diving** off Mallorca is something of an anticlimax: there may be lots of companies offering this service, but the island's underwater world lacks colour and clarity with the exception of the clear and reefy waters around the island of Sa Dragonera. Menorca, on the other hand, offers first-rate diving with visibility averaging around 30m, lots of reefs and a scattering of shipwrecks. Some divers swear by Menorca's north coast, but others prefer the west.

Shopping

Big-city Palma has its full share of chain and department stores (see p.87) as well as lots of specialist food and drink shops (see box, p.88), but everywhere else – on both Mallorca and Menorca – is much too small to offer much of a shopping "scene". That said, **open-air markets** (see box below), mostly selling fresh fruit and vegetables, but some also featuring every tourist trinket known on earth, are extremely popular and

Principal open-air markets (mercats)

For markets in Palma, see p.89.

Mondays
Calvià
Manacor

Tuesdays
Alcúdia
Artà
Maó

Wednesdays
Andratx
Capdepera
Petra
Port de Pollença
Santanyí
Sineu

Thursdays
Alaior
Inca

Fridays
Algaida
Binissalem
Ciutadella

Saturdays
Alaró
Bunyola
Cala Rajada
Ciutadella
Maó
Santanyí
Sóller

Sundays
Alcúdia
Felanitx
Pollença
Porto Cristo
Valldemossa

Clothing and shoe sizes

Women's dresses and skirts

American	4	6	8	10	12	14	16	18
British	8	10	12	14	16	18	20	22
Continental	38	40	42	44	46	48	50	52

Women's blouses and sweaters

American	6	8	10	12	14	16	18
British	30	32	34	36	38	40	42
Continental	40	42	44	46	48	50	52

Women's shoes

American	5	6	7	8	9	10	11
British	3	4	5	6	7	8	9
Continental	36	37	38	39	41	42	43

Men's suits

American	34	36	38	40	42	44	46	48
British	34	36	38	40	42	44	46	48
Continental	44	46	48	50	52	54	56	58

Men's shirts

American	14	15	15.5	16	16.5	17	17.5	18
British	14	15	15.5	16	16.5	17	17.5	18
Continental	36	38	39	41	42	43	44	45

Men's shoes

American	7	7.5	8	8.5	9.5	10	10.5	11	11.5
British	6	7	7.5	8	9	9.5	10	11	12
Continental	39	41	41	42	43	44	44	45	46

lots of towns have one, either once or twice weekly; go early – at about 8am – to get the best deals. As for **local specialities**, look out for artificial pearls from Manacor; Camper shoes; fancy green-tinted glass chandeliers; and *siurells*, white clay whistles flecked with red and green paint and shaped to depict a figure, an animal or rural scene – they are almost always mass-produced today, but have a long island pedigree as tokens of friendship. In addition, Mallorcan wine (see box, p.32) and Menorcan cheese, gin and honey come highly recommended and you shouldn't leave the Balearics without having at least one *ensaimada* (spiralled flaky pastry).

Shopping hours are normally Monday to Friday 9.30/10am to 1.30/2pm and 5 to 7/8pm, plus Saturday morning 9.30/10am to 1.30/2pm, though big department stores operate longer hours, typically Monday to Saturday 9.30am to 9.30pm. In the resorts, many shops and stores are open daily from 9.30am till late.

Travel essentials

Costs

Solely in terms of transport do Mallorca and Menorca remain budget destinations for northern Europeans, North Americans, Australians and New Zealanders; hotel and restaurant prices are now on a par with most of Europe. On **average**, if you're prepared to buy your own picnic lunch, stay in inexpensive *hostales* and hotels, and stick to the cheaper bars and restaurants, you could get by on around €60 per person per day, assuming you're sharing a room. If you intend to stay in three-star hotels and eat at quality restaurants, you'll need more like €120 a day per person, with the main variable being the cost of your room – and bear in mind that room prices rise steeply as the season progresses. On €180 a day and upwards, you'll be limited only by your energy reserves, unless you're planning to stay in a five-star hotel, in which case this figure won't even cover your bed. One additional cost is **IVA**, a seven percent sales tax levied on most goods and services. Check in advance to see if IVA is included in the price of your bigger purchases; otherwise, especially in more expensive hotels and restaurants, you may be in for a bit of a shock. As for **tipping**, taxi drivers, restaurant and bar staff anticipate a tip of between ten and fifteen percent.

Crime and personal safety

Setting aside the ETA bombings of 2009, thousands of expatriates love Mallorca and Menorca for their lack of **crime** – and with good reason. In the islands' villages and small towns petty crime is unusual, and serious offences, from burglary to assault and beyond, extremely rare. Of the three larger towns, only Palma presents any problems, mostly low-key stuff such as the occasional fight and minor theft, and commonsense precautions are normally enough to keep you out of any trouble. Nevertheless, you should be aware that noisy and **aggressive males** commonly colonize some of the late-night bars at the seedier resorts – S'Arenal and Magaluf have the worst reputations – though it's more a question of which bar you're in, rather than the resort you're staying at. **Theft from parked cars** (as distinct from car theft) is also a problem, especially at major tourist attractions, so whatever you do, don't leave anything in view when you park. If you are a **victim of crime**, you'll need to go to the **police** (see p.44) to report it, not least because your insurance company will require a police report or number. In dealing with the police, remember that, although they are polite enough in the normal course

Spanish embassies abroad

Australia 15 Arkana St, Yarralumla, Canberra, ACT 2600 ☎02/6273 3555, ⓦwww.maec.es

Canada 74 Stanley Avenue, Ottawa, Ontario K1M 1P4 ☎1-613/747 2252, ⓦwww.maec.es

Ireland 17A Merlyn Park, Ballsbridge, Dublin 4 ☎01/269 1640, ⓦwww.maec.es

New Zealand See Australia. Consulates in Auckland and Christchurch

South Africa 169 Pine St, Arcadia, 0083 Pretoria ☎344 3877, ⓦwww.maec.es

UK 39n Chesham Place, London SW1X 8SB ☎0207/235 5555, ⓦwww.conspalon.org. Consulates in Edinburgh and Manchester

USA 2375 Pennsylvania Ave NW, Washington DC 20037-1736 ☎1-202/452-0100, ⓦwww.spainemb.org. Also consulates in Boston, Chicago, Houston, Los Angeles, Miami, New Orleans, New York, and San Francisco

of events, they can be extremely unpleasant if you get on the wrong side of them. At all times, keep your cool and remember, especially if you are British, just how unpleasant some of your compatriots can be when they're tanked up.

Electricity

Spanish **electricity** runs at 220 volts AC, with standard European-style two-pin plugs. Brits will need a plug adaptor to connect their appliances, North Americans both an adaptor and a transformer.

Entry requirements

Citizens of all EU and EEA countries only need a **valid passport or national identity card** to enter Spain, where – with some limitations – they also have the right to work, live and study. US, Australian, Canadian and New Zealand citizens need only a valid passport for visits of **up to ninety days**, but are not allowed to work. Non-EU/EEA citizens who wish to visit Spain for **longer than ninety days** must get a special visa from a Spanish consulate or embassy before departure (see p.40 for addresses). Visa requirements do change and it is always advisable to check the current situation before leaving home.

Gay and lesbian travellers

The **gay and lesbian scene** is fairly low-key in Mallorca and almost invisible in Menorca – in striking contrast to neighbouring Ibiza. Most of the action takes place in Palma on Avinguda Joan Miró, just south of Plaça Gomila. In 2005, Spain became the fourth country (after Canada, the Netherlands and Belgium) to legalize gay marriage and there is now a battery of laws against discrimination on the grounds of sexual preference.

Health

Under reciprocal health care arrangements, all citizens of the EU (European Union) and EEA (European Economic Area) are entitled to **free medical treatment** within Spain's public health care system. Non-EU/EEA nationals are not entitled to free treatment and should, therefore, take out their own

B

medical insurance. EU/EEA citizens may, however, also want to consider private health insurance, both to cover the cost of items not within the EU/EEA scheme, such as dental treatment and repatriation on medical grounds, and to enable them to seek treatment within the private sector. For more on insurance, see p.42. No **inoculations** are currently required for Mallorca or Menorca.

The **public health care system** in the Balearics is of a good standard and widely available with clinics and hospitals in all the larger towns. If you're seeking treatment **under EU/EEA reciprocal health arrangements**, it may be prudent to double check that the medic you see is working within (and seeing you as a patient of) the public system. That being the case, you'll receive free treatment just as the locals do. Sometimes you will be asked to produce documentation to prove that you are eligible for EU/EEA health care, sometimes no one bothers, but technically you should have your passport and your **European Health Insurance Card (EHIC)** to hand. If, on the other hand, you have a travel insurance policy covering medical expenses, you can seek treatment in either the public or private health sectors, the main issue being whether – at least in major cases – you have to pay the costs upfront and then wait for reimbursement or not. Note that in the larger resorts your hotel will probably be able to arrange an appointment with an English-speaking doctor, who will almost certainly see you as a private patient; elsewhere, you'll be lucky if the medic speaks English.

Minor complaints can often be remedied at a **pharmacy** (*farmàcia*): pharmacists are highly trained, willing to give advice (often in English), and able to dispense many drugs which would only be available on prescription in many other countries. Pharmacies are ubiquitous and are listed in the Yellow Pages. **Condoms** are available from most *farmàcias* and from all sorts of outlets in the

Rough Guides travel insurance

Rough Guides has teamed up with WorldNomads.com to offer great **travel insurance** deals. Policies are available to residents of over 150 countries, with cover for a wide range of **adventure sports**, 24 hour emergency assistance, high levels of medical and evacuation cover and a stream of **travel safety information**. Roughguides.com users can take advantage of their policies online 24/7, from anywhere in the world – even if you're already travelling. And since plans often change when you're on the road, you can extend your policy and even claim online. Roughguides.com users who buy travel insurance with WorldNomads.com can also leave a positive footprint and donate to a community development project. For more information go to Ⓦ **www.roughguides.com/shop**.

resorts, such as bars and vending machines. It's a good job: a recent survey of 18- to 30-year-old visitors found that the average time between arrival and first sexual contact was 3hr 42min.

Insurance

Even though EU/EEA health care privileges apply in Spain, EU/EEA citizens are still best off taking out an **insurance policy** before travelling to cover against theft, loss and illness or injury. For non-EU/EEA citizens, an insurance policy is a must. A typical policy usually provides cover for the loss of baggage, tickets and – up to a certain limit – cash or cheques, as well as cancellation or curtailment of your journey. Many policies can be chopped and changed to exclude coverage you don't need: sickness and accident benefits can often be excluded or included at will. Taking out private insurance also means the cost of items not within the scope of the EU scheme, such as dental treatment and repatriation on medical grounds, can be covered. In the case of major expense, the more worthwhile policies promise to sort matters out before you pay rather than after, but if you do have to pay upfront, make very sure that you always keep full doctors' reports, signed prescription details and all receipts. In the event that you have anything stolen, you must obtain an official statement from the police.

Internet and email

Many hotels and *hostales* provide **internet access** for their guests either free or for a small charge. Failing that, head for the nearest library, where internet access is almost always free, if sometimes for a fixed period only – usually about an hour.

Mail

On both islands, there is a **post office** (*correu*) in every town and in most of the larger villages; the majority are handily located on or near the main square. Opening hours are usually Monday to Friday 9am to 2pm, though the post offices in Palma, Maó and Ciutadella are open much longer. All post offices close on public holidays. **Outbound post** is slow but reasonably reliable, with letters or cards taking about a week to reach Britain and Ireland, up to two weeks to North America and Australasia. You can buy stamps (*segells*) at tobacconists (look for the brown and yellow *tabac* or *tabacos* sign) and at scores of souvenir shops as well as at post offices. **Post boxes** are yellow; where you have a choice of slots, pick the flap marked *províncies i estranger* or *altres destinos*. **Postal rates** are inexpensive, with postcards and small letters attracting two tariffs: one to anywhere in Europe, the other worldwide. **Inbound post** is reasonably reliable too.

Maps

Detailed **road maps** of Mallorca and/or Menorca are widely available from island newsagents, tourist offices, petrol stations, souvenir shops and bookshops; for the most part they cost €4–8. The quality of these road maps varies enormously and many are hopelessly out of date, so before you buy a map check the **road numbers**: all Balearic road numbers were changed in 2006, so – for example – the main road running along Mallorca's north coast was the C710, but is now the MA-10, and Menorca's one and only main road is now the ME-1 (not the C721). You're also better off buying a **Catalan** map as distinct from a Castilian (Spanish) or even an English or German map: in this case, check out the spelling of Port de Pollença on Mallorca's north coast – if it reads "Puerto de Pollensa", you've got a Castilian map; similarly, on Menorca, check the capital is marked Maó, not the Castilian "Mahón".

Currently, the most **accurate road map of Mallorca** is Firestone's *Mallorca Tourist map* (1:75,000), which comes with an index and a large-scale map of Palma (1:6500). This can, however, be hard to get hold of both on Mallorca and at home – and a good second bet is the *Rough Guide Map to Mallorca* (1:80,000), which also has an index, displays topographical features and is rip-proof and waterproof. This Rough Guide map is not sold in the Balearics, so you will need to order it before departure (Ⓦwww.roughguides .com). Easily the most **accurate road map of Menorca** is the *Mapa Menorca: Reserva de la Biosfera* (1:60,000), published by Triangle Postals (Ⓦwww.trianglepostals.com). This has an index, marks major cycling and hiking routes and has large-scale inset maps of Ciutadella and Maó. It's widely available in Menorca – the tourist offices in both Maó and Ciutadella sell them.

The **best Mallorca hiking guides** are produced by Editorial Alpina (Ⓦwww .editorialalpina.com), who publish five Mallorca guides at €10 to 20 each. Three of the five combine to cover the whole of the northwest coast – "Mallorca Tramuntana Sud", "Mallorca Tramuntana Central" and "Mallorca Tramuntana Norte". The English-language editions of these three are clearly written and the **maps** (at 1:25,000) are well presented and very detailed. The company also publishes a walking guide and map (1:50,000) to the whole of the island and a (Spanish only) guide and map (1:50,000) to 26 selected Mallorca hikes. The only problem is one of availability: Sóller tourist office (see p.105) should have copies as should one of the town's bookshops, but otherwise it's best to buy before you leave

home. **Menorca hiking maps** are much thinner on the ground and the best you'll do is the very competent *Menorca Tour & Trail Map* (1:40,000) produced by Discovery Walking Guides (Ⓦwww.walking.demon .co.uk). This publication is not available on the island, so once again buy before you leave home.

Money and exchange

Spain's currency is the **euro** (€). Each euro is made up of 100 cents. The **exchange rate** for the euro at time of writing was 0.86 to the British pound; 1.40 to the US dollar; 1.56 to the Canadian dollar; 1.71 to the Australian dollar; 2.09 to the New Zealand dollar; and 11.35 to the South African Rand. There are euro notes of €500, €200, €100, €50, €20, €10 and €5, and coins of €2, €1, 50c, 20c, 10c, 5c, 2c and 1c, but note that many retailers will not touch the €500 and €200 notes with a barge pole – you have to break them down into smaller denominations at the bank. All well-known brands of **traveller's cheque** in all major currencies are widely accepted in Mallorca and Menorca, and you can change them as well as foreign currency into euros at most Balearic banks and savings banks, which are ubiquitous; **banking hours** are usually Monday to Friday from 9am to 2pm, with many banks opening on Saturday mornings from 9am to 1pm from October to April. **ATMs** are commonplace in Palma, Maó, Ciutadella and all the larger resorts. Most ATMs give instructions in a variety of languages, and accept a host of **debit cards** without charging a transaction fee. **Credit cards** can be used in ATMs too, but in this case transactions are treated as loans, with interest accruing daily from the date of withdrawal. All major credit cards, including American Express, Visa and Mastercard, are widely accepted.

Opening hours and public holidays

Although there's been some movement towards a northern European **working day** in Menorca and Mallorca – especially in Palma and the major tourist resorts – most shops and offices still close for a **siesta** of

Public holidays

January 1 New Year's Day (*Cap d'Any*)
January 6 Epiphany (*Reyes Magos*)
Maundy Thursday (*Dijous Sant*)
Good Friday (*Divendres Sant*)
May 1 Labour Day (*Día del Treball*)
August 15 Assumption of the Virgin (*Assumpció*)
October 12 Spanish National Day (*Día de la Hispanidad*)
November 1 All Saints (*Tots Sants*)
December 6 Constitution Day (*Día de la Constitució*)
December 8 Immaculate Conception (*Inmaculada Concepción*)
December 24 Christmas Eve
December 25 Christmas Day (*Nadal; Navidad in Castilian*)
December 26 Boxing Day/St Stephen's Day (*Dia de Sant Esteban*)

at least two hours in the hottest part of the afternoon. There's a lot of variability, but basic working hours are typically Monday to Friday 9am to 1pm & 4pm to 7pm, Saturday 9am to 1pm; notable exceptions are the extended hours operated by the largest department stores, some important tourist attractions and most tourist and souvenir shops. Government offices are not open on Saturdays. In winter (Nov–March), Menorca's tourist industry pretty much shuts up shop and although things aren't so clear cut in Mallorca most of the resorts scale right down.

Local festivals (see pp.35–36) are a prominent feature of island life and they work in tandem with **public holidays**, whose precise dates and details are fixed annually – so there may be some (minor) variations to the list in the box above. The island's resorts are generally oblivious to public holidays as are hotels and most restaurants, but almost all businesses and shops close and public transport is reduced to a skeleton service.

Phones

The **international phone code** for Spain is 34. Note that most Balearic phone numbers begin with ☎971, but this is an integral part of the number, not an (optional) area code. In the Balearics, **phone cards** can be bought from tobacconists and newsstands in several denominations, beginning at €5, but **phone boxes** are disappearing fast as a

concomitant of the irresistible rise of the mobile phone. There is good coverage for **mobile phones/cell phones** on both Mallorca and Menorca. Your mobile/cell needs to be on the 900/1800 MHz band, the band common to the rest of Europe, Australia and New Zealand. The North American cell network is not compatible with the GSM band, so you'll need a tri-band phone, which is able to switch from one band to the other.

The **Spanish phone directory** is available (in Spanish) at ☻www.paginas-amarillas.es.

The police

There are three main types of **police** in the Balearics: the Guardia Civil, the Policía Nacional and the Policía Local, all of them armed. The **Guardia Civil,** who are dressed in green, police the highways and the countryside; the brown-uniformed **Policía Nacional**, who are mainly seen in Palma, guard key installations and/or personnel and control crowds and demonstrations; and the **Policía Local**, who wear blue uniforms, operate in the towns. The Policía Local are generally reckoned to be the most sympathetic. Many police officers speak English, especially in the towns and resort areas, but you can't bank on it.

Smoking

On January 1, 2006, new **anti-smoking legislation** was passed in Spain, making smoking illegal in all theatres, bars and restaurants as well as on public transport, though the positive effects of this ban have been partly negated by local exemptions allowing smoking in scores of restaurants and bars. Owners of these establishments must display their exemption certificate.

Time zones

Spain is one hour ahead of Greenwich Mean Time, six hours ahead of US Eastern Standard Time, nine hours ahead of US Pacific Standard Time, nine hours behind Australian Eastern Standard Time and eleven hours behind New Zealand – except for periods during the changeovers made in the respective countries to and from daylight saving. In Spain, the clocks go forward an hour on the last Sunday of March and back an hour on the last Sunday of October.

Tipping

Taxi drivers, restaurant and bar staff anticipate a tip of between ten and fifteen percent.

Tourist information

In **Mallorca**, there's a helpful **provincial tourist office** at the airport (see p.53) and another in the centre of Palma (see p.54). Both will provide free road maps of the island and leaflets detailing all sorts of island-wide practicalities. In addition, most towns and almost every resort has its own **tourist office**. These vary enormously in quality, and while they are generally useful for local information, they cannot be relied on to know anything about what goes on outside their patch. In **Menorca**, there are extremely efficient year-round **tourist offices** in the two main towns, Maó and Ciutadella, and a tourist information desk at the airport.

Travelling with children

Most Balearic *hostales*, pensions and hotels welcome **children** and many offer rooms with three or four beds. Restaurants and cafés almost always encourage families too. Many package holidays have **child-minding facilities** as part of the deal and many more organize a programme of kids' activities. Younger children will, of course, be quite happy to play around on the beach, but pre- and early teens may well want a bit more crash, bang and wallop, which is available on Mallorca at three water/theme parks: Hidropark in Port d'Alcúdia (see p.171); Western Water Park in Magaluf (see p.96); and Aqualand in S'Arenal (see p.91). **Concessionary rates** for children under 14/15 years are commonplace and infants go free. For babies, eating out seems to work quite well (some places will prepare food specially) though you might want to bring powdered milk – babies, like most Spaniards, are pretty contemptuous of the UHT stuff generally available. Disposable nappies and other basic supplies are widely available in the resort areas and the larger towns.

Calling home from abroad and useful numbers

Note that the initial zero is omitted from the area code when dialling the UK, Ireland, Australia and New Zealand from abroad.
Australia international access code + 61
New Zealand international access code + 64
UK international access code + 44
US and Canada international access code + 1
Ireland international access code + 353
South Africa international access code + 27

Useful telephone numbers in the Balearics:
Directory enquiries (national) ☎11888
Directory enquiries (international) ☎11886
Emergencies ☎112
Operator Services ☎1009

Travellers with disabilities

Despite their popularity as holiday destinations, facilities for **travellers with disabilities** on both Mallorca and Menorca lag some way behind most of the EU. That said, things are improving. Hotels with wheelchair access and other appropriate facilities are increasingly common and, by law, all new public buildings in Spain are required to be fully accessible. On the other hand, toilet facilities for people with disabilities are rare; car rental firms are very ill-stocked with adapted vehicles, even though there are designated disability parking bays; and, although most EMT buses in Palma have low-floor access, some don't and few do elsewhere on the island. More positively, **flying** to the islands should pose few problems as almost all the scheduled airlines concerned are more than willing to assist.

Useful websites

ⓦ **www.conselldemallorca.net** Extensive government site.

ⓦ **www.mallorcaweb.com** and ⓦ **www.menorcaweb.com** Compendious websites dedicated to many aspects of island life.

ⓦ **www.okspain.org** Official site of the USA's Spanish National Tourist Office. (SNTO).

ⓦ **www.spain.info** The official website of the Spanish National Tourist Office (SNTO) provides an excellent general introduction to the country as a whole, and its myriad synopses – on everything from national parks to accommodation – are concise and clearly, even temptingly written.

ⓦ **www.tourspain.co.uk** Official site of the UK's SNTO.

ⓦ **www.spain.info/ca/tourspain** Official site of the Canadian SNTO.

ⓦ **www.visitbalears.com** The Balearic government's official, English-language tourist site with separate sections for all of the islands. Covers a wide range of topics – from shopping through to nature – but many of the synopses are more than a little terse. Clearly laid out; a useful introduction.

Guide

Guide

Palma and around

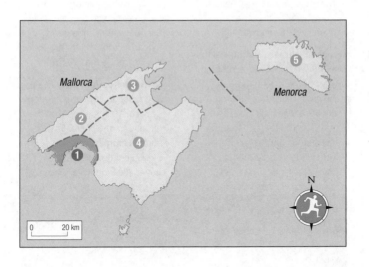

CHAPTER 1

Highlights

* **Palma Cathedral** The city's outstanding attraction, and one of Spain's finest Gothic cathedrals, whose honey-coloured walls and buttresses dominate the waterfront from the crest of a hill. See p.60

* **Mallorcan Primitives** The Museu de la Catedral is home to a fascinating selection of works by the distinctive school of medieval island painters known as the Mallorcan Primitives. See pp.64–65

* **The Old Town, Palma** Palma's old town is the most intriguing part of the city, its narrow lanes and alleys intercepted by attractive little piazzas and flanked by a handsome medley of Gothic churches and Renaissance mansions. See pp.70–76

* **Eating in Palma** Palma has the island's widest and liveliest selection of cafés, restaurants and tapas bars, ranging from informal local joints to Michelin-starred palaces offering the latest in international culinary chic. See pp.84–86

* **Platja de Palma, S'Arenal** Perhaps the most self-conscious beach in Mallorca, awash with preening sunbathers who come to enjoy the fine white sands which extend for some 4km around the Bay of Palma. See p.91

* **Miró Foundation, Cala Major** The artist Joan Miró hunkered down in Mallorca to avoid the attentions of General Franco and his cronies, creating some of his finest paintings here during his long exile. See p.92

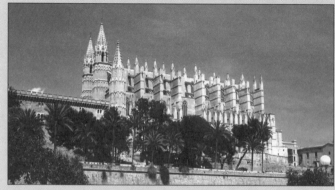

▲ Palma Cathedral

Palma and around

P**ALMA** is an ambitious city. In 1983 it became the capital of one of Spain's newly established autonomous regions, the **Balearic islands**, and since then it has shed its dusty provincialism, developing into a go-ahead and cosmopolitan commercial hub of over 380,000 people. The new self-confidence is plain to see in the city centre, a vibrant and urbane place of careful coiffures and well-cut suits, which is akin to the big cities of the Spanish mainland and a world away from the heaving tourist enclaves of the surrounding bay. There's still a long way to go – much of suburban Palma remains obdurately dull and somewhat dilapidated – but the centre now presents a splendid ensemble of lively shopping areas and refurbished old buildings, mazy lanes, fountains, gardens and sculpture, all enclosed by what remains of the old city walls and their replacement boulevards.

This geography encourages downtown Palma to look into itself and away from the sea, even though its **harbour** – now quarantined by the main highway – has always been the city's economic lifeline. The Romans were the first to recognize the site's strategic value, establishing a military post here known as Palmaria, but real development came with the Moors, who made their **Medina Mayurka** a major seaport protected by no fewer than three concentric walls. Jaume I of Aragón captured the Moorish stronghold in 1229 and promptly started work on the **cathedral**, whose mellow sandstone still towers above the waterfront, presenting from its seaward side – in the sheer beauty of its massive proportions – one of Spain's most stunning sights.

As a major port of call between Europe and North Africa, Palma boomed under both Moorish and medieval Christian control, but its wealth and prominence came to a sudden end with the Spanish exploitation of the New World: from the early sixteenth century, Madrid looked west across the Atlantic and Palma slipped into Mediterranean obscurity. One result of its abrupt decline has been the preservation of much of the **old town**, with its beguiling tangle of narrow, labyrinthine streets and high-storeyed houses. The pick of Palma's other historic attractions are the fourteenth-century **Castell de Bellver** and the heavyweight Baroque **Basílica de Sant Francesc**.

Yet for most visitors, Palma's main appeal is its sheer vitality: at night scores of excellent **restaurants** offer the best of Spanish, Catalan and Mallorcan cuisine, while the city's **cafés** buzz with purposeful chatter. Palma also boasts **accommodation** to match most budgets, making it a splendid base from which to explore the island. In this respect, the city is far preferable, at least for independent travellers, to the string of resorts along the neighbouring **Badía de Palma** (Bay of Palma), where most of the accommodation is block-booked by tour operators. If you are tempted by a cheap package, however, it's as well to bear in

PALMA & AROUND

5 km

0

Manacor   Llucmajor   Llucmajor

Inca   Inca   Sóller   Puigpunyent & La Granja   Estellencs

MA-15

MA-19A

MA-19

Aqualand

N

Palma Aquarium

Platja de Palma

Sometimes   S'Arenal Harbour   S'Arenal

Ses Maravelles   Cala Blava

Ca'n Pastilla   Cap Enderrocat

MA-13

MA-13A

MA-15   MA-19

MA-20

CMTURA

MA-11

Cala Gamba

Es Portixol   Es Molinar

PALMA

Cathedral

Es   Badia de Palma

MA-1

Ferry Port

Fundació Pilar
Joan Miró

Castell de
Bellver

Cala
Major

Gènova   Illetes

Marineland

Portals
Nous

MA-1C

Palma Nova

Torrenova

Magaluf

Cala Mago

Portals Vells

Cap de Cala Figuera

Calvià

MA-1

Western
Water Park

Galilea

Capdellà

MA-1032

MA-1031

Andratx

MA-1

Peguera

Cala
Fornells

Santa Ponça

Camp
de Mar

MA-10

Port d'Andratx   Port d'Andratx

mind that the more agreeable of the resorts lie to the west of the city, where a hilly coastline of rocky cliffs and tiny coves is punctuated by small, sandy beaches. Development is ubiquitous, but **Cala Major** is of interest as the site of the former home and studio of Joan Miró; well-to-do **Illetes** has several excellent hotels and a couple of lovely cove beaches; and pint-sized **Cala Fornells** has a fine seashore setting and several good hotels – and it's also within easy reach of the spacious sandy shorelines of family-oriented **Santa Ponça** and **Peguera**. Places to avoid include lager-swilling **Magaluf** and all the resorts to the east of Palma, where the pancake-flat shoreline is burdened by a seamless band of skyscrapers stretching from **Ca'n Pastilla** to **S'Arenal** – behind what is, admittedly, one of the island's longest and most impressive beaches, the **Platja de Palma**.

Arrival

Mallorca's international **airport** is 11km east of downtown Palma, immediately behind the resort of Ca'n Pastilla. It consists of one enormous terminal, which handles both scheduled and charter flights, with separate floors for arrivals (downstairs) and departures (upstairs). Both floors have **airport information desks** – a good job, as the airport can be very confusing. On the arrivals floor, a flotilla of **car rental** outlets jostle for position by the luggage carousels. Beyond, through the glass doors, is the main **arrivals hall**, which has 24-hour **ATMs** and **currency exchange** facilities, dozens of package-tour agents plus a **provincial tourist office** (Mon–Sat 8.30am–8pm, Sun 9am–1.30pm) with a wide range of brochures, key public transport timetables, maps, and lists of hotels and *hostales*; it's beside Exit 4. The tourist office will not, however, help arrange **accommodation** and neither will most of the package-tour travel agents. An exception is the extremely helpful **Prima Travel** (May–Oct; ☎971 78 93 22, ⓦwww.prima-travel.com), who have a good selection of hotels, apartments and villas in all price ranges, plus English-speaking staff.

The airport is linked to the city and the Bay of Palma resorts by a busy highway, which shadows the shoreline from S'Arenal in the east to Palma Nova and Magaluf in the west. The least expensive way to reach Palma from the airport is by **EMT bus #1** (daily every 15min from 6am–2.30am; €2), which

---

Parking in Palma

Trying to find an **on-street car parking space** in downtown Palma can be a nightmare – and you're well advised to either leave your vehicle on the city's outskirts, especially for visits of more than an hour or two, or head for one of the city's several **car parks** – the Parc de la Mar near the cathedral often has spaces when others do not; car parks charge around €1.70 per hour. Note also that if you're staying downtown, you should consider choosing a hotel which either has its own car park or has an arrangement with a local one (some hotels offer parking discounts). On-street parking in the city centre requires an **ORA ticket** during busy periods (Mon–Fri 9am–2pm & 4.30–8pm, Sat 9am–2pm). At other times, when the centre is much less congested and vacant spots more common, parking is free. Tickets are readily available from ORA parking meters but, although the cost is very reasonable (around €1.60 per hour), the longest-lasting ticket only provides two hour's parking – and fines are immediate and steep. Note also that if the time allowed overlaps into a free period, your ORA ticket is still valid when restricted time begins again.

leaves from the main entrance of the terminal building, just behind the taxi rank. They reach the city's inner ring road near the foot of Avinguda Gabriel Alomar i Villalonga, at the c/Joan Maragall junction, then head on to Plaça Espanya, on the north side of the centre, before continuing west to the Passeig Mallorca and then south to the top of Avinguda Jaume III. There are frequent stops along the way. A **taxi** from the airport to the city centre will set you back about €20; taxi rates are controlled and a list of island-wide fares should be available from the provincial tourist office in the arrivals hall.

Palma **ferry terminal** is about 4km west of the city centre. Acciona Trasmediterranea and Iscomar ferries arrive at Terminal 2; Balearia ferries at Terminal 3, about 150m away. **EMT bus #1** (daily every 15min from 6am–2.30am; €1.25) leaves every fifteen minutes from outside Terminal 2 to the Plaça Espanya. There are also **taxi** ranks outside both terminal buildings; the fare to the city centre is about €10.

Orientation

Almost everything of interest in Palma is located in the city centre, a roughly circular affair whose southern perimeter is defined by the cathedral and the remains of the old city walls, which in turn abut the coastal motorway and the harbour. The city centre's landward limits are determined by a zigzag of wide boulevards built beside or in place of the old town walls. Two of these boulevards, **Avinguda de la Argentina** and **Avinguda Gabriel Alomar i Villalonga**, connect with the coastal motorway, **the Ma–1**, thereby completing the circle. The **Ma–20** ring road around the suburbs loops off from the coastal motorway to create a much larger, outer circle.

The city centre itself is crossed by four interconnected avenues: **Passeig d'es Born**, **Avinguda Jaume III**, **c/Unió** (which becomes **c/Riera** at its eastern end) and **Passeig de la Rambla**. Your best bet is to use these four thoroughfares to guide yourself round the centre – Palma's jigsaw-like side streets and squares can be very confusing. Central Palma is about 2km in diameter, roughly thirty minutes' walk from one side to the other. If you're in a hurry, **taxi** fares are reasonable. There are several city-centre taxi ranks, with one on Plaça Espanya, another on Avgda Jaume III; alternatively, phone Radio Taxi Palma (☎971 76 45 45).

Information

There's a **provincial tourist office** bang in the centre just off Passeig d'es Born at Plaça de la Reina 2 (Mon–Fri 9am–8pm, Sat 9am–2pm; ☎971 71 22 16). The main **municipal office** is on the north side of Plaça Espanya (daily 9am–8pm; ⓦwww.palmavirtual.es) and there's another, much smaller municipal office inside Can Solleric, at Passeig d'es Born 27 (daily 9am–8pm). The first two provide city- and island-wide information, dispensing free maps, accommodation lists, bus schedules, ferry timetables, lists of car rental firms and all sorts of special-interest leaflets, including a free listings magazine, *youthing*, and the useful *Palma: Best Mediterranean Shopping* brochure, which details many of the city's most distinctive shops. The third office only has a limited range of city information. Palma's official website, ⓦwww.palmavirtual.es, is multilingual and has a battery of information, including a calendar of events and festivities.

City transport

City buses are operated by **EMT** (Empresa Municipal de Transports) and almost all their services, which combine to link the centre with the suburbs and the nearer tourist resorts, pass through **Plaça Espanya**; several of the more useful services also pass through Placa de la Reina. In the city centre, each EMT bus stop displays a schematic plan showing the route followed by – and the timetable of – those buses that halt at that particular stop; in addition, an electronic display shows when the next bus or buses will arrive. **Tickets** are available from the driver and cost €1.25 per journey within the city limits. You can buy a **carnet** of ten at a discount (€8) from most *tabacs* (tobacconists) and some newsagents. EMT also has an **enquiry telephone line** in Spanish and Catalan on ☎900 70 07 10, or visit their multilingual website at ⓦwww.emtpalma.es.

Alternatively, **Citysightseeing** (☎902 10 10 81, ⓦwww.citysightseeing -spain.com) operates double-deck, hop-off, hop-on bus trips around the major sights throughout the year (May–Sept daily 10am–8pm & Oct–April daily 10am–6pm; every 20–30min). Their buses head round the city centre's enclosing boulevards and venture west as far as the ferry terminal, but frankly EMT's buses are a much better bet with one exception: EMT does not provide a bus service from the city centre to either the Poble Espanyol (see p.82) or the Castell de Bellver (see p.82), whereas Citysightseeing does – it's **Bus Ciutat Línia 50** (Daily: May–Sept 10am–8pm & Oct–April 10am–6pm; every 20–30min).

Moving on from Palma

Buses along the Badía de Palma coast are fast and efficient. The resorts in the immediate vicinity of Palma are served by **EMT** (☎900 70 07 10, ⓦwww.emtpalma .es), all of whose buses pass through Plaça Espanya; most EMT buses also have several other city-centre stops. Principal EMT services include **bus #3**, heading to Cala Major and Illetes; and **bus #15**, running east through Es Portixol to Ca'n Pastilla and S'Arenal. **Ticket prices** are incredibly low – the 25-minute journey to S'Arenal, for instance, costs just €1.25.

Island-wide bus services – including the remaining Badía de Palma resorts of Portals Nous, Magaluf and Peguera, plus the likes of Port d' Andratx (see p.138) and Sant Elm (see p.136) – are operated by several companies under the auspices of **tib** (Transportes de les Illes Baleares). All services depart from the subterranean **Estació Intermodal**, the combined **bus and train station** on the north side of Plaça Espanya. For **timetable information**, tib has a Spanish/Catalan information line on ☎971 17 77 77, maintains a website on ⓦhttp://tib.caib.es/ and operates a very helpful **information desk** (daily 6am–9pm), where most of the staff speak at least some English. For information on bus services in and around Palma, see p.97.

Mallorca has **two train lines**: one, the modern line, links Palma with most of the larger towns of the central plain, including Binissalem, Inca, Sineu, Manacor and Sa Pobla; the second is the delightful antique train line running from Palma to Sóller (see p.104). The train station for the modern line is part of the Estació Intermodal on the north side of Plaça Espanya. The Sóller train station is a few metres to the west, also on the north side of Plaça Espanya. There are ticket offices at both stations.

Driving is straightforward: the *autovia* (motorway) shoots along the coast from S'Arenal right round to Palma Nova and then slices across a narrow peninsula to reach Santa Ponça and Peguera. Alternatively, you can choose to take the old coastal road through most of the resorts, heading east from Palma to Es Portixol and ultimately S'Arenal, or west from Cala Major to Magaluf.

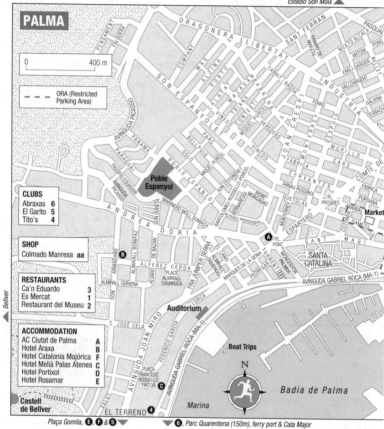

Citysightseeing **tickets**, covering all their services, are available on board all of their buses, cost €13, and are valid for 24 hours. The most popular departure point is Avinguda d'Antoni Maura, near the cathedral.

Finally, a more poised way of seeing Palma is to take a traditional **horse-and-carriage ride** – they hang around next to the cathedral; count on around €30 for half an hour.

Accommodation

There are several dozen **hotels and hostales** dotted around Palma, but nevertheless demand can still outstrip supply in peak periods, most notably in June, early July and September, which is when you really need to book ahead. Perhaps surprisingly, things are not usually as tight from the middle of July to late August, when many Spaniards try to avoid the searing heat of this and every other Spanish city, but even so vacant rooms can still get mighty sparse. Note also that in periods of high demand, some places insist on a minimum stay of two or three nights. The city's tourist offices (see p.54) will not help you

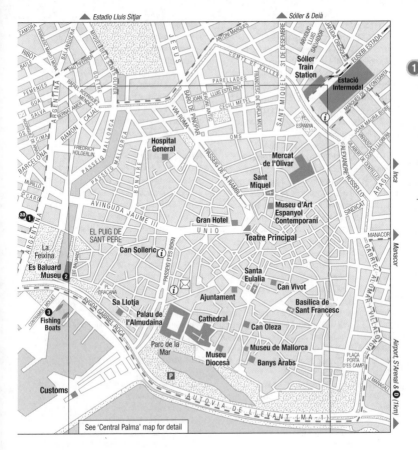

find a room – though they will give you a full list of hotels and *hostales* – and if you need assistance one good contact is Prima Travel (☎971 78 93 22, ⓦwww.prima-travel.com), who specialize in last-minute accommodation and have an office at the airport.

Many of Palma's more enticing hotels and *hostales* are in the centre, which is a good job given that this is by far the most engaging part of the city. In particular, there's a cluster of **budget** places along the narrow, cobbled side streets off the Passeig d'es Born and a number of more modern **mid-range hotels** on the Passeig Mallorca, a particularly attractive portion of the inner ring road, where two sections of old city wall run down the middle of the boulevard on either side of a deep watercourse-cum-moat. There's another cluster of modern high-rises, including some quite plush places, to the west of the centre, overlooking the waterfront along Avinguda Gabriel Roca (also known as the Passeig Marítim), but the city's most **distinctive hotels** – and not necessarily the most expensive – are concentrated in the old town, in a string of beautifully converted old mansions.

One final word of caution: many hotels and *hostales*, especially at the bottom end of the market, have some pretty ropey rooms as well as some good ones. If you are not satisfied, ask for a transfer.

Inexpensive

Hostal Apuntadores c/Apuntadors 8
☎971 71 34 91, ⊛www.palma-hostales.com.
A long-established *hostal* with simple, straightforward rooms in a centrally located old house just off Passeig d'es Born. Some rooms are en suite, others have shared facilities, but light sleepers should bag a room at the back as c/Apuntadors can get very noisy at night. Breakfast is served in the café in the reception area. ❶

Hostal Brondo c/Ca'n Brondo 1
☎971 71 90 43, ⊛www.hostalbrondo .net. In a central but quiet street, this stylish little place occupies a sympathetically modernized old house complete with ancient stone arches and traditional whitewashed plasterwork. The guest rooms, some of which are quite small, are decorated in plain but pleasant modern style and come either en suite or with shared facilities. Shared bath ❶, en suite ❷

Hotel Casa Padrina c/Tereses 2 ☎971 42 53 00, ⊛www.casapadrina.com. Operated by the owners of the *Hotel Dalt Murada* (see p.59), this six-room hotel occupies a late nineteenth-century townhouse complete with beamed ceilings and antique Spanish furniture. It's all very pleasant (after registration you have your own key) and you are right in the centre, albeit in a somewhat gloomy location in the side streets off the Passeig de la Rambla. Very competitively priced with rooms from ❷

Hostal-residencia Regina c/Sant Miquel 77
☎971 71 37 03, ⊛www.hostalreginapalma.com. Small, family-run hotel in an unusual, long and low-slung 1920s building. The interior has recently been refurbished in (vaguely) retro style and the twelve guest rooms, all of which are on the first floor, are mostly en suite; some also have a/c. A three-minute walk from Plaça Espanya. Shared bath ❶, en suite ❷

Hostal Ritzi c/Apuntadors 6 ☎971 71 46 10, ⊛www.hostalritzi.com. Well-regarded and long-established one-star *hostal* in the centre of the city, just off Passeig d'es Born. Occupies an ancient but well-kept five-storey house and although the rooms, both en suite and with shared facilities, could hardly be described as super comfortable, they are perfectly adequate. Shared bath ❶, en suite ❷

Hotel Rosamar Avgda Joan Miró 74
☎971 73 27 23, ⊛www.rosamarpalma.com. A gay-friendly gathering place for an international crew of men and a few women, the *Rosamar* occupies a well-kept, modern block 3km west of the centre, at the junction of c/Patrimoni and Avgda Joan Miró. Has forty guest rooms and no less than three sun terraces with views out over the bay; ask for a room with a sea view. Reachable on EMT bus

#3 from several points in the city including Plaça Joan Carles I (every 15min). Open March to October only. ❶

Hostal Terminus Plaça Espanya 5 ☎971 75 00 14, ⊛www.terminushostal.com. Fetching two-star establishment with a quirkily old-fashioned foyer and fairly large and frugal but still comfortable rooms. Very handy for the Sóller train station – which is a plus – but also within earshot of the traffic-clogged inner ring road. ❶

Moderate

AC Ciutat de Palma Plaça Pont 3 ☎971 22 23 00, ⊛www.ac-hotels.com. Gleaming chain hotel in a stylishly revamped, six-storey high-rise on the edge of the groovy Santa Catalina quarter. The interior is resolutely modern, all angular lines and big vases, and the bedrooms, of which there are 85, are very comfortable with all mod cons. To get there catch EMT bus #3 from several places in the centre, including Plaça Rei Joan Carles I. Rack rate ❺, but prices can soar at peak periods.

Hotel Almudaina Avgda Jaume III, 9 ☎971 72 73 40, ⊛www.hotelalmudaina.com. Dapper modern rooms in one of the attractive 1940s blocks overlooking the city's premier shopping street. Popular with Spanish business folk. Great rooftop views from the uppermost floors. ❹

Hotel Araxa c/Alférez Cerdá 22 ☎971 73 16 40, ⊛www.hotelaraxa.com. Attractive four-storey modern hotel with pleasant gardens and an outdoor swimming pool, located in a quiet residential area about 2km west of the centre, not far from the Castell de Bellver. Most of the rooms, which are decorated in comfortable modern style, have balconies. To get there by public transport, take EMT bus #3 from Plaça Rei Joan Carles I and get off at c/Marquès de la Sènia, just before the start of Avgda Joan Miró; it's a five- to ten-minute walk from the bus stop. ❺

Hotel Born c/Sant Jaume 3 ☎971 71 29 42, ⊛www.hotelborn.com. Delightful hotel in an excellent downtown location, set in a refurbished mansion with big wooden doors and a lovely courtyard, where you can have breakfast under the palm trees. The rooms, most of which face onto the courtyard, are comfortable if a little plain, and all have a/c. It's a popular spot, so book early in high season. ❸

Hotel Catalonia Majórica c/Garita 3 ☎971 40 02 61, ⊛www.hoteles-catalonia.com. Big and modern four-star hotel overlooking the coast from near the ferry port about 4km west of the centre. Some 170 rooms kitted out in brisk and efficient chain-hotel style. Ask for a room with a sea view. Competitively priced from ❹

Hotel Dalt Murada c/Almudaina 6 ☎971 42 53 00, ⓦwww.daltmurada.com. One of the most delightful hotels in the city, this family-run place occupies a splendid old mansion in a great location down an old cobbled alley metres from Plaça Cort. The house still retains many of its original eighteenth-century – and even earlier – features. Each of the guest rooms has its own character, but they are all large and extremely well-appointed and most hold antique furnishings. Breakfast is served in the garden courtyard, weather permitting. Great location too – the family also own the small and much plainer, six-room *Hotel Casa Padrina* (see p.58). ➏

Hotel H M Jaime III Passeig Mallorca 14 ☎971 72 59 43, ⓦwww.hmjaimeiii.com. Agreeable four-star hotel with smart modern rooms kitted out in crisp, minimalist style. The public areas are a little over-done – what on earth is a canoe sculpture doing in the foyer? – but that's hardly a major drawback. The front guest rooms, overlooking the Passeig Mallorca, have the advantage of a balcony, but try to keep to the upper floors away from the noise of the traffic. ➏

Hotel Melià Palas Atenea Passeig Marítim (Avgda Gabriel Roca) 29 ☎971 28 14 00, ⓦwww .solmelia.com. A vast, classy 1960s-style foyer, which looks like it has been imported from Las Vegas, leads to attractively furnished, comfortable rooms with balconies overlooking the bay. ➎

Hotel Palau Sa Font c/Apuntadors 38 ☎971 71 22 77, ⓦwww.palausafont.com. This smooth and polished, four-star hotel, decorated in earthy Italian colours and graced by modern works of art, manages to be both stylish and welcoming. There's a small pool on the roof terrace, and some rooms enjoy inspiring views of the cathedral. Breakfast included. ➏

Hotel Palladium Passeig Mallorca 40 ☎971 71 28 41, ⓦwww.hotelpalladium.com. Proficient three-star hotel offering spick-and-span accommodation in a modern tower block overlooking the handsome Passeig Mallorca. ➌

Hotel San Lorenzo c/Sant Llorenç 14 ☎971 72 82 00, ⓦwww.hotelsanlorenzo.com. Amongst the narrow lanes of what was once the fishermen's quarter of Sant Pere, this chi-chi, four-star hotel has been cleverly squeezed into an old seventeenth-century mansion. The antique details have been lovingly preserved, while modern facilities, such as the swimming pool in the garden, have been tastefully added. Every mod con. ➏

Hotel Saratoga Passeig Mallorca 6 ☎971 72 72 40, ⓦwww.hotelsaratoga.es. Bright, modern, centrally located hotel in a smart seven-storey block complete with a rooftop café-bar and garden

swimming pool. Rooms are neat and trim, with marble floors and balconies either overlooking the boulevard (which can be noisy) or an interior courtyard (much quieter). Substantial banquet-breakfast included. ➏

Expensive

Hotel Convent de la Missió c/de la Missió 7A ☎971 22 73 47, ⓦwww.conventdelamissio.com. Über cool, fourteen-room hotel, whose slick minimalism has been intelligently shoehorned into the wide spaces of a former convent. The location is, however, really rather drab – on a dull side street off c/Sant Miquel. Also home of the headline-hitting *Simply Fosh* restaurant (see p.86). ➑

Hotel-residencia Palacio Ca Sa Galesa c/Miramar 8 ☎971 71 54 00, ⓦwww .palaciocasagalesa.com. Charmingly renovated seventeenth-century mansion set amongst the narrow alleys of the oldest part of town, with just twelve luxurious and tastefully furnished rooms and suites. There's an indoor heated swimming pool (set in a renovated ancient Roman bath) and fine views of the city from the roof terrace. Opened in the early 1990s, this was one of the first deluxe hotels to occupy an old island mansion and its success set something of a trend. ➒

Hotel Portixol c/Sirena 27 ☎971 27 18 00, ⓦwww.portixol.com. Es Portixol, just a couple of kilometres east of Palma Cathedral, was once the preserve of local fishermen, who docked their boats at either of its sheltered coves. The district hit the skids in the 1960s, but it's now championed as an exemplar of urban renewal, its terrace houses all cleaned and dusted, one cove turned into a marina, the other into a tiny beach resort. Leading the aesthetic charge is this high-rise, seafront hotel, a very urban and urbane spot with all sorts of finessed details, from creative backlighting through to guest room TV cabinets that look like mini beach huts. It's all good fun, but note that it's worth paying extra for a room with a sea view. There's an outside swimming pool and a restaurant, where you can dine either inside or outside looking out over the ocean. ➑, sea view ➒

Hotel Puro Oasis Montenegro 12 ☎971 42 54 50, ⓦwww.purohotel.com. Self-conscious designer hotel much admired by the likes of *Condé Nast*. Aimed at the 'hip' city dweller, there are rugs on the ceiling, cushions on the floor, and a sort of erotic charge to the public areas aided and abetted by the house music. As you might expect, the guest rooms are similarly slick and á la mode. The hotel is in an old house amongst the narrow side streets west of the Passeig d'es Born. ➑

The City

There's not much argument as to where to start a tour of Palma – it's got to be the **cathedral**, which dominates the waterfront from the crest of a hill. Central Palma's other landmark is the **Palau de l'Almudaina** next door, an important royal residence from Moorish times and now, much modified, the repository of a mildly engaging assortment of municipal baubles. Spreading northeast behind the cathedral are the narrow lanes and ageing mansions of the most intriguing part of the **old town**. A stroll here is a pleasure in itself, and tucked away among the side streets are three good diversions: the **Museu de Mallorca**, the island's most extensive museum, the ecclesiastical treasures of the **Museu Diocesà**, and the Baroque **Basílica de Sant Francesc**.

North of the old town lies the heart of the early twentieth-century city, where the high-sided tenements are graced by a sequence of flamboyant buildings in the *Modernisme* style (the Spanish, and especially Catalan, form of Art Nouveau), particularly on and around **Plaça Weyler**.

West of the city centre, you should consider a visit to the **Castell de Bellver**, an impressive hilltop castle, and perhaps also to the much less interesting **Poble Espanyol**, which comprises detailed, scaled-down reproductions of characteristic buildings from every region of Spain.

The cathedral

Legend has it that when the invasion force of Jaume I of Aragón and Catalunya stood off Mallorca in 1229, a fierce gale threatened to sink the fleet. The desperate king promised to build a church dedicated to the Virgin Mary if the expedition against the Moors was successful. It was, and Jaume fulfilled his promise, starting construction work the following year. The king had a political point to make too – he built his cathedral, a gigantic affair of golden sandstone, bang on top of the Great Mosque inside the Almudaina, the old Moorish citadel. The Reconquista – the expulsion of the Moors by the Christians – was to be no temporary matter.

As it turned out, the **cathedral** ("La Seu" in Catalan) was five hundred years in the making. Nonetheless, although there are architectural bits and bobs from several different eras, the church remains essentially Gothic, with massive exterior buttresses – its most distinctive feature – taking the weight off the pillars within. The whole structure derives its effect from its sheer height, impressive from any angle, but startling when viewed from the waterside esplanade.

The doors and bell tower

The finest of the cathedral's three doors is the **Portal del Mirador** ("Lookout Door"), which overlooks the Bay of Palma from the south facade. Dating from the late fourteenth century, the newly buffed and scrubbed Mirador features a host of Flemish-style ecclesiastical figurines set around a tympanum where heavily bearded disciples sit at a Last Supper. In contrast, the west-facing **Portal Major** ("Great Door"), across from the Palau de l'Almudaina, is a neo-Gothic disaster, an ugly reworking – along with the sixty-metre-high flanking turrets – of a far simpler predecessor that was badly damaged by an earthquake in 1851.

On the north side is a third door, the **Portal de l'Almoina**, decorated in a simple Gothic design of 1498. Above rises the solid squareness of the **bell tower** (closed to the public), an incongruous, fortress-like structure that clearly did not form part of the original design. When the largest of the bells, the 5700-kilo N'Eloi, was tolled in 1857, it shattered most of the cathedral's windows.

The nave
You **enter the cathedral** (April, May & Oct Mon–Fri 10am–5.15pm, Sat 10am–2.15pm; June–Sept Mon–Fri 10am–6.15pm, Sat 10am–2.15pm; Nov–March Mon–Fri 10am–3.15pm, Sat 10am–2.15pm; €4; **W** www.catedral demallorca.org) on the north side through the museum (see p.64). The majestic proportions of the interior are seen to best advantage from the western end – from the Portal Major. In the central **nave**, fourteen beautifully aligned, pencil-thin pillars rise to 21m before their ribs branch out, like fronded palm trees, to support the single-span, vaulted roof. The nave, at 44m high, is one of the tallest Gothic structures in Europe, and its 121-metre length is of matching grandeur. This open, hangar-like construction, typical of Catalan Gothic architecture, was designed to make the high altar visible to the entire congregation and to express the mystery of the Christian faith, with kaleidoscopic floods of light filtered in through the **stained-glass windows**. Most of the original glass was lost long ago, but recent refurbishment has returned a number of windows to their former glory and, now that many others have been un-bricked, the cathedral has re-emerged from the gloom imposed by Renaissance, Baroque and neo-Gothic architects. There are seven rose windows, the largest of which crowns the triumphal arch of the apse towards the east end and boasts over 1200 individual pieces of glass; providing the morning sun is out, it showers the nave with a wonderful, dappled light. The cathedral's designers also incorporated a specific, carefully orchestrated artifice: twice a year, at 6.30am on Candlemas and St Martin's Day, the sun shines through the stained glass of the eastern window onto the wall immediately below the rose window on the main, western facade.

Gaudí's restoration
The first attempt to return the church to something like its original Gothic splendour was made at the beginning of the twentieth century when an inspired local bishop commissioned the *Modernista* Catalan architect **Antoni Gaudí** (1852–1926) to direct a full-blown restoration. At the time, Gaudí was renowned for his fancifully embellished metalwork, and his functionalist extrapolation of Gothic design was still evolving. This experimentation led ultimately to his most famous and extravagant opus, the church of the Sagrada Familia in Barcelona, but here in Palma his work was relatively restrained – though still deeply controversial. Indeed, certain Catholic dignitaries took the aesthetic hump over the revamp and when, in 1926, a Barcelona tram flattened Gaudí they must have thought their prayers had been answered.

Gaudí worked on Palma's cathedral intermittently between 1904 and 1914, during which time he removed the High Baroque altar and shifted the ornate choir stalls from the centre to the side of the cathedral, placing them flat against the walls. The new high altar, a medieval alabaster table of plain design, was then located beneath a phantasmagorical **baldachin**, a giant canopy, enhanced by hanging lanterns, which was supposed to symbolize the Crown of Thorns. It's not a great success, though to be fair Gaudí never had time to complete it – he wanted it to be made of wrought iron, but what you see today is in fact a trial piece fashioned from cork, cardboard and brocade.

Other examples of Gaudí's distinctive workmanship are dotted around the cathedral. The **railings** in front of the high altar are twisted into shapes inspired by Mallorcan window grilles, while the wall on either side of the **Bishop's**

CENTRAL PALMA

Castell de Bellver ▲

Teatre Municipal

Estació Intermodal

Sóller Train Station

PLAÇA ESPANYA

MARIE CURIE

PORTA PINTADA

JOAN XXIII

Mercat de l'Olivar

CAPUTXINS

PLAÇA DE L'OLIVAR

SANT MIQUEL

Sant Miquel

FRANCESC DE BORJA MOLL

CAN MAÇANET

CAN PERPINYA

MISSIO

MISSIO

TERESES

POSADA DE LA REAL

Museu d'Art Espanyol Contemporani

SANT MIQUEL

Teatre Principal

PL. MAJOR

PL. MARQUES DEL PALMER

BOSSERIA

L'Aguila

Can Rei

CAN GATER

MOLINERS

VILANOVA

COSTA D'EN BRASA

VOLTA DE LA MERCE

HOSTAL DE L'ESTE

SINDICAT

CAN VALLORI

LLOTGETA

HOSTALS

CORDERIA

FERRERIA

RIERA

Gran Hotel

PL. WEYLER

kk

BARTOMEU

SANTA CILIA

PL. CAN TAGAMENT

CAN

BELDANS

BROSSA

MONTEROS

CECILI METEL

CARDENAL POU

OMS

SANT ELIES

CARME

HORTS

PL. BISBE BERENGUER DE PALOU

JERONI ANTIC

P. DE JESUS

PASSEIG DE LA RAMBLA

CAN OLIVA

CAN PUEYO

CAN JAQUOTOT

CAPUTXINES

CAN CAMPANER

ROSA

SANT NICOLAU

UNIO

PL. MERCAT

CAN SERINYA

Can Balaguer

CAN BRONDO

CAN OMS

BARO DE PINOPAR

VIA ROMA

CAMPINS

PL. STA. MAGDALENA

ANGELS

BISBE

SASTRE ROIG

SANT JAUME

C. DE STA. MAGDALENA

SECRETA DE SANT JAUME

CAN MERCADA

SANT JAUME

PALMA

GAVARRERA

Can Solleric

Can Oleza

JOVELLANOS

SANT GAIETA

PL. REI JOAN CARLES I

AVINGUDA JAUME III

CAN DURETA

CAN OFRE

SANT FELIU

Hospital General

PL. HOSPITAL

CATANY

C. TORRELLA

HERMITA

C. CATALINA

CAN RIBERA

CONCEPCIO

AIGUA

MONTCADES

MISERICORDIA

BISBE

BOTIA

SANTIAGO RUSIÑOL

JOAQUIM

SANT MARTI

SANT FELIU

CONCEPCIO

CONCEPCIO

Can Pavesi

Can Moner

EL PUIG DE SANT PERE

CAN SALES

BERENGUER

PAU

Can Oleza

RUBEN DARIO

CERDANYA

CONFLENT

OMELADES

CARLADES

BERENGUER SANT JOAN

HUG DE BESALERS

ARAGONES

JOAN DE CREMONA

METGE MATAS

STA MARIA DEL SEPULCRE

BONAIRE

AVINGUDA DE PORTUGAL

PASSEIG MALLORCA

PASSEIG MALLORCA

RAMON CAJAL

EIVISSA

MENORCA

PL. PORTA DE SANTA CATALINA

N

ACCOMMODATION

Hotel Almudaina	H
Hostal Apuntadores	N
Hotel Born	G
Hostal Brondo	J
Hotel Casa Padrina	E
Hotel Convent de la Missió	D
Hotel Dalt Murada	P
Hotel H M Jaime III	F
Hotel-residencia Palacio Ca Sa Galesa	Q
Hotel Palau Sa Font	K
Hotel Palladium	C
Hotel Puro Oasis	M
Hostal-residencia Regina	B
Hostal Ritzi	O
Hotel San Lorenzo	L
Hotel Saratoga	I
Hostal Terminus	A

RESTAURANTS

Aramis	8
Caballito del Mar	21
Ca'n Carlos	3
Celler Pagès	11
Forn de Sant Joan	13
La Cuchara	1
Simply Fosh	D

CAFÉS & TAPAS BARS

Bar Bosch	6
Bon Lloc	9
Café Lírico	17
Ca N'Ignasi de Pollença	2
Ca'n Joan de S'Aigo	10
Cappuccino	16
El Pilon	7
Gran Hotel Café	5
La Bodeguilla	4
La Taberna del Caracol	23
Orient Express	18
Taberna de la Bóveda	22

LATE-NIGHT BARS

Abaco	15
Escape	12
Gotic	20
Jazz Voyeur Club	14
La Lonja	19

SHOPS

Camper	cc
Camper	ee
Colmado Santo Domingo	oo
El Corte Inglés	ff
Fet a Mà	aa
Fine Books	rr
Forn des Teatre	kk
Forn Fondo	hh
Frasquet	mm
H&M	jj
La Casa del Mapa	pp
La Concha	nn
La Favorita	bb
Libreria Fondevila	dd
Loewe	ii
Majorica	gg
Vidrias Gordiola	qq
Zara	ll

Map labels:

Es Baluard Museu
Consolat de Mar
Can Alomar
Sa Llotja
Palau March
Costa de la Seu
Cathedral
Ajuntament
Arc de l'Almudaina
Can Bordils
Can Marques
Can Oleza
Santa Eulalia
Museu de Mallorca
Banys Àrabs
Museu Diocesà
Museu Lladó
Palau de l'Almudaina
Parc de la Mar
Basílica de Sant Francesc
Can Vivot
Joan S'Aigo
Monti-Sion
Templar Chapel
Sant Jeroni
Gateway
Walls
Portella

PASSEIG D'ES BORN
AVGDA. D'ANTONI MAURA
AVINGUDA GABRIEL ROCA (MA-1)
AUTOVIA DE LLEVANT (MA-1)
Badia de Palma

100 m
0

Throne, at the east end of the church, sports ceramic inlays with brightly painted floral designs. Yet Gaudí's main concern was to revive the Gothic tradition by allowing extra light. To this end he introduced **electric lighting**, bathing the apse in bright artificial light and placing lamps and candelabra throughout the church. This was all very innovative: at the time, no choir had ever before been removed in Spain and electric lighting was a real novelty. The artistic success of the whole project, though, was undeniable, and it was immediately popular with the congregation. Like the rest of his work, however, it did not bring Gaudí much international acclaim: it was only in the 1960s that his techniques were championed and copied across western Europe, and that his crucial role in the development of modernism was finally acknowledged.

The chapels

The aisles on either side of the central nave are flanked by a long sequence of **chapels**, dull affairs for the most part, dominated by dusty Baroque altars of gargantuan proportions and little artistic merit. The exception, and the cathedral's one outstanding example of the Baroque, is the **Capella del Corpus Christi**, at the head of the aisle to the left of the high altar. Begun in the sixteenth century, the chapel's tiered and columned altarpiece features three religious scenes, cramped and intense sculptural tableaux depicting – from top to bottom – the temptations of St Anthony, the presentation of Jesus in the temple, and the Last Supper. Just in front and across from the chapel is a massive stone **pulpit** that was moved here by Gaudí, a makeshift location for this excellent illustration of the Plateresque style. Dated to 1531, the pulpit's intricate floral patterns and bustling Biblical scenes cover a clumsy structure, the upper portion of which is carried by telamons, male counterparts of the more usual caryatids (supporting columns draped in female clothing).

There's also the **Capella de la Trinitat** (Trinity Chapel) at the east end of the church directly behind the high altar. You can't actually get to it today, but this tiny chapel is of considerable interest and there are vague plans to open it up at some point. Completed in 1329, the chapel accommodates the remains of Jaume II and Jaume III, two notable medieval kings of Mallorca (for more on whom, see pp.275–278). Initially, the bodies were stored in a tomb that operated rather like a filing cabinet, allowing the corpses to be venerated by the devout. They were viewed in 1809 by the first British traveller to write an account of a visit to Mallorca, the unflappable Sir John Carr, who calmly observed that, "considering the monarchs had been dead for five hundred years…they were in a state of extraordinary preservation". This gruesome practice was finally discontinued during the nineteenth century, and alabaster sarcophagi now enclose the royal bones.

Visitors either regain the cathedral museum (see below) from the north side of the nave or exit via the cloisters.

The Museu de la Catedral

The ground floor of the bell tower and two adjoining chapterhouses have been turned into the **Museu de la Catedral** (same times and ticket as the cathedral), which holds an eclectic assortment of ecclesiastical knick-knacks. The first room's most valuable exhibit, in the glass case in the middle, is a gilded silver monstrance of extraordinary delicacy, its fairy-tale decoration dating from the late sixteenth century. On display around the walls is a hotchpotch of chalices and reliquaries and a real curiosity, the portable altar of Jaume I, a wood and silver chessboard with each square containing a bag of relics.

The second room is devoted to the Gothic works of the **Mallorcan Primitives**, a school of painters that flourished on the island in the fourteenth and fifteenth centuries, producing strikingly naive devotional works of bold colours and cartoon-like detail. The work of two of the school's leading fourteenth-century practitioners is displayed here, beginning with the so-called **Master of the Privileges**, noted for his love of warm colours and minute detail. His work is shown to good advantage in a large (though unlabelled), cartoon-like panel painting of *The Life of St Eulalia*, whose martyrdom fascinated and excited scores of medieval Mallorcan artists. A Catalan girl-saint, Eulalia defied the Roman emperor Diocletian by sticking to her Christian faith despite all sorts of ferocious tortures, which are depicted here in ecstatic detail. She was eventually burnt at the stake and at the moment of her death, white doves flew from her mouth. The Master of the Privileges was greatly influenced by Italian painters, but his contemporary, the **Master of Montesión**, looked to his Catalan contemporaries for his sense of movement and tight draughtsmanship as in two panels displayed here, one of the *Crucifixion*, the other of the *Virgin Mary*. Later, the work of the Mallorcan Primitives shaded into the new realism of the Flemish style, which was to dominate Mallorcan painting throughout the sixteenth century. **Joan Desi**'s (unlabelled) *Panel of La Almoina* illustrates the transition – it's the large panel showing St Francis, complete with stigmata, at the side of Christ. One of Desi's pupils was **Alonso de Sedano**, who adopted a similar style in his *Martyrdom of St Sebastian*, which has the saint pierced by so many arrows that he looks like a sort of pin cushion.

The third and final room, the **Baroque chapterhouse**, is entered through a playful Churrigueresque doorway, above which a delicate Madonna is entertained by lively cherubic angels. Inside, pride of place goes to the High Baroque **altar**, a gaudy, gilded affair surmounted by the Sacred Heart, a gory representation of the heart of Jesus that was very much in vogue during the eighteenth century. Some imagination went into the designation of the reliquaries displayed round the room, comprising an unlikely collection of bits and pieces of various saints. Of more appeal are a pair of finely carved, Baroque **crucifixes**, each Christ a study in perfect muscularity swathed in the flowing folds of a loincloth.

The Palau de l'Almudaina

Opposite the cathedral stands the **Palau de l'Almudaina**, originally the palace of the Moorish *walis* (governors), and later of the Mallorcan kings (April–Sept Mon–Fri 10am–5.45pm, Sat 10am–1pm; Oct–March Mon–Fri 10am–1pm & 4–5pm, Sat 10am–1pm; €3.20, audioguide €2; free on Wed to EU citizens showing their passport). The present structure, built around a central courtyard, owes much of its appearance to Jaume II (1276–1311), who spent the last twelve years of his life in residence here. Jaume converted the old fortress into a lavish palace that incorporated both Gothic and Moorish features, an uneasy mixture of styles conceived by the Mallorcan Pedro Selva, the king's favourite architect. The two most prominent "Moorish" attributes are the fragile-looking outside walls, with their square turrets and dainty crenellations, and the delicate arcades of the main loggia, which can be seen from the waterside esplanade below.

Once Mallorca was incorporated within the Aragonese kingdom, the Palau de l'Almudaina became surplus to requirements, though it did achieve local notoriety when the eccentric Aragonese king Juan I (1387–95) installed an **alchemist** in the royal apartments, hoping he would replenish the treasury by turning base metal into gold. He didn't succeed. Today the palace serves a variety of official functions, has a small garrison to protect it, and holds a series

▲ Palau de l'Almudaina

of state apartments kept in readiness for visiting dignitaries and the king, which is presumably why those exhibits that are labelled carry Castilian inscriptions. When the king or some other bigwig is in residence, parts of the palace are cordoned off.

At the **reception**, you can pick up a free plan and/or opt for an audioguide.

The Sàlon de Consejos and Comedor de Oficiales

A visit begins with a series of medieval corridors and rooms whose rough stonework is almost entirely devoid of ornamentation, but things pick up in the **Salón de Consejos** (Hall of Councils), where the walls sport a group of admirable Flemish tapestries, fifteenth- and sixteenth-century imports devoted to classical themes. Amongst them is a Roman Triumph, a blood-curdling war scene, and, best of the lot, the suicide of Cleopatra, showing a particularly wan-looking queen with the guilty asp slithering discreetly away. Moving on, the **Comedor de Oficiales** (Officers' Mess) possesses a handful of Flemish genre paintings, fine still-life studies including one by the seventeenth-century Antwerp-based artist Frans Snyders – there's no label, but it's the painting with the man, the woman, the cat and several carcasses. Snyders was a contemporary of Rubens and odd-jobbed for him, painting in the flowers and fruit on many of his canvases.

The Sala de Guardia and the Baños Árabes

Next door, there are charming views across the city and harbour from the outside **terraza** (terrace), which holds a small formal garden, and then it's inside again for the **Sala de Guardia** (Guard Room), where there are several dire eighteenth-century Spanish tapestries. Crude and inexact, these are in striking contrast to the Flemish tapestries exhibited elsewhere, but by then Spain had lost control of the Netherlands and the Spanish court could no longer acquire pieces from its traditional suppliers. In 1725, the Spanish king founded a tapestry factory in Madrid, but its products – as demonstrated here – were poor, and there must have been some aesthetic gnashing of teeth when the Spanish court took delivery. Nearby, the **Baños Árabes** (Arab Baths) are, like the city's other Banys Àrabs at c/Can Serra 7 (see p.70), a rare survivor from Moorish times, comprising three stone-vaulted chambers, one each for cold, tepid and hot baths. Enough remains to see how this sophisticated set-up worked and why the Christian kings who supplanted the Moors adopted them lock, stock and barrel.

The Salón Mayor and the Capella de Santa Ana

After the Arab Baths, you move into the central **courtyard**, from where the **Escalera Real** (Royal Staircase), installed by Philip II, leads up to the **state apartments** that fill out the palace's upper level. These apartments are really rather sterile, but there are several splendidly ornate Mudéjar wooden ceilings and one architectural peculiarity: extra floors were inserted into the original structure and the result is most clearly visible on the top floor, where the **Salón Mayor** (Main Hall) is framed by heavy stone arches. In this room also is a magnificent seventeenth-century tapestry, *The Siege of Carthage*, which covers most of the back wall. The adjoining **Despacho de Su Majestad el Rey** (Office of the King), with its attractive Gothic gallery, was where the Moors surrendered to Jaume I in 1229.

Afterwards, it's back into the courtyard for the **Capella de Santa Ana** (Chapel of St Anne), a largely fourteenth-century Gothic structure that is still used for army officers' masses and weddings. The interior, with its fine vaulted and embossed ceiling, is decidedly intimate, almost cosy, a suitable home for the **Capella de St Praxedis**, which, with its medieval effigy and reliquary, is devoted to a much venerated saint. A fourth-century figure, Praxedis survived the massacre of her Christian companions and had the presence of mind to mop up their blood with a sponge and preserve it for later worship; Jaume III brought the reliquary back with him from Rome. Incidentally, the delicate marble carving above the chapel entrance is carved in the Romanesque style, a deliberate use of what was by then an archaic tradition. The three figures above the door depict the Virgin Mary with saints Anne and Joachim to either side.

The Museu Diocesà

The smartly turned out **Museu Diocesà** (Diocesan Museum; Mon–Sat 10am–2pm; €3) occupies part of the old bishop's palace, a handsome courtyard complex round the back of the cathedral – and directly above the old city walls – at c/Mirador 5. The museum's highlight is its collection of **Mallorcan Primitives**, the city's largest, displayed on the ground floor alongside an assortment of religious statuary and a scattering of reliquaries. Later – and lesser - items are displayed upstairs.

The Master of the Passion of Mallorca and Pere Niçard

Beside reception is the striking *Passion of Christ* by an unknown artist dubbed the **Master of the Passion of Mallorca**. Dated to the end of the thirteenth century, the painting follows a standard format, with a series of small vignettes outlining the story of Christ, but the artistry is in the warm and gentle detail: the Palm Sunday donkey leans forward pushing his nose towards a child; one of the disciples reaches out across the Last Supper table for the fish; and two of Jesus' disciples slip their sandals off in eager anticipation during the Washing of the Feet. Close by is another fine work, **Pere Niçard**'s large and dramatic, late fifteenth-century *St George and the Dragon*, a panel painting in which the stern fortifications of Palma appear in the background. Below the saint, to either side of Christ emerging from his tomb, are smaller paintings depicting the conquest of Mallorca by Jaume I – the storming of Palma on the right and the administering of (rough) justice to the left.

The Master of Bishop Galiana and Pere Terrencs

The museum also holds an intriguing *St Paul* retable by the **Master of Bishop Galiana**, whose tight lines are very much in the Catalan tradition. This particular panel painting is a didactic cartoon-strip illustrating the life of St Paul, who is shown with his Bible open and sword in hand, a view of the Church militant that must have accorded well with the preoccupations of the powerful bishops of Mallorca. Look out also for the way Galiana portrays the Conversion on the road to Damascus, with Saul-Paul struck by a laser-like beam of light. There are several paintings by **Pere Terrencs**, but it is the *Crucifixion* that catches the eye, a sophisticated, early sixteenth-century work of strong, deep colours set within a triangulated structure. Above is the blood-spattered, pale-white body of Christ, while down below – divided by the Cross – are two groups, one of hooded mourners, the other a trio of nonchalant Roman soldiers in contemporary Spanish dress. Terrencs has chosen to ignore the two thieves who were crucified with Christ, showing him suffering alone on a bare and barren hill.

Upstairs, the museum's first floor has a few modest paintings from the seventeenth century onwards, a room full of ceramics, and a graffiti wall where generations of bored priests doodled and dawdled. Curiously, there are also a few bits of furniture designed by **Gaudí**, who lodged here at the palace when he was working on the cathedral (see p.61).

The Palau March

Just along c/Palau Reial from the Almudaina, across the top of the wide flight of stone steps that leads up from Plaça de la Reina, is the **Palau March** (April–Oct Mon–Fri 10am–6pm, Sat 10am–2pm; Nov–March Mon–Fri 10am–5pm, Sat 10am–2pm; €3.60; ⓦ www.fundbmarch.es), whose arcaded galleries and imperious Italianate bulk fill out the entire block between c/Palau Reial and c/Conquistador. The palace was built between 1939 and 1945 in the general style of the city's earlier Renaissance mansions on behalf of **Joan March**, long the island's most powerful inhabitant (see box, p.69). A visit begins with the palace's most enjoyable feature, its splendid **Italianate courtyard**, which offers attractive views over the city centre and displays a potpourri of modern **sculpture** drawn from the March collection. Amongst the twenty or so pieces exhibited, there are two Henry Moores, a Rodin torso and a fetchingly eccentric *Orgue del Mar* (Organ of the Sea) by Xavier Corberó (b.1935).

After the courtyard, the **interior** of the *palau* is a distinct anticlimax, its cold stone walls displaying an odd and distinctly unsatisfying mix of curios with almost no labelling at all. Entering the building on the right-hand side of the courtyard, beside the Rodin, the first room gives some background information on the kitsch, eighteenth-century Neapolitan figurines that are the villa's main exhibit – as displayed in a second room, which is dominated by a **Nativity Scene**, complete with a veritable army of small models packed into a large glass cabinet. It's difficult to know quite what to make of all this – and things get worse on the first floor, where the Spanish painter **Josep Maria Sert** (1874–1945) was responsible for both the brutal muscularity of the ceiling painting at the top of the stairs and the March family's one-time

Joan March

One of the most controversial figures in Mallorca's recent history, **Joan March** (1880–1962) was born a peasant's son in the small town of Santa Margalida on the east side of the island. At school, he showed his entrepreneurial flair by loaning money to his classmates at a high rate of interest and deciding, so the story goes, to start a trade in cigarettes, charging by the puff. March's father was a pig herder and at the age of 20 Joan negotiated the first of his major business deals, supplying meat direct to a sausage factory in Barcelona. In the next few years he allegedly established a dominant position in the **tobacco smuggling** trade with Algeria, displaying a ruthlessness that made him feared and loathed in equal measure.

March made more money in World War I, when both the British and the Germans paid him for his services, and took advantage of the difficulties experienced by the island's landed aristocracy to make yet more. For a variety of reasons, including the phylloxera infestation of the vineyards (see box, p.32), many of Mallorca's large estates had become uneconomic. March bought them up for a song and then sold them back to the farm hands who had previously worked them. The profit on each transaction was small, but there was the economy of scale: March sold no fewer than forty thousand land titles, an enormous number for a small island, and by these means transformed the structure of Mallorcan society as an accidental corollary to his greed.

During the Spanish Civil War, it seems likely that March loaned Franco money on generous terms and helped the Fascists with military supplies. Whatever the truth, March did become the richest man in Franco's Spain and was much favoured by the regime. In 1955, for reasons that remain obscure, he decided to reinvent himself, becoming a **patron of the arts**, buying up dozens of sculptures and paintings and giving millions of pesetas to a new charitable foundation, the **Fundació Joan March**. In Palma, the *fundació* runs the Museu d'Art Espanyol Contemporani (see p.80) and March's old house, the Palau March (see p.68) is open to the public. However, the man is mainly recalled by the bank he set up in 1926, the **Banca March**, which now has branches right across the island.

music room just beyond. The latter is decorated with racist murals depicting New Orleans jazz scenes of frolicking "Negroes" – Sert did much better elsewhere. The only modest light in the cultural gloom is the adjoining **book and curio room**, which holds an idiosyncratic collection of old volumes and illuminated manuscripts.

The city walls and Parc de la Mar

A wide flight of steps leads down from between the cathedral and the Palau de l'Almudaina to a handsomely restored section of the **Renaissance city walls**, whose mighty zigzag of bastions, bridges, gates and dry moats once encased the whole city. These replaced the city's **medieval walls**, portions of which also survive – look back up from the foot of the steps and a large chunk is clearly visible beneath the cathedral. Constructed of sandstone blocks and adobe, the earlier fortifications depended for their efficacy on their height, with a gallery running along the top from which the defenders could fire at the enemy. By the middle of the fifteenth century, however, the development of more effective artillery had shifted the military balance in favour of offence, with cannons now able to breach medieval city walls with comparative ease. The military architects of the day soon evolved a new design in which walls were built much lower and thicker to absorb cannon shot, while four-faced bastions – equipped with artillery platforms – projected from the line of the walls, providing the defenders with a variety of firing lines. The whole caboodle was protected by a water-filled **moat** with deep, sheer sides. The costs of refortifying the major cities of western Europe were astronomical, but every country joined in the rush. In Palma, the Habsburgs ordered work to start on the new (Renaissance) design in the 1560s, though the chain of bastions was only completed in 1801.

Strolling the city wall

From the foot of the steps below the cathedral, a wide and pleasant **walkway** travels along the top of the Renaissance walls, providing delightful views of the city and harbour plus an insight into the tremendous strength of the fortifications. Heading **west**, the walkway leads to the **tiered gardens** of a lush Moorish-style park, which tumbles down to – and runs along beside – Avinguda d'Antoni Maura, an extension of the tree-lined Passeig d'es Born (see p.77). In the opposite direction – **east** from the steps below the cathedral – the walkway passes above the planted trees, concrete terraces and ornamental lagoon of the **Parc de la Mar**, an imaginative and popular redevelopment of the disused land that once lay between the walls and the coastal motorway. Indeed, it has proved so popular that the municipality are considering shoving the highway underground so that they can extend the park to the seashore.

Wall and walkway zigzag along the south side of old Palma before eventually fizzling out at Plaça Llorenç Villalonga, but long before that – just a couple of minutes from the cathedral – you reach the double **Portella gateway**, where you go down one of the wide stone ramps to reach the foot of c/Portella.

The old town

The medina-like maze of streets to the rear of the cathedral constitutes the heart of the **old town**, which extends north to Plaça Cort and east to Avinguda Gabriel Alomar i Villalonga. Long a neglected corner of the city, most of the district has now been refurbished in an ambitious and massively expensive project that has restored much of its antique charm. The area's general appearance is its main appeal, rather than any specific sights, and you can spend hour after hour wandering down narrow lanes and alleys, loitering in the squares, gazing at Renaissance mansions and peering at imposing Baroque and Gothic churches. Nonetheless, there are a couple of obvious targets, namely the district's two finest churches – the **Església de Santa Eulalia** and the **Basílica de Sant Francesc** – plus the city's most extensive museum, the **Museu de Mallorca**.

The Banys Àrabs

Leaving the city walls at the Portella gate (see above), you'll find yourself on the edge of the old town at the foot of c/Portella. North of the gate, take the first turning on the right for the **Banys Àrabs**, at c/Can Serra 7 (Arab Baths; daily: June–Sept 9am–8pm; Oct–May 9am–6pm; €1.20). One of the few genuine reminders of the Moorish presence, this tenth-century brick *hammam* (bath house) consists of a small horseshoe-arched and domed chamber that was once heated through the floor. The arches rest on stone pillars, an irregular bunch thought to have been looted from the remains of the island's Roman buildings. The baths are reasonably well preserved, but if you've been to the baths in Girona or Granada, or even the Baños Árabes in the Palau de l'Almudaina (see p.66), these are really rather dull. The lush garden outside, with tables where you can picnic, is perhaps nicer.

Casa Museu J. Torrents Lladó

Close to the Banys Àrabs, at c/Portella 9, the old house and studio of the Catalan artist J. Torrents Lladó (1946–93) has been pleasantly converted into a small museum, the **Casa Museu J. Torrents Lladó** (mid-June to mid-Sept Tues–Fri 11am–7pm, Sat 10am–2pm; mid-Sept to mid-June Tues–Fri 10am–6pm, Sat 10am–2pm; €3), celebrating his life and work. Lladó trained in Barcelona but, after some initial dabblings, he rejected Modernism in the late 1960s, moving to Mallorca in 1968. Here, he became well known as a society portraitist, painting pictures of the rich and famous – or at least the rich – in a dark and broody Baroque style, examples of which hang alongside a number of landscapes, both watercolours and sticky oils.

The Museu de Mallorca

From the Lladó museum, it's a few metres north up along c/Portella to the expansive **Museu de Mallorca** (Tues–Sat 10am–7pm, Sun 10am–2pm; €3), which occupies **Can Aiamans**, a rambling Renaissance mansion whose high-ceilinged rooms make a delightful setting for an enjoyable medley of Mallorcan artefacts. The earliest exhibits date from prehistoric times, but there's also a superb assortment of Gothic paintings and some excellent examples of *Modernista* fittings and furnishings. The labelling is a tad patchy but hopefully the major revamp, which is currently underway, will rectify matters; it's also possible that the layout of the museum will change – so the description below should be treated with caution.

Prehistory, the Romans and the Moors

Currently, the collection begins in the **basement**, on the right-hand side of the entrance courtyard, with a series of rooms that track through the island's early history. Here you'll find a ragbag of **archeological finds** and displays on the *navetas* and *talayots* typical of Mallorca's prehistoric Talayotic culture (for more on which, see p.271). Archeologists have been arguing for decades about exactly when the island was first settled, an arcane dispute focused on a confusing series of finds made in the scattering of caves where the earliest islanders took shelter: the museum plays it safe by hedging its chronological bets.

By comparison, the **Late Talayotic Period** (500/400 BC–123 AD) is much more clearly defined and it's then that the islanders either made – or possibly imported – the finely detailed and extremely bellicose statuettes that presently have a whole room to themselves. Of the dozen or so statuettes on display, most are of nude men, helmeted and armed, aggressive figurines clearly representative of a warlike culture: indeed, such was the islanders' reputation as warriors that the Carthaginians recruited hundreds of them to fight in their armies during the Punic Wars against Rome in the third century BC. Equally striking, and in the same room, is the **Bou de Talapí**, an angular carving of a bull's head that exudes a brutish strength of almost disconcerting proportions.

After the Talayotic section, there is a modest display on **Roman** Mallorca, including a number of finely worked funerary tablets, and another on the **Moorish** period, where the highlights are some ornate Mudéjar wooden panelling and an exquisite selection of Arab and Moorish jewellery. The Moorish section leads back to the main courtyard, which you cross to reach the rest of the collection.

The Mallorcan Primitives

On the left-hand side of the entrance courtyard, an old stone stairway leads up to the first of a couple of rooms devoted to the city's second largest collection of **Mallorcan Primitive painters** after the Museu Diocesà (see p.67). On display in this first room are works by the Masters of Montesión and Castellitx and, best of the lot, a panel painting entitled *Santa Quiteria*, whose lifelike, precisely executed figures – right down to the king's wispy beard – are typical of the gifted **Master of the Privileges**. In the same room there's also a curious thirteenth-century work of unknown authorship dedicated to St Bernard of Clairvaux, with the saint on his knees devotedly drinking the milk of the Virgin Mary. It is an appropriate image: St Bernard, the founder of the Cistercian order, played a crucial role in the development of the cult of the Virgin Mary, elevating her to a key position as the intercessor between humankind and God.

Beyond is a room of religious statues and carved capitals and then a second room of Gothic paintings, which is distinguished by a sequence of works by **Francesc Comes** (1379–1415), whose skill in catching subtle skin textures matches his Flemish contemporaries and represents a softening of the early Mallorcan Primitives' crudeness. In his striking *St George*, the saint – girl-like, with typically full lips – impales a lime-green dragon with more horns/hooks than could possibly be useful. One of the last talented exponents of Mallorcan Gothic, the **Master of the Predellas** – probably a certain Joan Rosató – is represented by his Bosch-like triptych of the *Life of Santa Margalida*, with each group of onlookers a sea of ugly, deformed faces and cruelly curious eyes. The work outlines the life of Margaret of Antioch, one of the most venerated saints in medieval Christendom. During the reign of the Roman emperor Diocletian (284–305 AD) she refused to marry a pagan prefect and was consequently executed after being tortured with extravagant gusto. As if this weren't enough, she also had to resist more metaphysical trials: Satan, disguised as a dragon, swallowed her, but couldn't digest her holiness, so his stomach opened up and out she popped unharmed. This particular tribulation made Margaret the patron saint of pregnant women.

The ensuing rooms display the stodgy art of the **Counter-Reformation**, with Palma's own Miquel Bestard (1590–1633) making a successful appearance with his whopping *Feeding of the Five Thousand*. Miraculously, Jesus feeds the hungry crowd from a meagre supply of loaves and fishes, but the subtext is much more revealing: Bestard's crowds are well behaved and respectful of authority – just what the Catholic hierarchy had in mind.

Modern art

The museum's **top floor** currently holds a mildly engaging assortment of nineteenth- and early twentieth-century paintings by both native artists and foreign artists once resident in Mallorca. This includes a neat sample of works by Mallorca's own **Juli Ramis** (1909–90), whose striking style is illustrated by his oil-on-fabric *Tres Cavalls* (Three Horses) and the radiant blues of *Tardor en blau* (Blue Autumn). A native of Sóller, Ramis left the island when he was nineteen to spend the next sixty years abroad, travelling widely and becoming acquainted with some of the leading artistic lights of his day, notably Picasso and his mates. Ramis mixed his styles, but was essentially an Expressionist with Surrealistic leanings. He returned to Mallorca in the last years of his life and died in Palma.

Also on this floor are two rooms of **Modernista** fittings and furnishings, mostly retrieved from shops and houses that have since been demolished. Of particular interest are the charming wall tiles manufactured at the island's **La Roqueta** works. The pottery was in production for just twenty years (1897–1918), but this coincided with the vogue for the *Modernista* pieces in which La Roqueta excelled.

North to Can Marquès

Continuing on up the hill from the Museu de Mallorca, c/Portella leads into c/Morey where, at no. 9, you'll find **Can Oleza** (no public access), a sixteenth-century mansion with an elegant shaded courtyard embellished by a handsome balustrade and a set of Ionic columns. Close by, turn left up c/Almudaina for a peek at the chunky remains of the old east gate, the **Arc de L'Almudaina**, a rare remnant of the Moorish fortifications topped with medieval barbicans. On this street also, at no. 9, is **Can Bordils**, one of the city's oldest mansions, but drably recycled as municipal offices with only two splendidly carved windows left to recall its better days.

Opposite Can Bordils, just along the street at c/Zanglada 2A, is **Can Marquès** (Mon–Fri 10am–2pm; €6; ⓦwww.canmarques.net), one of the few old mansions to be open to the public, which sounds really promising, yet the interior is disappointingly dull. Visitors slope round half a dozen rooms equipped with an insipid assortment of mostly late nineteenth- and early twentieth-century furniture, the only highlight being several superb chandeliers – long an island speciality.

Santa Eulalia and Can Vivot

Overshadowing the square at the top of c/Morey is the **Església de Santa Eulalia** (Mon–Fri 7am–12.30pm & 5.45–8.30pm, Sat 7am–1pm & 4.30–8.45pm, Sun 8am–1pm & 6.30–8.30pm; free), which was built on the site of a mosque in the mid-thirteenth century. It took just 25 years to complete and consequently possesses an architectural homogeneity that's unusual for ecclesiastical Palma, though there was some later medieval tinkering, and nineteenth-century renovators added the belfry and remodelled the main (south) facade. The church is typically Gothic in construction, with a yawning nave originally designed – as in the cathedral – to give the entire

---

Mansions in Palma

Most of medieval Palma was destroyed by fire, so the patrician **mansions** that characterize the old town today usually date from the reconstruction programme of the late seventeenth and early eighteenth centuries. Consequently they are surprisingly uniform in layout, built in the fashionable Renaissance style, with columns and capitals, loggias and arcades tucked away behind outside walls of plain stone three or four storeys high. Entry to almost all of these mansions was through a great arched **gateway**, which gave onto a rectangular courtyard around which the house was built. Originally, the **courtyard** would have been cheered by exotic trees and flowering shrubs, and equipped with a fancy stone and ironwork well-head, where visitors could water their horses. From the courtyard, a stone **exterior staircase** led up to the main public rooms – with the servants' quarters below and the family's private apartments up above. For the landed gentry, it was a very comfortable life indeed: as one British gentleman stated approvingly in the 1840s, "The higher classes lead a life of perfect inactivity – doing little, but eating occasionally...It is difficult to imagine a less agitated or more objectless existence."

Very few of these mansions are open to the public, and all you'll see for the most part is the view from the gateway – the municipality actually pays people to leave their big wooden gates open. Several have, however, passed into the public domain, the Can Aiamans, now the home of the Museu de Mallorca (see p.71), being the prime example. Others meriting a quick gander are Can Bordils (p.73), Can Oleza (p.73), Can Vivot (see p.74), Can Marquès (see p.73) and Can Solleric (p.77), but only the last two of these are open to the public.

congregation a view of the high altar. The bricked-up windows of today – as well as the darkness of the stained glass – keep out much of the light and spoil the effect, but suggestions that they be cleared have always been ignored. Framing the nave, the aisles accommodate twelve shallow **chapels**, one of which (the first on the right) sports a delightful Gothic panel-painting in finely observed Flemish style. In kitsch contrast, the other chapels are standard-issue Baroque, though they pale into insignificance when compared with the hourglass-shaped **high altarpiece**, a flashy Baroque extravagance of colossal proportions. This holy ground witnessed one of the more disgraceful episodes of Mallorcan history. During Easter week, 1435, a rumour went round that Jewish townsfolk had enacted a blasphemous mock-up of the Crucifixion. There was no proof, but the Jews were promptly robbed of their possessions and condemned to be burnt at the stake unless they adopted Christianity. The ensuing mass baptism was held here at Santa Eulalia.

Just west of the Plaça Santa Eulalia lies the fetching Plaça Cort (see p.76), whilst around the back of the church, at c/Can Savella 4, is **Can Vivot**, an especially opulent early eighteenth-century mansion, whose spacious main courtyard, with its handsome columns and arches, is distinguished by a lovely staircase. Built on top of a Moorish palace, the interior of the mansion is decorated in fine Neoclassical style, especially the sumptuous library, which is filled with scientific instruments of the age, though the house and library are only occasionally open to the public.

The Basílica de Sant Francesc

Anchoring this part of the old town, a short walk east of Plaça Santa Eulalia, the **Basílica de Sant Francesc** (daily 9.30am–12.30pm & 3.30–6pm; closed Sun afternoon; €1) is a domineering pile that occupies the site of the old Moorish soap factory. Built for the Franciscans towards the end of the thirteenth century, the original church was a vast Gothic edifice that benefited from royal patronage after King Jaume II's son, also named Jaume, became a member of the monkish order in 1300. Subsequent medieval remodellings replaced the initial wooden ceiling with a single-span, vaulted stone roof of imposing dimensions and added stately chapels to the nave and apse. The Basílica became the most fashionable church in medieval Palma and its friars received handsome kickbacks for entombing the local nobility within its precincts. Increasingly eager to enrich themselves, the priests came to compete for possession of the corpses, while the various aristocratic clans vied with each other in the magnificence of their sarcophagi. These tensions exploded when a certain Jaume Armadams had a jug of water emptied over his head inside the church on All Saints' Day, 1490. The congregation went berserk and over three hundred noblemen fought it out in the nave before the priests finally restored order. The scandal caused the Basílica to be closed by decree for several decades.

The main facade

In the seventeenth century the church was badly damaged by lightning, prompting a thoroughgoing reconstruction, which accounts for most of its present-day appearance. The main **facade**, which dates from this period, displays a stunning severity of style, with its great rectangular sheet of dressed sandstone stretching up to an arcaded and balustraded balcony. The facade is pierced by a gigantic rose window of Plateresque intricacy and embellished by a **Baroque doorway**, the tympanum of which features a triumphant Virgin Mary engulfed by a wriggling mass of sculptured decoration. Above the Madonna is the figure of St George, and to either side and below are assorted

Ramon Llull

The life of **Ramon Llull** (1235–1315) – a figure much beloved of Catholic propagandists – was an exercise in redemption through carnal excess. As a young man, Llull was an ebullient rake in the retinue of the future Jaume II. His sexual adventures were not impeded in the least by his marriage, but they ground to a dramatic halt when a certain Ambrosia de Castillo, his latest amatory target, whom he had pursued into the church of Santa Eulalia on horseback, revealed to him her diseased breasts. A deeply shocked Llull devoted the rest of his life to the Catholic faith, becoming a fearless missionary and dedicated scholar of theology, philosophy and alchemy. Exemplifying the cosmopolitan outlook of thirteenth-century Mallorca, Llull learnt to read, write and speak several languages, including Arabic, and travelled to France, much of Spain and North Africa. He also founded a monastery and missionary school on **Puig Randa** (see p.186), east of Palma, where he spent ten years in seclusion, writing no fewer than 250 books and treatises. It was Llull's scholarship that attracted the attention of his old friend Jaume II, who summoned him to court in 1282. With royal patronage, Llull then established a monastic school of Oriental languages in the mountains near Valldemossa, and it was here he trained his future missionary companions. Llull was killed on his third evangelical excursion to Algeria in 1315, his martyrdom ensuring his subsequent beatification.

saints – look out for the scholar and missionary Ramon Llull, shown reading a book. The strange statue in front of the doorway of a Franciscan monk and a young Native American celebrates the missionary work of **Junipero Serra** (see p.183), a Mallorcan priest despatched to California in 1768, who subsequently founded the cities of San Diego, Los Angeles and San Francisco.

The interior

The church's **interior**, approached through a neat and trim Gothic cloister, is distinguished by its monumental **high altar**, a gaudy Baroque affair featuring balustrades, lattice-work and clichéd figurines beneath a painted wooden statue of *St George and the Dragon*. It's heady stuff as are the rolling scrollwork and trumpeter-angel of the eighteenth-century **pulpit** on the wall of the nave, and the ornate Gothic-Baroque frontispiece of the **organ** just opposite. Close by, recessed chapels enclose the ambulatory and the first one on the left holds the **tomb of Ramon Llull**, whose bones were brought back to Palma after his martyrdom in Algeria in 1315. Considering the sanctity of the man's remains, it's an odd and insignificant-looking memorial, with Llull's alabaster effigy set high up on the wall to the right of the chapel altarpiece at a disconcertingly precarious angle.

The Templar chapel

Follow c/Ramon Llull east from the Basílica de Sant Francesc and you'll spy the large and distinctive fortified **gateway** at the end of the street. Dating from the thirteenth century, the gateway once marked the entrance to the castle-like compound of the **Knights Templar**, a military order founded to support the Crusades. The knights established bases right across the Mediterranean and this was one of the more important – though they were soon to be dispossessed. The order was rich and secretive, its independence resented by the papacy and just about every secular ruler in Europe. In 1312, following trumped-up charges of heresy, sorcery and bestiality, the pope disbanded the order and their Palma compound passed into the hands of the Hospitallers of St John, a rival knightly order. The Knights Hospitallers survived until 1802, when the Spanish king disbanded them and confiscated their property.

An alley leads through the gateway to the only other surviving part of the military compound, the **Templar chapel** (in theory open Mon–Fri 9.30am–1pm & 3.30–7pm, Sat 9.30am–1pm), whose Gothic and Romanesque features were extensively remodelled in the 1880s. Inside, the gloomy nave is divided into three bays with ribbed vaulting and a wooden ceiling over the atrium.

Plaça Sant Jeroni

From the Templar gateway, head south along c/Temple for a couple of minutes to reach **Plaça Sant Jeroni**, a pretty little piazza set around a diminutive water fountain. The severe stone walls of a former convent, now a college, dominate one side of the square, while the **Església de Sant Jeroni** fills out another. The church facade is mostly a plain stone wall, but it is broken up by two doorways, the one on the left displaying a swirl of carved foliage and garlands of fruit. The door's tympanum portrays the well-known story of Saint Jerome in the desert, during which the saint endures all sorts of tribulations and temptations, but still sticks true to the faith; above, two heraldic lions stand rampant. The **interior**, with its heavy stone vaulting and oversized organ, is mostly seventeenth-century, but it's rarely open to the public – a shame given that the church holds several good paintings by the Mallorcan Primitives, including Pere Terrencs' striking *Sant Jeroni*.

Monti-Sion

From Plaça Sant Jeroni, c/Seminari and then c/Monti-Sion run west through the depths of the old town past the **Església de Monti-Sion** (most likely to be open Mon–Fri 7–8.30am), whose thundering facade is a hectic heap of angels and saints, coats of arms and wriggling foliage. Below the figure of the Virgin, look out for a strangely inconclusive representation of the Devil – half-sheep, half-dragon. Beyond the church, c/Monti-Sion leads to a crossroads: turn right along c/Pare Nadal to reach the Basílica de Sant Francesc (see p.74) or keep dead ahead and the twisting side streets will deliver you onto Plaça Santa Eulalia, footsteps from Plaça Cort.

Plaça Cort

Bustling **Plaça Cort**, with its elegant nineteenth-century facades and grizzled olive tree, was named after the various legal bodies – both secular and religious – which were once concentrated here. Along with much of the rest of Spain, Mallorca possessed a truly Byzantine legal system until the whole caboodle was swept away and rationalized during the Napoleonic occupation. Today, one side of the square is dominated by the **Ajuntament** (Town Hall), a debonair example of the late Renaissance style: pop in for a look at the grand and self-assured foyer, which mostly dates from the nineteenth century, and the six folkloric *gigantones* (giant carnival figures) stored here – four in a corner, the other two tucked against the staircase.

From Plaça Cort, it's a pleasant five-minute stroll to Plaça de la Reina via **c/Sant Domingo**, which weaves downhill lined by attractive nineteenth-century town houses with wrought-iron grilles and stone balconies. Alternatively, it's a short walk from Plaça Cort along c/Palau Reial to the Palau March (see p.68) and the cathedral (see pp.60–65).

Plaça de la Reina and Avinguda d'Antoni Maura

Tiny, leafy **Plaça de la Reina** is at the very heart of Palma with one of the city's most sociable avenues – the Passeig d'es Born – extending north, and

Avinguda d'Antoni Maura running south. Also from the square, a wide and good-looking flight of steps, the **Costa de la Seu**, leads up beneath the spiky walls of the Palau de l'Almudaina to the cathedral (see pp.60–65) and the Palau March (see p.68). The *palau* originally extended right down to the Plaça de la Reina, incorporating what is now the *Cappuccino* café as well as the tiny Biblioteca March Servera (library), but these parts were hived off years ago.

South of Plaça de la Reina, **Avinguda d'Antoni Maura** slices down to the wide breakwater that marks the start of Palma harbour. The avenue takes its name from **Antoni Maura** (1853–1925), a Mallorcan who served as prime minister of Spain four times between 1903 and 1921. An outstanding orator and extraordinarily forceful personality, Maura was a conservative who saw universal suffrage as "the politics of the mob", preferring a limited franchise and a constitution which gave power to the middle classes, as long as they marched to the tune of the Church and the Crown. To give the man some credit, his conservatism with regard to universal suffrage – which was in place from 1887 – was prompted by Spain's particular circumstances. In a backward, largely agrarian society, most Spaniards were largely indifferent to national issues and power was concentrated in the hands of district bosses, or *caciques*, who would bring out the vote for any candidate provided they were guaranteed control of political patronage. Some bosses ruled by intimidation, others by bribery, but the end result was a dense mixture of charity and jobbery, dubbed *caciquismo*, which made national government well-nigh impossible. Maura struggled against this chicanery, and his assertive nationalism was quite enough for Franco to have this avenue named after him; no one has bothered to change it since.

The Passeig d'es Born

North of Plaça de la Reina, the **Passeig d'es Born** is distinguished by its long line of plane trees and by the stone sphinxes at its top and bottom. The avenue has been the city's principal promenade since the early fifteenth century, when the stream that ran here was diverted following a disastrous flash flood. In recent years, it has suffered badly from traffic congestion, but newly imposed restrictions have restored some of its pleasantries and a concerted effort has also been made to clean up its decaying mansions, large and decorous affairs that once housed the island's most powerful families. One of the last to receive the treatment is **Can Alomar**, an imposing stone extravagance with its own courtyard at the corner of c/Sant Feliu.

One mansion that has already been scrubbed and polished is **Can Solleric**, Passeig d'es Born 27 (Tues–Sat 10am–2pm & 5–9pm, Sun 10am–1.30pm; free), a lavish affair of heavy wooden doors, marble columns and vaulted ceilings that comes complete with a fine Italianate loggia and an elegant double stone stairway leading up from an internal courtyard. Built for a family of cattle and olive oil merchants in 1763, the house now displays temporary exhibitions of modern art and has a small tourist information desk.

El Puig de Sant Pere

The ancient neighbourhood of **El Puig de Sant Pere** (St Peter's Mount) covers the area west of the Passeig d'es Born and north to Avinguda Jaume III. The district comprises a cobweb of narrow lanes and alleys that shelter a sprinkling of old stone mansions, though most were divided up years ago to cater for the district's sailors, dockers and fishermen. It's the general flavour of Sant Pere that appeals rather than specific sights, but it's still worth seeking out two late Renaissance facades on c/Sant Feliu, which runs off Passeig d'es Born. At no. 8 is **Can Moner**, whose ornate doorway sports telamons, cherubs and cornucopia, whilst no. 10, **Can Pavesi**, offers a mythical beast with its tongue stuck right out.

There's a gruesome story behind the name of a lane off nearby c/Estanc. **Mà del Moro**, "The Hand of the Moor", harks back to Ahmed, an eighteenth-century slave who murdered his master in a house on this alley. Ahmed was executed for the crime, and his hand was chopped off and stuck above the doorway of the house where the murder was committed – "pour encourager les autres" as Voltaire would have it.

From Passeig d'es Born to Avinguda Jaume III and Es Baluard

Avinguda Jaume III marches west from the top of Passeig d'es Born flanked by a matching set of long and sturdy stone arcades, which encase some of the island's chicest clothes shops and downtown's biggest department store, **El Corte Inglés** (Mon–Sat 9.30am–9.30pm). Dating to the 1940s, this is Francoista architecture at its most appealing – very symmetrical and self-consciously Spanish – and there's something very engaging about the airs and graces of the avenue, with its jostle of beshorted tourists and besuited Spaniards. Furthermore, the web of ancient alleys immediately to the north of the avenue, focused on **c/Concepció**, is another attractive corner of the city, all high stone walls and dignified old mansions.

At the top of the avenue, the **Passeig Mallorca** is bisected by the deep, walled watercourse which once served as the city moat and is now an especially handsome feature of the city. Turn left here, on this side of the *passeig*, and you soon reach the mammoth **bastion** that was built to anchor the southwest corner of the Renaissance city wall and now holds the **Es Baluard museu d'art modern i contemporani**, on Plaça Porta Santa Catalina (Modern & Contemporary Art Museum; mid-June–Sept Tues–Sun 10am–10pm; Oct to mid-June Tues–Sun 10am–8pm; €4.50). It's a handsome setting with the stern lines of the bastion augmented by both a wide view over the bay and a series of large, geometric **sculptures** carefully positioned across the fortification in a perfect match of style and setting. In particular, look out for the irregular, rusting cubes of *Almagra* by Gerardo Rueda (1926–96) and the plaque-like severity of *Triplico* by José Luís Sanchez (b.1926). This is, however, as good as it gets: inside, the museum has three floors – the top floor for a regularly rotated selection from the permanent collection, the other two for temporary exhibitions – but, at the risk of sounding churlish, the most striking feature is just how few exhibits there are on display and, given the lavishness of the setting, the limited range of the permanent collection. That said, there are a handful of Mirós, a few Mallorcan landscapes by Anglada Camarasa (1872–1959), and a rare and unusual sample of Picasso ceramics, most memorably a striking white, ochre and black vase-like piece entitled *Big Bird Corrida*.

Doubling back from Es Baluard, cross the footbridge that spans the Passeig Mallorca to reach **La Feixina**, a pleasant terraced **park**, whose trees, lawns, flower beds and fountains step south to the foot of **Avinguda Argentina** across from the jetties where the fishing boats come in. The park's only scenic blot is the whopping **column** erected by Franco to honour those Balearic sailors who were loyal to the Fascist cause.

From Passeig d'es Born to Passeig de la Rambla

Eastwards from the top of the Passeig d'es Born runs **c/Unió**, a new if rather unimaginative appellation – it means "unity" – for a street Franco had previously named after **General Mola**, one of the prime movers of the Nationalist rebellion of 1936. Mola was killed in a plane accident during the Civil War, possibly to Franco's relief. Hitler, for one, thought that Mola was the more competent, remarking that his death meant that "Franco came to the top like Pontius Pilate in the Creed".

Near the start of c/Unio, at no. 3, **Can Balaguer** is a sprawling Renaissance mansion with imposing doors and a grand cobbled courtyard. A mouldy sort of place, it has long been in need of a major refurbishment – and one has at last just started. A few metres further east is tiny **Plaça Mercat**, the site of two identical *Modernista* buildings commissioned by a wealthy baker, Josep Casasayas, in 1908. Each is a masterpiece of flowing, organic lines tempered by graceful balconies and decorated with fern-leaf and butterfly motifs. Just down the street, on **Plaça Weyler**, stands a further *Modernista* extravagance, the magnificent **Gran Hotel** of 1903. Recently cleaned and buffed, the facade boasts a playful turret-tower, balconies, columns and bay windows enlivened with intricate floral trimmings and brilliant polychrome ceramics inspired by Hispano-Arabic designs. The interior houses a café-bar (see p.85) and the spacious **Caixa Forum art gallery** (Tues–Sat 10am–9pm, Sun 10am–2pm; free), which organizes an excellent and wide-ranging programme of temporary exhibitions. The permanent collection is essentially confined to a large sample of work by the Catalan impressionist-expressionist **Hermen Anglada–Camarasa** (1871–1959), who is best known for the evocative Mallorcan land- and seascapes he produced during his sojourn on the island from 1914 to 1936. Unfortunately, the gallery only possesses one or two of these island scenes and instead Camarasa is ill-represented by two huge and drearily folkloric canvases entitled *Valencia* and *El Tango de la Corona*, though a couple of sombre women's portraits do leaven the artistic loaf.

There's another excellent example of *Modernisme* across the street from the Gran Hotel in the floral motifs and gaily painted wooden doorway of the **Forn des Teatre** (theatre bakery) at Plaça Weyler 9. From here, it's a few paces more to the Neoclassical frontage of the **Teatre Principal**, whose tympanum sports a fanciful relief dedicated to the nine Muses of Greek mythology. The theatre has long been the city's main auditorium for classical music, ballet and opera.

At the theatre, the main street – now c/Riera – does a quick about-face to join the **Passeig de la Rambla**, whose plane trees shelter Palma's main flower market. The two statues at the foot of the boulevard, representing Roman emperors, were placed here in 1937 in honour of Mussolini's Italy – one set of Fascists tipping their municipal hats to another.

Plaça Major and around

On both sides of the Teatre Principal, a steep flight of steps leads up to **Plaça Major**, a large pedestrianized square built on the site of the former headquarters of the **Inquisition** (see box, p.81). The square, a rather plain affair with a symmetrical portico running around its perimeter, once housed the fish and vegetable market, but nowadays it's mainly popular for its pavement cafés. On the south side of Plaça Major lies the much smaller **Plaça Marquès del Palmer**, a cramped setting for two fascinating *Modernista* edifices. The more dramatic is **Can Rei**, a five-storey apartment building splattered with polychrome ceramics and floral decoration, its centrepiece a gargoyle-like face set between a pair of winged dragons. The facade of the adjacent **L'Àguila** building is of similar ilk, though there's greater emphasis on window space, reflecting its original function as a department store.

To the south, the shopping area between Plaça Marquès del Palmer and Plaça Cort retains an agreeably old-fashioned air, with the three- and four-storey buildings that frame its main streets – principally pedestrianized **c/Jaume II** – embellished with an abundance of fancy iron-grilled balconies.

The Museu d'Art Espanyol Contemporani and Església Sant Miquel

Running north from Plaça Major, **c/Sant Miquel** is another popular and pleasant shopping street. Here, at no. 11, the **Banca March** occupies a fine Renaissance mansion whose *Modernista* flourishes date from a tasteful refurbishment in 1917. The building has two entrances, one to the old bank, the other to the upper-floor **Museu d'Art Espanyol Contemporani** (Mon–Fri 10am–6.30pm, Sat 10.30am–2pm; free), which showcases a prime sample of contemporary art drawn from the collection of the March family (for more on Joan March, see p.69). The collection features seventy works by 52 twentieth-century Spanish artists, the intention being to survey the Spanish contribution to modern art – a theme which is further developed by temporary exhibitions on the top floor. The earliest piece, Picasso's *Tête de Femme* (1907), is of particular interest, being one of the first of the artist's works to be influenced by the primitive forms that were to propel him, over the following decade, from the re-creation of natural appearances into abstract art. Miró and Dalí are also represented, and there's one still life by the Spanish Cubist Juan Gris, as well as a number of harsh abstractions by the leading contemporary Catalan artist Antoni Tàpies (b.1923). Rather harder to negotiate are the allegedly "vigorous" abstractions of both the El Paso (Millares, Feito, Canogar) and the Parpalló (Sempere, Alfaro) groupings of the late 1950s.

From the museum, it's a brief hoof north along c/Sant Miquel to the **Església Sant Miquel** (Mon–Sat 8am–1.30pm & 4.30–7.30pm; free), whose sturdy exterior is the result of all sorts of architectural meddlings. Inside, the barrel-vaulted nave is almost entirely windowless, a dark and gloomy space where the one highlight is the high altarpiece, a Baroque classic with a central image celebrating St Michael in smiting mode. The altarpiece is a good example of the intricate work of Francesc Herrara (1590–1656), a much-travelled Spanish painter of religious and genre subjects known for his purposeful compositions and tangy realism.

West along the harbourfront

The various marinas, shipyards, fish docks and ferry and cargo terminals that make up Palma's **harbourfront** extend west for several kilometres from the bottom of Avinguda d'Antoni Maura to the edge of Cala Major (see p.92). The harbour is at its prettiest along its eastern, city-centre-skirting stretch, where a cycling and walking path hugs the seashore, with boats to one side and bars, restaurants, apartment blocks and the smart hotels of the **Avinguda Gabriel Roca** – often dubbed the Passeig Marítim – across the main road on the other.

The Spanish Inquisition

In 1478, mindful of his need for their military support, the **pope** granted Spain's Isabella I and Fernando V the right to establish their own **Inquisition**. It was much appreciated. The dual monarchs had realized that the Catholic faith was the most powerful force binding a fragmented Spain together, and were sure the Inquisition would both consolidate the Church's position and buttress their own. Installed in Castile in 1480 and in Aragón and Catalunya – including the Balearics – seven years later, the Inquisition began its work with the **Jews**. During the Middle Ages, the Jews had played a leading role in Spain's cultural and economic life and were generally treated with tolerance. This began to change in the late fourteenth century, when many Spaniards became increasingly resentful of the Jews' commercial clout and their role as rent collectors for the big landowners. In 1391, anti-Semitic riots broke out across much of Spain – including Mallorca – and many Jews, in fear for their lives, hastily submitted to baptism. These new Christians were subsequently called **conversos**, but in the event baptism merely staved off disaster. The riots continued – like the disturbance in Palma in 1435 (see p.74) – and matters came to a head after the capture of Spain's last Moorish kingdom, Granada, in 1492. Flush with military success but short of cash, Fernando and Isabella **expelled** from Spain all those Jews who had not turned Christian – about 120,000 – and confiscated their property, leaving the remaining *conversos* isolated and vulnerable.

Following the Reformation, the Inquisition turned its attention to the **Protestants**, though in truth there were very few of them in Iberia – only two thousand were indicted in Spain in the whole of the sixteenth century. Nevertheless, despite the limited nature of the Protestant threat, the Inquisition was profoundly influential. Most Spaniards regarded it as a bastion against heresy and, acting in this spirit, the Inquisitors kept all progressive thought at bay. Thus, whereas much of Europe was convulsed by disputation, Spain sank into ritual and dogma with the threat of the Inquisition in the background: in Palma few potential heretics could ignore the louring presence of its headquarters, plonked on a hill overlooking the city (now occupied by Plaça Major). Furthermore, by its very processes the Inquisition created an atmosphere of fear and mistrust. The Inquisitors acted on charges of heresy brought to them by the public, but these accusations were often frivolous or motivated by personal enmity. Worse still, even the most orthodox Catholic could not be sure of acquittal. The Inquisitor's examinations were often so theologically complex and long-winded that the danger of self-condemnation was ever-present – and under torture, many would confess to anything and everything.

Opposed by reforming clerics in the eighteenth century and increasingly ignored by the state, the Inquisition gradually lost influence. It was finally **abolished** during the Napoleonic occupation of Spain in 1808. Fifteen years later, in 1823, the headquarters of the Inquisition in Palma was demolished.

Sa Llotja

The first harbourfront landmark is the fifteenth-century **Sa Llotja**, the city's former stock exchange. This carefully composed late-Gothic structure was designed by Mallorca's own **Guillermo Sagrera**, one of the most original European architects of his day, and it is distinguished by its four octagonal turrets, slender, spiralling columns and tall windows. The building now hosts frequent, and occasionally excellent, exhibitions. It also boasts a series of fierce-looking gargoyles and a muscular angel – appropriately the Guardian Angel of Commerce – above the front door.

Next door, the dignified **Consolat de Mar** was built in the 1660s to accommodate the Habsburg officials who supervised maritime affairs in this part of the empire. Today, as the home of the president of the Balearic islands, it's closed to the public, but the outside is worth a second look for its pair of crusty old cannons and elegant Renaissance gallery. The forlorn-looking gate between the two buildings – the **Porta Vella del Moll** – originally stood at the end of Avinguda d'Antoni Maura, where it was the main entrance into the city from the sea; it was moved here when portions of the town wall were demolished in the 1870s.

To the Parc Quarentena

From the Consolat, it's just a few minutes' walk west to the foot of **Avinguda Argentina** and a further fifteen or twenty minutes' stroll along the hotel- and palm-lined esplanade to the next worthwhile objective, the delightful **Parc Quarentena**. The cool and shaded terraces of the park clamber up the hillside from the harbourfront and you can exit at the top on c/Patrimoni, metres from the dreary modernity of Plaça Gomila and Avinguda Joan Miró.

Northwest of the centre: the Poble Espanyol

The kitsch **Poble Espanyol** (Spanish Village; April–Nov Mon 9am–8pm, Tues–Thurs 9am–2am, Fri & Sat 9am–4am, Sun 9am–midnight; Dec–March Mon–Thurs 9am–8pm, Fri & Sat 9am–4am, Sun 9am–midnight; €8.50; Ⓦ www .poble-espanyol.com) was constructed between 1965 and 1967, its Francoist intentions apparent in its celebration of everything Spanish. Walled like a medieval city, the "village" contains accurate, scaled-down reproductions of a number of old and important buildings, such as Barcelona's Palau de la Generalitat, Seville's Torre del Oro, a segment of Granada's Alhambra, El Greco's house in Toledo, and the Ermita de San Antonio in Madrid. These are dotted round the village's streets and squares, where you'll also find souvenir shops, restaurants and bars. It's all a bit daft – and school parties swamp the place during the day – but it's one way of introducing yourself to Spanish architecture.

The Poble Espanyol is about 2.5km northwest of the city centre, and reachable direct on Citysightseeing double-decker buses (see p.55).

West of the centre: the Castell de Bellver

Boasting superb views of Palma and its harbour from a wooded hilltop some 3km west of the city centre, the **Castell de Bellver** (April–Sept Mon–Sat 8.30am–8.30pm, Sun 10am–5pm; Oct–March Mon–Sat 8.30am–7pm, Sun 10am–5pm; €2, but free on Sun, when the castle museum is closed) is a handsome, strikingly well-preserved fortress built for Jaume II at the beginning of the fourteenth century. Of canny circular design, the castle's immensely thick walls and steep ditches encircle a central **keep** that incorporates three imposing towers. In addition, an overhead, single-span **stone arch** connects the keep to a massive, freestanding tower, built as a final refuge. To enhance defence, the walls curve and bend and the interconnecting footbridges are set at oblique angles to each other. It's all very impressive – and looks well-nigh impregnable – but the castle was also intended to serve as a royal retreat from

Raixa, the old country home of Cardinal Despuig, has also passed into public ownership and its terraced gardens are a delight – or at least they will be when they have been revamped as part of a project that looks like extending into 2012. Raixa is in between Palma and Sóller (see p.113).

▲ Castell de Bellver

the summer heat, and so the austere outside walls hide a commodious, genteel-looking **circular courtyard**, surrounded by two tiers of inward-facing arcades that once belonged to the residential suites. The whole construction is ingenious, incorporating many skilful touches: the flat roof, for example, was designed to channel every drop of rainwater into a huge underground cistern.

Soon after its construction, improvements in artillery rendered the original fortress obsolete and although modifications were made, they were never very convincing. Neither did it last long as a royal residence. As early as the 1350s the keep was in use as a prison, a function it performed until 1915. More recently, the castle interior has been turned into a **museum** with a plodding history of the city on the ground floor and a small but delightful collection of **Roman statuary** up above. A local antiquarian and ecclesiastical bigwig by the name of **Cardinal Antonio Despuig** (1745–1817) gathered together these classical pieces and bequeathed the whole lot to the city on his death. The only problem is that there's absolutely no labelling, so unless you're a classical expert it's impossible to know quite what you're looking at. Nevertheless, amongst the miscellany of busts and effigies, there's no mistaking a rare and perfectly preserved column of strikingly patterned *cippolino* marble and, most extraordinary of all, a small and exquisite alabaster of a sleeping hermaphrodite, apparently troubled by a confusing dream, half-in but mainly out of her toga. Other exhibits include carved seals, marble inscriptions, first-century medallions, a funeral stele, and a fearsome bust of Medusa, her head crawling with snakes. After you've explored the castle, you can wander through the pine-scented woods that surround it: there's a network of **footpaths**, but few signs.

Citysightseeing double-decker buses (see p.55) link the city centre with the Castell, but otherwise you're stuck with a stiff, thirty-minute walk uphill from Avingvda Joan Miró, the site of the nearest bus stop (EMT bus #3). If you're driving, follow the signs from Avinguda Joan Miró (one-way west from the centre towards Plaça Gomila).

Eating and drinking

There's more gastronomic variety in Palma than anywhere else in Mallorca. **Cafés** and **tapas bars** are liberally distributed around the city centre, with a particular concentration in the side streets off the Passeig d'es Born and Avinguda d'Antoni Maura, though those on and around c/Apuntadors, at the heart of the city's nightlife, tend to charge over the odds. Some downtown cafés are up and running by 9am, but – with most visitors taking **breakfast** at their hotel – there's not much demand for early-morning cafés. For light **lunches** and snacks (tapas), however, you're spoiled for choice. You can chomp away in chic Modernist surroundings or join the crowds in simple formica-and-wallpaper-diners where the food more than compensates for the decor – and then there's everything in between. Tapas can cost as little as €5 per dish and should never cost more than €12.

There's not much distinction between tapas bars and **restaurants**, as many of the former serve full meals as well as snacks – and, of course, put a couple of tapas together and you've got a full meal anyway. In fact, the differences often have more to do with appearance than food: if you've got a tablecloth, for instance, you're almost certainly in a restaurant. Most Palma restaurants concentrate on Catalan and/or Mallorcan dishes, but there are lots of Spanish places too as well as a couple of vegetarian café-restaurants. At all but the most expensive of places, €20 should cover the price of a main course in the evening, and you can usually cut costs by opting for a lunchtime *menu del día*.

Most of Palma's cafés, restaurants and tapas bars are geared up for the tourist trade to some extent at least and **multilingual menus** (in English, German, Catalan and Castilian) are commonplace. The following are marked on the **map** on pp.62–63 unless otherwise stated.

Cafés and tapas bars

Bar Bosch Plaça Rei Joan Carles I. One of the most popular and inexpensive tapas bars in town, the traditional haunt of the city's intellectuals and usually humming with conversation. At peak times you'll need to be assertive to get served. Open daily 8am–1am.

Bon Lloc c/Sant Feliu 7. One of the few vegetarian café-restaurants on the island, with good food at low prices and an informal, homely atmosphere in old and pleasant wood-beamed premises; mains at around €10. Open Mon–Sat 1–4pm.

Café Lirico Avgda d'Antoni Maura 6. Most of Palma's downtown cafés have been modernized, but not this one – its large mirrors, imitation marble and weatherbeaten clientele reminiscent of Spanish cafés of yesteryear. Not much in the way of choice, but certainly good fun – and good coffee. Snacks from €4. Open Mon–Sat 8am till late.

Ca N'Ignasi de Pollença Passeig Mallorca 16. The salads and snacks here at this pleasant modern café are OK, but it's the cakes you come for – none better than the earth-moving, ground-shattering chocolate cake (at €4). Open daily 9am–10pm.

Ca'n Joan de S'Aigo c/Can Sanç 10. A long-established coffee house with wonderful, freshly baked *ensaimadas* (spiral pastry buns) and fruit-flavoured mousses to die for. Charming decor too, from the kitschy water fountain to the traditional Mallorcan green-tinted chandeliers. It's on a tiny alley near Plaça Santa Eulalia – take c/Sant Crist and its continuation c/Canisseria then turn right. Open daily (except Tues) 8am–9pm.

Cappuccino c/Conquistador. Occupying the lower part of the Palau March near the cathedral, this attractive terrace café (one of a small island chain) offers first-rate, nicely presented sandwiches and salads. Service is attentive, the furnishings and fittings slick and the soundtrack jazzy, all of which contribute to what is a very popular spot, with prices from around €10. Open daily 9am–1am.

El Pilon c/Can Cifre 4. Vibrant, cramped and crowded tapas bar in stone-vaulted, cave-like premises on a side street off the north end of Passeig d'es Born. Offers a first-rate variety of tapas (and full meals) – try the meatballs (*albondigas*) – and electrifyingly fast service. Excellent value too, with tapas from as little as €5. Open Mon–Sat 1pm till late.

Gran Hotel Café Plaça Weyler 3. Smart, modern café that makes a good spot for lunch, with tables inside or out on a pleasant, little square. The *menú del día* is excellent value at €15.

La Bodeguilla c/Sant Jaume 3. Located in a glossily refurbished old town house just off Avgda Jaume III, this establishment has a ground-floor wine bar offering tasty tapas from €9 and up. Open Mon–Sat 1–11.30pm.

La Taberna del Caracol c/Sant Alonso 2 ☎971 71 49 08. Deep in the depths of the old town, this smashing tapas bar-cum-restaurant occupies charming old premises, all wooden beams and ancient arches. Choose from thirty different sorts of tapas from just €5. Reservations advised throughout the summer, but note that they sometimes appear to be reluctant to accept single customers. Open Mon–Sat 7.30–11.30pm.

Orient Express c/Llotja de Mar 6. Beside Sa Llotja, this idiosyncratic café-restaurant has a railway carriage-like interior. Crêpes are the speciality – and served as mains they average out at about €10. Open Mon–Fri 1.30–4pm & 8pm–midnight, Sat 8pm–midnight.

Taberna de la Bóveda Passeig de Sagrera 3. Just off Plaça Llotja, this relaxing tapas bar and restaurant serves up an excellent range of tapas from as little as €10 – try the squid in ink. Particularly pleasant pavement terrace too. Open daily 1.30–4pm & 8–11.30pm.

Restaurants

Aramis c/Montenegro 1 ☎971 72 52 32. Set in a sympathetically refurbished old stone mansion on a side street off Passeig d'es Born, this smart, top-flight restaurant has an imaginative menu with an international range of dishes – ravioli and pumpkin, wild mushrooms *en croute*, for example – plus a wonderful house red. Mains average €22. Reservations required. Open Mon–Fri 1–3.30pm & 8–11pm, Sat 8–11pm.

Caballito del Mar Passeig de Sagrera 5 ☎971 72 10 74. Harbourside restaurant metres from Sa Llotja, which has long been a favourite with well-heeled British holidaymakers. There was a time when this was undoubtedly the best seafood restaurant in town and although this probably isn't the case today, it does excel with its house speciality – the *daurada amb sal al forn* (sea bream oven-baked in salt). The terrace is the place to eat here – the interior is really rather glum. Main courses average €20–25, but the extras soon mount up. Reservations well-nigh essential. Open daily 1–4pm & 8–11.30pm, but closed Mon in winter.

Ca'n Carlos c/Aigua 5 ☎971 71 38 69. Charming, family-run restaurant featuring first-class Mallorcan cuisine that takes in such delights as cuttlefish and snails. The menu isn't extensive but everything is carefully prepared and there's a daily special as well as a fish of the day. Good dishes to sample are the suckling pig, *fava parada* (dried-bean stew) and *caragols de la mallorquina* (snails). Attentive service and smartly turned out premises. Main courses average €17–25. Open Tues–Sat 1–4pm & 8–11pm.

Ca'n Eduardo Contramoll Mollet 4 (see map, pp.56–57) ☎971 72 11 82. Spick-and-span restaurant located upstairs in one of the plain modern buildings beside the fish dock, just across from – and east of – the foot of Avgda Argentina. There's an enjoyable view of the harbour, but the real treat is the fresh fish – a wonderful range, all simply prepared, though grilled is best. Main courses average €22. Open Tues–Sat 1–3.30pm & 8.30–11pm.

Celler Pagès c/Felip Bauza 2, off c/Apuntadors at ☎971 72 60 36. Small, intimate restaurant with an easy-going family atmosphere in a pleasantly decorated two-room basement. Serves traditional Mallorcan food – try the stuffed marrows with home-made mayonnaise on the side, the delicious roast leg of duck with dried plums and grilled vegetables or the tongue with capers. Mains are an amazing bargain here – from just €8. Reservations pretty much essential. Open Mon–Sat 1–3.30pm & 8–11pm.

Es Mercat c/Pursiana 14 ☎971 45 38 40. See map, pp.56–57. Located in the fashionable, vaguely New Age district of Santa Catalina, this attractively furnished modern restaurant features a creative Mediterranean menu – try, for example, the black tagliatelle with salmon. Mains at around €15. Open Mon 1–3.30pm, Tues–Sun 1–3.30pm & 8.30–11pm.

Forn de Sant Joan c/Sant Joan 4 ☎971 72 84 22. Set in an old bakery, this smart and extremely popular restaurant offers a wide range of seafood dishes (€15–20) and does an excellent line in tapas (from €10) – try the red peppers stuffed with shellfish, followed by the lemon and cinnamon mousse. The location, bang in the centre of the city's nightlife, pumps up the prices, albeit not unbearably so. Open Mon 6–11pm, Tues–Sun 1–11pm.

La Cuchara Passeig Mallorca 18 ☎971 72 22 23. The premises may lack a little atmosphere – they are routinely modern – but the food at this reliable restaurant is first rate with the focus on Spanish dishes with a Mallorcan twist. Great wine cellar. Mains €14–18. Open daily from 8pm.

Restaurant del Museu Es Baluard Museu, Plaça Porta Santa Catalina s/n ☎971 90 81 99. Adjacent to the Es Baluard gallery, this excellent restaurant occupies two Modernist glass cubes with views out across the bay. The menu is based on Mallorcan cuisine, but there are all sorts of international flourishes – try the lamb. Main courses cost around €15 in the evening, slightly less during the day. See map, pp.56–57. Open Tues–Sun 1–3.30pm & 8–11pm; café open Tues–Sun 10am–8pm.

Simply Fosh in the Hotel Convent de la Missió, c/de la Missió 7A ☎971 72 01 14. Taking its name from Mallorca's leading chef, Marc Fosh, this newly opened restaurant has garnered lavish praise from all and sundry. The premises are super cool/very minimalist and you can eat either inside or on the shaded terrace. The food is light, well balanced and finely flavoured with local, seasonal ingredients to the fore. Try such delights as smoked ham in a pea and truffle broth or pork belly with orange and rosemary. A two-course lunch with a glass of wine costs an affordable €40–50 and there's a *menú del día* for around €20. Great service too. Reservations essential. Open Mon–Fri 1–3.30pm & 7.30–10.30pm, Sat 7.30–10.30pm.

Nightlife and entertainment

Most of the cafés and tapas bars listed above are quite happy just to ply you with drink until midnight or beyond. In addition, there is a cluster of lively **late-night bars** – mostly with music as the backdrop rather than the main event – amongst the narrow and ancient side streets backing onto **Plaça Llotja**. Alternatively, a number of more modish bars can be found strung out along **Avinguda Gabriel Roca** in the vicinity of the Jardins La Quarentena, an area of ritzy hotels and apartment blocks which hums at night with fashionable locals dressed to the nines, hopping from bar to bar. **Clubs** (*discotecas*) are not Palma's forte, but there are a couple of decent ones on Avinguda Gabriel Roca. They're rarely worth investigating until around 1am and entry charges will cost you anything up to €20, depending on the night and what's happening (although entry is sometimes free). The door staff usually operate an informal dress code of one sort or another – if you want to get in, avoid beach gear and (heaven forbid) white trainers.

Performing arts

Traditionally, Palma has had little to offer in terms of **performing arts**, but matters are on the mend. The grand nineteenth-century **Teatre Principal**, Plaça Weyler 16 (☎971 71 33 46, ⓦwww.teatreprincipaldepalma.cat), features classical music, theatre and opera, whilst the **Teatre Municipal**, Passeig Mallorca 9 (☎971 73 91 48, ⓦwww.palmademallorca.es), offers a varied programme of contemporary drama, classic films, dance and ballet. In summer, there's almost always something going on at the open-air Parc de la Mar, just below the cathedral, and other summer venues for music and dance include the Castell de Bellver (see p.82), and the **Auditorium**, Avingvda Gabriel Roca 18, ☎971 73 47 35, ⓦwww.auditoriumpalma.es). Ask at the tourist office (see p.54) for a complete listing of upcoming events. The following are marked on the map on pp.62–63 unless otherwise stated.

Late-night bars

Abaco c/Sant Joan 1 ☎971 71 49 39. Set in a charming old mansion in the city centre, just off c/ Apuntadors, this is easily Palma's most unusual bar, with an interior straight out of a Busby Berkeley musical: fruits cascading down its stairway, caged birds hidden amid patio foliage, elegant music and a daily flower bill you could live on for a month. Drinks, as you might imagine, are extremely expensive (cocktails cost as much as €15) but you're never hurried into buying one. It is, however, rather too sedate to be much fun if you're up for a big night out. Open Tues–Sat 9pm–2am, but closed for most of Jan.

Escape Plaça Draçana 13. Friendly little place, and always lively, located just off a square that gets busier if not exactly prettier every year. Close to the harbourfront too.

Gotic Plaça Llotja 2. Popular bar and café with a tiny interior but a large candlelit pavement terrace. Hums till the early hours.

Jazz Voyeur Club c/Apuntadors 5 ☏ 971 72 07 80, ⓦ www.jazzvoyeur.com. Pocket-sized jazz club in the heart of the city, metres from Sa Llotja. Live sounds most nights – check out the website for who is coming when.

La Lonja c/Llotja de Mar 2. A popular, well-established haunt, with revolving doors and pleasantly old-fashioned decor; the background music caters for (almost) all tastes and you can sit out in the square right in front of Sa Llotja.

Clubs

Abraxas Avgda Gabriel Roca 42 (see map, pp.56–57) ☏ 665 55 46 29, ⓦ www .mallorcaclubs.com. Formerly *Pacha*, this loud, popular and raucous superclub has a gyrating dance floor and a couple of bars inside, as well as a bar outside in the garden. A ten-minute walk west of the Jardins La Quarentena, and 800m east of the ferry terminal. Dress up to get in – no

dullards. Entrance (usually) €15. July–Aug daily 11pm–6am, Sept–June Thurs–Sun 11pm–6am.

El Garito Dàrsena de Can Barbarà s/n (see map, pp.56–57) ☏ 971 73 69 12, ⓦ www.garitocafe .com. Cool club that covers all its musical bases, from house to disco classics. Attractive terrace too. West of the centre just off Avgda Joan Miró. Daily 8pm–4am.

Tito's Plaça Gomila 3 (see map, pp.56–57) ☏ 971 73 00 17, ⓦ www.titosmallorca.com. With its stainless steel and glass exterior, this long-established nightspot looks a bit like something from a sci-fi film. Outdoor lifts carry you up from Avgda Gabriel Roca (the back entrance) to the dance floor, which pulls in huge crowds from many countries – or you can go in through the front entrance on Plaça Gomila. The music (anything from house to mainstream pop) lacks conviction, but it's certainly loud. The Avgda Gabriel Roca entrance is just on the city-centre side of the Jardins La Quarentena. June to early Sept daily 11.30pm–5am, Oct–May Fri–Sun 11.30pm–5am.

Shopping

Like every other big city in Spain, Palma has its share of multinational stores and most of them have extended **opening hours**, whereas the smaller, more local companies tend to stick to the traditional norm – Monday to Friday 9/10am to 1.30pm or 2pm and 5.30/6pm to 8.30/9pm and Saturday 9/10am to 1/2pm. As for the specifics, there's a particular concentration of up-market and/or designer **clothes shops** on and around Avingvda Jaume III. Here, on Plaça Rei Joan Carles I, there are, for example, two Zara stores – one for men and one for women – an H&M, and a Loewe. **Camper shoes** are made on the island – and they have two stores in Palma, one at Avgda Jaume III, 16, the other at c/Sant Miquel 17 (both Mon–Sat 10am–8.30pm) – and so are **artificial pearls** (see p.188): the largest pearl manufacturer is Majorica, who have dozens of official agents in Palma as well as their own outlet at Avgda Jaume III, 11 (Mon–Fri 9.30am–1.30pm & 4.30–8pm, Sat 9.30am–1.30pm). **Glass-making** is a traditional island craft; Vidrias Gordiola, near the Ajuntament at c/Victoria 2 (Mon–Fri 10.15am–2pm & 4.30–8pm, Sat 10.15am–2pm), has a fine range of clear and tinted glassware, from bowls, vases and lanterns through to some wonderfully intricate chandeliers. For **pottery** and other handmade wares, including flowers in bottles, try Fet a Mà, c/Sant Miquel 52 (Mon–Fri 9.30am–1.30pm & 4.30–8pm, Sat 9.30am–1.30pm), or the delightfully old-fashioned La Concha, c/Jaume II, 19 (Mon–Fri 10am–1.30pm & 5–8pm, Sat 9.30am–1pm), which also stocks cheap and cheerful **souvenirs** such as brightly coloured Spanish fans, garish Spanish plates, model cherubs and mini-*gigantones* (carnival figures). Both sell **siurells**, white clay whistles flecked with red and green paint and shaped to depict a figure, an animal or a scene (a man sitting on a donkey, for instance); *siurells* have been given as tokens of friendship in Mallorca for hundreds of years.

For **new books and maps**, El Corte Inglés, Avgda Jaume III, 15 (Mon–Sat 9.30am–9.30pm), sells a small and rather eccentric assortment of

Specialist food and drink shops

Amongst the city's specialist food shops, **Colmado Santo Domingo**, c/Sant Domingo 1 (Mon–Fri 10am–1.30pm & 5–7.30pm, Sat 10am–1pm), is a tiny, cave-like, old-fashioned store packed with hanging sausages and local fruit and veg; it's right in the centre, metres from Plaça Cort. The **sausages** you should try carry the "Sobrasada de Mallorca de Cerdo Negro" label, which guarantees they are made from the island's own indigenous black pig. There are more sausages, amidst much else, to the north of the centre in Palma's main covered market, the **Mercat de l'Olivar**, on Plaça de l'Olivar (Mon–Sat 7am–2pm; for more on markets, see p.89), which has literally dozens of fresh food and seafood stalls. Near the market, the cheerily painted **La Favorita**, c/Sant Miquel 38 (Mon–Fri 9.30am–1.30pm & 5–7.30pm, Sat 10am–1pm), is one of the city's best delis, with all sorts of Spanish and Italian treats and a superb range of pastas. In Santa Catalina, a groovy part of the city immediately to the west of Avinguda Argentina, is one of its main rivals, **Colmado Manresa**, c/Fàbrica 19 (Tues–Fri 9am–2pm & 5–8pm, Sat 9am–2pm; see map, pp.56–57), founded in 1949 and stuffed with all manner of island delicacies, including premium, black-pig *sobrasadas*, salted cod (*bacalao*) and rice from the island's central plain, Es Pla.

Palma has a platoon of good cake and pastry shops (pastelerías), including **Forn des Teatre**, Plaça Weyler 9 (Mon–Sat 9am–12.30pm & 4.30–7.30pm), and the excellent **Forn Fondo**, c/Unió 15 (Mon–Sat 8am–8.30pm & Sun 8am–2pm), where the fig cake (*higos* in Castilian) is especially delicious. Both sell the freshly baked *ensaimadas* (spiral pastry buns) that are so much a feature of island life, but the best – though this is the subject of much fierce argument – come from *Ca'n Joan de S'Aigo*, a charming coffee house near Plaça Santa Eulalia (see p.73). Palma also possesses a first-rate chocolatier and confectioner, **Frasquet**, just off Plaça Mercat beside the church at c/Orfila 4 (Mon–Fri 9.30am–2pm & 5–8pm, Sat 9.30am–2pm) – try the *torrons*, almond-paste balls doused in roasted pine nuts.

Many Palma shops and most supermarkets stock a reasonable range of Spanish wines, and a goodly proportion also carry Balearic vintages. The biggest department store in the city centre, **El Corte Inglés**, Avgda Jaume III, 15 (Mon–Sat 9.30am–9.30pm), has an especially wide selection of both Spanish and Mallorcan wine in its basement, all at competitive prices – a top-notch Binissalem red only costs about €7.

English-language novels from Ken Follett to Anne Frank, and also has a modest selection of Mallorca guidebooks and maps. Librería Fondevila, near the Teatre Principal at Costa de Sa Pols 18 (Mon–Fri 9.45am–1.30pm & 4.30–8pm, Sat 9.45am–1.30pm), has a rather better selection of general maps of Mallorca, but easily the best map shop in town is La Casa del Mapa, in the mini-arcade below street level at c/Sant Domingo 11 (Mon–Fri 9.30am–2pm & 5–7.30pm). Palma also possesses a large and very browseable English-language **secondhand bookshop**, Fine Books, c/Morey 7 (Mon–Fri 9am–7pm, Sat 9am–4pm & Sun 9am–1pm).

For specialist food and drink shops, see box above.

Listings

Airlines Air Berlin ☎902 32 07 37; British Airways ☎902 11 13 33; bmibaby ☎971 78 79 06; easyJet ☎807 26 00 26; Iberia ☎902 40 05 00; Ryanair ☎971 78 96 47; Spanair ☎902 131 415; Thomas Cook Airlines ☎971 78 82 42. For a full list of airlines, consult the Yellow Pages (ⓦwww .paginasamarillas.es) under *Linies aèries* (*Lineas aéreas* in Castilian).

Airport information ☎971 78 95 56.

Banks and exchange There are plenty of banks on and around the Passeig d'es Born and Avgda Jaume III. ATMs are commonplace here too.

Beaches The closest beach to the city centre is the narrow strip of sand next to the *autovia* just east of Avgda Gabriel Alomar i Villalonga. Swimming is not, however, recommended here as the water is too polluted. Instead most locals make the twenty-minute trip on EMT bus #15 east to the Platja de Palma (see p.91).

Bike rental Palma on Bike, just southeast of Plaça Major at Plaça Salvador Coll 8 (☎971 71 80 62, ⓦwww.palmaonbike.com), rents out city and mountain bikes from just €12 per day. Advance reservations, at least 24hrs ahead of time, are advised. They also do bike tours, kayak and roller-blade rentals.

Boat trips Several companies offer two-hour excursions round the Badía de Palma; there are regular daily departures from May–October and the cost is about €10 per person. There are also excursions to Sant Elm (mid-May to mid-Oct 3 weekly; 2hr each way; €52 including meal) and Portals Vells (mid-May to mid-Oct 1 daily; 1hr 30min each way; €52 including meal). Boats depart from the jetty near the Auditorium, on the harbourfront at Avgda Gabriel Roça 18. The two main tourist offices have the full list of boat trips.

Bullfights Palma's bullfighting ring, the Plaça de Toros, is a few blocks northeast of the Plaça Espanya along c/Reina Maria Cristina in El Coliseo Balear, on c/Arquitecte Gaspar Bennàzar. The season is short, running from mid-July to late August. You can get tickets and details from travel agents and hotel receptions.

Buses Details of all island bus services are available from the information desk at Palma's combined bus and train station, the Estació Inter-modal, on Plaça Espanya. The city's two main tourist offices (see p.54) supply bus timetables too. Alternatively, call/check out ☎971 17 77 77, ⓦhttp://tib.caib.es/ for information on island-wide bus services, or ☎900 70 07 10, ⓦwww.emtpalma.es for details of EMT city buses – though in both cases, you'll (probably) need to speak either Spanish or Catalan to get anywhere.

Car rental Mallorca's airport heaves with car rental companies, as does Palma – there's a concentration of both large and small companies along Avgda Gabriel Roca. Amongst the big companies, there are branches of Atesa at Avgda Gabriel Roca 25 ☎971 45 66 02; Betacar-Europcar, Avgda Gabriel Roca 19 ☎971 73 77 58 (airport ☎971 78 91 35); and Hertz, Avgda Gabriel

Roca 13 ☎971 73 47 37 (airport ☎971 78 96 70). The city's two main tourist offices (see p.54) can supply a complete list.

Consulates Ireland, c/Sant Miquel 68A ☎971 71 92 44; UK, Plaça Major 3D ☎971 71 20 85. For a complete list, look under *consolats* (Castilian *consulados*) in the Yellow Pages (ⓦwww.paginasamarillas.es).

Doctors and dentists In the resort areas and in Palma most hotel receptions will be able to find an English-speaking doctor or dentist. For complete lists look under *metges* (Castilian, *médicos*) or *clíniques dentals* (*clínicas dentales*) in the Yellow Pages (ⓦwww.paginasamarillas.es).

Email and internet Most hotels and *hostales* now provide internet access for their guests either free or at minimum cost. Otherwise, head for the library (see below).

Emergencies ☎112.

Ferries and catamarans Palma's two main tourist offices have ferry and catamaran schedules and tariffs. Tickets can be purchased either at most travel agents or direct from the three ferry companies concerned. These are Acciona Trasmediterranea (☎902 45 46 45, ⓦwww.trasmediterranea.es); Balearia (☎902 16 01 80, ⓦwww.balearia.com); and Iscomar (☎902 11 91 28, ⓦwww.iscomar.com). All three have offices down at the ferry port, about 4km west of the city centre along Avgda Gabriel Roca, but they are only open before and just after sailings. For details of ferry services to Mallorca from mainland Spain, Menorca and Ibiza, see p.20 & p.21.

Football Mallorca's premier team is Real Club Deportivo Mallorca (ⓦwww.rcdmallorca.es), who play at the Estadio Son Moix stadium on the north side of town. Fixture details either direct or from the tourist office.

Gay and lesbian scene The suburb of El Terreny, about 3km west of the centre below the Castell de Bellver, remains the focus of the city's gay life, with a rainbow-flagged hotel, the *Rosamar* (see p.58), and a decent selection of gay and lesbian bars. For general information, venues and events, contact Ben Amics ("Good Friends"), which operates a website (Spanish/Catalan only, ⓦwww.benamics.com) and an info line (☎971 71 56 70; Tues–Sat 6pm–9pm).

Library There's a quaint old municipal library inside the Ajuntament (Town Hall) on Plaça Cort (Mon–Fri 8.30am–8.30pm & Sat 9am–1pm).

Maps See "Shopping" p.87.

Markets Palma's big *Rastrillo* (flea market) is held every Saturday morning (8am–2pm) on Avgda Gabriel Alomar i Villalonga, between Plaça Porta d'es Camp and c/Manacor. There's also a flower market on Passeig de la Rambla (Mon–Fri 8am–2pm & 5–8pm, Sat 8am–2pm). Mercat de l'Olivar, the city's main covered market, is on Plaça de l'Olivar (Mon–Sat 7am–2pm).

Pharmacies Central pharmacies include Farmacia Castañer, Plaça Rei Joan Carles I, 3. A full list of pharmacies is in the Yellow Pages (ⓦwww.paginasamarillas.es) under *farmàcies* (Castilian *farmacias*).

Post office The central *correos/correu* is at c/Constitució 5 (Mon–Fri 8.30am–8.30pm, Sat 9.30am–2pm).

Trains Both main tourist offices (see p.54) as well as the information desk at the Estació Intermodal (see p.55) have train timetables. Or you can phone direct: Palma to Inca, Manacor and points east on ⓣ971 17 77 77, ⓦhttp://tib.caib.es/; Palma to Sóller on ⓣ902 36 47 11, ⓦwww.trendesoller.com.

Travel agencies There are dozens of travel agencies in Palma, listed in full in the Yellow Pages (ⓦwww.paginasamarillas.es) under *agències de viatges* (Castilian, *agencias de viajes*). One helpful downtown choice is Viajes Pafu, Plaça Weyler 1 (ⓣ971 21 41 58), where they sell ferry tickets.

Around Palma

Spread around the sheltered waters of the **Badía de Palma** are the package tourist resorts that have made Mallorca synonymous with the cheap and tacky. In recent years the Balearic government has done its best to improve matters – greening resorts, restricting high-rise construction and redirecting traffic away from the coast – but their inherited problems remain. In the 1960s and 1970s, the bay experienced a building boom of almost unimaginable proportions as miles of pristine shoreline sprouted concrete and glass hotel towers, overwhelming the area's farms and fishing villages. There were few planning controls, if any, and the legacy is the mammoth sprawl of development that now extends, almost without interruption, from **S'Arenal** in the east to **Magaluf** in the west – with Palma roughly in the middle. To make matters worse, it is also debatable as to whether the recent move away from high-rise construction is well-conceived. The new villa complexes that are now the fashion gobble up the land at an alarming rate and multiply traffic. Furthermore, although the new villas are rarely more than three storeys high and built in a sort of pan-Mediterranean style they end up looking terribly, remorselessly suburban. As a consequence, although the thirty-kilometre-long stretch of coast between S'Arenal and Magaluf is divided into a **score or more resorts**, it's often impossible to pick out where one ends and the next begins. That said, most of the resorts have evolved their own identities, either in terms of the nationalities they attract, the income group they appeal to, or the age range they cater for.

East of Palma lies **S'Arenal**, mainly geared up for young German tourists, with dozens of pounding bars and all-night clubs. S'Arenal also fringes one of Mallorca's best **beaches**, the **Platja de Palma**, which stretches from S'Arenal round to **Ca'n Pastilla**, but although the beach is superb, the flat shoreline behind it accommodates an unprepossessing, seemingly endless strip of restaurants, bars and souvenir shops.

West of Palma, the coast bubbles up into the low, rocky hills and sharp coves that prefigure the mountains further west. The sandy beaches here are far smaller – and some are actually artificial – but the terrain makes the tourist development seem less oppressive. **Cala Major**, the first stop, was once the playground of the jetset. It's hit grittier times today, but some of the grand old buildings have survived and the **Fundació Pilar i Joan Miró**, which exhibits a fine selection of Miró's work in what was once his home and studio, makes an enjoyable detour. The neighbouring resort of **Illetes** is a good deal more polished, boasting comfortable hotels and attractive cove beaches, and is perhaps the best place to stay hereabouts, though you might also consider neighbouring **Portals Nous**, which has an affluent and exclusive air born of its swanky marina. Next up comes British-dominated **Palma Nova**, a major package holiday destination popular with all ages, and the adjacent **Magaluf**, where modern high-rise hotels, thumping nightlife and a substantial sandy beach cater to a youthful and very British crowd. South of Magaluf, the charming cove beach of **Portals Vells** is a real surprise, hidden away on an undeveloped, pine-studded peninsula. West of Magaluf, the coastal highway leaves the Badia de Palma for large and sprawling **Santa Ponça** before pushing on to **Peguera**, a large, rambling resort with attractive sandy beaches and a relaxed family atmosphere. Next door – and much more endearing – is tiny **Cala Fornells**, where pretty villas thread along the coastal hills and a trio of first-rate hotels overlook a wooded cove – and concrete-slab beaches, which are not as bad as they sound; the development is fairly restrained here and, if you're after a straightforward resort holiday hereabouts, this is as good as it gets. From Cala Fornells, it's another short hop to the good-looking bay, which encloses the burgeoning resort of **Camp de Mar**.

Practicalities

Although the Badía de Palma resorts boast hundreds of **hotels**, *hostales* and apartment buildings, the bulk are block-booked by the package tourist industry from May or June through to September or October, with frugal pickings for the independent traveller; out of season, many places simply close down. We've selected several of the more interesting and enjoyable package hotels where there's a reasonable chance of finding a vacancy independently in high season, but left it at that. Neither have we described resort **nightlife** since the liveliest discos and clubs are, as a general rule, concentrated in the tackier spots. This stretch of coast also has hundreds of **restaurants and cafés**, but the choice is not as diverse as you might expect, and for the most part standards are not very high: the vast majority of places serve either low-price pizzas and pastas or a sort of pan-European tourist menu. For bus connections, see box on p.55.

East of Palma

The motorway rushes **east** out of Palma with tourist resorts on one side and the airport on the other. The flatlands backing onto the coast were once prime agricultural land, hence the multitude of ruined **windmills**, built to pump water out of the marshy topsoil and now gaunt reminders of earlier, more pastoral times. The alternative route, along the old coastal road, is a bit more interesting and a lot slower; take the turning off the *autovía* just beyond the city walls (signposted to Ca'n Pastilla) and follow the road as it tracks through a series of resorts, beginning with **ES PORTIXOL**, an intelligently revamped old quarter with its own small beach and top-ranking *Hotel Portixol* (see p.59). Pushing on, you soon reach **CA'N PASTILLA**, the first substantial tourist resort on this part of the coast, its fifty-odd hotels and apartment buildings set in a rough rectangle of land pushed tight against the seashore. The place is short on charm and certainly too close to the airport for sonic comfort, but it does herald the start of the fine Platja de Palma beach.

Sometimes, Ses Maravelles and S'Arenal

The **Platja de Palma**, the four-kilometre stretch of sandy beach that defines the three coterminous (and indistinguishable) resorts of **SOMETIMES**, **SES MARAVELLES** and **S'ARENAL**, is crowded with serious sun-seekers, a sweating throng of bronzed and oiled bodies slowly roasting in the heat. The beach is also a busy pick-up place, the spot for a touch of verbal foreplay before the night-time bingeing begins. It is, as they say, fine if you like that sort of thing – though older visitors can't but help look marooned. A wide and pleasant walkway lined with palm trees runs behind the beach and this, in turn, is edged by a long sequence of bars, restaurants and souvenir shops. A toy-town tourist "train" shuttles up and down the walkway, but there's so little to distinguish one part of the beach from another that it's easy to become disoriented. To maintain your bearings, keep an eye out for the series of smart, stainless-steel beach bars, each numbered and labelled, in Castilian, "*balneario*", dotted along the shore.

Singling out any part of this massive complex is a pretty pointless exercise, but the area around **S'Arenal harbour** does at least have a concentration of facilities. S'Arenal also boasts **Aqualand** (late May to late Sept daily 10am–5/6pm; €22, children €15; Ⓦwww.aqualand.es), a huge leisure complex of swimming pools, water flumes and kiddies' playgrounds on the eastern edge of the resort about 15km east of Palma. To get there, follow the signs from the motorway (Exit 13) or take EMT bus #23 from Palma bus station. Similarly, Sometimes, at the west end of the Platja de Palma, is home to the top-ranking, 55-tank **Palma Aquarium** (daily: mid-June to mid-Sept 10am–8pm, mid-Sept to mid-June 10am–6pm; €18.50; Ⓦwww.palmaaquarium .com). To get there, leave the motorway at Exit 10 or take bus #15 or #23 from the bus station.

West of Palma

Located just a couple of kilometres to the **west** of Palma's ferry port, cramped and crowded **CALA MAJOR** snakes its way along a hilly stretch of coastline bisected by its main street (the Ma-1C). This modest, modern pile-up is brightened by the occasional *Modernista* building, reminders of halcyon days when the resort was a byword for elegance as exemplified by the ritzy, five-star *Hotel Nixe Palace* (Ⓣ971 70 08 88, Ⓦwww.hotelnixepalace.com; ❸), a large and attractive structure which hogs the shoreline beside the main road. There's also the small matter of a royal palace, the **Palacio de Marivent**, and although you can't go in, you can glimpse it from the main street – it's close to the Ma-1 motorway at the east end of the resort.

Cala Major's Fundació Pilar i Joan Miró

Opposite the Palacio de Marivent, the (poorly) signposted road to Gènova dog legs up the hill for 500m to run past the **Fundació Pilar i Joan Miró**, c/Joan de Saridakis 29, where the painter **Joan Miró** (1893–1983) lived and worked for much of the 1950s, 1960s and 1970s (mid-May to mid-Sept Tues–Sat 10am–7pm; Sun 10am–3pm; mid-Sept to mid-May Tues–Sat 10am–6pm, Sun 10am–3pm; €6); EMT bus #46 (every 10–30min) from central Palma stops 100m below the entrance.

Initially – from 1920 – the young Miró was involved with the **Surrealists** in Paris and contributed to all their major exhibitions: his wild squiggles, supercharged with bright colours, prompted André Breton, the leading theorist of the movement, to describe Miró as "the most Surrealist of us all". In the 1930s he adopted a simpler style, abandoning the decorative complexity of his earlier work for a more minimalist use of symbols, though the highly coloured forms remained. Miró **returned to Barcelona**, the city of his birth, in 1940, where he continued to work in the Surrealist tradition, though as an avowed opponent of Franco his position was uneasy. In 1957

▲ Fundació Pilar i Joan Miró

he **moved to Mallorca**, its relative isolation offering a degree of safety. His wife and mother were both Mallorcan, which must have influenced his decision, as did the chance to work in his own purpose-built studio with its view of the coast. Even from the relative isolation of Franco's Spain he remained an influential figure, prepared to experiment with all kinds of media, right up until his death here in Cala Major in 1983.

The expansive hillside premises of the Fundació includes the bright-white **Espai Estrella** (Star Space), an angular modern gallery which holds a rotating and representative sample of the prolific artist's work. Miró was nothing if not productive, and the Fundació owns 134 paintings, 300 engravings and 105 drawings, as well as sculptures, gouaches and preliminary sketches – more than six thousand works in all. There are no guarantees as to what will be on display, but you're likely to see a decent selection of his paintings, most notably the familiar dream-like squiggles and half-recognizable shapes that are intended to conjure up the unconscious, with free play often given to erotic associations. The gallery also hosts temporary exhibitions of modern and contemporary art, though these mostly take place in another part of the main complex, the **Espai Cubic** (Cubic Space). In between the two, the **Biblioteca** (Library) stores a comprehensive collection of Miró documents.

From the main complex, it's a brief stroll over to the **Taller Sert** (Sert Workshop; hourly guided visits; free), a striking Modernist structure with a roof partly shaped like seagull wings. The workshop takes its name from the architect who designed it, Josep Sert, but this was very much Miró's studio where he spent a large slice of his life. The interior has been left pretty much as it was at the time of the artist's death and it certainly gives the flavour of how the man worked – tackling a dozen or so canvases at the same time. Just beyond the studio is **Son Boter** (mid-May to mid-Sept hourly guided visits; free), a traditional Mallorcan farmhouse dating from the seventeenth century. Miró bought the place in 1959 and used it as a reserve studio for some of his larger compositions. He also doodled on the walls and his graffiti has survived intact.

Illetes

Prosperous **ILLETES**, just off the Ma-1C coastal road immediately to the west of Cala Major – and 7km from Palma – comprises a ribbon of restaurants, hotels and apartment buildings which bestride the steep hills that rise high above a rocky shoreline. There's precious little space left, but at least the generally low-rise buildings are of manageable proportions and one of the hotels, the *Bon Sol*, about halfway along the main drag (☎971 40 21 11, Ⓦwww.hotelbonsol.es; ❼), is particularly appealing, its assorted terraces tumbling down the cliffs to the seashore and its own artificial beach. A string of tiny cove beaches punctuates the coast here, the most attractive being the pine-shaded **Platja Cala Comtesa**, at the southern end of the resort, alongside a military zone.

▲ Illetes

Portals Nous

Just to the west of Illetes, **PORTALS NOUS** (aka Puerto Portals) is a ritzy settlement where polished mansions fill out the green and hilly terrain between the coast and the dull and drab main street (Ma-1C). There's a tiny **beach** too, set beneath the cliffs and reached via a flight of steps at the foot of c/Passatge del Mar, but the big deal is the **marina**, one of Mallorca's most exclusive, where the boats look more like ocean liners than pleasure yachts. What you make of all this glitz and the flock of celebrities that it attracts is very much a matter of taste (and politics), but the marina is certainly a lively spot. One of the most hyped of its many **bars and restaurants** is the Michelin-starred *Restaurant Tristán* (T 971 67 55 47), where you can expect to pay an arm and a leg, maybe two. In striking contrast, the resort's **Marineland** is one of the tackier attractions on the island, with shark tanks and a tropical aquarium, as well as dolphin and sea-lion shows (late Feb to mid-Nov daily 9.30am–6pm; €22, children €16; W www.marineland.es). Young children love the place; adults mostly suffer in silence.

Portals Nous has precious few **hotels** – much of the shoreline is occupied by private villas and apartments – and the best local accommodation is about 3km to the west of the marina beside the old coastal road, the MA-1C. It's here you'll find the four-star *Hotel Punta Negra Resort* (T 971 68 07 62, W www.h10hotels .com; O), whose deluxe accommodation spreads over two rugged coves beside crystal clear waters.

Palma Nova

Old Mallorca hands claim that **PALMA NOVA**, 4km west of Portals Nous, was once a beauty spot, and certainly its wide and shallow bay, with its excellent beaches and pine-clad headlands, still has its moments. But for the most part, the bay has been engulfed by a broad, congested sweep of tourist facilities. With the development comes a vigorous (mainly British) nightlife and a platoon of hotels on or near the seashore – though, as elsewhere, most are block-booked by tour operators throughout the season.

Calvià

Tucked away in the hills behind the coast, about 6km north of Palma Nova, is the tiny town of **CALVIÀ**, the region's administrative centre – hence the oversized town hall, paid for by the profits of the tourist industry. The parish church of **Sant Joan Baptista** (Mon–Sat 10am–1pm) is the town's key building, a large and much modified thirteenth-century structure whose Gothic subtleties mostly disappeared during a nineteenth-century refurbishment – hence the crude bas-relief carving of the Garden of Gethsemane above the main door. There are pleasant views across the surrounding countryside from outside the church, and the adjacent square is home to a modern mural showing a rather neat depiction of the island's history.

TransaBús **bus** #L111 links Palma with Calvià via Portals Nous between four and six times daily.

Magaluf

TORRENOVA, on the chunky headland at the far end of Palma Nova, is a cramped and untidy development that slides into **MAGALUF**, whose high-rise towers march across the next bay down the coast. For years a cheap-as-chips package holiday destination, Magaluf finally lost patience with its youthful British visitors in 1996. The local authorities won a court order allowing them to demolish twenty downmarket hotels in an attempt to end – or at least control – the annual binge of "violence, drunkenness and open-air sex" that, they argued, characterized the resort. The high-rise hotels were duly dynamited and an extensive clean-up programme subsequently freshened up the resort's appearance. However, short of demolishing the whole lot, there's not too much anyone can do with the deadening concrete of the modern town centre – and the demolished blocks will anyway be replaced, albeit by more upmarket hotels. These draconian measures have brought some improvement, but the resort's British visitors remain steadfastly determined to create, or at least patronize, a bizarre caricature of their homeland: it's all here, from beans-on-toast with Marmite to *Tom Brown's Chicken & Steak Inn.*

Stuck on the western edge of Magaluf, **Western Water Park** (May to mid-Oct daily 10am–5/6pm; €24, children 4–12 years €16; ⓦ www.westernpark .com) contrives to weld together a replica Wild West town – one of the most incongruous sights in Spain – with a platoon of water rides and water shutes.

South to Cala Mago and Portals Vells

Things pick up on the edge of Magaluf with the spatulate **peninsula** that extends to the south of the resort, poking its knobbly head out into the ocean. The west side of the peninsula has been extensively developed, but the east side has been barely touched, its pine-clad coves bumping down to Portals Vells – though note that there is no public transport. The **road to Portals Vells** begins at Exit 14 on the Ma-1 motorway just where it merges with the Ma-1C to the northwest of Magaluf. From the Ma-1 exit, the road cuts south, running past the Western Water Park and keeping straight at a fork where the road to Santa Ponça curves off to the right; the fork is 2.5km from the Ma-1. South of the fork, the road narrows into a country lane, passing a golf course before heading off into the woods. After about 3km, a steep, 1km-long turning on the left leads down to **CALA MAGO** (still signposted in Castilian as Playa El Mago), where a rocky little headland with a shattered guard house has lovely beaches to either side. Park and walk down to whichever cove takes your fancy: the nudist beach on the right with its café-restaurant, or the delightful pine-shaded strand on the left with its beach bar, tiny port and sprinkling of villas.

Continuing a further 600m past the Cala Mago turning, a second side road branches off for the kilometre-long trip down to the cove beach of **PORTALS VELLS**. Despite a bar-restaurant and a handful of villas, this remains a pleasant, pine-scented spot of glistening sand, rocky cliffs and clear blue water, especially appealing early in the morning before the crowds arrive. Clearly visible from the beach are the **caves** of the headland on the south side of the cove. A rough footpath leads to the most interesting, an old cave church where the holy-water stoup and altar have been cut out of the solid rock – the work of shipwrecked Genoese seamen, according to local legend.

Santa Ponça

West of Magaluf, the Ma-1 trims the outskirts of **SANTA PONÇA**, one of the less endearing of the resorts that punctuate this stretch of coast. Mostly a product of the 1980s, this sprawling conurbation has abandoned the concrete high-rises of yesteryear for a pseudo-vernacular architecture that has littered the hills with suburbanite villas. More positively, the setting is attractive, with rolling hills flanking a broad bay, and the resort's white sandy beaches offer safe bathing.

Peguera

Sprawling **PEGUERA**, about 6km northwest of Santa Ponça, is strung out along a lengthy, partly pedestrianized main street – the Avinguda Peguera – immediately behind several generous sandy beaches. There's nothing remarkable about the place, but it does have an easy-going air and is a favourite with families and older visitors. The Ma-1 loops right round Peguera and the easiest approach, if you're just after the **beach**, is from the south. Head into the resort along the main street and park anywhere you can before you reach the pedestrianized zone, where the town's baffling one-way system sends you weaving through the resort's side streets – best avoided, if you can.

Cala Fornells

Next door to Peguera is the much prettier – and much smaller – resort of **CALA FORNELLS**, which is reached via either of two signed turnings on the Avinguda Peguera just to the west of the pedestrianized centre. Take the more easterly turning and the road climbs up to a string of chic, *pueblo*-style houses that perch on the sea cliffs and trail round to the tiny centre of the resort, where a wooded cove is set around a minuscule beach and concreted sunbathing slabs. Although Cala Fornells tends to be overcrowded during the daytime, at night the tranquillity returns, and it makes a good base for a holiday.

Cala Fornells has two fetching **hotels**, both behind the beach at the end of the access roads: the sprucely modern, four-star *Coronado* (☎971 68 68 00, ⓦ www.hotelcoronado.com; ❻), where all 150-odd bedrooms have sea views and balconies; and the more sympathetic, green-shuttered and white-painted *Cala Fornells* (☎971 68 69 50, ⓦ www.calafornells.com; ❻).

Camp de Mar

Burgeoning **CAMP DE MAR**, flanking a hilly cove just 3km west of Peguera, has an expansive beach and fine bathing, though the scene is marred by the presence of two thumping great **hotels** dropped right on the seashore – the *Hotel Playa Camp de Mar*, a British favourite, and the smarter, four-star *Hotel Riu Camp de Mar*, which caters mainly to Germans. Both are modern high-rises equipped with spacious, balconied bedrooms, and both are essentially the preserve of the package industry – which gives you a clear idea of what this resort is like. Camp de Mar and its surroundings are also in the middle of a massive expansion, with brand-new villa complexes trailing back from the beach in an all-too-familiar semi-suburban sprawl. All the same, the **beach** is an amiable spot to soak up the sun, and it's hard to resist the eccentric café stuck out in the bay and approached via a rickety walkway on stilts.

A minor road twists west from Camp de Mar over wooded hills to **Port d'Andratx** (see p.138).

Travel details

City buses

Palma to: the airport (#1; every 15min; 25min); Cala Major (#3; every 10min; 15min); Fundació Miró (#46; every 20min; 30min); Illetes (#3; every 10min; 20min); S'Arenal (#15; every 10min; 30min).
For further information, call ☎900 70 07 10, or consult ⓦ www.emtpalma.es.

Island-wide buses

Palma to: Alcúdia (Mon–Sat hourly, 5 on Sun; 1hr); Algaida (Mon–Sat every 1–2hr, 5 on Sun; 25min); Andratx (every 30min to hourly; 1hr); Artà (Mon–Sat 4–5 daily, 2 on Sun; 1hr 20min); Banyalbufar (6–7 daily; 1hr); Binissalem (3–6 daily; 20min); Bunyola (Mon–Fri hourly, Sat 7 daily, Sun 4 daily; 20min); Cala d'Or (Mon–Sat 6 daily, 3 on Sun; 1hr 10min); Cala Figuera (May–Oct Mon–Sat 2 daily; 1hr

30min); Cala Millor (Mon–Sat 10 daily, 3 on Sun; 1hr 15min); Cala Rajada (2–6 daily; 1hr 35min); Ca'n Picafort (4–6 daily; 1hr 30min); Colònia de Sant Jordi (May–Oct Mon–Sat 5–9 daily, 3 on Sun; 1hr); Coves del Drac (Mon–Sat 3 daily, 2 on Sun; 1hr); Deià (5–7 daily; 45min); Esporles (Mon–Fri hourly, 6 on Sat & Sun; 30min); Estellencs (6–7 daily; 1hr 20min); Felanitx (May–Oct Mon–Sat every 1–2hr, 5 on Sun; 1hr); Inca (Mon–Sat hourly, Sat & Sun 3–5 daily; 30min); La Granja (6–7 daily; 35min); Lluc: train to Inca (see below), then bus from Inca to Lluc (Mon–Fri every 1–2 hours, 1 on Sat & Sun; 35min); Magaluf (hourly; 25min); Manacor (Mon–Sat 10 daily, 5 on Sun; 45min); Peguera (hourly; 35min); Platja de Formentor (May–Oct Mon–Sat 1 daily; 1hr 30min); Pollença (Mon–Fri hourly, 7 on Sat & Sun; 1hr 10min); Port d'Alcúdia (Mon–Sat hourly, 5 on Sun; 1hr 15min); Port d'Andratx (every 30min to hourly; 1hr 10min); Port de Pollença (Mon–Fri hourly, 7 on Sat & Sun; 1hr 15min); Port de Sóller (via the tunnel: Mon–Fri hourly, Sat 7 daily, Sun 4 daily; 35min; via Valldemossa: 5–7 daily; 1hr 30min); Porto Cristo (May–Oct Mon–Sat 8 daily, 3 on Sun; 1hr 10min); Porto Petro (May–Oct 3-6 daily; 1hr 35min); Santanyí (May–Oct Mon–Sat 6 daily, 3 on Sun; 1hr); Sóller (via the tunnel: Mon–Fri hourly, Sat 7 daily, Sun 4 daily; 30min; via Valldemossa: 5–7 daily; 1hr 15min); Valldemossa (Mon–Fri every 9 daily, Sat 7 daily, Sun 5 daily; 30min). For further information, call ☎971 17 77 77, or check out ⓦhttp://tib.caib.es/.

Trains

Palma to: Binissalem (every 20min; 30min); Inca (every 20min; 40min); Lloseta (every 20min; 35min); Manacor (hourly; 1hr); Muro (hourly; 50min); Petra (hourly; 55min); Sineu (hourly; 50min). For further information, call ☎971 17 77 77, or check out ⓦhttp://tib.caib.es/. **Palma** to: Sóller (6–7 daily; 1hr). For further information, call ☎902 36 47 11, or consult ⓦwww.trendesoller.com.

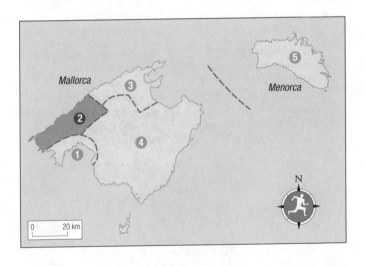

2

Western Mallorca

CHAPTER 2 # Highlights

✳ Sóller This delightful town boasts handsome stone mansions, a dinky main square and an exquisite setting amidst craggy mountains – and it's still within easy striking distance of the beach. See pp.103–108

✳ Palma-Sóller train Ride the antique train over the mountains from Palma to Sóller for a wonderful introduction to the island's jagged, searing mountains. See p.104

✳ Jardins d'Alfábia First established by the Moors, these are the finest gardens in Mallorca, with lush trellises and verdant terraces leading to the sweetest of lily-choked pools. See p.112

✳ Deià One of Mallorca's most beguiling villages, where a huddle of ancient stone houses are set against a spectacular mountain backdrop. See p.116

✳ Hiking in the Serra de Tramuntana Criss-crossed by scores of exhilarating trails, the rugged mountains that range along the length of the island's northwest shore offer the finest hiking in the Balearics. See pp.122–123 & pp.132–133

✳ Valldemossa Monastery The old stone town of Valldemossa zeroes in on its splendid medieval monastery, whose echoing cloisters once sheltered George Sand and Frédéric Chopin. See p.127

▲ Valldemossa Monastery

2

Western Mallorca

M allorca is at its scenic best in the gnarled ridge of the **Serra de Tramuntana**, the imposing mountain range which stretches the length of the island's northwestern shore, its rearing peaks and plunging seacliffs intermittently punctuated by valleys of olive and citrus groves. Midway along and cramped by the mountains is **Sóller**, an antiquated merchants' town that serves as a charming introduction to the region, especially when reached on the scenic narrow-gauge **train line** from Palma. From Sóller, it's a short hop down to the coast to **Port de Sóller**, a one-time port and fishing village that has become a popular resort set around a deep and handsome bay: this geographical arrangement – the town located a few kilometres inland from its port – is repeated across Mallorca, a reminder of more troubled days when marauding corsairs forced the islanders to live away from the coast. The mountain valleys in the vicinity of Sóller were once remote and isolated, but today they shelter three bucolic stone-built villages – **Biniaraix**, **Fornalutx** and **Orient** – and near at hand also are two of the island's finest gardens, the oasis-like **Jardins d'Alfàbia** and the Italianate terraces of **Raixa**, though the latter is closed for a revamp at the time of writing.

Southwest of Sóller, the principal coastal road, the **Ma-10**, threads up through the mountains to reach the beguiling village of **Deià**, tucked at the base of formidable cliffs and famous as the former home of Robert Graves. Beyond lies the magnificent Carthusian monastery of **Valldemossa**, whose shadowy cloisters briefly accommodated George Sand and Frédéric Chopin during the 1830s, and the *hacienda* of **La Granja**, another compelling if perhaps over-visited stop. Continuing southwest, the Ma-10 wriggles high above the shoreline, slipping through a sequence of mountain hamlets, of which **Banyalbufar** and **Estellencs** are the most picturesque, their tightly terraced fields tumbling down the coastal cliffs. A few kilometres further and you leave the coast behind, drifting inland out of the mountains and into the foothills that precede the market town of **Andratx**. Beyond, on Mallorca's western tip, lie the safe waters of **Port d'Andratx**, a medium-sized resort draped around a handsome inlet, its villas announcing the start of the intense tourist development that eats up the coast eastwards to Palma.

Hiking and beaches

The Serra de Tramuntana provides the best **hiking** on Mallorca, with scores of **hiking trails** latticing the mountains. There are trails to suit all aptitudes and all levels of enthusiasm, from the easiest of strolls to the most gruelling of long-distance treks, and generally speaking paths are well marked, though apt to be

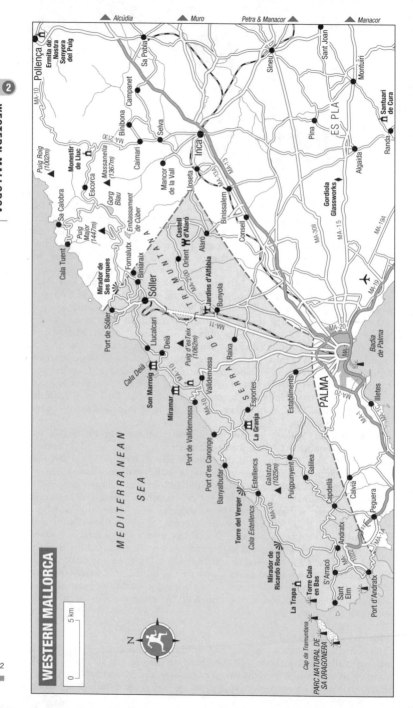

WESTERN MALLORCA

N

0 ___ 5 km

MEDITERRANEAN SEA

Badia de Palma

Alcúdia   *Muro*   *Petra & Manacor*   *Manacor*

Pollença
Ermita de Nostra Senyora del Puig
MA-10

Sa Pobla
Campanet
Binibona
Selva
Caimari
Monestir de Lluc
Puig Roig (1002m)
Escorca
Massanella (1367m)
MA-2130
Gorg Blau
Embassament de Cúber
Sa Calobra
Puig Major (1447m)
Cala Tuent
Fornalutx
Biniaraix
Mirador de Ses Barques
Sóller
Port de Sóller

Sant Joan
Sineu
Muro
Montuïri
Inca
Mancor de la Vall
Loseta
MA-13
Binissalem
Consell
Pina
Randa
Santuari de Cura
Algaida
Gordiola Glassworks
MA-19A
MA-30ll
MA-15
ES PLA
MA-13A

Castell d'Alaró
Alaró
Orient
MA-2100
Jardins d'Alfàbia
Bunyola
MA-11
TRAMUNTANA
SERRA DE

Llucalcari
Deià
Cala Deià
Son Marroig
Puig d'es Teix (1062m)
Valldemossa
Raixa
Miramar
Port de Valldemossa
Esporles
La Granja
Establiments
PALMA
MA-20
MA-1
Illetes
MA-1A

Port d'es Canonge
Banyalbufar
Estellencs
Galatzó (1025m)
Puigpunyent
Galilea
Capdellà
Calvià
Torre del Verger
Cala Estellencs
MA-10
Peguera

Mirador de Ricardo Roca
Torre Cala en Bas
La Trapa
S'Arracó
Sant Elm
Andratx
Port d'Andratx
MA-1A

Cap de Tramuntana
PARC NATURAL DE SA DRAGONERA

The best Mallorcan **hiking guides** are produced by Editorial Alpinaa (Ⓦwww .editorialalpina.com), who publish three guides at around €12 each that combine to cover the whole of the northwest coast – "Mallorca Tramuntana Sud", "Mallorca Tramuntana Central" and "Mallorca Tramuntana Norte". The English-language editions of all three are clearly written and the **maps** (at 1:25,000) are well presented and very detailed, the only problem being one of availability: Sóller tourist office should have copies as should one of the town's bookshops, but otherwise it's probably best to buy a copy before you leave home either at a specialist map shop or via the company's website.

clogged with thorn bushes. Broad details of several walks are given in the text and **two day-long hikes**, one beginning in Valldemossa and the other in Deià, are described in depth. The region is also crossed by Mallorca's main long-distance hiking trail, the **Ruta de Pedra en Sec** (Dry-stone Route, the **GR221**), which begins in Sant Elm and threads its way through the mountains to Sóller before proceeding onto Pollença – or at least it will do when everything is sorted out: at the time of writing, access disputes with local landowners mean that a section of the GR221 west of Sóller – and in between Banyalbufar and Estellencs – is inaccessible, though the trail to the east of Sóller is in full working order (for more details, see p.143). There are two **hikers' hostels** (*refugis*; Ⓦwww.conselldemallorca.net) on the Sant Elm–Sóller section of the GR221 – one each at Deià (see p.118) and Port de Sóller (see p.110) – and one more is under construction at Sant Elm. See the box above for information on hiking guides.

If you're looking for **beaches**, Port de Sóller has a pleasant sandy strip, but otherwise it's all rock and pebble, though there is compensation in the scenery, wild and wonderful at both **Cala Estellencs** and **Cala Deià**.

Accommodation and getting around

Port d'Andratx, Deià, Sóller and Port de Sóller have the widest range of **accommodation**, but all the villages in the region have at least a couple of places to stay. Nevertheless, from June to early September (and sometimes beyond), vacancies are extremely thin on the ground and advance reservations are strongly advised. To compensate, distances are small – from Andratx to Sóller via the Ma-10 is only about 70km – the roads are good and the **bus** network is adequate to good for most destinations. **Taxis** can work out as a reasonable deal too, especially if you're travelling in a group: the fare for the seventy-kilometre trip from Sóller to Andratx, for instance, is about €70, central Palma to Sóller €35. If you're driving, note that although all the villages hereabouts have small **car parks**, in summer finding a spare lot between about 10am or 11am and 5pm can be problematic, and very frustrating – as is Sóller's convoluted one-way system.

Sóller and around

At the end of the train line from Palma lies **Sóller**, one of the most laid-back and enjoyable towns on Mallorca, and an ideal and inexpensive base for exploring the surrounding mountains. Most visitors, though, stick religiously to the coast, taking the vintage tram on from Sóller down to the popular and eminently amenable seaside resort of **Port de Sóller**, which has the nicest **beach** hereabouts as well as a clutch of good restaurants and hotels. However, the best of the scenery lies just inland to the northeast, where Sóller's mellow mansions fade seamlessly into the orchards and farmland that precede the charming hamlets of **Biniaraix** and **Fornalutx**. Further afield, on the landward side of the Serra de Tramuntana, spread the verdant gardens of the **Jardins d'Alfàbia** and the hamlet of **Orient**, which is on the road to the remote hilltop ruins of the **Castell d'Alaró**. Beyond the castle are the attractive little towns of **Alaró** and Binissalem (see p.179), the centre of Mallorca's wine industry and a station on the Palma to Inca train line.

Getting to Sóller and Port de Sóller

Fast and straight, the **Ma-11** cuts straight across the island from Palma to Sóller, tunnelling straight through the mountains as it approaches its destination. The twenty-kilometre journey takes about thirty minutes to drive and the **tunnel**, which is 3023m long and ends 2.5km from the centre of Sóller, costs €4.45 per car. You can avoid the tunnel – and the toll – by driving over the mountains along a zigzagging minor road, an enjoyable detour with smashing views that adds 7km to the trip; **cyclists** are not allowed in the tunnel because of vehicle fumes.

There's a frequent direct **bus** service from Palma to Sóller and Port de Sóller via the tunnel. This is supplemented by a good service linking Palma with Sóller and Port de Sóller via Valldemossa and Deià. On the Ma-10, there's a seasonal service running in from Lluc and Pollença to the east, but nothing from points west of Valldemossa. The **trains** from Palma to Sóller (see box below) link with the clanking vintage **trams** that roll their way down to the coast at Port de Sóller, 5km away. The trams, some of which date back to 1912, depart every hour on the hour daily from 7am to 7pm, sometimes later; the fifteen-minute journey costs €4 each way; pay the conductor.

The train from Palma to Sóller

The 28-kilometre **train** journey from Palma to Sóller is a delight, dipping and cutting through the mountains and fertile valleys of the **Serra de Tramuntana**. The line was completed in 1911 on the profits of the orange and lemon trade: the railway was built to transport the fruit to Palma, at a time when it took a full day to make the trip by road. The rolling stock is tremendously atmospheric too, with narrow carriages – the gauge is only 914mm – that look like they've come out of an Agatha Christie novel, though it has to be admitted that it is something of a clanky, bumpy ride.

First the train has to clear the scratchy suburbs of Palma, but within about fifteen minutes it's running across pancake-flat farmland with the impenetrable-looking peaks of the Serra de Tramuntana dead ahead. After clunking through the outskirts of **Bunyola**, the train threads upwards to spend five minutes tunnelling through the mountains, where the noisy engine and dimly lit carriages give the feel of a roller-coaster ride. Beyond, out in the bright mountain air, are the steep valleys and craggy thousand-metre peaks at the heart of the Serra de Tramuntana, and everywhere there are almond groves, vivid with blossom in January and February.

There are six or seven **departures** daily from Palma station throughout the year and the whole ride takes just under an hour. An ordinary one-way **ticket** costs €10, a return €17. For further information, call ☎902 36 47 11, or check out ⊛www.trendesoller.com.

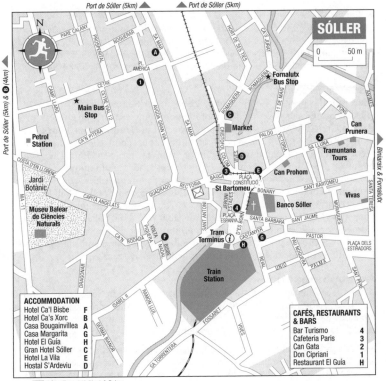

Port de Sóller (5km)

Port de Sóller (5km)

SÓLLER

0   50 m

N

PARE CALANY

PROSPERITAT

NOGUERAR

SA MAR

HORT DE SES TIES

CAS JURAT

Port de Sóller (5km) & B (4km)

CETRE

CETRE VELL 12

AVUDA GRAN VIA

ROMAGUERA

ROMAGUERA

11 DE MAIG

PONS

XIMELIS

Biniaraix & Fornalutx

CAMP LLARG

CA'N PITERA

Main Bus
Stop

COSTA D'EN LLORENÇ

Petrol
Station

MA-11

Jardí
Botànic

Museu Balear
de Ciències
Naturals

CAPITÀ ANGELATS

QUADRADO

RECTORIA

SANT ANTONI

CA'N RODADA

VOLTA PIQUERA

BISBE
NADAL

DRAGONAR

ISABEL II

RAMON LLUL

GERMA BIANOR

SA TORRENTERA

FOSSARET

VIVES

Pt.
AMÉRICA

Market

CRISTÒFOL COLOM

BAUÇA

JERÓNI
ESTADES

ANTONI

PLAÇA
ESPANYA

Tram
Terminus

Train
Station

Fornalutx
Bus Stop

CASTANYER

SA MAR

PALOU

VICTÒRIA

SA LLUNA

PLAÇA
CONSTITUCIÓ

St Bartomeu

SANTA BARBARA

Can
Prunera

Tramuntana
Tours

Can Prohom

BONANY

SANT BARTOMEU

Banco Sóller

SANT JAUME

PAU NOGUERA

UNIO

REIAL

PALMA

SANT PERE

Vivas

MORAGUES

PASTOR

SANTA TERESA

PLAÇA DELS
ESTIRADORS

ACCOMMODATION
Hotel Ca'l Bisbe   F
Hotel Ca's Xorc   B
Casa Bougainvillea   A
Casa Margarita   G
Hotel El Guía   H
Gran Hotel Sóller   C
Hotel La Vila   E
Hostal S'Ardeviu   D

CAFÉS, RESTAURANTS
& BARS
Bar Turismo   4
Cafeteria Paris   3
Can Gata   2
Don Cipriani   1
Restaurant El Guía   H

Sóller Tunnel (2.5km) & Palma

Sóller

Rather than any specific sight, it's the general flavour of **SÓLLER** that appeals, with the town's narrow, sloping lanes cramped by eighteenth- and nineteenth-century **stone houses** adorned with fancy grilles and big wooden doors – the former dwellings of the region's rich fruit merchants. A couple of low-key attractions fill out a wander around the town and it's also an easy stroll east to the picturesque village of **Biniaraix**, with the deluxe hamlet-hidey-hole of **Fornalutx** a further couple of kilometres to the northeast.

Arrival and information

Though there's a chance that things may change yet again, **buses** to Sóller should pull in and depart from the **main bus stop**, on the west side of the centre, just off the Ma-11 on c/Cetre; from here, it's a five- to ten-minute walk to Plaça Constitució. Note also that when it comes to **leaving Sóller by bus**, services heading both east and west along the coast are often full; to be sure of a seat, you'll need to go down to Port de Sóller, where these services usually originate.

Sóller **train station** and adjacent **tram terminus** are immediately to the south of the main square and here also, in an old train carriage plonked in the middle of Plaça d'Espanya, is Sóller **tourist office** (Mon–Fri 10am–2pm & 3–5pm, Sat 9am–1pm; ☎971 63 80 08, ⓦwww.sollernet.com). They issue free town maps, have a comprehensive list of accommodation, and sell hiking guides, including all three of the Editorial Alpina series covering the entire Serra de Tramuntana (see box, p.103). If the tourist office has sold out, as is sometimes the case, try either of two bookshops, the Librería Papererîa, on Plaça Constitució, or the Librería Calabruix, close by at c/Sa Lluna 7. If you want a **taxi**, go to the taxi rank beside the tourist office or call ℡971 63 84 84.

Getting around

Bike rental is possible in Sóller with *Vivas*, c/Sant Teresa 20 (℡971 63 02 34), who charge €8 per day for their more basic mountain bikes, up to €18 for a Racing Conor. A comparable service is provided by **Tramuntana Tours**, c/Sa Lluna 72 (℡971 63 24 23, ⓦwww.tramuntanatours.com), though their main preoccupation is an extensive programme of tours and excursions. They offer mountain-bike tours, canyoning, fishing trips and an ambitious range of day-long **guided walks** with something to suit most aptitudes. There are, for example, medium-to-difficult guided walks to Alaró Castle (14km), Valldemossa (16km) and up the Barranc de Biniaraix (16km); a difficult clamber down the Torrent de Pareis gorge (8km); and an easy jaunt round the Sóller valley (11km). Costs vary considerably, but reckon on a minimum of €30 per trip per person. Transport is provided to and from the trailhead as required and the operators will, within reason, collect hikers from where they are staying.

Accommodation

Until a few years ago, there was hardly anywhere to stay in Sóller, but recently the town has mushroomed **hotels** as if there were no tomorrow. Even better, standards are generally high, there's a good chance of finding a vacant room here in high season and prices are very competitive.

Hotel Ca's Xorc Ctra Sóller–Deià (Ma-10) Km 56.1 ℡971 63 82 80, ⓦwww.casxorc.com. Located high in the hills, about 4km west of Sóller along the Ma-10, this superb hotel occupies a renovated old olive mill in which each of the twelve guest rooms has been decorated in sleek modern style. There's an outside pool and handsome terraced gardens, and the food is simply fabulous, featuring local ingredients and variations on traditional Mallorcan dishes. Reservations essential. ❻

🏃 **Hotel Ca'l Bisbe** Bisbe Nadal 10 ℡971 63 12 28, ⓦwww.hotelcalbisbe.com. This appealing four-star hotel occupies a sensitively refurbished former bishop's palace, complete with beamed ceilings, pool and garden. Each of the 25 guest rooms is generously appointed, unfussily decorated and comes with every mod con. Very competitively priced. ❸

Casa Bougainvillea c/Sa Mar 81 ℡971 63 31 04, ⓦwww.casa-bougainvillea.com. This enjoyable B&B occupies an old, sympathetically modernized three-storey terrace house on a busy side street a short walk from Plaça Constitució. There are eight guest rooms here, all en suite, and each is decorated in a pleasingly unfussy style. Weather permitting, breakfast is served in the garden, where guests can idle away their time reading and relaxing. Competitively priced too. ❷

Casa Margarita c/Reial 3 ℡971 63 42 14, ⓦwww.sollernet.com/casamargarita. Pleasant, traditional rooms with large and rather grand wooden furniture in an attractive old terraced house close to the train station. Stay at the back (away from the road) if you're a light sleeper. ❶

🏃 **Hotel El Guía** c/Castanyer 2 ℡971 63 02 27, ⓦwww.sollernet.com/elguia. There may be a batch of glossy new hotels in Sóller, but this long-established, two-star, family-run place is hard to beat. Set behind a pretty little courtyard, the hotel's layout and decor are very traditional and although the guest rooms are a tad spartan, they are perfectly adequate and really rather engaging. To get there, walk down the steps from the train station platform and turn right. Closed Dec–Feb. ❷

🏃 **Gran Hotel Sóller** c/Romaguera 18 ℡971 63 86 86, ⓦwww.granhotelsoller .com. There are four good things about this five-star hotel: the central location, the rooftop café, pool and breakfast bar, the garden, and the building, a grand structure whose *Modernista* flourishes date back to the 1880s – amazingly enough, considering its size, the building started out as a private house. Less positively, the interior has been kitted out in a plush but pedestrian modern style and although the guest rooms have every convenience, they hardly stir the imagination. And it is expensive. ❼

Hotel La Vila Plaça Constitució 14 ☎ 971 63 46 41, ⓦ www.lavilahotel.com. Right in the centre of Sóller, in an attractive old building above a café on the main square, this self-styled boutique hotel has eight double rooms, half of which overlook the square, the rest the garden at the back. The rooms are really rather appealing – especially as they each have a big old Spanish bed board – if a tad small. Competitively priced at ❹

Hostal S'Ardeviu c/Vives 14 ☎ 971 63 83 26, ⓦ www.sollernet.com/sardeviu. Down an unbecoming alley just a stone's throw from the main square, the *S'Ardeviu* is a small, family-run hotel in an intelligently revamped old mansion. Many of the house's original features have been maintained and the bedrooms are neat and trim. Small double ❸, large ❹

The Town

All streets lead to the main square, **Plaça Constitució**, an informal, pint-sized affair of big old plane trees, crowded cafés and grouchy mopeds just down the hill from the train station. The square is dominated by the hulking mass of the church of **St Bartomeu** (Mon–Thurs 11am–1pm & 3–5.15pm, Fri & Sat 11am–1pm), a crude but somehow rather fetching neo-Gothic remodelling of a medieval original with a couple of Art Nouveau flourishes thrown in. Its most appealing features are the enormous and precisely carved rose window stuck high in the main facade and the heavy-duty but apparently pointless balustrade above it. Inside, the cavernous nave is suitably dark and gloomy, the penitential home of a string of gaudy Baroque altarpieces. Next door, the **Banco de Sóller,** now gobbled up by the Banco Santander, is a *Modernista* extravagance, sheathed in a coat of roughly dressed stone and adorned by miniature balconies and almost frantic wrought iron grilles, all the work of Joan Rubiò, a Gaudí acolyte. Rubiò was also responsible for the elaborate stone façade of **Can Prunera**, just east of the square at c/Sa Lluna 90. The building has recently been converted into the **Museu del Modernisme** (Tues–Sun 10.30am–6.30pm), its handsome *Modernista* furnishings and fittings supplemented by a small collection of *Modernista* paintings. On the way to Can Prunera, at c/Sa Lluna 16, is **Can Prohom**, a grand eighteenth-century mansion where the district's landed gentry used to stay when they came to town.

Train station

Sóller **train station** is a handsome building, its wide stone staircases and high-ceilinged old waiting rooms witnessing the days when it was crucial to the town's merchants. Four of the station's rooms have been turned into **exhibition** areas (daily 10.30am–6.30pm; free) – two rooms each for a selection of cheery, sometimes tongue-in-cheek ceramics by **Picasso** and another two for the flamboyant squiggles of his friend **Miró**, whose maternal grandfather came from Sóller. The merchants may have welcomed the railway, but the peasantry wasn't so sure – they had already proved themselves decidedly reluctant to accept technological change. In the 1860s, telegraph poles were erected between Sóller and Palma in an effort to improve communications. At first, groups of farm labourers snipped the wires and chopped the poles down, but when they heard that messages could be sent down the wires, they concluded that the same applied to goods. As a result, according to a visiting British captain, one J. W. Clayton, "bundles of clothes, pairs of knickerbockers, petti-coats, baskets of edibles, and even wigs…[were] neatly ticketed and addressed" and hung on the wires for onward transmission. When they stayed put, there were more attacks on the poor old telegraph poles.

Museu Balear de Ciències Naturals

Back on Plaça Constitució, take c/Bauçà for the five- to ten-minute walk west to the house and gardens that comprise the mildly diverting **Museu**

Balear de Ciències Naturals, on the main Palma-Sóller road (Balearic Museum of Natural Sciences; Tues–Sat 10am–6pm, Sun 10am–2pm; €5; Ⓦ www.jardibotanicdesoller.org). The house is an old merchant's villa that has been stripped out to accommodate a series of modest displays with temporary exhibitions on the top floor and the permanent collection on the two floors down below. This **permanent collection** begins with a fairly good section on the leading botanists of yesteryear, including Archduke Ludwig Salvator (see p.124), and continues with an assortment of island fossils and rocks. The labelling is in Catalan, but English leaflets are available in each of the rooms. Outside, the neat and trim **Jardí Botànic** (same hours) rolls down the hillside divided into thirteen small areas, half of which (M1–M6) are dedicated to Balearic species, including dune and sea-cliff species in M2, shade-loving plants in M4, and mountain plants in M5. A free English-language brochure identifying and illustrating many of the plants is issued at the main gate (for both the house and the gardens).

Eating and drinking

Sóller's main square and its immediate surroundings heave with **cafés** and **café-bars**, and although prices are very reasonable, the quality of the food on offer – with one or two exceptions – is very disappointing. The **restaurant** scene is similarly constrained and although there are two or three good spots, you may decide to pop down to Port de Sóller (see below) for a bite to eat instead.

Bar Turismo Avgda d'es Born 8. By the tram lines just up from Plaça Constitució, this convivial and rather old-fashioned little bar is an amenable spot to nurse a drink.

Cafeteria Paris Plaça Constitució. The premises may be standard-issue modern, but this is where you'll get the best coffee in town. Better-than-average snacks too.

🏃 **Can Gata** c/Sa Lluna 51 ☏ 971 63 86 34. Arguably the best restaurant in town, a laid-back, easygoing place in an old town house where the focus is on all things Mallorcan. Great home-cooking at bargain-basement prices – the daily special is a snip at €10. Garden terrace too.

Open daily: April to mid-Oct 12.30–9pm; mid-Oct to March 12.30–4pm.

Don Cipriani Avgda Gran Via 43 ☏ 971 63 30 49. One of the better restaurants in town, this pleasantly decorated Italian place specializes in home-made pastas with main courses averaging around €12. Has a small outside terrace at the back. Open Tues–Sun noon–3.30pm & 7.30–11pm.

Restaurant El Guia c/Castanyer 2 ☏ 971 63 02 27. In the hotel of the same name, this trim little restaurant sticks to Mallorcan dishes, which it does very well. Mains from around €15. Open Tues–Sun 1–3pm & 8–10pm, plus limited opening hours Nov–March.

Port de Sóller

PORT DE SÓLLER is one of the most popular spots on the west coast, and its handsome, horseshoe-shaped bay, ringed by forested hills, must be one of the most photographed places on the island after the package destinations around Palma. The high jinks of the Badía de Palma are, however, a world away from this low-key, family-oriented resort, which has been slowly grafted onto an old fishing port and naval base. Attractions here include one pleasant strip of **beach**, the **Platja d'en Repic**, right at the back of the bay and with generally clean and clear water, plus a wide selection of restaurants. It's also worth making the enjoyable hour-long hike – or brief drive – west to the **lighthouse** (far) guarding the cliffs of Cap Gros above the entrance to the bay. From here, the views out over the wild and rocky coast and back across the harbour are truly magnificent, especially at sunset. There's a surfaced road all the way: from the tram terminus, walk round the southern side of the bay past Platja d'en Repic and keep going, following the signs.

Sa Fira i Es Firó

If you're around Sóller and Port de Sóller in the second week of May, be sure to catch the **Sa Fira i Es Firó**, which commemorates the events of May 1561 when a large force of Arab pirates came to a sticky end after sacking Sóller. The Mallorcans had been taken by surprise, but they ambushed and massacred the Arabs as they returned to their ships and took grisly revenge by planting the raiders' heads on stakes. The story – bar decapitations – is played out in chaotic, alcoholic fashion every year at the festival. The re-enactment begins with the arrival of the pirates by boat, and continues with fancy-dress Christians and Arabs battling it out through the streets of the port, to the sound of blanks being fired in the air from antique rifles. On the days preceding this knees-up, there are also sporting and cultural events as well as a large, open-air market. The tourist office can give you a rough idea of the schedule of events, plus details of the dances and parties that follow.

Arrival and information

Trams from Sóller shadow the main road and clank to a stop beside the jetties bang in the centre of town. From here, it's a couple of minutes' walk east to the **tourist office**, located beside the church on c/Canonge Oliver 10 (Mon–Fri 9.30am–1pm & 3–5pm; ☎971 63 30 42, ⊛www.sollernet.com). They carry a reasonable range of local information, including restaurant and accommodation lists, maps and boat-trip details. In addition, Tramuntana Tours (see p.106) has a seasonal outlet down by the bay at Passeig Es Través 12 (March–Oct). **Buses** stop round the corner from the tourist office, beside the church on c/Església.

In summer, **boats** leave the dock by the tram terminus for day trips along the coast to either Sa Calobra (May–Oct 4 daily; €20) or Port Andratx (June–Sept 1 daily; €30). Amongst several companies, both these routes are serviced by Barcos Azules (⊛www.barcosazules.com).

Accommodation

Most of the port's hotels and *hostales* overlook the bay and although **rooms** are hard to find in high season thanks to the tour operators, there are usually lots of vacancies the rest of the year. Pleasingly, there are no massive hotel tower blocks here, but rather a ring of 1960s three- to four-storey blocks, several of which have benefited from the upgrading of the resort in general and its hotels in particular.

Hotel Aimia c/Santa Maria del Camí 1 ☎971 63 12 00, ⊛www.aimiahotel.com. In this slick, four-star hotel the 43 guest rooms have all the unmistakeable signs of the designer with flush ceiling lights and several shades of brown. Naturally, there's a spa, a gym and a pool – and it's all reassuringly smart, comfortable and expensive. ❼

Hotel Espléndido Passeig des Través 5 ☎971 63 18 50, ⊛www.esplendidohotel.com. The stylish remodelling of a 1950s, five-storey hotel block has created this ultra-chic establishment, where the guest rooms have been equipped in the full flush of Modernist style with lots of greys and whites plus crafty overhead lighting. The better guest rooms have a sea-facing balcony and there's a large outside pool, spa and garden. ❻

Hotel Es Port c/Antoni Montis s/n ☎971 63 16 50, ⊛www.hotelesport.com. Sited in its own lush gardens at the back of the port, a few minutes' walk from the waterfront, this three-star establishment is one of the resort's more distinctive hotels, occupying a one-time fortified country house that dates back to the seventeenth century. The interior displays many original features and the guest rooms are generally commodious and well appointed with traditional furnishings and fittings, though some are in the modern – and less appealing – annexe. There's also a large outside swimming pool. ❹

Hotel Los Geranios Passeig de Sa Platja 15 ☎971 63 14 40, ⊛www.hotel-losgeranios.com. Straightforward, three-star seafront hotel overlooking the Platja d'en Repic, with twenty-odd

◄ Cap Gros Lighthouse, C & 2

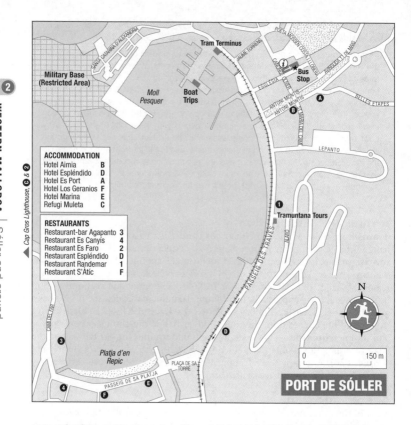

ACCOMMODATION
Hotel Aimia	**B**
Hotel Espléndido	**D**
Hotel Es Port	**A**
Hotel Los Geranios	**F**
Hotel Marina	**E**
Refugi Muleta	**C**

RESTAURANTS
Restaurant-bar Agapanto	**3**
Restaurant Es Canyis	**4**
Restaurant Es Faro	**2**
Restaurant Espléndido	**D**
Restaurant Randemar	**1**
Restaurant S'Àtic	**F**

PORT DE SÓLLER

rooms on four floors, mostly with sea views. The place is independently managed, but the rooms are equipped in standard chain style. ⑤
Hotel Marina Passeig de Sa Platja 3 ☏ 971 63 14 61, ⓦ www.hotelmarinasoller.com. Large, long-established and competitively priced two-star hotel overlooking the Platja d'en Repic. The rooms are decorated in standard-issue modern style, but most of them are spacious, many have cooking facilities and most have balconies. Also does apartments (②). ①

Refugi Muleta Cap Gros s/n ☏ 971 63 42 71, ⓦ www.conselldemallorca.net. Government-run hikers' hostel in an old stone building beside the lighthouse up on the headland immediately to the west of Platja d'en Repic, and within easy walking distance of the GR221 long-distance hiking trail (see p.103). Offers dormitory accommodation in bunk beds at just €11 per person per night, plus €4.50 for breakfast. Open all year; advance reservations required. ①

Eating and drinking

Port de Sóller heaves with **cafés** and **restaurants**, but standards are very variable: some serve up mediocre food with the package tourist in mind, others are more authentically *Mallorquín* – or at least Spanish. The selection below describes several of the better places; nearly all of them have bayside locations.

Restaurant-bar Agapanto Camí del Far 2 ☏ 971 63 38 60, ⓦ www.agapanto.com. At the west end of Platja d'en Repic, beside the

seashore at the start of the road up to the lighthouse, the *Agapanto* is a modish bar and restaurant dabbling in fusion food with "ambient" sounds to match. Vegetarian main courses start at €13, a few euros more for the meat and fish. Open daily noon–midnight.

Restaurant Es Canyís Passeig de Sa Platja 32 ☎971 63 14 06. Bright and cheerful bistro-style restaurant offering an excellent and extensive range of Spanish dishes from its bayshore premises behind the Platja d'en Repic. The snails are a house speciality, but the paella is tempting, as is the chicken breast in almond sauce. Main courses begin at a very competitive €12. Open Tues–Sun 1–4pm & 8–11pm.

Restaurant Es Faro Cap Gros ☎971 63 37 52. Set in a wonderful location, high up on the cliffs at the entrance to the harbour (and an easy 1.7km drive – or stiff walk – up from Platja d'en Repic), this well-known restaurant offers spectacular views from its outside terrace. During the day, the *Es Faro* serves up coffees, light meals and an excellent *menú del día* and at night it's à la carte with the seafood being the main event. Mains from €20. Reservations essential in the evening. Open daily:

March–Sept 10am–midnight, with more restricted hours in winter.

Restaurant Espléndido Passeig des Través 5 ☎971 63 18 50. In the hotel of the same name, this fast-moving bistro has smashing bay views and an all-purpose menu, featuring everything from fish and chips to classic Spanish dishes. Mains average €15–20. Open all day, every day.

Restaurant Randemar Passeig des Través 16 ☎971 63 45 78. Much praised restaurant occupying a good-looking 1920s villa down by the bay. Covers many of the Spanish classics, but it's the Italian dishes that steal the limelight – lip-smacking pastas and pizzas from as little as €8 for a main course. Daily 12.15–4pm & 7–11pm.

Restaurant S'Àtic On the top floor of the *Hotel Los Geranios*, Passeig de Sa Platja 15 ☎971 63 81 13. Elegantly understated establishment, with views over the bay and outstanding nouvelle Mediterranean-meets-Mallorcan cuisine. Mains from €20. Open Tues–Sun 7.30–10.30pm, plus Sat & Sun 1.30–3.30pm.

East of Sóller: Biniaraix and the Barranc de Biniaraix

Strolling along c/Sa Lluna (and its continuation) east from Sóller's main square, it takes about half-an-hour to reach the village of **BINIARAIX**, passing orchards and farmland criss-crossed with ancient irrigation channels and dry-stone walls. Nestled in the foothills of the Serra de Tramuntana, Biniaraix is tiny – just a cluster of old stone houses surrounding a dilapidated church and the smallest of central squares – but it is extraordinarily pretty. It is also a useful starting point for **hiking** into the surrounding mountains, the most popular route being the stiff but particularly scenic, two-hour haul up to the L'Ofre farmhouse at the top of the **Barranc de Biniaraix**, a beautiful ravine of terraced citrus groves set in the shadow of the mountains. To get to the Biniaraix **trailhead**, walk uphill from the square along c/Sant Josep. After about 200m you'll reach a spring and cattle trough, where a sign offers a choice of hiking trails, including the one east up the *barranc*, on (one small part of) the **GR221** long-distance footpath (see p.103).

Sections of the trail up the *barranc* use the old **cobbled roadway** that was once part of the pilgrims' route between Sóller and the monastery at Lluc (see p.147). Built in the fifteenth century, the roadway's maintenance proved a real headache for a long line of bishops: sometimes they had to threaten the peasantry with fines to keep the road in good order, sometimes they offered indulgences, but the snail hunters who regularly broke down the retaining walls to collect these tasty creatures proved indifferent to both. At the top of the ravine, you can extend your walk by clambering your way up to the **Es Cornadors** viewpoint – allow 45 minutes each way – or by heading northeast to the Cúber reservoir (see p.146), a comparatively easy walk across even ground – allow about two hours. Otherwise, the quickest way to get back to Sóller is by returning the way you came.

Northeast of Sóller: Fornalutx

Good-looking **FORNALUTX**, about 4km northeast of Sóller, is often touted as the most attractive village on Mallorca, and it certainly has a superb location, its honey-coloured stone houses huddling against a mountainous backdrop with the surrounding valley perfumed by orange and lemon groves. Matching its setting, the quaint centre of Fornalutx fans out from the minuscule main square, its narrow cobbled streets stepped to facilitate mule traffic, though nowadays you're more likely to be hit by a Mercedes than obstructed by a mule: foreigners love the place and have helped turn it into a bijou-deluxe settlement that is well able to sustain several prime hotels.

Practicalities

If you're **driving from Sóller**, the easiest way to get to Fornalutx is to take the Ma-10 east and watch for the turn; this will bring you straight to the car park at the north end of the village. There's also a limited **bus** service between the two (Mon–Fri 4 daily, Sat 2 daily; 15min) or you can take a **taxi** – the fare from Sóller to Fornalutx is about €12. Fornalutx does not have a tourist office, but there are a pair of smart and appealing **hotels** a stone's throw from the square. First up is the charming *Fornalutx Petit Hotel*, c/Alba 22 (☎971 63 19 97, ⓦwww.fornalutxpetithotel.com; ❻), which occupies an immaculately furnished and spotlessly clean old stone house with a terraced garden and pool; it also offers splendid views down the valley below. Reservations are essential here and at the neighbouring – and very similar – British-owned *Ca'n Reus*, c/Alba 26 (☎971 63 11 74, ⓦwww.canreushotel.com; ❹), though the chic-rustic decor here is a tad more self-conscious. To get to c/Alba, walk down the main street from the square (in the Sóller direction) and take the first left just beyond the conspicuous railings – a minute's stroll.

Amongst the village's **restaurants**, you might try the homely *Es Turó* (☎971 63 08 08; daily except Thurs 8am–11pm; closed Dec & Jan), which offers good-quality Mallorcan cuisine at very reasonable prices – mains begin at about €15. The restaurant has a pleasant outside terrace with valley views and is located just a couple of minutes' walk uphill from the main square near the car park. It is, however, the neighbouring *Ca N'Antuna* (☎971 63 30 68; closed Sun eve & Mon) that has garnered all the PR praise: again, the emphasis is on island dishes, with the baked lamb the house speciality, and the lemon tart is famous from one end of the island to the other.

South of Sóller: to the Jardins d'Alfàbia and Raixa

Heading south from Sóller, the main road to Palma tunnels through the Serra de Tramuntana, but there is an alternative, much more scenic route along a minor road that hairpins up and over the mountains, threading its way past the **Coll de Sóller**, a rocky pass with a lookout point offering splendid views out over the coast. Whichever route you choose, be sure to drop by the **Jardins d'Alfàbia**, lush and beautiful terraced gardens to be found a few metres from the south end of the tunnel (April–Sept Mon–Sat 9.30am–6.30pm; Oct–March Mon–Fri 9.30am–5pm & Sat 9.30am–1pm; €4.50). Shortly after the Reconquista, Jaume I granted the estate of Alfàbia to a prominent Moor by the name of Benhabet. Seeing which way the historical wind was blowing, Benhabet, as governor of Pollença, had given his support to Jaume, provisioning the Catalan army during the invasion. There was no way Jaume I could leave his Moorish ally in charge of Pollença (and anyway

Great places to stay

While the mere mention of the word "Mallorca", and to a lesser extent "Menorca", is usually enough to summon images of sky-rise hotels jammed tight against gently roasting tourists, the fact is that the islands offer a surprisingly diverse wealth of accommodation, from funky *fincas* tucked away in the depths of the countryside to handsome old mansions and merchants' houses. Unlike many of the identikit beach hotels, most of these places have a story to tell, a history interwoven with the islands' very cultural fabric.

Hotel Ca's Xorc ▲

Hotel Es Molí ▼

Stone by stone: fincas

There's never been any shortage of **stone** on either Mallorca or Menorca and neither – at least until recently – has there been a problem with labour: right up until the 1950s, hundreds of farm workers were desperately keen to supplement their meagre incomes by working on any building project that came along, providing it wasn't forced labour – in the countryside big landowners often had the right to make the local peasantry repair roads without payment. The main beneficiaries of all this hard graft were the island's landowners, who had a ready workforce when it came to the construction of their stone farmhouses, or **fincas**, which remain a prominent part of the Balearic landscape. Some of these *fincas* – for example *La Granja* near Valldemossa – are to all intents and purposes rural palaces (or *haciendas*); others, like *Ca's Xorc*, near Sóller, are rather more modest country houses. One fortunate consequence of the speed with which tourism washed over the islands was that many of these old *fincas* were modernized for use as holiday homes and hotels, rather than being demolished, and the charm of lodging in one lies at least in part in the solidity and simplicity of its architectural form: a stone or stone-and-rubble exterior, a flagged exterior courtyard, shuttered and grilled rectangular windows, high, wood-beamed ceilings and cellar/basement service quarters. It's also usual to find these *fincas* surrounded by a raft of often fascinating specialist buildings, from olive presses and workshops through to barns, workers' lodgings and store houses.

Town houses, mansions and monasteries

The larger landowners and merchants also possessed handsome, honey-coloured stone **town houses** and it's these that give the likes of Sóller, Binissalem, Ciutadella and Fornalutx their particular character. In Binissalem, for example, *Scott's Hotel* occupies a sympathetically revamped, eighteenth-century almond grower's house, whilst Fornalutx's *Petit Hotel* is sited in a charming old stone house that dates back to the seventeenth century, if not beyond. It is, however, the patrician mansions of Palma that take the architectural prize. Most of medieval Palma was destroyed by fire, so the city's gentry were obliged to rebuild in a hurry in the late seventeenth and early eighteenth centuries, lining the city's narrow streets with a wonderful ensemble of Renaissance-style mansions, a string of which are now immensely appealing hotels. By the late nineteenth century, however, many a well-heeled islander felt vaguely embarrassed by the austere stone mansions of yesteryear and was only too pleased to latch onto **Modernisme**, the local version of Art Nouveau. Consequently, there are *Modernisme* buildings all over the islands and several of them have been turned into deluxe hotels, most memorably the *Gran Hotel Sóller*, in Sóller. A world apart from the whims of architectural fashion, Mallorca's monasteries have likewise been converted, despite their isolated and often spectacular locations. The monks are long gone, but five former monasteries now offer some of the quietest and least expensive lodgings on Mallorca.

▲ Gran Hotel Sóller

▼ Monestir de Lluc

Hotel Dalt Murada ▲

Hotel Costa d'Or ▼

Santuari de Sant Salvador ▼

Great places to stay

- **Hotel Dalt Murada, Palma** Family-run hotel in a marvellous old mansion where the large and well-appointed guest rooms are kitted out with all manner of antiques. See p.59.

- **Gran Hotel, Sóller** Five-star extravagance in an immaculately restored *Modernisme* mansion. See p.106.

- **Scott's Hotel, Binissalem** Amenable hotel in an old merchant's house, where each room is kitted out in immaculate taste and style. See p.181.

- **Hotel Ca's Xorc, near Sóller** Charming hotel in a creatively revamped old olive mill set among the mountains outside Sóller. See p.106.

- **Petit Hotel, Fornalutx** Charming, family-run hotel in a lovely old stone town house in one of Mallorca's most beguiling little villages. See p.112.

- **Hotel Costa d'Or, near Deià** The Costa d'Or has several virtues, but its superb coastal location, high above the ocean, is well-nigh unbeatable. See p.117.

- **Hotel Es Molí, Deià** Top-notch, genteel hotel that offers the very best of food and hospitality. See p.118.

- **Es Castell, Binibona** Intelligently modernized old *finca* in the foothills of the Serra de Tramuntana mountains – there's nowhere better. See p.181.

- **Biniarroca Hotel, Menorca** Swish hotel in an immaculately restored old *finca*. See p.221.

- **Monestir de Lluc** The most visited and commercialized of those monasteries which provide accommodation, Lluc is also a major tourist attraction in its own right. See p.149.

- **Santuari de Sant Salvador, near Felanitx** Grand views over the east coast and a handsome setting make this Santuari an appealing proposition. See p.202.

it was already pledged to a Catalan noble), but he was able to reward him with this generous portion of land. Benhabet planned his new estate in the Moorish manner, channelling water from the surrounding mountains to irrigate the fields and fashion oasis-like gardens. Generations of island gentry added to the estate without marring the integrity of Benhabet's original design, thus creating the lovely gardens of today.

There are no **buses** to the gardens, but the Sóller–Palma tunnel bus stops – or should stop – at the Bunyola turn-off, from where it's a 2km walk back up along the hard shoulder of the Ma-11 to the clearly signposted entrance.

The gardens and the house

From the roadside, you follow a stately avenue of plane trees towards the gatehouse. In front of the gatehouse is the **ticket office** and a sign that directs visitors up a wide flight of stone steps and into the **gardens**, where the footpath leads through trellises of jasmine and wisteria, creating patterns of light and shade. Near the start there's even a visitor-operated water feature – press the button and retire. Beyond, brightly coloured flowers cascade over narrow terraces to the sound of gurgling watercourses and, at the end of the path, lies a verdant jungle of palm trees, bamboo and bullrushes tangling a tiny pool choked with water lilies. It's an enchanting spot, especially on a hot summer's day, and an outdoor **bar** (usually) sells big glasses of freshly squeezed orange juice – a snip at just €1.70.

A few paces away is the **house**, a rather routine, verandaed *hacienda* whose handful of high-ceilinged rooms contain an eccentric mix of antiques and curios. Pride of place goes to a superb **oak chair** adorned with delightful bas-relief scenes depicting the story of **Tristan and Isolde**. There were several versions of this well-known medieval tale, but the one on the chair is all about jealousy: on the front the two protagonists are shown playing chess, an innocent enough pastime, but one that stirs the jealousy of Isolde's husband the king. On the back of the chair, the king's head appears in the tree peering down at the two of them as they walk in the garden – and you know it will all end in tears. The chair has been in the house for centuries and local legend asserts that the uncrowned Jaume IV ordered it, but never had the chance to take possession. Jaume was captured – and his father, King Jaume III, killed – by the Aragonese at the battle of Llucmajor in 1349, and the younger Jaume spent the rest of his days in exile. Unfortunately, it's all poppycock as the chair was actually made in the fifteenth century in Flanders.

At the front of the house, the cobbled **courtyard** is shaded by a giant plane tree and surrounded by good-looking, rustic outbuildings. Beyond lies the **gatehouse**, an imposing structure sheltering a fine coffered ceiling of Mudéjar design, with an inscription praising Allah.

Raixa

Pressing on south from the Jardins d'Alfàbia, along the Ma-11, it's about 5km to the short unpaved lane that leads west to **Raixa**, the one-time country estate of the eighteenth-century antiquarian Cardinal Antonio Despuig (whose collection of classical sculpture can be seen in Palma – see p.83). The cardinal carved a sequence of terraced **gardens** out of the hill beside his country home and then proceeded to decorate them with Neoclassical statues, water fountains and even bits of old masonry recovered from medieval buildings in Palma – all in the fashionable Italian style of his day. Despuig saw himself as a leading light of the Enlightenment, but underneath the cultured cassock was a medieval piety: he died in Italy and on his deathbed he left instructions for his heart to be cut out and buried close to the body of Mallorca's favourite saint, Catalina Thomàs (see p.130). At the time of writing, the manor house and the gardens are being refurbished, but should be open again by 2012.

Southeast of Sóller: to Orient and Alaró

In between Alfàbia and Raixa, a country road forks east off the Ma-11, looping past the sun-bleached walls of the unremarkable market town of **BUNYOLA** before snaking across the forested foothills of the Serra de Tramuntana. It's a beautiful drive – though some of the bends are nerve-jangling – and after about 12km you reach **ORIENT**, a tiny hamlet of ancient houses scattered along the edge of the Vall d'Orient, a valley where hills crimp and crowd olive and almond groves. The main part of the village slopes up the hill from the road and at the top is a dinky little parish **church** named in honour of Sant Jordi (St George), whose effigy cuts a striking pose on the high altar. For most of its history, Orient was as poor as it was remote, but tourism has transformed the place and now the locals, who only number about thirty, share their bucolic retreat with second-home owners and a cluster of smart, rural-chic hotels.

Practicalities
Local bus #221 links Bunyola with Orient twice daily and the journey takes twenty minutes; seats need to be reserved ahead of time on ☎971 61 52 19. There are no buses between Orient and Alaró (see p.115). The most engaging **hotel** in Orient is the four-star *Hotel Dalt Muntanya* (☎971 61 53 73, ⓦwww .daltmuntanya.net; ❸; closed Nov–Jan), which occupies a sympathetically remodelled old house with eighteen individually styled bedrooms, many of which have mountain views. Its two rivals are the recently renovated *Agroturismo Son Palou*, in the lavishly restored old *hacienda* next to the church (☎971 14 82 82 ⓦwww.sonpalou.com; ❺); and *Hotel L'Hermitage*, located about 1km east of Orient on the Ma-2100 (☎971 18 03 03, ⓦwww.hermitage-hotel.com; closed Dec to mid-Feb; ❻). *L'Hermitage* has 24 immaculate rooms – a handful in the original medieval monastery and the rest in the surrounding chalets – and bills itself as a spa. As you would expect, all three hotels have a full range of facilities, including gardens and outside pools, and each has a deluxe restaurant. The **restaurant** at the *Hotel Dalt Muntanya* probably shaves its rivals in terms of price and Mallorcan specialities, but there's also the rather more traditional/authentic *Restaurant Orient* (☎971 61 51 53; closed Tues), opposite the *Hotel Dalt Muntanya*, where the wine is produced by the owner and the speciality is a superb suckling pig, though you can also sample such delights as partridge with mushrooms and rabbit with prawns; mains begin at about €15.

The Castell d'Alaró
Beyond Orient, the Ma-2100 edges along the narrow valley of the Torrent d'en Paragon for around 3km, before veering south to slip between a pair of molar-like hills whose bare rocky flanks tower above the surrounding forest and scrub. The more westerly of the two sports the sparse ruins of the **Castell d'Alaró**, originally a Moorish stronghold but rebuilt by Jaume I. Visible for miles around, the castle looks impregnable on its lofty perch, and it certainly impeded the Aragonese invasion of 1285; when an Aragonese messenger suggested terms for surrender, the garrison's dual commanders responded by calling the Aragonese king Alfonso III "fish-face", punning on his name in Catalan (*anfos* means "perch"). When the castle finally fell, Alfonso had the two roasted alive – goodness knows what he'd have done if they'd called him something really rude.

The side road that leads up towards the castle branches off the Orient-Alaró road just to the north of the town of Alaró – watch for the signposted right turn just beyond the Kilometre-18 stone marker. The first 3km of this side road are bumpy and narrow but reasonably easy, whereas the last 1.3km is gravel and dirt with a perilously tight series of hairpins negotiating a very steep hillside – especially hazardous after rain. The road emerges at a car park and an old **farmstead**, which now holds the *Es Verger* restaurant (Tues–Sun 1–9pm; ☎971 18 21 26). It's tempting to linger here: the views down over the plain are sumptuous and the food tasty, particularly the house speciality, oven-baked lamb. From the restaurant, you can also spy the ruins of the castle above, about an hour and a half's walk away along a clearly marked track. The trail leads to the castle's stone gateway, beyond which lies an expansive wooded plateau accommodating the fragmentary ruins of the fortress and the tiny pilgrims' church of Mare de Déu del Refugi.

There's a simple café-bar up here too as well as a soon-to-be-completed **hikers' hostel**, the *S'Hostatgeria Castell d'Alaró* (☎971 18 21 12; ⓦwww .conselldemallorca.net), whose construction has involved all sorts of difficulties: much of the building gear had to be lifted in by helicopter. The hostel will have thirty bunk beds in dormitory accommodation and the charge will be just €11 per person per night.

Alaró

Back on the Ma-2100, it's about 1.5km south from the castle turn-off to the town of **ALARÓ**, a sleepy little place of old stone houses fanning out from an attractive main square, **Plaça Vila**. A long and elegant arcaded gallery flanks one side of the square, and a second is shadowed by the **church**, a fortress-like, medieval affair whose honey-coloured sandstone is embellished with a Baroque doorway. The town was once at the centre of the trade between the mountains and the plain, with farm produce going one way, animal skins and charcoal the other, but it really hit the headlines in 1901 when it became the first place on the island to install electric street lighting – even ahead of Palma, much to the chagrin of that city's ruling council.

Alaró's main square holds several cafés and **restaurants**, where local families gather on the weekend. The pick of the bunch is *Es Traffic*, at no. 8 (☎971 87 91 17; daily except Tues noon–4pm & 8–11.30pm), which serves up Mallorcan specialities – notably casseroles – in an attractively renovated old mansion or in the spacious garden out the back; mains average €15. The restaurant shares its premises with a first-rate **hotel**, the family-owned *Can Xim* (same number, ⓦwww.canxim.com; ❸), whose eight guest rooms are kitted out in a smart, modern style that fits in nicely with the old house.

Just south of Alaró, you leave the foothills of the Serra de Tramuntana and slip down onto the central plain, Es Pla, near to **Binissalem** (see p.179). Local bus #320 (Mon–Fri every 20min, Sat & Sun hourly; 10min) links Alaró with the **Alaró/Consell train station** on the Palma-Inca train line – one stop away from Binissalem.

Deià to Port d'Andratx

The western reaches of the **Serra de Tramuntana** rise out of the flatlands around Palma, with the range's forested foothills and sheltered valleys soon giving way to the craggy, wooded mountains that crimp most of the **southwest coast**. Several fast roads link Palma with the coast – the prettiest runs to Valldemossa – and a delightful network of country roads pattern the foothills, but the key sights and the best scenery are most readily reached along the main coastal road, the **Ma-10**.

West of Sóller, the Ma-10 skirts the broad and wooded slopes of the Puig d'es Teix to reach **Deià**, an ancient mountain village which perches on the steep terraced slopes above the seashore, clinging to the fame brought by its association with the writer **Robert Graves**, whose former house has recently been opened to the public. The next 20km of coastline boasts four of Mallorca's star attractions, allied to some of its finest coastal scenery: **Son Marroig** and **Miramar**, two complementary mansions once owned by a Mallorca-loving Habsburg, Archduke Ludwig Salvator; the hilltop monastery of **Valldemossa**, complete with its echoing cloisters and choice examples of modern art; and the old grandee's mansion and estate of **La Granja**. This captivating quartet is hard to beat, although the tiered hamlets that decorate the coast further down the road are also instantly beguiling. Of these, both **Banyalbufar** and **Estellencs** occupy fine sites and are well worth at least a fleeting visit, probably more. The Ma-10 emerges from the Serra de Tramuntana at **Andratx**, a crossroads town with easy access to the tiny port and often underestimated mini-resort of **Sant Elm**, where you can hike out into the mountains or catch the passenger boat over to **Sa Dragonera**, the humpy island nature reserve that lies just offshore. Andratx is also within easy striking distance of the more commercialized harbour-cum-resort of **Port d'Andratx**, long a popular holiday spot for Germans and Brits alike.

Beach lovers have meagre pickings in this part of the island. There's a good sandy beach with safe swimming at Sant Elm, but further up the coast, shingle strips will have to suffice. The most impressive of these is **Cala Deià**, set beneath the mountains at the end of a narrow ravine. **Accommodation** can be hard to find, too. Each of the destinations mentioned above has at least a couple of places to stay, but you're strongly advised to book ahead if you're visiting between June and September or even October. Deià and Port d'Andratx have the widest choice of hotels and *hostales*, and so represent the best bets for a last-minute vacancy, with Sant Elm, Valldemossa, Estellencs and Banyalbufar the runners up.

Getting around

There is a regular **bus** service from Palma to Port de Sóller via Valldemossa, Deià and Sóller, and another from Palma to Esporles, La Granja, Banyalbufar and Estellencs. There are also fast and frequent buses from Palma to Andratx and Port d'Andratx, plus a regular service from Andratx to Sant Elm. The only major gaps are along the Ma-10 coast road between Estellencs and Andratx and between Banyalbufar and Valldemossa. For frequencies and journey times, see p.140.

Distances between destinations are short, so **taxis** can work out a reasonable proposition if you're in a group: the fare for the thirteen-kilometre trip from Port de Sóller to Deià, for example, is just €21.

Deià

DEIÀ, 10km west of Sóller, is beautiful. The mighty Puig d'es Teix (1062m) meets the coast here, and, although the mountain's lower slopes are gentrified by the villas of the well-heeled and well-to-do, it retains a formidable, almost mysterious presence, especially in the shadows of a moonlit night. Deià's long main street, Arxiduc Lluis Salvador, which doubles as the coastal highway (Ma-10), skirts the base of the Teix and shows off the bulk of the village's

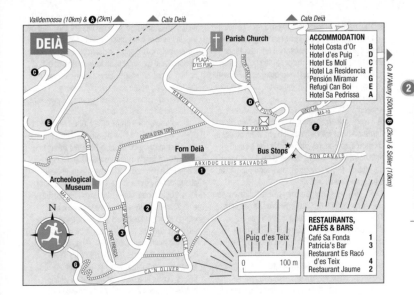

hotels and restaurants to fine advantage. Holed up in his den, **Ca N'Alluny**, it was Robert Graves (see box, p.120) who made Deià famous and at its peak, in the 1960s and 1970s, the village literally heaved with writers and poets, painters and musicians. The literati have, however, moved on and the affluent have moved in – a classic case of money following (as distinct from having) talent.

Arrival and information

Buses from points east and west along the coast scoot through Deià at regular intervals, travelling along the main drag, which doubles as the coastal highway, the Ma-10. The main **bus stop** is towards the east end of the village. There's no tourist information office as such, but most if not all of the hotels and pensions will gladly provide advice on local walks and have bus timetables. Look out also for the locally produced *Deià Pocket Guide*, which details almost everything you could possibly want to know: a new version is promised as the old one needs updating and is now in short supply. For a **taxi**, call ☎609 38 61 68. It takes about fifteen minutes to walk from one end of the village to the other along the main street.

Deià is the haunt of long-term expatriates, who sustain several cultural festivals, most notably the **Festival de Deià** (☎971 63 91 78, Ⓦwww.dimf .com) whose classical music concerts begin in April and end in September.

Accommodation

Deià boasts accommodation to match every size of wallet. The village possesses two of the island's most luxurious hotels as well as a hikers' hostel, and then there's pretty much everything in between. There's a reasonable chance of finding a room on spec at any time of the year, but you're really much better off making a reservation at least a day or two in advance.

 Hotel Costa d'Or 2km east of Deià along the Ma-10 coast road at the hamlet of

Llucalcari ☎971 63 90 25, Ⓦwww.hoposa.es. This splendid four-star hotel occupies a wonderful setting, overlooking an undeveloped slice of coast and surrounded by pine trees and olive groves. There's a shaded terrace bar and a fine outdoor swimming pool. The rooms are kitted out in slick, modern style and the best look out over the ocean. Part of a medium-sized island chain. Closed Nov–March. ⑥

Hotel d'Es Puig c/Es Puig 4 ☎971 63 94 09, ⓦwww.hoteldespuig.com. A smart and tastefully furnished hotel with eight bedrooms in an elegantly converted, four-storey old stone house located in the centre of the village, between the Ma-10 and the church. Pay a few euros more for a room with a balcony. Closed Jan. ⑤

Hotel Es Molí Carretera Deià-Valldemossa s/n ☎971 63 90 00, ⓦwww.esmoli.com. This long-established, four-star hotel has an excellent, fully deserved reputation. The hotel buildings, one of which dates back to the seventeenth-century, overlook the main road from the wooded slopes at the far west end of town. Inside, the public areas are smart if certainly not minimalist, large enough to accommodate all of the guests with lots of room to spare. Ninety well-appointed, a/c bedrooms and suites are divided between the main building and the annexe at the back, and each is decorated in comfortable, somehow rather reassuring style; most have a balcony and many have wide coastal views. The terraced gardens are particularly lovely, providing a lush setting for the outside pool, and the breakfast terrace is simply charming. As a bonus, the hotel minibus takes guests – the majority of whom are British, and who come back year after year – to a private (rocky) beach, a twenty-minute drive to the east. Closed Nov to March. ⑧

Hotel La Residencia c/Son Canals s/n ☎971 63 90 11, ⓦwww.hotel-laresidencia.com. Models and nannies, big cars and flash clothes are the order of the day here in what must be one of Mallorca's ritziest hotels. The decor is minimalist-meets-rustic Mallorca and the hotel itself is an extended extrapolation of two old stone manor houses. It overlooks the main drag at the east end of the village. Facilities abound – pools, bars, restaurants, tennis court, a spa and so on and so forth. ⑨

Pensión Miramar c/Ca'n Oliver s/n ☎971 63 90 84, ⓦwww.pensionmiramar.com. You don't get many good deals in Deià, but this is one of them – a family-run *pension* in a traditional stone *finca* perched high above the main road about halfway through the village. There are nine fairly frugal rooms here – some en suite, some with shared facilities – and the views over the village from the courtyard in front of the house are stunning. On foot, it's a stiff ten-minute walk up from the main road. Closed Dec–Feb. ❶

Refugi Can Boi c/Es Clot 5 ☎971 63 61 86, ⓦwww.conselldemallorca.net. Government-run hikers' hostel in a neat and trim new building handily located below the Ma-10 coastal road – in the valley below the church, with 32 bunk beds in dorms at just €11 per person per night. Advance reservations required. On the GR221 long-distance footpath (see p.103). ❶

Hotel Sa Pedrissa Carretera Deià-Valldemossa s/n ☎971 63 91 11, ⓦwww.sapedrissa.com. This hotel, on its own about 2km west of Deià on the Ma-10 coastal road, occupies an immaculately revamped old stone farmhouse, which, along with its assorted outhouses, perches high above – and has wide views over – the coast. Stone and marble floors, exposed wooden beams and oodles of white paint set the tone, there's a terrace pool and each of the nine bedrooms is impeccably turned out. ❹–⑨

The Town

At times, Deià's main drag is too congested to be much fun, but the tiny heart of the village, tumbling over a high and narrow ridge on the seaward side of the road, still retains a surprising tranquillity. Labyrinthine alleys of old peasant houses curl up to a pretty **parish church**, in the precincts of which is buried **Robert Graves**, the village's most famous resident – his headstone marked simply "Robert Graves: Poeta, E.P.D." (*En Paz Descanse*, "Rest In Peace"). From the graveyard, there are memorable views out over the coast and of the Teix, with banks of tightly terraced fields tumbling down from the mountain towards the sea. The church itself is unremarkable, but one of its outbuildings does hold a modest **museum** (Sat 9am–7pm; €2), which possesses a folksy assortment of religious bric-a-brac.

The Robert Graves House – Ca N'Alluny

Graves put Deià on the international map and his old home, **Ca N'Alluny** (Mon–Fri 10am–5pm & Sat 10am–3pm; €5; ⓦwww.lacasaderobertgraves .com), is a substantial stone building located beside the main road about 500m

▲ Deià

east of the village. Opened to the public in 2006, the house has been returned to something like its 1940s appearance and comes complete with the family's own furnishings and fittings. A visit begins with a short and well-made film introducing the author's life and times and then it's onto the house, where the living rooms seem surprisingly modest and very homely. The study, where Graves produced much of his finest work, is of modest proportions too and beyond is an exhibition area with yet more biographical information, old photographs, letters and manuscripts plus a recording of Graves reading a poem – *The Face in the Mirror*. Finally, you emerge into the small but well-kept garden, where there are olive, carob, fruit and almond trees. For more on Graves see the box on p.120.

Deià Archeological Museum

Deià's other specific sight, its **Archeological Museum** (Tues, Thurs & Sun 5–7pm; free), is hidden away in the wooded ravine below and between the old centre of the village and the *Hotel Es Molí* up on the main road. The archeologists William and Jacqueline Waldren founded the museum in 1962 to display the items they had retrieved from a number of local prehistoric sites. In particular, the couple had just hit the archeological headlines with their investigations into a prehistoric cave dwelling near Deià. Here they found a great hoard of bones, the remains of a veritable herd of *Myotragus balearicus*, a small, goat-like animal unique to the Balearics, whose precise prehistoric importance has sparked much debate: some have argued that it was once the nutritional mainstay hereabouts, others have suggested that the island's early inhabitants brought the animals with them, but they proved hard to domesticate. More importantly, the bones were found at a level in the subsoil that pushed back the date at which the earliest islanders were thought to have lived here by several hundred years – to 4000 or even 5000 BC. The Waldrens carried on with their archeological explorations after they hit the news, and the museum displays many of the key finds they retrieved in forty years of work.

Cala Deià

Much loved by Graves, **Cala Deià** is the nearest thing the village has to a beach, comprising some 200m of shingle at the back of a handsome rocky cove of jagged cliffs, boulders and white-crested surf. It's a great place for a swim, the water is clean, deep and cool, and there are two summer-only, beach bar-restaurants to keep the swimmers happy. Most of the time, the cove is quiet

Robert Graves in Deià

The English poet, novelist and classical scholar **Robert Graves** (1895–1985) spent two periods living in Deià, the first in the 1930s, and the second from the end of World War II until his death. During his first stay he shared a house at the edge of the village with **Laura Riding**, an American poet and dabbler in the mystical. Riding had arrived in England in 1926 and, after she became Graves's secretary and collaborator, the two of them began an affair that was to break up both of their marriages. The tumultuous course of their relationship created such a furore that they decided to leave England, settling in Mallorca on the advice of Gertrude Stein in 1930. The fuss was not simply a matter of morality – many of their friends were indifferent to adultery – but more to do with the self-styled "**Holy Circle**" they had founded, a cabalistic and intensely self-preoccupied literary-mystic group. The last straw came when Riding, in her attempt to control the group, jumped out of a window, saying "Goodbye, chaps", and the besotted Graves leapt after her. No wonder his mate T.E. Lawrence ("of Arabia") wrote of "madhouse minds" and of Graves "drowning in a quagmire".

Both recovered, but the dottiness continued once they'd moved to Deià, with Graves acting as doting servant to Riding, whom he reinvented as a sort of all-knowing matriarch and muse. Simultaneously, Graves thumped away at his prose: he had already produced *Goodbye to All That* (1929), his bleak and painful memoirs of army service in the World War I trenches, but now came his other best-remembered books, **I, Claudius** (1934) and its sequel **Claudius the God** (1935), historical novels detailing the life and times of the Roman emperor. Nonetheless, to Graves these "potboilers", as he styled them, were secondary to his poetry – usually carefully crafted love poems of melancholic tenderness in praise of Riding – which were well received by the critics of the time.

At the onset of the Spanish Civil War, Graves and Riding left Mallorca, not out of sympathy for the Republicans – Graves was far too reactionary for that – but to keep contact with friends and family. During their exile Graves was ditched by Riding, and he subsequently took up with a mutual friend, **Beryl Pritchard**. After Graves had returned to Deià in 1946, he worked on *The White Goddess*, a controversial study of prehistoric and classical myth that argued the existence of an all-pervasive, primordial religion based on the worship of a poet-goddess. Pritchard joined him in the midst of his labours (the book was published in 1948), and in 1950 they were married in Palma. They were not, however, to live happily ever after. Graves had a predilection for young women, claiming he needed female muses for poetic inspiration, and although his wife outwardly accepted this waywardness, she did so without much enthusiasm.

Meanwhile, although Graves's novels became increasingly well known and profitable, his poetry, with its preoccupation with romantic love, fell out of fashion, and his last anthology, *Poems 1965–1968*, was widely criticized by the literary establishment. Nevertheless, Graves's international reputation as a writer attracted a steady stream of visitors to Deià from the ranks of the literati, with the occasional film star dropping by to add to the self-regarding stew. By the middle of the 1970s, however, just as an acclaimed BBC TV production of *I, Claudius* was bringing his books to a wider public in his native country, Graves had begun to lose his mind and he ended his days in sad senility. The house where Graves lived in Deià from 1946 onwards is now open to the public (see p.118).

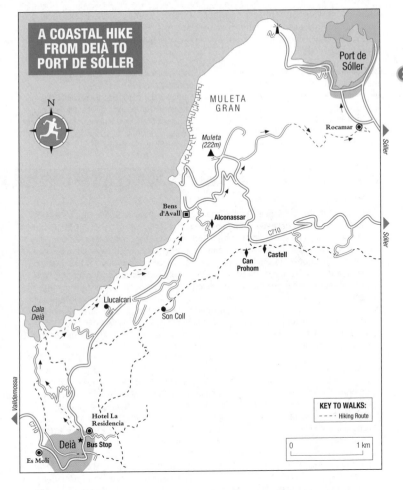

A COASTAL HIKE FROM DEIÀ TO PORT DE SÓLLER

N

MULETA GRAN

Muleta (222m)

Port de Sóller

Rocamar

Sóller

Sóller

Bens d'Avall

Alconassar

C710

Castell

Can Prohom

Cala Deià

Llucalcari

Son Coll

KEY TO WALKS:
- - - - Hiking Route

Valldemossa

C710

Hotel La Residencia

Bus Stop

Deià

Es Molí

0   1 km

and peaceful, but parties of day-trippers do sometimes stir things up. There are two ways to get there **on foot**. The more obvious route is signed from the bend in the road 80m or so northeast of the bus stop; it leads down a wooded ravine and takes about thirty minutes to complete – and directions are given in the first part of the "Coastal Hike" route to Port de Sóller described on p.122. Even more bucolic, however, is the path that threads its way through the wooded and terraced gulch in between the old centre of the village and the *Hotel Es Molí*; this takes about forty minutes. To **drive** there, head northeast along the main road out of Deià and watch for the (easy-to-miss) sign about 700m beyond the *Hotel La Residencia*, but note that finding a parking space down at the beach can be a nightmare.

Eating and drinking

You're spoiled for choice when it comes to eating out in Deià. Dotted along the main street – c/Arxiduc Lluís Salvador (Ma-10) – are several smart and polished **restaurants** plus a number of more modest **café-bars**, ideal for nursing a drink and, especially in the off-season, checking out the expat scene. The village also has a good **grocery-store-cum-bakery**, Forn Deià, about 200m west of the main bus stop.

Café Sa Fonda c/Arxiduc Lluís Salvador 5. If you're looking for island simplicities, Deià is the wrong place for you, but this busy café-bar, up a flight of steps off the main drag, is the nearest thing you'll get to a locals' favourite. There's a large shaded terrace and although drinks are the main event, they serve snacks and light meals too. Open daily Tues–Sun noon to midnight.

Patricia's Bar c/Felip Bauça s/n. Cordial little café-bar just off the main street at the west end of the village. Snacks and light meals plus occasional live music, usually in the wintertime. Open daily except Wed noon–midnight.

A coastal hike from Deià to Port de Sóller

12km; 4hr–4hr 30min. Mainly easy; difficult in parts.

This delightful **walk** starts in Deià village and ends in **Port de Sóller**. There's a fairly regular bus service between the two places (see p.140), which makes the round trip relatively straightforward, but be sure to confirm bus times before you set out. The coast north of Deià is dotted with pine trees and abandoned olive terraces, and slopes steeply down to the sea from the high massif of Sa Galera. On such steep terrain, run-off water plays havoc with terrace walls and paths, so although this walk is mainly easy, care is needed where erosion has occurred. The views are superlative all the way, beginning with the panorama of the blue-green waters of **Cala Deià** (see p.120). The hiking route is partially waymarked with red paint and cairns, although a certain amount of route-finding is required due to gully erosion and fallen trees. There are stiles at all the boundary fences the path crosses. The last stretch of the walk is along the **GR221** long-distance footpath (see p.103).

The route

From the **bus stop** in Deià, walk in the Sóller direction and turn left down c/Vinyeta, which is signed "Sóller 2hr 30 min, Cala de Deià 30min". After five minutes, where the road ends, cross a makeshift stile and take the path through an olive grove. Continue on downhill following the path, which crosses another stile, criss-crosses a road several times and then joins this same road. Continue along it to reach **Cala Deià** with its beach bars, beached boats and rumbling surf.

To access the **coastal path** retrace your steps from the beach to find a flight of steps located some 50m back from where the road ends (there is another flight of steps closer to the beach, but this just leads to a public toilet). Ascend the steps and you're on the coastal path. After about five minutes you will see a path to the left: ignore this and continue on. After a further two minutes, a stone path swings right off the main path. Again, ignore this and continue on along the unsurfaced track marked with a line of **red painted stones**. This track bears left then turns right before crossing a low wall. After bearing right again, it then turns sharp left downhill beside the wall. One minute later turn right again and continue straight on, passing a *mirador* (viewpoint) with a private path descending to it from an unseen house above. Continue, ascending around a big boulder on your right and you will now be walking along an attractive headland through pine trees overlooking the sea and the rocks at Cala Deiá.

After a further five to ten minutes you will reach a clearing with a **small stone circular table** and log seats. Pass through the clearing and bear right, keeping close to a stone wall. Stay well to the right as there is a steep drop to the left. After about one minute negotiate a stile and continue through pine woods. Further on you will cross another stile. Beyond this the path bears left, crosses a wall and drops down to a clearing: take care not to go wrong here as there are some private paths to houses and also fallen trees obscuring your way.

Restaurant Es Racó d'es Teix c/Vinya Vella 6 ⊕971 63 95 01. Delightful restaurant in an old stone house with an attractive shaded terrace; it's located a steep 30m or so above the main road, about halfway into the village – watch for the sign. The Mediterranean cuisine features local ingredients and is strong on island dishes, but it doesn't come cheap with main courses from €30. Reservations well-nigh essential. Open daily except Mon & Tues 1–3pm & 8–11pm.

Restaurant Jaume c/Arxiduc Lluís Salvador 22 ⊕971 63 90 29. First-rate terraced restaurant on the main drag about halfway into the village, specializing in traditional Mallorcan cuisine – try, for instance, the pork in cabbage leaves. Being family-owned, every dish is carefully prepared and the service is very attentive. Reservations advised. Main courses average around €22. Open daily except Mon 1–4pm & 7.30–10.30pm, but restricted opening hours for much of the winter.

Your route continues alongside the coast and you will soon reach a **large circular stone table** with log seats. At this point the path forks left downhill and leads you via a gap in a wall and after a few minutes towards a stone enclosure. Pass below this and along the left side of a wall where the ground rises steeply inland. A minute or so further on you will pass a house on the right. Beyond this the path zigzags towards the sea and then reaches a clearing with a view of a rocky cove. Negotiate an eroded gully and continue on passing walled terraces and then a house, both to your right. The path then crosses a stile and then ascends inland. Look out for a stone marker on the path which looks like a small **Z** and at this point go right uphill and then immediately left under a pine tree. You will now be on a terrace. Ahead of you will be fallen trees, so bear sharp right, then left while climbing upwards to reach a small clearing in the pine trees. Bear left along the lowest terrace and then downhill to reach the next gully. Cross it, negotiating fallen trees and go up the other side towards the next gully which is heavily eroded, cross it and climb steeply out.

Continue on, via a gap in a wall to reach the headland at the top. On reaching a barbed wire fence turn left and walk steeply downhill towards the sea with the fence on your right. Follow the fence until you reach a stile. Beyond the stile the path is well waymarked. It crosses a stone wall and descends to an olive grove and pine trees with large boulders to either side. Follow the path as it ascends to another stile. Cross this, pass a stone shack and further on, near a barbed wire gate, go over a further stile. Continue on, and upon reaching a newish stone wall climb the steps towards its end. Follow the path through tall trees and descend to a concreted road. Turn right on to this and follow it uphill, passing houses on the left until you reach the rear of the chi-chi **Restaurant Bens d'Avall** (⊕971 63 23 81; closed Mon & most Tues), one of Mallorca's swishest restaurants with wide coastal views and a modern take on traditional Balearic cuisine.

The path swings right at this point. Immediately to your left is a canalized stream – usually dried up in summer – and beyond it the access road to the *Bens d'Avall*. You need to cross over the streambed to get to the road. Continue up the path from the right turn and look very carefully for a gap in the top of the streambed wall. This marks the point below which are a series of **metal pegs** that allow you to climb down the side of the streambed and up the other side. Having crossed the stream turn right and follow the road uphill for 1.5 km to reach the Muleta road junction. At this point turn left along the unsurfaced road, then right by a small electricity substation. After five minutes turn left and continue straight on following signs to **Port de Sóller**. The route is clearly signed from this point and leads directly to the now derelict **Rocamar Hostal**. Below the Rocamar, turn left for the Platja d'en Repic, Port de Sóller's largest beach (see p.108), or right for the main road to Sóller (see p.103).

Son Marroig

Beyond Deià, the Ma-10 snakes its way along the coast for 3km to reach **Son Marroig** (Mon–Sat 9.30am–6pm; €3), an imposing L-shaped mansion perched high above the seashore – and just below the road. The house dates from late medieval times, but was refashioned in the nineteenth century to become the favourite residence of the Habsburg archduke **Ludwig Salvator** (see box below). Dynastically insignificant but extremely rich, the Austrian aristocrat was a man in search of a hobby – and he found it in Mallorca. He first visited the island at the tender age of 19, fell head-over-heels in love with the place, and returned to buy Son Marroig along with a sizeable slice of the west coast between Deià and Port de Valldemossa.

The Son Marroig estate comprises the house, its gardens and the headland down below. Despite its setting and long history, the **house** actually conspires to be rather dull with all its key exhibits piled into two large and gloomy first-floor rooms. Here you'll find a small sample of Hispano-Arabic pottery, a display featuring some of the archduke's manuscripts and pamphlets, and several ducal photographs: whatever else he did on the island, the duke certainly must have enjoyed his food, ballooning up from a regular-sized young man to a real heavy-weight. There are also photographs of the duke's two other Mallorcan houses,

The Archduke Ludwig Salvator

Cousin to the Habsburg Emperor Franz Josef of Austria no less, the young **Ludwig Salvator** (1847–1915) was supposed to join the imperial army, but he cleared off and took his sea captain's certificate instead. Mightily miffed at this insubordination, the emperor decided a carrot was better than a stick and appointed him the Governor of Bohemia hoping that this would settle him down. It might have worked too, but for a freak accident: Salvator's young wife, **Mathilde**, was watching the archduke inspect his soldiers from a balcony until, bored out of her brain, she decided to have a furtive cigarette. It was a bad decision. The cigarette set her dress on fire and she burnt to death in double quick time. Out of sympathy, his family was now inclined to indulge Salvator's wanderlust and the archduke headed south to the Mediterranean in 1866. It was on his travels that the archduke first visited Mallorca and it made such an impression on him that he returned to live here, buying a chunk of the west coast and building (or at least adopting) no fewer than **three homes** – Son Marroig (see above), Miramar (see opposite) and S'Estaca, now a home of Michael Douglas.

Once in residence, Ludwig immersed himself in all things *Mallorquín*, learning the dialect and chronicling the island's topography, archeology, history and folklore in astounding detail. He churned out no fewer than **seven volumes** on the Balearics and, perhaps more importantly, played a leading role as a proto-environmentalist, conserving the coastline of his estates and, amongst many projects, paying for a team of geologists to chart the Coves del Drac (see p.200).

Salvator may have been hard working, but he also squeezed in a lot of R&R, allegedly sleeping with a platoon of local women and fathering a merry band of children. Back at Habsburg HQ, rumours of Salvator's endeavours – both in and out of the sack – went down badly: it was not so much that "Don Balearo", as he was nicknamed, slept with peasant girls, but more that he recognized them and their (his) children, giving them money and land. To add grist to the mill, Salvator even brought one of his women – **Catalina Homar** – back to the Habsburg court in Vienna and, after her untimely death, publicly dedicated one of his books to her. It was, however, World War I rather than Vienna's disapproval that brought a sudden end to the archduke's stint in Mallorca. In 1914, at the outbreak of war, Salvator was summoned back to the Austro-Hungarian Empire to do his royal duty; he died within a year.

Miramar (see below) and **S'Estaca** (no public access), down near Port de Valldemossa and currently owned by Michael Douglas. These distractions won't detain you for long, however, and you'll soon want to head out to the **garden**, whose terraces are graced by a Neoclassical belvedere of Tuscan Carrara marble. The views west along the jagged, forested coast are gorgeous.

Down below the garden is a slender shank of a promontory known as **Sa Foradada**, "the rock pierced by a hole", where the archduke used to park his yacht. The hole in question is a strange circular affair sited high up in the rock face at the end of the promontory. It takes about forty minutes to **walk** the 3km down to this rock, a straightforward excursion to a delightfully scenic spot, though the estate itself is a little scruffy and ill-kempt. There should be few problems with direction-finding on the walk, which begins at the gate just up the slope and to the left of the house. A sign on the gate insists you need to get permission at Son Marroig before setting out, but this is just to make sure you pay the admission fee. Walkers usually have to clamber over the gate's stile – though sometimes the gate is left open – and then, about 100m further on, need to keep right at the fork in the track; as you approach the tip of the promontory, think carefully before deciding to attempt the precarious climb beyond the old jetties. On your return, you can slake your thirst at the **café-bar** overlooking the coast from beside the car park near the house.

Miramar

From Son Marroig, it's just 2km southwest along the coast to **Miramar** (Tues–Sun 9.30am–6pm; €4), once the site of a medieval monastery – hence the signs for the "**Monestir de Miramar**" – and the last of the houses bought by the Archduke Salvator during his long sojourn on the island. The house and its grounds hold an improbable assortment of remains and memorials, beginning with a line of thirteenth-century **stone pillars**, all that is left of the original monastery built for the scholar-missionaries of Ramon Llull (see p.75). Beyond the pillars is the **house**, whose handful of rooms holds a horridly romantic stone memorial to the archduke's first secretary, a certain Vratislav Vyborny, a mock-up of part of the archduke's yacht, the *Nixe II*, and two rooms devoted to the life of Ramon Llull. Outside, the **grounds** offer tremendous views along the coast, so you don't really need to pay much attention to the geometric shapes that were originally – and allegedly – laid out by Llull or to the stone shrine the archduke built in Llull's honour.

Valldemossa

Beyond Miramar, the Ma-10 stays high above the coast, twisting through what was once the archducal estate en route to the intriguing hill-town of **VALLDEMOSSA**. Approaching from Deià, first impressions are not encouraging as the road cuts through the town's drab western outskirts, and it's probably worth driving right round Valldemossa to start again, driving in from the south on the Ma-1110 Palma road – five minutes each way should do the trick. **Arriving from the south**, the Ma-1110 squeezes through a narrow, wooded defile before entering a lovely valley, whose tiered and terraced fields clamber up towards a sloping jumble of rusticated houses and monastic buildings backclothed by the mountains.

The origins of Valldemossa date to the early fourteenth century, when the asthmatic **King Sancho** built a royal palace here in the hills where the air was easier to breathe. Later, in 1399, the palace was gifted to Carthusian monks from Tarragona, who converted and extended the original complex into a

VALLDEMOSSA

▲ *Palma*

Return from Puig d'es Teix

CAMI DE SA COMA

PARE CASTANYEDA

RECTORIA

Santa Thomàs Shrine

Sant Bartomeu

SA DRAGONERA

PLAÇA SANTA CATALINA TOMAS

DONANTS DE SANG

PLAÇA PUBLICA

BUGER

P. CONSTITUCIÓ

ROSA

A

B

FILOSES

PARE FRANCESC FRAU

LLUIS VIVES

AMETLERS

REI SANXO

ROSA

UETAM

2

PLAÇA RAMON LLULL

1

Palau Sancho

PINS

SON GUAL

CANONGE

Valldemossa Monastery

PLAÇA CARTOIXA

MAS

AVINGUDA PALMA

JOAN MIR DE LA CONCEPTION

P

School

VIA BLANQUERNA

Costa Nord

i

P

Jardines Joan Carles

PINS

ALZINES

URUGUAI

◀ *Hike to Puig d'es Teix*

OLIVARES

JOAN FUSTER

JOAN MIR

VENERABLE SOR ANNA

ANER

ES COS

PILAR MUNT

Bus Stop ★

AVGDA AL SALVADOR

JOAN MIR

N

0   100 m

ACCOMMODATION
Es Petit Hotel — A
Hotel Valldemossa — B

CAFÉS & RESTAURANTS
Ca'n Mario — 2
Cappuccino — 1

▲ *Deià, MA-10 & Port de Valldemossa*

monastery, now Mallorca's most visited building after Palma Cathedral. An enjoyable place to spend the night, Valldemossa has two appealing hotels as well as a couple of good restaurants and it's also within striking distance of its old seaport, tiny **Port de Valldemossa**, whose gaggle of modern villas and micro-beach of churning surf are reached along the dramatic hairpins of a narrow country road.

Arrival and information

There is a good daily **bus service** to Valldemossa from Palma, Deià, Sóller and Port de Sóller, but nothing from Esporles, Banyalbufar and points west. The main **bus stop** is beside the most westerly of the car parks that flank the modern bypass as it skirts the town centre to the north. From here, it's a couple of minutes' walk to the monastery and about the same to the **tourist office**, back along the bypass towards Palma (Mon–Fri 9am–1.30pm & 3–5pm, Sat 10am–1pm; ☏971 61 20 19, ⓦwww.valldemossa.com).

Accommodation

Valldemossa has two enticing **options**, the cheaper being the *Es Petit Hotel*, which occupies a tastefully renovated old stone house metres from the monastery at c/Uetam 1 (☏971 61 24 79, ⓦwww.espetithotel-valldemossa .com; ❹). There are eight, en-suite guest rooms here, each decorated in a pleasant, unfussy style with creams and browns to the fore; several also have smashing views down the valley. A second and much more lavish option is the *Hotel Valldemossa*, Carretera Vieja de Valldemossa s/n (☏971 61 26 26, ⓦwww .valldemossahotel.com; ❾), about five minutes' walk south from the monastery along the old Palma road. A grand Italianate stairway climbs up to what was originally a pair of nineteenth-century, hilltop farmhouses, but is now a sleek, rural-chic hotel with a heated indoor pool, a restaurant and an expansive terrace. Lush gardens tumble down the hillside and the twelve rooms – three doubles and nine suites – as you might expect from the price, come with every mod con: all very chi-chi.

Valldemossa Monastery

Remodelled and restructured on several occasions, most of Valldemossa's **Real Cartuja de Jesús de Nazaret** (Royal Carthusian Monastery of Jesus of Nazareth; March–May & Oct Mon–Sat 9.30am–5.30pm, Sun 10am–1pm; June–Sept Mon–Sat 9.30am–6.30pm, Sun 10am–1pm; Nov–Feb Mon–Sat 9.30am–4pm, Sun 10am–1pm; €8.50) is of seventeenth- and eighteenth-century construction. It owes its present notoriety almost entirely to the novelist and republican polemicist **George Sand** (1804–76), who, with her companion, the composer **Frédéric Chopin** (1810–49), lived here for four months in 1838–39. They arrived just three years after the last monks had been evicted during the liberal-inspired suppression of the monasteries, and so were able to rent a commodious set of vacant cells. Their stay is commemorated in Sand's *A Winter in Majorca*, a sharp-tongued and sharp-eyed epistle that is available hereabouts in just about every European language (an extract is given on p.129). Reading the book today, what comes through strongly is Sand's frustration with the ossified social structures on the island, though her diatribes against reaction sometimes merge into a mean-spirited contempt for her Spanish neighbours. Ungraciously, Sand explains that her nickname for Mallorca, "Monkey Island", was coined for its "crafty, thieving and yet innocent" inhabitants, who, she asserts, are "heartless, selfish and impertinent". Quite what the islanders made of Sand is unknown, but her trouser-wearing, cigar-smoking image – along with her "living in sin" – could hardly have made the woman popular in rural Mallorca. There's an obvious, though limited curiosity in looking around Sand and Chopin's old quarters, but the monastery boasts far more interesting diversions, and it's easy to follow the signs around the place.

A visit begins in the gloomy **church**, a square and heavy construction, which is distinguished by its late Baroque ceiling paintings and barrel vaulting, though the lines of the nave are spoiled by the clumsy wooden stalls of the choir. It also possesses a kitsch high altar and a fanciful bishop's throne, which somehow manages to look a little self-conscious. Beyond the church lie the shadowy **cloisters**, where the first port of call is the **pharmacy**, which survived the expulsion of the monks to serve the town's medicinal needs well into the twentieth century. Its shelves are crammed with a host of beautifully decorated majolica jars, antique glass receptacles and painted wood boxes, each carefully inscribed with the name of a potion or drug.

The cells

Close to the pharmacy, the **prior's cell** is, despite its name, a comfortable suite of bright, sizeable rooms, enhanced by access to a private garden with splendid views down the valley. The cell incorporates a chapel, a library, an audience chamber, a dining room and a bedroom, and it is graced by a potpourri of religious *objets d'art*. These include a number of handsome majolica pieces and two unattributed medieval triptychs displayed in the library. These are the *Adoration of the Magi*, a charmingly naive painting in the Flemish style, and an intricate three-panel marble sculpture celebrating the marriage of Pedro II of Aragón (1174–1213), who – if you're after an English connection – came a fatal cropper in a battle with the army of Simon de Montfort outside Toulouse. This degree of luxury was clearly not what the ascetic St Bruno had in mind when he founded the Carthusian order in the eleventh century. Nevertheless, it's hard to blame the monks at Valldemossa for lightening what must have been a very heavy burden. Bruno's rigorous regime, inspired by his years as a hermit, had his monks in almost continuous isolation, gathering together only for certain church services and to eat in the refectory on Sundays. At other times, lay brothers fed the monks through hatches along the cloister corridors, though this was hardly an onerous task: three days a week the monks had only bread and water, and they never ate meat. The diet and the mountain air, never mind the celibacy, seem to have suited them: the longevity of the Valldemossa monks was proverbial.

Along the corridor, **Cell no. 2** exhibits miscellaneous curios relating to **Chopin and Sand**, from portraits and a lock of hair to musical scores and letters; it was in this cell that the composer wrote his *Raindrop* Prelude, but not on the Steinway piano that is here today – that arrived long after the composer's departure. There's more of the same in **Cell no. 4**, where pride of place goes to Chopin's piano, which was finally installed just three weeks before the couple left for Paris after months of unbelievable complications. Considering the hype, these incidental Chopin mementos are something of an anticlimax and neither do things improve much in the ground-floor galleries of the adjacent **Museu Municipal**, which concentrates on local landscape painters and takes a stab at tracing the diligent endeavours of Archduke Ludwig Salvator (see box, p.124), photographed out and about on his horse. But don't give up: the upstairs section of the museum, entitled the **Museu Municipal Art Contemporani**, has a small but outstanding collection of modern art, including work by Max Ernst, Francis Bacon and Henry

George Sand at Valldemossa

Mallorca has been the subject of many foreign jottings, beginning with the well-heeled travellers who nosed around the island in the nineteenth century. Amongst these assorted travellers, the most distinguished was **George Sand** (1804–76), the pen name of the French aristocrat Armandine Lucile Aurore Dupin, the Baroness Dudevant. Sand married the eponymous baron in 1822, and left him nine years later for the literary life of Paris, where she embraced the Republican cause. A prolific author, dramatist and journalist, Sand became a well-known figure in French political circles and her occasional travels included an extended stay in Valldemossa (1838–39) in the company of her partner, the pianist and composer **Frédéric Chopin**. Sand was not overly impressed with the islanders, but she did take a liking to Valldemossa, as she recorded in her **memoir** of the time, *A Winter in Majorca*.

"To reach the Cartuja [Valldemossa monastery] you have to leave the coach, for it is impossible for any vehicle to clamber up the stony track that leads to it. It is a fascinating approach with its sudden twists and bends among magnificent trees, and with wonderful views that are unfolded at every step, and increase in beauty the higher one rises. … At the head of the valley …[the Carthusian monks]… have made a vast garden ... [which occupies]... the whole inclined background of the valley, and rises in a succession of wide terraces on the lower slopes of the mountain. By moonlight, and when its irregularity is masked by the darkness, it could be taken for an amphitheatre carved out for the battles of giants. In the centre and under a group of lovely palms, a stone-built reservoir collects the water from the mountain springs, and distributes it to the lower terraces by means of paved channels, similar to those which irrigate the environs of Barcelona. …

The Cartuja, situated at the highest point of this gorge, looks on the north side over an extensive valley, which widens out and rises in a gentle slope to the coastal cliffs, whose base is battered and eroded by the sea. One arm of the cordillera points towards Spain, and the others towards the Orient. From this picturesque Carthusian monastery therefore, the sea can be glimpsed or sensed on two sides. Whilst its roar is audible to the north, it can be descried to the south like a fine, brilliant line beyond the descending mountain slopes and the immense plain which is revealed to the eye. It is a surpassing picture, framed in the foreground by dark, pine-covered crags; beyond that by the sharply outlined profiles of mountains set off by superb trees; and in the background by the rounded humps of hills, which the setting sun gilds with the warmest shades, and on whose crests one can still distinguish, from a distance of a league, the microscopic outlines of the trees, as fine as the antennae of butterflies, as black and distinct as a trace of Chinese ink on a backdrop of sparkling gold."

Moore. There's also a room full of characteristic squiggles by Joan Miró and a substantial sample of paintings by the Spanish modernist **Juli Ramís** (1909–90), from geometric abstractions through to forceful, expressionistic paintings like *The Blue Lady* (*Dama Blava*).

Palau Sancho

Doubling back to the prior's cell, be sure to take the doorway that leads outside the cloisters and across the courtyard to the **Palau Sancho** (Palace of King Sancho; same times & ticket as the monastery). It's not the original medieval palace – that disappeared long ago – but this fortified mansion is the oldest part of the monastery complex and its imposing walls, mostly dating from the sixteenth century, accommodate a string of appealing period rooms cluttered with faded paintings and other curios, from fans and a head of a suffering Christ to old halberds and muskets. The palace was the first home of the monks, but it has also seen service as the residence of local bigwigs and as a political prison, its most celebrated internee being the liberal reformer Gaspar de Jovellanos, a victim of the royal favourite Manuel de Godoy, who had him locked up here from 1801 to 1802. On your way round the palace, you'll glimpse the original entrance, which comes complete with fortified towers and an eccentric wooden drawbridge linking two internal rooms, but this is much better viewed from the narrow side street that runs along the east side of the palace – on the side away from the cloisters. The palace also hosts free and frequent **concerts** of **Chopin's piano music** in the small auditorium beside today's entrance.

The rest of Valldemossa

The monastery is very much the main event in Valldemossa, though there are a couple of minor attractions amongst the cobbled lanes and old stone houses of the town centre, which tumbles prettily down the hillside beneath it. First up is the church of **Sant Bartomeu**, an imposing Gothic edifice with a handsome bell tower that lords it over a tiny piazza. Close by, round the back alongz a narrow alley at c/Rectoria 5, is the humble birthplace of **Santa Catalina Thomàs**, a sixteenth-century nun revered for her piety. The interior of the house has been turned into a simple little shrine, with a statue of the saint holding a small bird.

Eating and drinking

The centre of Valldemossa is packed with **cafés and restaurants**. Many are geared up for the day-trippers and offer pretty dire food at inflated prices, but there are exceptions. One sound choice is the first-floor *Ca'n Mario*, c/Uetam 8 (℡971 61 21 22), a family-run place with engagingly traditional décor, where they serve traditional Mallorcan food with main courses averaging around €15. Very different is the slick and ultra-modern café-restaurant *Cappuccino*, at Plaça Ramon Llull 5, where the prices may be over the odds, but the quality is first rate. The food on offer changes with the time of day, from breakfast in the morning to hot dishes – beef carpaccio, lasagne and so forth – from lunch times onwards; *Cappuccino* is in fact a small but buoyant Mallorca chain.

Around Valldemoss: Port de Valldemossa

The closest spot to Valldemossa for a paddle is **PORT DE VALLDEMOSSA**, where a handful of seaside villas huddle together in the shadow of the mountains at the mouth of a narrow, craggy cove. There's no public transport, but the drive down to the port, once Valldemossa's gateway to the outside world, is stimulating: head west out of Valldemossa to rejoin the Ma-10 and, after about 1.5km, turn right at the sign and follow the twisty side road for 6km down through the mountains. Port de Valldemossa's beach is small and shingly, and tends to get battered by the surf, but the scenery is stunning and the village sports a popular seashore **restaurant**, *Es Port* (daily: Feb–June & Sept–Nov 10am–6pm; July & Aug 10am–10pm; ℡971 61 61 94), which has a good reputation for its seafood – try the shellfish and lobster paella at just €12 per head; times may vary, so ring ahead to confirm.

Southwest to La Granja and Esporles

Heading southwest from Valldemossa, the Ma-10 threads a scenic route along the coastal mountains for about 9km until it reaches the 1.5km-long turning for **La Granja** (daily 10am–6pm; €11; ⓦwww.lagranja.net), a grand *hacienda*

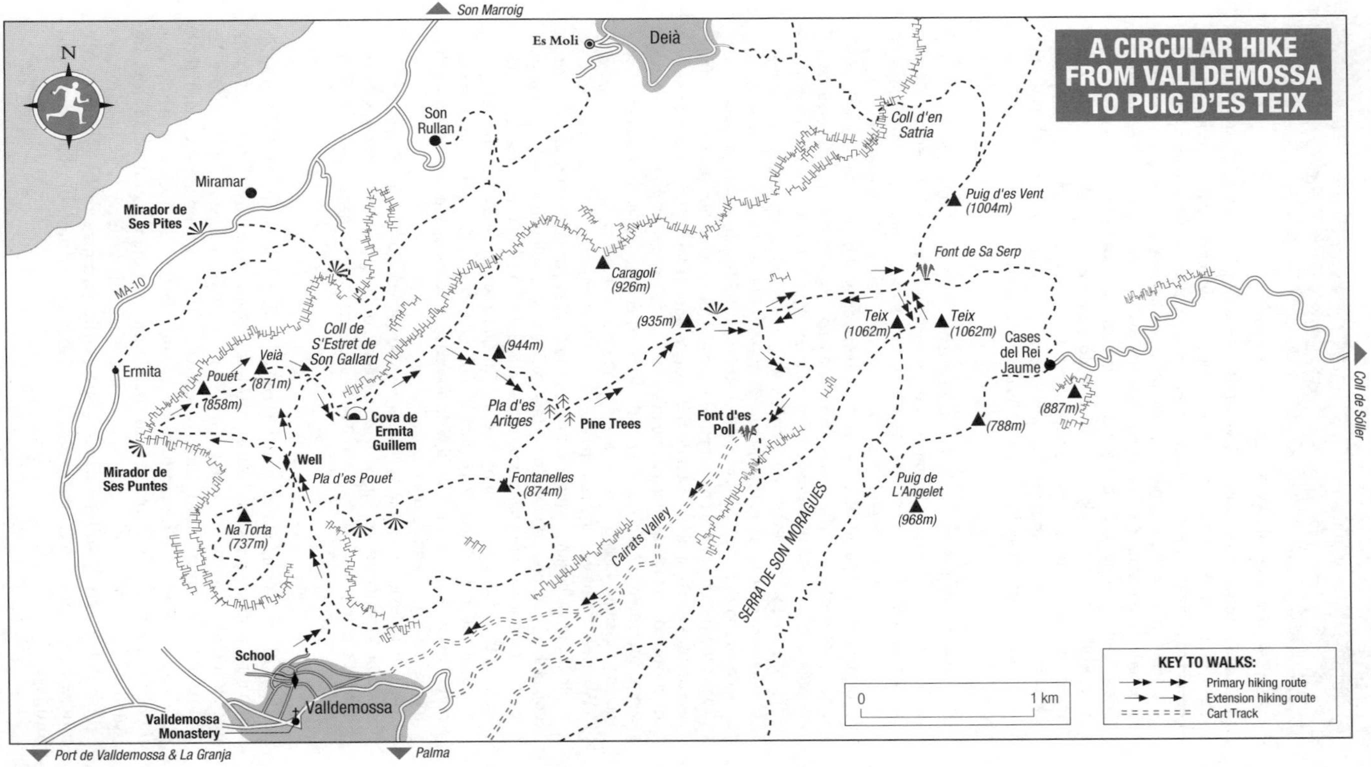

A CIRCULAR HIKE FROM VALLDEMOSSA TO PUIG D'ES TEIX

2

WESTERN MALLORCA

1 km

N

Coll de Sóller

(887m)

Puig d'es Vent (1004m)

Font de Sa Serp

Teix (1062m)

Cases del Rei Jaume

(788m)

Teix (1062m)

Puig de L'Angelet (968m)

Coll d'en Satria

Deià

Es Moli

Son Marroig

Carapoli (926m)

(935m)

Font d'es Poll

SERRA DE SON MORAGUES

Son Rullan

(944m)

Pla d'es Aritges Pine Trees

Fontanelles (874m)

Cairats Valley

Miramar

Coll de S'Estret de Son Gallard

Cova de Ermita Guillem

Well Pla d'es Pouet

Valldemossa

Veià (871m)

Pouet (658m)

Na Torta (737m)

School

Mirador de Ses Piites

Ermita

Mirador de Ses Puntes

Valldemossa Monastery

Port de Valldemossa & La Granja

Palma

www.roughguides.com

131

A circular hike from Valldemossa to Puig d'es Teix by the Archduke's Path

12.5km; 674m of ascent; 4hr 30min–5hr. Medium difficulty.

The terrain between **Valldemossa and Deià** is mountainous and wild, abounding in steep cliffs and rocky summits; the lower slopes are wooded but the tops are almost devoid of vegetation, with numerous dramatic viewpoints, many of them overlooking the ocean. The land is rough but, as elsewhere in Mallorca, the mountains are criss-crossed by footpaths first made by charcoal burners, olive growers and hunters. These paths can be stony but this area was also subject to the attentions of the nineteenth-century Austrian archduke **Ludwig Salvator** (see box, p.124), who had some wonderful paths constructed so that he could ride around on horseback admiring the scenery. This **circular walk** – which can be lengthened or shortened to suit – is a classic, showing the area to its best advantage.

The route

From near the monastery on Valldemossa's bypass (Avinguda Palma), proceed along **c/Venerable Sor Aina** past the car park and take the first right up to the school. Climb the **steps** at the left-hand side of the school, then turn right and almost immediately left onto c/Alzines. Follow this road round, turn right onto c/Olivares and then keep straight up a wide path that leads into the woods, entered by a stile over a gate. The stony path twists up quite steeply to reach an opening in the wall at the edge of a wooded plain, the **Pla d'es Pouet**; a shortcut near the top is waymarked but it makes little difference which way you go. From the wall, go straight on across the level ground to reach an old **well** (now polluted) in a large clearing. This well is a vital reference point in a confusing area and it is essential that you take your bearings carefully here.

Take the path bearing slightly right of the well (northeast at first, and then north), which leads easily up to the **Coll de S'Estret de Son Gallard**. On the col is a barrier of brushwood set up by hunters who still practise the traditional *caza a coll* method, which you can observe: birds are lured into flying along artificial tunnels created by cutting passages through the trees, then captured in nets.

From the nearby v-shaped stone seats, the path continues uphill to the right. To the south of the main path lies the **Cova de Ermita Guillem**, an interesting hermit's cave, containing icons and candles; this offers excellent shelter if you're unlucky with the weather – look for a branch path on the right and a gap in a wall to the left, which leads to the enclosure in front of the cave. To rejoin the uphill main path, retrace your steps for about 100m and then branch sharply off to the right. The most spectacular part of the walk begins here: it's a wide and easy walkway on the edge of cliffs with a breathtaking view and a good place for picnics.

As you approach the summit of **Caragolí**, you can spy Port de Sóller down on the coast and the mountains Major, Teix and Galatzó rising high above the seashore. Then the path climbs southeast to 944m before descending gently over a sloping,

nestling in a tranquil wooded and terraced valley. The house and its grounds make for a popular package-tourist trip, but, despite the many visitors, the estate just about manages to maintain a languorous air of old patrician comfort. La Granja was occupied until fairly recently by the Fortuny family, who took possession in the mid-fifteenth century; after about the 1920s it seems that modernization simply never crossed their minds. At the ticket desk, visitors are issued with a leaflet outlining a numbered self-guided tour.

The **Palma to Estellencs bus** stops by the entrance to La Granja pretty much every hour Monday through Friday, six times on Saturdays and Sundays.

arid plain, the **Pla d'es Aritges** (*aritge* is smilax, a plant with vicious backward-curving thorns). A path junction at an isolated group of pine trees offers a shortcut back to Valldemossa via Fontanelles. To continue on the main route, take the left fork northeast, which brings you over a 935m top and shortly after, to a viewpoint overlooking Deià. After this the path swings southeast and begins to descend to the Teix path junction.

A metre-high **cairn** marks the Teix path junction. Here, branch left (northeast) on a path that scrambles up a little gully and then continues over a sandy plateau towards a high stone wall. Cross this using the ladders provided and walk on to the **Pla de Sa Serp**, a plain where there is a spring – the **Font de Sa Serp**. A well-used path then leads up to the col between the two summits and on to the main west summit of Puig d'es Teix (1062m). From here the views over the Sóller valley and the western summit of Puig Major are especially fine, while the tops of Cornadors, L'Ofre and the Alfàbia ridge form a stunning skyline.

Return to the Teix path junction by the same route (avoid the difficult-to-follow route southwest from Teix towards Sa Bussa) and turn left to follow the main track down the **Cairats valley**. First you'll come to an old "snowhouse" (a deep hole used for storing ice in winter), then a stone mountain refuge and below that a spring and picnic site, the **Font d'es Poll** (Well of the Poplar). The wide track beyond is stony but you'll have no trouble finding the route. On the way down the valley you'll see reconstructions of a *sitja*, a charcoal-worker's shelter. Keep on the main track down the Cairats valley, going over a wall via stone steps to the left of a locked gate. Ignore two branch paths to the left and continue to some iron gates. Go straight on to join c/Xesc Forteza, then bear left into c/Lluis Vives at the end of which is a large old house with a square tower. From here there is a splendid view over the old part of Valldemossa. Continue on down c/Son Gual, turn left into c/Mas, then right onto Avinguda Palma for the centre of Valdemossa.

Extension of the walk to Mirador de Ses Puntes and Veià
1.5km; 116m of ascent; 45min

From the well in the clearing on the Pla d'es Pouet, take the path which leads northwest at first, before zigzagging uphill and swinging west. Fork left shortly after passing an old bread oven to reach the **Mirador de Ses Puntes**. From this superb viewpoint, return to the fork and take the right branch, which rises through the trees to the top of **Pouet** (858m) and, after a little dip, **Veià** (871m). For much of the way, the path is the wide bridleway built by the archduke and from it you can look down on Sa Foradada, a rocky headland near his old house, Son Marroig (see p.124). From the ruined shelter on Veià the path descends to the **Coll de S'Estret de Son Gallard**, where you rejoin the main path a little up from the well.

The house and the estate

From the **entrance** in front of the main forecourt, signs direct you up round the back of the house, past an incidental collection of well-weathered agricultural tackle and farmyard animals. At the back of the house, you can either detour up to the old bath house, which offers a wide view over the estate, or proceed into the main **house**, where a sequence of apartments is strewn with domestic clutter. A highlight is the delightful little theatre, where plays were once performed for the household in a manner common amongst Europe's nineteenth-century rural landowners. Thereafter, amongst much else, there's a children's games room, an ironing room, a graceful first-floor loggia, and a dining room, which, with its faded paintings and tapestries, has a real touch of country elegance.

Tagged onto the house, a series of **workrooms** recall the days when La Granja was a profitable and almost entirely self-sufficient concern. A wine press as well as almond and olive-oil mills prepared the estate's produce for export, whilst plumbers, carpenters, cobblers, weavers and rope makers all kept pace with domestic requirements from their specialized workshops. After the workrooms, one option is to go for a twenty-minute **walk** through the surrounding woods, or you can go directly to the **cellars**, the site of the farm kitchen. The Fortunys were one of Mallorca's more enlightened landowning families, and employees were well fed by the kitchen staff, who made cheeses, bread and preserves by hand. Also in the cellars are two entirely unauthentic additions – a display of torture instruments and a torture chamber. Moving on, you'll soon reach the family **chapel**, a diminutive affair with kitsch silver-winged angels, and then the expansive **forecourt**, shaded by plane trees and surrounded by antiquated workshops where costumed artisans "practise" traditional crafts such as wood-turning and candle-making. This part of the visit is more than a little bogus, but good fun all the same – and the home-made pastries and doughnuts (*bunyols*) are lip-smacking. Your visit may coincide with a mildly diverting display of Mallorcan **folk dancing**, which also takes place in the forecourt.

Esporles

It's a couple of kilometres along the Palma road from La Granja to **ESPORLES**, an amiable, leafy little town whose elongated main street follows the line of an ancient stone watercourse. This is Mallorca away from the tourist throng, and although there's no special reason to stop, you might drop by the town's finest building, its thirteenth-century **church**: a massive, heavily buttressed affair at the top of the town overlooking Plaça Espanya. This certainly wasn't the place to be in 1452, when local landowners finally managed to crush a peasants' revolt that had spread across the island from the Esporles district. The leader of the insurrection, a certain Miquel Forns, was tortured to death on Plaça Espanya and his body was left swinging on a gibbet to ram home the point.

The Palma to Estellencs bus (see p.140) passes through Esporles, and there's a frequent Palma-Esporles service too.

Banyalbufar

Back on the Ma-10, just beyond the turning for La Granja, a narrow side road forks down to the coast at **PORT D'ES CANONGE**. The five-kilometre journey down through thickly forested hills is splendid, but the settlement itself is disappointing, a scrawny, modern *urbanització* flanking a shingle beach. Consequently, you're far better off staying on the main coast road for a further 6km, enjoying spectacular views as you approach **BANYALBUFAR**, a drowsy little village whose terraced fields cling gingerly to the coastal cliffs. The land here has been cultivated since Moorish times, with a spring above the village providing a water supply that's still channelled down the hillside along slender watercourses into open storage cisterns, the unlikely looking home for a few carp. The village itself is bisected by its main street, which doubles as the Ma-10, with ancient houses and steep cobbled lanes to either side. The cute **main square** perches above the main street, overlooked by a chunky parish **church** dating from the fifteenth century. Banyalbufar is a fine place to unwind and there's a rough and rocky **beach** fifteen minutes' walk down the hill from the main drag – just follow the signs.

Arrival and information

The regular Palma to Estellencs **bus** passes through Banyalbufar and the **bus stop** is on the main street, a short stroll from the square. The village does not have a tourist office, but there are several appealing **places to stay** and a passable **café and restaurant** scene.

Accommodation

Considering its size, Banyalbufar has a good range of **accommodation** and prices are reasonable throughout.

Hotel Mar i Vent c/Major 49 ☎971 61 80 00, ⓦ www.hotelmarivent.com. In a conspicuous 1940s building on the main street towards the east end of the village, this old-fashioned hotel has thirty rooms, the pick of which are reasonably large and have sea-facing balconies with fantastic views out along the coast. There's also an outside pool and help for drivers: the staff will park your car for you – a real blessing given the village's steep and narrow lanes. ❹

Hotel Sa Baronia c/Baronia 16 ☎971 61 81 46, ⓦ www.hbaronia.com. Traditional – some would say old-fashioned – hotel, parts of which inhabit an ancient fortified house. The forty-odd guest rooms are simple and straightforward, all white walls and varnished furniture, the bonus being that all of them have sea-facing balconies. Large outside pool and handily located at the west end

of the village, beside the main street. Closed Nov–March. ❷

Hotel Sa Coma Camí des Molí 3 ☎971 61 80 34, ⓦ www.hotelsacoma.com. Small and engaging, family-run hotel in a medium-sized, three-storey modern block down below the main drag on the way to the beach. The décor is pretty predictable but there are great sea views, home cooking and an outside pool. Closed Nov–April. ❹

Hotel Son Borguny c/Borguny 1 ☎971 14 87 06, ⓦ www.sonborguny.com. This hotel occupies a sympathetically modernized old stone terrace house that dates back to the fifteenth century, with eight guest rooms kitted out in a cheerful version of modern-meets-traditional style; the only drawback is that most of the rooms do not have sea views. ❸

Eating and drinking

Most visitors to Banyalbufar **eat** where they sleep – no bad thing if you're staying at the *Sa Coma* in particular – but there are a couple of good alternatives.

Es Trast c/Comte de Sallent 10 ☎971 14 85 44. Down below the high street, this creative little restaurant serves a good range of Mediterranean dishes at reasonable prices. Closed Wed.

Pegasón c/Pont 2. The *Pegasón* café-bar is the busiest place in the village, serving up pizzas (from €8) and a limited range of meat and fish dishes in two cosy little rooms; it's just below the main

street across from the main square. Mon–Sat except Thurs 7–11.30pm & Sun 1.30–11.30pm.

Restaurante Son Tomas c/Baronia 17 ☎971 61 81 49. At the west end of the village, this modern restaurant has great steaks and a delicious fish of the day (for around €23), as well as an excellent *menú del día*. Wide sea views too. Wed–Sun 12.30–4pm & 7.30–10.30pm.

Southwest to Estellencs

Pressing on from Banyalbufar, it's about 1.5km to the **Torre del Verger**, a sixteenth-century watchtower built as a sentinel against pirate attack and now providing stunning views along the coast. **ESTELLENCS**, 5km further on, is similar to Banyalbufar, with steep coastal cliffs and tight terraced fields, though if anything it's even prettier, its narrow, winding alleys crimped by old stone houses and a trim, largely eighteenth-century parish **church**. A steep, but driveable, two-kilometre lane leads down from the village, past olive and orange orchards, to **Cala Estellencs**, a rocky, surf-buffeted cove that shelters a shingly beach and summertime bar.

Practicalities

Buses to Estellencs stop in the centre of the village beside the main street, which doubles as the Ma-10. The best **hotel** is the lovely little ⚐ *Hotel Nord*, in the middle of the village – and below the main street – at Plaça Triquet 4 (☎971 14 90 06, ⓦ www.hotelruralnord.com; ❹; closed Nov–Jan). Family-run, the hotel occupies a cleverly reworked and modernized old stone house and olive press. There are just eight guest rooms, two with a private terrace and one with a balcony, and each has been decorated in creams and whites with the original architecture – especially the wooden beamed ceilings – respected wherever possible. The only problem can be finding the place: you have to keep your eyes peeled to spot the sign on the west side of the village. No such difficulty affects the large and conspicuous *Hotel Maristel* (☎971 61 85 50, ⓦ www.hotelmaristel .com; ❹; closed Nov–Feb), whose two substantial modern blocks straddle the main road at the west end of the village. The fifty or so rooms here are large and well appointed and many have balconies offering great views down over the coast. There's also an outside pool, as there is at a third – and slightly cheaper – choice, the delightful *Sa Plana Hotel*, just above the main road at the west end of the village (☎971 61 86 66, ⓦ www.saplana.com; ❸). This rusticated, family-run *finca* comprises five guest rooms, each of which has a distinctly period appearance.

Of the village's several **restaurants**, the pick is the ⚐ *Montimar* (Tues–Sun noon–3.30pm & 7–10.30pm; ☎971 61 85 76), up a flight of steps from the main street near the church. The menu here bristles with Mallorcan favourites like suckling pig, snails and rabbit and every effort is made to source things locally. The premises themselves are attractively antique, too, and there's a pleasant outside terrace; mains average €13.

To Andratx

Travelling southwest from Estellencs, the **Ma-10** scuttles along the coast before turning inland to weave its way up and over forested foothills to **ANDRATX**, a busy but unremarkable town 19km southwest of Estellencs – and just 23km from Palma. The main event here is the **Wednesday morning market**, a tourist favourite, but otherwise there's not much to detain you, though the old houses and cobbled streets of the upper town do form an harmonious, ochre ensemble, culminating in the fortress-like walls of the thirteenth-century church of **Santa Maria**, built high and strong to deter raiding pirates, its balustraded precincts offering panoramic views down to the coast.

Andratx is well connected by **bus** with Palma, Sant Elm and Port d'Andratx, but there are currently no services from Estellencs and points northeast along the coast.

Sant Elm and the Parc Natural de Sa Dragonera

From Andratx, it's 3km west along a pleasant country road to the hillside hamlet of **S'Arracó**, which is itself the prelude to a pretty, orchard-covered landscape that buckles up into wooded hills and dipping valleys as it approaches the seashore, another 5km or so away. At the end of the road is the low-key, pocket-sized resort of **SANT ELM**, whose main street strings along the shoreline with a pretty and sandy cove beach at one end and a **harbour** at the other – and, mercifully, no tower blocks in between.

From Sant Elm's tiny harbour, **passenger boats** (Feb–March & Oct to mid-Nov Mon–Sat 4 daily; April–Sept 8 daily; €10 return; 15min; ☎639 61 75 45 or 696 42 39 33) take a few minutes to shuttle across to the austere

▲ Sant Elm beach with views to Sa Dragonera

offshore islet that comprises the **Parc Natural de Sa Dragonera** (April–Sept daily 10am–5pm; Oct–March daily 10am–3pm; free). This uninhabited hunk of rock, some 4km long and 700m wide, lies at an oblique angle to the coast, with an imposing ridge of seacliffs dominating its northwestern shore. Behind the ridge, a rough road travels the length of the island, linking a pair of craggy capes and their lighthouses. The boat docks at a tiny cove-harbour – **Cala Lladó** – about halfway up the east shore, which puts both ends of the island within comfortable walking distance, though the excursion north to **Cap de Tramuntana** is both shorter and prettier – allow about an hour each way. There's also a much more challenging, three- to four-hour trail that clambers up to the **Puig de na Pòpia** lighthouse on the northwest coast. Most people visit Sa Dragonera for the scenic solitude, but the island is also good for **birdlife** – ospreys, shags, gulls and other seabirds are plentiful, and you may also see several species of raptor. To confirm **sailing times**, call ahead or inquire at the tourist office (see p.138), which has both schedules and park maps. Incidentally, be sure to check the times of your return boat trip on the outward journey.

The rugged coastal district just to the north of Sant Elm is devoid of development and boasts several enjoyable **hikes**. The most popular is the hour-long (5km) hike to **La Trapa**, where the small monastery, which was built by Trappist monks in the early nineteenth century, is being turned into a hikers' hostel, the *Refugi La Trapa*, at the start of the **GR221** long-distance footpath (see p.103); for the latest news on the hostel, check out ⓦ www.conselldemallorca.net. Part of the hiking route from Sant Elm is along a steep and narrow path that offers superlative views over the coast. The start of the hike is on the north side of Sant Elm: keep going along the shoreline until you reach Plaça Mossen Sebastia Grau, where buses terminate. From this square, take Avinguda La Trapa and keep going. Sant Elm tourist office issues maps of the resort as well as free, if rudimentary, hiking maps.

Practicalities

There is a good daily bus service to Sant Elm from Andratx and Port d'Andratx. **Buses** pull in at the south end of the main street, opposite a large dirt car park. From both the bus stop and the car park, it's a couple of minutes' walk to the **tourist office** (May–Sept Mon–Thurs 9am–4pm, Fri 9am–3pm, Sat 9am–2pm & Sun 9am–4pm; ☎971 62 80 19), which has information on local hikes, bus timetables, and the sailing times of the boat to Sa Dragonera (see p.136). The same boat company also operates passenger ferries between Sant Elm and Port d'Andratx (April–Oct 1 daily; 20min; €7 each way).

The resort has two **hotels** and there's a reasonable chance of a vacancy in high season at one of them, the *Hostal Dragonera*, on the main drag at c/Jaume I, 5 (☎971 23 90 86, ⓦwww.hostaldragonera.net; ❸; closed Nov–Feb), though at peak times they often insist on a minimum stay of one week. This one-star *hostal* occupies a simple modern building with clean and neat rooms, the best of which have balconies with sea views. The other hotel, the *Aquamarín*, at c/Cala Es Conills 4 (☎971 23 91 05; ❸; closed Nov–April) is a package-tour favourite with rarely a spare room in sight. The hotel is a lumpy concrete structure built in the general style of an old watchtower and plonked next to the beach at the south end of the main street.

Sant Elm has a wide choice of **cafés and restaurants** and the vast majority are dotted along its main street. One good choice is the harbourside *Vista Mar* (☎971 23 75 47; closed Tues), which has fine sea views from its terrace and does an excellent fish soup as well as fishy main courses from around €17. Close by, there's also the first-rate *Na Caragola* (☎971 23 90 06), again with enjoyable sea views and with seafood its forte; again, mains cost around €17.

Port d'Andratx

In the last decade, the picturesque port and fishing harbour of **PORT D'ANDRATX**, 5km southwest of Andratx, has been transformed by a rash of low-rise shopping complexes and Spanish-style villas. Nevertheless, it's not at all a classic case of overdevelopment: the heart of the **old town**, which slopes up from the south side of the bay, preserves a cramped network of ancient lanes, and there's no denying the prettiness of the setting, with the port standing at the head of a long and slender inlet flanked by wooded hills. Sunsets show the place to best advantage, casting long shadows up the bay, and it's then that the old town's gaggle of harbourside restaurants crowd with holidaymakers and expatriates, a well-heeled crew, occasionally irritated by raucous teenagers, who come here to while away the night. Port d'Andratx may be rather sedate, but it's still an enjoyable place to spend a night or two, especially as it possesses several outstanding seafood restaurants and is easy to reach. The one thing it doesn't have is a sandy beach – the nearest one is east over the hills at Camp de Mar (see p.97).

Arrival and information

There are fast and frequent **buses** to Port d'Andratx from Palma, Andratx and all the larger Badía de Palma resorts to the west of the capital as well as a reasonably frequent service from Sant Elm. Buses pull in at the back of the bay, a brief walk from both the old town (on the left as you face the sea) and the big, modern marina (on the right). From April to October, there are also once-daily **boats except on Sundays** from Sant Elm. The journey takes twenty minutes and costs €7; for timetable details call ☎639 61 75 45 or 696 42 39 33. There's a **taxi** rank on the old town harbourfront near the back of the bay, or you can call Radio Taxi Andratx on ☎971 13 63 98; the fare to Camp de Mar is about €6, to Sant Elm about €10.

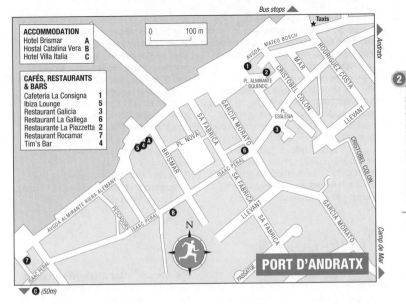

Accommodation

Even in the height of the season, there's a good chance of finding a vacant **room** in Port d'Andratx, but you're much safer booking ahead. The options are, however, limited to an inexpensive *hostal* and two hotels, one a bargain, the other full-blown luxury. All are located on or near the old town's harbourfront.

Hotel Brismar Avgda Almirante Riera Alemany 6 ☎971 67 16 00, ⓦwww.hotelbrismar.com.
A pleasant, old-fashioned three-star place with fifty spotless, en-suite rooms, the pick of which have port-facing balconies (though avoid these if you're a light sleeper – there's a bar next door). Closed Dec–Feb. ❸

Hostal Catalina Vera c/Isaac Peral 63 ☎971 67 19 18, ⓦwww.hostalcatalinavera.es. This appealing establishment occupies a neatly shuttered and whitewashed 1950s two-storey house in a quiet location, flanked by a small orchard one block up from the harbourfront. Packed with house plants, the foyer leads to twenty

guest rooms, which are smartly turned out in traditional Spanish style and each has its own balcony or terrace; all the doubles are en suite. Closed Nov–March. ❶

Hotel Villa Italia Cami Sant Carles 13 ☎971 67 40 11, ⓦwww.hotelvillaitalia.com. Located a five-minute stroll west of the old part of town along Camí Sant Carles (an extension of c/Isaac Peral) and set behind a steeply terraced garden, this is an opulent, 1920s twin-towered Italianate mansion with luxuries such as a rooftop swimming pool, as well as gorgeous views out over the bay. There are rooms and suites both in the old villa and in the more modern annexe. ❾

Eating and drinking

The old town is packed with **cafés and restaurants**, which line up along the harbourfront and crowd the more central portions of c/Isaac Peral, one block up the hill. Generally speaking, standards are high and a local feature is the seafood – good almost everywhere and superb at the town's two Galician places. Eating is the big deal here, but there are several **bars** too, lively little spots that hum till the early hours throughout the summer.

Cafeteria La Consigna Avgda Mateo Bosch 26. Popular and enjoyably modern coffee house-cum-patisserie about a third of the way along

the harbourfront with great cakes, croissants and coffees.

Ibiza Lounge c/Almirante Riera Alemany 7. The flashiest bar in town, with a wide range of sounds, from house through to jazz, and imaginative decor including art installations in the courtyard. Open from 10pm onwards.

Restaurant Galicia c/Isaac Peral 37 ☎971 67 27 05. Highly recommended, bistro-style Galician place serving mouthwatering seafood without the pretensions of some of its rivals down on the harbourfront. Especially strong on shellfish. Has simple, modern decor and very reasonable prices with mains from €17.

Restaurant La Gallega c/Isaac Peral 52 ☎971 67 13 38. Excellent and very popular bistro-style Galician restaurant specializing in seafood, with main courses from about €15.

Restaurante La Piazzetta Plaça Almirante Oquendo 2. Large, popular restaurant and pizzeria on a pleasant pedestrianized square just up from – and about one-third of the way along – the harbourfront from the head of the bay. Tasty pizzas and pastas from €7 as well as reasonably priced seafood dishes.

Restaurant Rocamar c/Almirante Riera Alemany 27 ☎971 67 12 61. A well-established restaurant at the west end of the harbourfront, away from the crowds and offering delicious seafood; also has a lovely bayside terrace. Seafood main courses from €22. Open daily in summer noon–11pm, restricted hours in winter.

Tim's Bar c/Almirante Riera Alemany 10. More subdued than the Ibiza Lounge next door, this cosy little bar caters to an older crowd.

Travel details

Buses

For further information, call ☎971 17 77 77, or check out ⊛http://tib.caib.es/.

Andratx to: Palma (every 30min to hourly; 1hr); Port d'Andratx (every 30min to hourly; 10min); Sant Elm (7 daily; 40min).

Banyalbufar to: Esporles (6–7 daily; 20min); Estellencs (6–7 daily; 20min); La Granja (6–7 daily; 15min); Palma (6–7 daily; 1hr).

Bunyola to: Orient (2 daily; 30min, but service by advance reservation only, see p.114); Palma (Mon–Fri hourly, 7 on Sat, 4 on Sun; 20min).

Deià to: Palma (5–7 daily; 45min); Port de Sóller (5–7 daily; 40min); Sóller (5–7 daily; 30min); Valldemossa (5–7 daily; 15min).

Estellencs to: Banyalbufar (6–7 daily; 20min); Esporles (6–7 daily; 40min); La Granja (6–7 daily; 35min); Palma (6–7 daily; 1hr 20min).

Palma to: Andratx (every 30min to hourly; 1hr); Banyalbufar (6–7 daily; 1hr); Bunyola (Mon–Fri hourly, 7 on Sat, 4 on Sun; 20min); Deià (5–7 daily; 45min); Esporles (Mon–Fri hourly, 6 on Sat & Sun; 30min); Estellencs (6–7 daily; 1hr 20min); La Granja (6–7 daily; 35min); Port d'Andratx (every 30min to hourly; 1hr 10min); Port de Sóller (via the tunnel: Mon–Fri hourly, 7 on Sat, 4 on Sun; 35min; via Valldemossa: 5–7 daily; 1hr 30min); Sóller (via the tunnel: Mon–Fri hourly, 7 on Sat, 4 on Sun; 30min; via Valldemossa: 5–7 daily; 1hr 15min); Valldemossa (Mon–Fri 9 daily, 7 on Sat, 5 on Sun; 30min).

Port d'Andratx to: Andratx (every 30min to hourly; 10min); Palma (every 30min to hourly; 1hr 10min); Sant Elm (7 daily; 30min).

Port de Sóller to: Deià (5–7 daily; 40min); Lluc (April–Oct Mon–Sat 2 daily; 1hr 20min); Palma (via the tunnel: Mon–Fri hourly, 7 on Sat, 4 on Sun; 35min; via Valldemossa: 5–7 daily; 1hr 30min); Pollença (April–Oct Mon–Sat 2 daily; 1hr 50min); Port de Pollença (April–Oct Mon–Sat 2 daily; 2hr); Sóller (Mon–Fri hourly, Sat & Sun every 1–2hr; 10min); Valldemossa (5–7 daily; 55min).

Sant Elm to: Andratx (7 daily; 40min); Port d'Andratx (7 daily; 30min).

Sóller to: Deià (5–7 daily; 30min); Lluc (April–Oct Mon–Sat 2 daily; 1hr 10min); Palma (via the tunnel: Mon–Fri hourly, 7 on Sat, 4 on Sun; 30min; via Valldemossa: 5–7 daily; 1hr 15min); Pollença (April–Oct Mon–Sat 2 daily; 1hr 40min); Port de Pollença (April–Oct Mon–Sat 2 daily; 1hr 50min); Port de Sóller (Mon–Fri hourly, Sat & Sun every 1–2hr; 10min); Valldemossa (5–7 daily; 50min).

Valldemossa to: Deià (5–7 daily; 15min); Palma (Mon–Fri 9 daily, 7 on Sat, 5 on Sun; 30min); Port de Sóller (5–7 daily; 55min); Sóller (5–7 daily; 50min).

Trains

Palma to: Binissalem (every 20min; 30min). For further information, call ☎971 17 77 77, or check out ⊛http://tib.caib.es/

Palma to: Sóller (6–7 daily; 1hr). For further information, call ☎902 36 47 11, or consult ⊛www.trendesoller.com.

3

Northern Mallorca

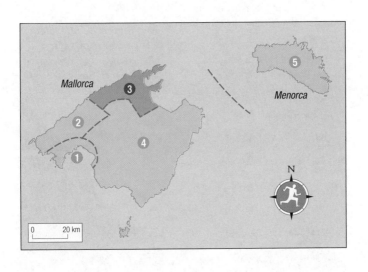

CHAPTER 3 # Highlights

✳ **Lluc** Home to the Balearics' most venerated icon, La Moreneta, this splendid monastery makes a smashing base for mountain hikes. See p.147

✳ **The Davallament, Pollença** Held in the beguiling little town of Pollença, the torchlit Lowering of the Cross – the Davallament – is the most evocative of the many events celebrating Easter Holy Week. See p.153

✳ **Ermita de Nostra Senyora del Puig** A rambling assortment of old stone buildings, this is one of the most appealing of Mallorca's several hilltop monasteries. See p.153

✳ **Península de Formentor** This tapered promontory of bleak sea-cliffs and pine-dusted hills offers gorgeous views and is a fruitful area for birdwatching. See p.161

✳ **Parc Natural de S'Albufera** A small pocket of wetland offering the best birdwatching on the island. See p.172

▲ Cap de Formentor

Northern Mallorca

The magnificent **Serra de Tramuntana** mountains reach a precipitous climax in the rearing peaks of northern Mallorca, beginning just to the northeast of Sóller. This is the wildest part of the island, long the haunt of brigands and monks, and even today the ruggedness of the terrain forces the main coastal road, the **Ma-10**, to duck and weave inland, offering only the occasional glimpse of the sea. A rare exception is the extraordinary side road that snakes down to both overcrowded **Sa Calobra** and the attractive beach at **Cala Tuent**, but it's the lovely monastery of Lluc that remains the big draw here – for religious islanders, who venerate an effigy of the Virgin known as La Moreneta, and tourists alike. Pushing on along the coast, the Ma-10 emerges from the mountains to reach **Pollença**, a tangle of stone houses clustered around a fine, cypress-lined Way of the Cross. Pollença is one of Mallorca's most appealing towns and it's also within easy reach of both the solitary coastal resort of **Cala Sant Vicenç** and the wild and rocky **Península de Formentor**, the bony, northernmost spur of the Serra de Tramuntana. This peninsula shelters the northern shore of the **Badía de Pollença**, which is home to the laid-back and low-key resort of **Port de Pollença**, whilst the next bay down holds the more upbeat and flashy **Port d'Alcúdia**. Close by, the old walled town of **Alcúdia** has a clutch of modest historical sights and pocket-sized **Muro** has a splendid main square. Here too is the **Parc Natural de S'Albufera**, which takes the prize as the best birdwatching wetland in the Balearics. This part of the Serra de Tramuntana offers **superb hiking**. Suggestions for several comparatively easy and/or short walks are given in the text, and we have also described in detail a half-day hike beginning in Port de Pollença and a second, shorter hike near Alcúdia. The region is also traversed by Mallorca's main **long-distance hiking trail**, the **Ruta de Pedra en Sec** (Dry-stone route; officially known as the **GR221**), which runs in from Sóller and worms its way through the mountains bound for Pollença. En route, it passes three **hikers' hostels** (*refugi*; ⓦwww.conselldemallorca.net): *Tossals Verds* (see p.146) in the mountains east of the Embassament de Cúber; *Son Amer*, near Lluc (see p.150); and *Pont Romà* in Pollença (see p.152). See the box on p.103 for information on hiking guides and where to get them; for more on the GR221 west of Sóller, see p.103. Northern Mallorca also boasts fine beaches, principally in the long, golden strands that stretch round the bays of Pollença and Alcúdia.

Practicalities

As regards **accommodation**, the resorts of northern Mallorca – primarily Port de Pollença, Port d'Alcúdia and Cala Sant Vicenç – muster a veritable phalanx

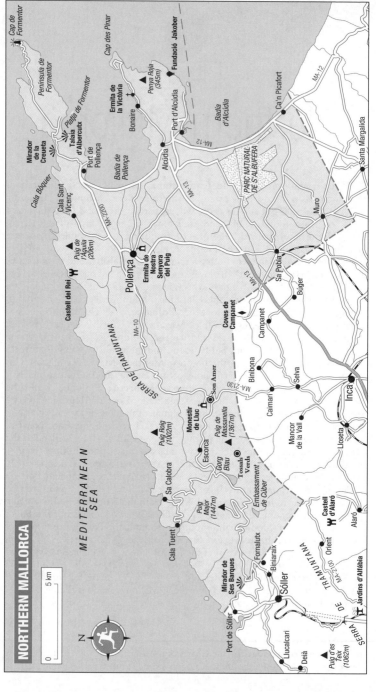

NORTHERN MALLORCA

0 5 km

N

MEDITERRANEAN
SEA

Cap de
Formentor

Península de
Formentor

Platja de Formentor

Cap des Pinar

Mirador de
la Creueta

Talaia
d'Albercutx

Port de Formentor

Port de
Pollença

Badia de
Pollença

Cala Boquer

Cala Sant
Vicenç

Ermita de
la Victoria

Penya Roja
(345m)

Fundació Jakober

Bonaire

Port d'Alcúdia

Alcúdia

Badia
d'Alcúdia

Ca'n Picafort

MA-12

Santa Margalida

MA-12

MA-12

MA-13

PARC NATURAL
DE S'ALBUFERA

Muro

Sa Pobla

Búger

MA-13

Puig de
l'Àguila
(206m)

Castell del Rei

Ermita de
Nostra
Senyora
del Puig

Pollença

MA-2200

SERRA DE TRAMUNTANA

MA-10

Coves de
Campanet

Campanet

Biniatró

Selva

Caimari

Inca

MA-2130

Son Amer

Monestir
de Lluc

Puig de
Massanella
(1367m)

Mancor
de la Vall

Lloseta

Puig Roig
(1002m)

Escorca

Gorg
Blau

Tossals
Verds

Embassament
de Cúber

Castell
d'Alaró

Alaró

Sa Calobra

Puig
Major
(1447m)

Cala Tuent

Fornalutx

Biniaraix

Mirador de
Ses Barques

Sóller

Orient

TRAMUNTANA

MA-2100

Jardins d'Alfàbia

Port de Sóller

Llucalcari

Deià

Puig d'es
Teix
(1062m)

SERRA DE

of hotels and *hostales*, but this is predominantly package territory, and from June to early September (and sometimes beyond), independent travellers are well advised to make advance **reservations**. In the shoulder season and in winter things are much easier and cheaper, though many places do close down. More promisingly, the number of inland *hostales* and hotels is on the increase – Pollença and Alcúdia both have places to stay – and there's not quite the seasonal crush here that there is on the coast. Finally, you could also stay at one of the region's two **monasteries** – at Lluc and just outside Pollença: the rooms are frugal but inexpensive, and there's usually space at any time of year.

Getting around by public transport is easy enough as even the smaller places have a reasonable **bus** service. Nonetheless, certain buses are seasonal and fairly infrequent – most notably the Sóller–Pollença service (April–Oct Mon–Sat 2 daily) – so advance planning is the order of the day; all the area's tourist offices carry bus timetables. Where the bus won't take you, a **taxi** will and rates, especially if you're travelling in a group, are very reasonable; drivers, on the other hand, should be aware that **parking** in all the more populous resorts and towns can be a real pain in the summertime between about 10 or 11am and 5pm.

The northern coast: from Sóller to the Formentor Peninsula

Beyond Sóller, the **Ma-10** forges through the highest and harshest section of the Serra de Tramuntana. For the most part, the mountains drop straight into the sea – precipitous and largely unapproachable cliffs with barely a cove in sight. The accessible exceptions are the comely beach at **Cala Tuent** and the horribly commercial hamlet of **Sa Calobra** next door. The best place to break your journey, however, is inland at the monastery and pilgrimage centre of **Lluc**, which offers a diverting museum, top-notch mountain hiking trails and a reliable supply of inexpensive rooms.

There's more low-priced monastery accommodation at the hilltop Ermita de Nostra Senyora del Puig, just outside **Pollença**, a beguiling old town of honey-coloured stone mansions sitting at the foot of a beautiful "calvary" walkway. Nearby, just down at the coast, is **Port de Pollença**, a medium-sized, remarkably amenable resort with a long sandy beach draped around the Badía de Pollença. The port is a popular summertime retreat for the inhabitants of Palma and abounds in places to stay; it's also within easy striking distance of the dramatic seacliffs of the **Formentor Peninsula** at the northernmost tip of the island.

Practicalities

There are good to excellent **bus services** to and between the towns and resorts stretching along the coast between Port de Pollença/Pollença and Ca'n Picafort. There are also fairly frequent buses from Inca train station to Lluc. However, the coastal bus linking Port de Sóller and Sóller with Lluc, Pollença and Port de Pollença only operates between April and October and only twice daily Monday through Saturday at that. What's more, demand for seats can sometimes outstrip supply, though you will have a better chance of grabbing a seat if you get on board at Port de Sóller rather than waiting at the second stop, Sóller. For the frequencies and journey times of all buses, see p.173.

Gorg Blau

Heading northeast from Sóller, the Ma-10 zigzags up into the mountains. After about 5km, the road passes the steep turning down to Fornalutx (see p.112) before offering a last lingering look over the coast from the **Mirador de Ses Barques** vantage point. Thereafter, the road snakes inland and tunnels through the western flanks of **Puig Major** (1436m), the island's highest mountain. Beyond the tunnel is the **Gorg Blau** (Blue Gorge), a bare and bleak ravine that was a well-known beauty spot until a hydroelectric scheme scarred the gorge and its immediate surroundings with a trio of puddle-like reservoirs. The second of the three – 3km beyond the tunnel – is the **Embassament de Cúber** (Cúber reservoir), an unappetizing expanse of water redeemed by its abundant birdlife, notably several different types of raptor. For a better look, stop at the lay-by to follow the easy footpath which circumnavigates the reservoir – it only takes a couple of hours to complete. The reservoir is also an obvious starting point for the four-hour hike west to the Barranc de Biniaraix along (part of) the **GR221** long-distance footpath; alternatively, it's a two-hour hike southeast to the *Refugi Tossals Verds* **hikers' hostel** (℡971 18 20 27, ⓦwww .conselldemallorca.net), in a remote spot high in the mountains. There are thirty bunk beds here at just €11 per person per night, with breakfast costing a further €4.50; reservations need to be made at least five days beforehand. The *refugi* is also on the GR221, but getting there involves a detour from the main route between Biniraix and Lluc.

To the immediate north of the reservoir rear the bare and craggy flanks of **Puig Major**, but the dramatic trail that twists up to the summit from the military base beside the main road remains off limits on account of its radar station. This makes **Puig de Massanella** (1365m), which looms over the Gorg Blau to the east, the highest mountain that can be climbed on Mallorca.

Cala Tuent

At the far end of Gorg Blau the Ma-10 bores into the mountains to emerge just short of a left turn leading down to Sa Calobra and Cala Tuent. This turn-off makes for an exhilarating, ear-popping detour to the seashore, the well-surfaced road hairpinning its way down the mountain slopes so severely that at one point it actually turns 270 degrees to run under itself.

About 10km down this road, there's a fork: head left over the hills for the five-kilometre journey to **CALA TUENT**, where a smattering of villas cling to the northern slopes of Puig Major as it tumbles down to the seashore. Ancient orchards temper the harshness of the mountain, and the gravel and sand beach is one of the quietest on the north coast. It's a lovely spot to while away a few hours – if you can wrangle a parking spot (space is limited) – and provided you stay close to the shore, the swimming is safe. There's nowhere to stay, but there is an excellent **restaurant** up on a ridge on the far side of the cove, the *Es Vergeret* (mid-Feb to Oct daily 12.30–4.30pm, plus July & Aug Sat 8.30–10.30pm; ☎971 51 71 05), which offers a tasty range of fish and meat dishes from €14, best devoured on the terrace in sight of the pounding surf.

Sa Calobra

Heading right back at the fork in the road, it's just 2km to **SA CALOBRA**, a modern resort occupying a pint-sized cove in the shadow of the mountains. The setting itself is gorgeous, but the place is an over-visited disaster: almost every island operator deposits a busload of tourists here every day in summer and the crush is quite unbearable – as is the overpriced and overcooked food at the local cafés. The reason why so many people come here is to visit the impressive box canyon at the mouth of the **Torrent de Pareis** (River of the Twins). It takes about ten minutes to follow the partly tunnelled walkway round the coast from the resort to the mouth of the canyon. Here, with sheer cliffs rising on every side, the milky-green river trickles down to the narrow bank of shingle that bars its final approach to the sea – though the scene is transformed after heavy rainfall, when the river crashes down into the canyon and out into the ocean.

Escorca

Back on the Ma-10, about 4km northeast of the Cala Tuent/Sa Calobra turn-off and 26km from Sóller, is **ESCORCA**, a poorly defined scattering of houses that is the starting point for the **descent of the Torrent de Pareis**, a famous though very testing and potentially dangerous hike-cum-climb which requires some basic rock-climbing skills. The river drops from here to Sa Calobra through a formidable, seven-kilometre-long limestone gorge, which takes about five hours to negotiate. The descent is not practicable in winter, spring, or after rainfall, when the river may be waist-high and the rocks dangerously slippery. The descent starts at the **sign** on the main road opposite the conspicuous *Restaurant Escorca*. The gorge is almost always hotter than its surroundings, so it's essential to take lots of water.

The Monestir de Lluc

Tucked away in a remote valley just off the Ma-10 about 10km east of Escorca, the austere, high-sided dormitories and orange-flecked roof tiles of the **Monestir de Nostra Senyora de Lluc** (Monastery of Our Lady of Lluc) stand out against the greens and greys of the surrounding mountains. It's a magnificent setting for what has been Mallorca's most important place of pilgrimage since the middle of the thirteenth century, though the religious significance of the place goes back much further: the valley's prehistoric animistic inhabitants deified the local holm-oak woods, and the **Romans** picked up on the theme, naming the place from *lucus*, the Latin for "sacred forest". Thereafter, the **monks** who settled here after the Reconquista were keen both to coin a purely Christian etymology and to enhance their reputation. They invented the story of a shepherd boy named Lluc (Luke) stumbling across a tiny, brightly painted **statue** of the Virgin in the woods. Frightened by his discovery, the lad collared the nearest monk and, lo and behold, when the pair returned, heavenly music filled their ears, bright lights dazzled their eyes, and celestial voices declared the statue to be an authentic heaven-sent image.

Buses to Lluc from points east and west along the coast, as well as Inca train station, stop in the large car park right outside the monastery.

The monastery church

The **monastic complex** (daily: April–Sept 10am–11pm; Oct–March 10am–8pm; free) is an imposing and formal-looking affair mostly dating from the eighteenth and early nineteenth centuries. At its centre is the main shrine and architectural highlight, the **Basílica de la Mare de Déu de Lluc**, which is graced by an elegant Baroque facade. To reach it, pass through the monastery's stately double-doored entrance and keep straight on till you reach the second – and final – courtyard, where there's a dreary statue of Bishop Campins, who overhauled Lluc in the early part of the last century and is shown kneeling and facing the entrance to the church. Dark and gaudily decorated, the church is dominated by heavy jasper columns, the stolidness of which is partly relieved by a dome over the crossing. On either side of the nave, stone steps extend the aisles round the back of the Baroque high altar to a small chapel. This is the holy of holies, built to display the statue of the Virgin, which has been commonly known as **La Moreneta** ("the Little Dark-Skinned One") ever since the original paintwork peeled off in the fifteenth century to reveal brown stone underneath. Just 61cm high, the Virgin looks innocuous, her face tweaked by a hint of a smile and haloed by a much more modern jewel-encrusted gold crown. In her left arm she cradles a bumptious baby Jesus, who holds the "Book of Life" open to reveal the letters alpha and omega.

Every day, the **Escolania de Lluc choir** performs in the basilica during the daily 11am Mass and again at evensong. Founded in the early sixteenth century with the stipulation that it must be "composed of natives of Mallorca, of pure blood, sound in grammar and song", the choir is nicknamed *Els Blauets*, "The Blues", for the colour of their cassocks. At the start of proceedings, a sliding door whizzes opens to reveal La Moreneta to the assembled congregation in the main body of the church.

The monastery museum

Just inside and to the right of the basilica's main entrance a small door leads through to a corridor that runs past the stairway up to the enjoyable **Museu de Lluc** (daily 10am–1.30pm & 2.30–5pm; €4). Immediately beyond the ticket desk, the exhibits lead with a section devoted to archeological finds from the Talayotic and Roman periods and then it's on into the so-called **Sala del Tresor** (Treasure Room), packed with all manner of folkloric items brought here to honour La Moreneta, from fancily painted fans, medallions, rosaries and crosses through to walking sticks discarded when the supplicants found they were no longer lame. Beyond, a room of incidental bric-a-brac, featuring examples of traditional island costume, precedes a section devoted to religious carvings and then a substantial collection of **majolica** (see box opposite), glazed earthenware mostly shaped into two-handled drug jars and show dishes or plates. Some two or three hundred pieces are on display, the pick coming from the eighteenth century, when the designs varied in sophistication from broad and bold dashes of colour to carefully painted naturalistic designs. The colours, however, remained fairly constant, restricted by the available technology to iron red, copper green, cobalt blue, manganese purple and antimony yellow. There is also a good sample of Balearic and Valencian **lustreware**, brown earthenware with a sheen – or lustre – and manufactured between the sixteenth and the eighteenth centuries. The final rooms on this floor are, by comparison, rather tame, devoted to the uninspiring island land- and village-scapes of **José Coll Bardolet** (1912–92).

Upstairs – and this is a welcome surprise – the museum displays an excellent cross section of **Mallorcan art**, either by native artists or artists once resident

Majolica

The fifteenth century witnessed a vigorous trade in decorative pottery sent from Spain to Italy via Mallorca. The Italians coined the term **"majolica"** to describe this imported Spanish pottery after the medieval name for the island through which it was traded, but thereafter the name came to be applied to all tin-glazed pottery. The process of making majolica began with the mixing and cleaning of clay, after which it was fired and retrieved at the "biscuit" (earthenware) stage. The biscuit was then cooled and dipped in a liquid glaze containing tin and water. The water in the glaze was absorbed, leaving a dry surface ready for decoration. After painting, the pottery was returned to the kiln for a final firing, which fused the glaze and fixed the painting. Additional glazings and firings added extra lustre. Initially, majolica was dominated by greens and purples, but technological advances added blue, yellow and ochre in the fifteenth century. Majolica of one sort or another was produced in bulk in Mallorca up until the early twentieth century.

here. Amongst them, there are the Goya-esque works of Salvador Mayol (1775–1834); the Neoimpressionist canvases of Llorenç Cerdà Bisbal (1862–1955); the romantic landscapes of Bartomeu Sureda (1769–1851); and the finely observed mountain landscapes of **Antoni Ribas Oliver** (1845–1911), arguably the most talented artist on display here. In particular, look out for Oliver's *Gorg Blau*, painted long before the gorge's rugged beauty disappeared under the waters of a reservoir (see p.146).

The rest of the monastery
Back outside the monastery's double-doored entrance, walk a few metres to the west and you'll soon spot the large, rough-hewn column at the start of the **Camí dels Misteris del Rosari** (Way of the Mysteries of the Rosary), a broad pilgrims' footpath that winds its way up the rocky hillside directly behind the monastery. Dating from 1913, the solemn granite stations marking the way are of two types: simple stone pediments and, more intriguingly, rough trilobate columns of Gaudí-like design, each surmounted by a chunky crown and cross. The prettiest part of the walk is round the back of the hill, where the path slips through cool, green woods with rock overhangs on one side and views out over the bowl-shaped **Albarca valley** on the other, with **Puig Roig** (1003m) rearing up beyond. It takes about ten minutes to reach the top of the hill, where a wrought-iron *Modernista* cross stands protected by ugly barbed wire. It's actually possible to stroll down into the Albarca valley on the country lane that begins to the left (west) of the monastery's main entrance, but the road fizzles out at a remote farmhouse long before you reach the coast.

On the east side of the monastery are the **Jardí Botanic** (botanical gardens; Mon–Sat 10am–1pm & 3–6pm; free) – they're signed through the conspicuous arches on the right as you face the main building. The gardens are laid out with local plants as well as exotics, plus small ponds and waterfalls, little footbridges and even a windmill. It takes about fifteen minutes to walk through the gardens on a well-defined path.

Practicalities
⚑ **Accommodation** at the monastery (☎971 87 15 25, ⓦ www.lluc.net; ❶) is highly organized, with simple, self-contained cells for up to four people (€32.50 singles, €37 doubles and €42.50 for four) and slightly more commodious apartments (❶), which offer self-catering but do not provide any utensils. In summer, **phone ahead** if you want to be sure of space; at other times simply book at

the monastery's information office on arrival. There's usually an 11pm curfew, except for the apartments, which have their own separate entrance. The main alternative is the *Refugi Son Amer* (☎971 51 71 09, ⓦ www.conselldemallorca .net; ❶), an all-year hikers' hostel close to the Ma-10 just 500m south of the Lluc turn as you head towards Escorca; it's also on the GR221 long-distance hiking route (see p.143). The hostel has a dining room and several bunk-bed dormitories (€11) with shared facilities; breakfast is available for €4.50.

For **food** in Lluc, there's a small general store and several adequate cafés and restaurants in between the monastery and the car park, but the star turn is the monks' former refectory, *Sa Fonda* (March–Oct daily 1–4pm & 7–9pm; Nov–Feb Mon 1–4pm & Wed–Sun 1–4pm & 7–9pm; ☎971 51 70 22), a beautifully restored old hall complete with wooden beams, wide stone arches and marble pillars. The food is traditional Spanish, with main courses from around €12; the meat dishes are much better than the fish.

Pollença and around

Founded in the thirteenth century, the pretty little town of **POLLENÇA** nestles among a trio of hillocks 20km northeast of Lluc, where the Serra de Tramuntana fades into coastal flatland. Following standard Mallorcan practice, the town was established a few kilometres from the seashore to militate against sudden pirate attack, with its harbour, **Port de Pollença** (see p.155), left as an unprotected outpost. For once the stratagem worked. Unlike most of Mallorca's old towns, Pollença successfully repelled a string of piratical onslaughts, the last and most threatening of which was in 1550, when the notorious Turkish corsair Dragut came within a hair's breadth of victory. In the festival of **Mare de Déu dels Àngels** on August 2, the townspeople celebrate their escape with enthusiastic street battles, the day's events named after the warning shouted by the hero of the resistance, a certain Joan Más: "Mare de Déu dels Àngels, assistiu-mos!" ("Our Lady of Angels, help us!").

Pollença is also within easy striking distance of **Cala Sant Vicenç**, a small, modern resort on the island's northern shore.

Arrival and information

Buses to Pollença from Palma, Inca, Port de Pollença and Cala Sant Vicenç pull in on the south side of the centre on c/Cecili Metel, a five-minute walk from the main square, Plaça Major. Less conveniently, buses from Sóller and Lluc currently drop passengers on the north side of town, beside the Ma-10, a good 1km from Plaça Major. The town's **tourist office** (Oct–April Mon–Fri 8am–3pm & Sat 10am–1pm; May–Sept Mon–Fri 9am–2pm & 2.30–4pm, Sat 10am–1pm; ☎971 53 50 77, ⓦ www.pollensa.com) is metres from Plaça Major on c/Antoni Maura. Pollença's tiny centre is best explored on **foot**, but outlying attractions such as the resort of Cala Sant Vicenç (see p.154) can be reached by bus (for frequencies, see p.173) or taxi. There's a taxi rank in the centre at the corner of Avinguda Pollentia and c/Reina Maria Cristina, or call ☎971 86 62 13. If you're **driving**, you can avoid the baffling one-way streets of the old town by entering Pollença from the south, turning off the main Inca–Port de Pollença road onto Avinguda Pollentia.

Accommodation

Pollença has a string of quality **hotels** right in the centre and most occupy sensitively modernized old stone town houses. Nearby, there's also bargain accommodation at a hilltop **monastery**.

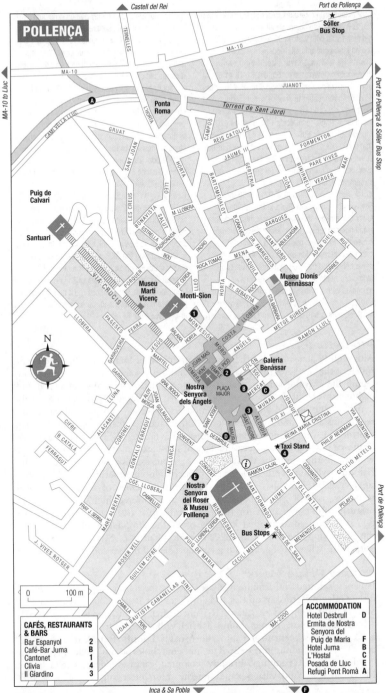

POLLENÇA

▲ Castell del Rei ▲ Port de Pollença ▲

★ Sóller
Bus Stop

3

NORTHERN MALLORCA

Puig de
Calvari

Santuari

Museu Marti Vicenç

Monti-Sion

Museu Dionís Bennàssar

Galeria Benàssar

Nostra Senyora dels Àngels

PLAÇA MAJOR

★ Taxi Stand

ⓘ

Nostra Senyora del Roser & Museu Pollença

Bus Stops ★

0   100 m

CAFÉS, RESTAURANTS & BARS

Bar Espanyol	2
Café-Bar Juma	B
Cantonet	1
Clivia	4
Il Giardino	3

ACCOMMODATION

Hotel Desbrull	D
Ermita de Nostra Senyora del Puig de Maria	F
Hotel Juma	B
L'Hostal	C
Posada de Lluc	E
Refugi Pont Romà	A

▼ Inca & Sa Pobla ▼   ▼ Ⓕ

Hotel Desbrull c/Marquès Desbrull 7 ☏ 971 53 50 55, ⊛ www.desbrull.com. Small, central hotel in an old stone villa with just six ultra-modern double rooms kitted out in brisk, modern style. ❹

Ermita de Nostra Senyora del Puig de Maria 2km south of town (see p.153) ☏ 971 18 41 32. At this hilltop monastery, the original monks' quarters have been renovated to provide simple rooms sleeping between two and six guests with shared facilities. A single room costs €14, doubles €22, triples €29, quads €36 and quins €43. Be warned that it can get cold and windy at night, even in the summer. There's a refectory, but the food is only average. Most guests turn up on spec: to be sure of a room, book ahead. ❶

Hotel Juma Plaça Major 9 ☏ 971 53 50 02, ⊛ www.hoteljuma.com. Right in the middle of town, overlooking the main square, this enjoyable, small hotel occupies an old stone merchant's house that functions rather like a traditional pension with reception on the first floor, a café down below and the a/c rooms up above. The rooms are neat and tidy and the best have balconies with views over the centre. ❹

L'Hostal c/Mercat 18 ☏ 971 53 52 81, ⊛ www .hostalpollensa.com. Six bright and breezy modern rooms with a/c in this family-owned hotel just metres from the main square. ❹

Posada de Lluc c/Roser Vell 11 ☏ 971 53 52 20, ⊛ www.posadalluc.com. This small and very comfortable hotel occupies an attractively restored old stone house in the centre of town. The monks from Lluc monastery (see p.147) used to lodge here when they popped into Pollença to pick up supplies – hence the statue of the Madonna over the front door – and many of the original features have been kept, most notably the deep stone arches and masonry walls. There's a small outside pool and each of the a/c guest rooms has been equipped in an appropriate modern version of period style. ❺

Refugi Pont Romà Camí Vell a Lluc s/n ☏ 971 53 36 49, ⊛ www.conselldemallorca.net. On the northern edge of town, this smart, new, all-year hikers' hostel has a dining area and half a dozen four- to twelve-bunk bedrooms with shared facilities. It's on the GR221 Serra de Tramuntana hiking route (see p.143) – and is a moderately difficult 5hr hoof from the Refugi Son Amer near Lluc (see p.150). Reservations must be made at least five days beforehand. Bunk beds cost €11, breakfast €4.50. ❶

Plaça Major

Although Pollença dodged the piratical attentions of Dragut and his mates, not much of the medieval town has survived and the austere stone houses that now cramp the twisting lanes of the centre mostly date from the seventeenth and eighteenth centuries. The heart of the town is **Plaça Major**, an especially amiable main square, which accommodates a cluster of laid-back cafés and restaurants and is also the site of a lively fruit and veg market on most Sunday mornings. Overlooking the square is the severe facade of the church of **Nostra Senyora dels Àngels**, a sheer cliff-face of sun-bleached stone pierced by a rose window. Dating from the thirteenth century, but extensively remodelled in the Baroque style five centuries later, the church's gloomy interior, with its mighty single-vaulted nave, has a mildly diverting sequence of ceiling and wall paintings, as well as a whopping, tiered and towered high altarpiece. The original church was built for the Knights Templar (for more on whom, see p.175) and passed to another knightly order, the Hospitallers of St John, after the pope suppressed them in 1312. The Hospitallers of St John struggled on until 1802, when the Spanish king appropriated all they owned.

Around Plaça Major

Pollença is dotted with commercial art galleries, the most conspicuous of which is the **Galeria Benàssar**, on Plaça Major (Tues–Sat 10am–1.30pm & 5–8.30pm, Sun 11am–1.30pm). The gallery is named after Dionís Benàssar (1904–67), a local artist whose former home, a brief walk northwest of Plaça Major at c/Roça 14, has been turned into the **Museu Dionís Benàssar** (call ☏ 971 53 09 97 for admission; €2). The museum holds a tidy collection of his Neoimpressionist paintings, brightly coloured canvases amongst which the Mallorcan land- and village-scapes are the most interesting. There's a second small museum – the **Museu Marti Vicenç** (Tues–Sat 10.30am–5.30pm & Sun 10.30am–2pm; free) – in a very old beamed building near the foot of the Via Crucis at c/Calvari 10. This comprises a shop and two rooms given over to the striking textiles created by Vicenç (b.1925), who was born into a family of local weavers, whose motifs he extended into the abstract designs on display here.

If you are roaming out this way, you might keep going north to the old Roman bridge – the **Pont Roma** – which has survived on the edge of town, about 600m away: it's not in itself a remarkable structure, but it has remained intact despite all the historical odds.

The Museu de Pollença

Walking south from Plaça Major, take c/Antoni Maura, and you soon reach a leafy square, whose greenery surrounds an antique water wheel and a stumpy, much battered watchtower. Behind looms the austere facade of **Nostra Senyora del Roser**, a deconsecrated church with a bright and gaudy Baroque interior that is sometimes used for temporary exhibitions. Otherwise, the church is usually closed, but the adjoining cloisters form part of the **Museu de Pollença** (July–Sept Tues–Sat 10am–1pm & 5.30–8.30pm, Sun 10am–1pm; Oct–June Tues–Sun 11am–1pm; €1.50), which houses a surprisingly good and regularly rotated collection of contemporary paintings, photography and video art, including pieces by winners of the town's annual art competition. There's also a modest assortment of local archeological finds, though these are poorly labelled, and a room of **Mallorcan primitive paintings**, most memorably a warm, tender and exquisitely detailed *Virgin and Musical Angels* by Francesc Comes (1379–1415). In the cloisters, look out for the memorial to Philip Newman (1904–66), the Manchester-born violinist who took a real shine to Pollença in the 1950s, founding and fostering its main musical festival, the **Festival de Pollença**, still held here every year throughout July and August (☎971 53 50 77, ⊛www.festivalpollenca.org), with the likes of flamenco star Diego El Cigala and Catalan folk legend Joan Manuel Serrat appearing in recent years.

North of the centre: the Puig de Calvari

Pollença's pride and joy is its **Via Crucis** (Way of the Cross), a long, steep and beautiful stone stairway, graced by ancient cypress trees, which ascends the **Puig de Calvari** (Calvary Hill) on the north side of the town centre. At the top, a much-revered thirteenth-century statue of **Mare de Déu del Peu de la Creu** (Mother of God at the Foot of the Cross) is lodged in a simple, courtyarded **santuari** (sanctuary), whose whitewashed walls sport some of the worst religious paintings imaginable, though the views out over coast and town are sumptuous. On Good Friday, a figure of Jesus is slowly carried by torchlight down from the *santuari* to the church of Nostra Senyora dels Àngels, a procession known as the **Davallament** (Lowering), one of the most moving religious celebrations on the island.

The Ermita de Nostra Senyora del Puig

There are more magnificent views from the **Ermita de Nostra Senyora del Puig**, a rambling, mostly eighteenth-century monastery perched on top of the Puig de Maria, a 330-metre-high hump facing the south end of town. The monastic complex, with its fortified walls, courtyard, chapel, refectory and cells, has had a chequered history, alternately abandoned and restored by both monks and nuns. The Benedictines now own the place, but the monks are gone and today a custodian supplements the order's income by renting out cells to tourists (see p.152). There's nothing specific to see, but the setting is extraordinarily serene and beautiful, with the mellow honey-coloured walls of the monastery surrounded by ancient carob and olive trees, a million miles from the tourist resorts clearly visible far below.

It takes around an hour to **walk** to the monastery from the centre of town: head for the main Pollença–Inca road (Ma-2200), where a signed turning leads up a steep lane that fizzles out after 1.5km to be replaced by a cobbled footpath winding up to the monastery's entrance. It's possible to drive to the top of the lane, but unless you've got nerves of steel, you're better off parking elsewhere. Note that there have been reports of cars left at the foot of the lane overnight being vandalized; although this is unusual, you might prefer to park in town instead.

Eating and drinking

Pollença does very well for **restaurants**, supported by the villa owners who congregate here every evening, strolling in from the surrounding countryside. The **café and bar** scene is less convincing, but there are several reasonably lively spots on and around Plaça Major. Almost all of the town's cafés and bars serve food of some description, mostly inexpensive tapas.

Bar Espanyol Plaça Major 2. Every other place on the main square may heave with the well-heeled and the well-tanned, but the renegades – or at least the semi-renegades – gather here at this old-fashioned, locals' favourite. Drinks are the big deal, but they also serve filling and inexpensive snacks.

Café-Bar Juma Plaça Major 9. Good range of tasty tapas sold in the brisk, modern bar of the *Hotel Juma*. Rapid-fire service and reasonable prices – a standard portion costs about €5. The outside terrace overlooking the main square is particularly pleasant.

Cantonet c/Monti-Sion 20 ☎971 53 04 29. This fashionable restaurant just north of Plaça Major offers top-notch international/Italian cuisine from a limited menu with main courses starting from as little as €12. In the summer, you can eat out on the terrace of the large church next door. Open daily except Tues 7–11pm.

Clivia Avgda Pollentia 5 ☎971 53 36 35. Very hospitable restaurant, and long-time expatriate favourite, offering an excellent range of Spanish dishes – try the squid in ink. If you choose fish, the waiter brings the uncooked version to the table so you can inspect it, which is really rather refreshing. The decor is traditional Spanish and attracts an older clientele. Mains €15–20. Open daily except Wed 1–3pm & 7–10pm.

Il Giardino Plaça Major 11 ☎971 53 43 02. Arguably the best restaurant in town, this smart bistro-style place offers a superb range of Italian dishes from about €14, pastas from €10, all prepared with vim and gusto and featuring the best of local ingredients; try the ravioli stuffed with wild mushrooms. To be sure of a seat on the terrace – where you will probably want to eat – either come early or book ahead. Great house wines too. Open daily 12.30–3pm & 7–11pm; closed Nov to mid-March.

Northeast of Pollença: Cala Sant Vicenç

Love or hate the place – and opinions are equally divided – there's no denying that **CALA SANT VICENÇ**, a modern resort 6km northeast of Pollença, boasts an attractive, solitary setting amongst a set of bare rocky outcrops which nudge gingerly out into the ocean. The problem is the resort itself: some visitors like the modern villas that spill over and around the wooded ravine at its heart, others think they are dreary in the extreme, but most are agreed that the *Hotel Don Pedro*, plonked on the minuscule headland separating two of the resort's beaches, is crass in the extreme. If you are staying in Cala Sant Vicenç, it may be comforting to know that it's easy enough to escape all the development by **hiking north** out onto the wild and wind-licked seashore. The obvious targets are the remote calas that punctuate the coastline, but you could also undertake the moderately strenuous hoof up to the top of **Puig de l'Àguila** (206m), from

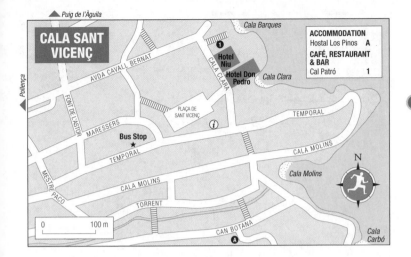

where there are grand views over the surrounding shoreline. This 6km-long hike takes around three hours; the first part uses a rough dirt and gravel road, the second follows a well-defined path that leads to the base of Puig de l'Àguila – but you'll still need a proper hiking map to find your way. If that sounds too much like hard work, the resort has three sandy **beaches**: two on either side of the *Hotel Don Pedro* and a third much larger strand – Cala Molins – on the south side of the resort.

Practicalities

Buses to Cala Sant Vicenç stop in the centre of the resort on c/Temporal, a few metres from the **tourist office** (June–Sept Mon–Fri 9am–1.30pm & 2–4pm, Sat 10am–1pm; ☏971 53 32 64) – and a couple of minutes more from the nearest beach. This is package territory, so vacant **rooms** are extremely thin on the ground, but you might try the two-star Hostal Los Pinos, c/Can Botana s/n (☏971 53 12 10, ⓦwww.hostal-lospinos.com; May to mid-Oct; ❷), which occupies an attractive modern villa with Art Deco flourishes on a wooded hillside on the south side of the resort. The rooms here are furnished in a spick-and-span version of traditional Spanish style, and there's an outside pool.

Amongst the resort's several **cafés and restaurants**, the pick is *Cal Patró*. (☏971 53 38 99; closed Tues), down the steps to the left of the *Hotel Don Pedro*, where the focus is firmly on the seafood – the catch of the day is usually first-rate and costs in the region of €25.

Port de Pollença

With the mountains as a shimmering backdrop, **PORT DE POLLENÇA** is a pleasantly low-key, family-orientated resort that arches through the flatlands behind the Badía de Pollença. The **beach** is the focus of attention here, a narrow, elongated sliver of sand, which is easily long enough to accommodate the crowds, while its sheltered waters are ideal for swimming. A rash of apartment buildings and hotels blights the edge of town, but there are no high-rises to speak of and the resort is dotted with attractive whitewashed and stone-trimmed villas. Altogether it's quite delightful, especially to the north of the marina, where a portion of the old beachside road – along **Passeig**

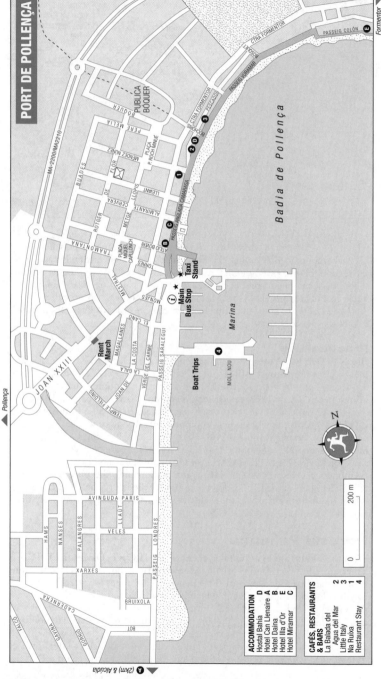

PORT DE POLLENÇA

▲ Cala Bóquer   ▲ Formentor

Formentor ▶

PASSEIG COLÓN   E

CTRA FORMENTOR

PASSEIG MIRAMAR

LIA PIXAR

CTRA FORMENTOR

PUBLICA
BÓQUER

PEREA MELIA

BÓQUER

3

2 D

PLAÇA
P. RIOR MIQUE

MÉNDEZ NÚÑEZ

ESCALAR

BÓQUER

1

BUADES

LLOR

LLEVANT

LLOPIS

ALMIRANTE

CERVERA

METGE

PASSEIG ANGLAD CAMARASA

MA-2200/MA2210

RÜTGER

C

TRAMUNTANA

PLAÇA
MIQUEL
CAPLLONCH

TORRES

B

BATLLE BOVER

MISTRAL

MONGES

Taxi
Stand

★ ★ Main
Bus Stop

i

Marina

Badia de Pollença

JOAN XXIII

MAGALLANES

EL CANO

LA COSTA

VERGE DEL CARME

JOAN DE

LA GALA

TEMPLE FIELDING

Rent
March

PASSEIG SARALEGUI

Boat Trips

4

MOLL NOU

▲ Pollença

AVINGUDA PARIS

HAMS

NANSES

PALANGRES

LLAÜT

VELES

XARXES

PASSEIG LONDRES

BRUIXOLA

BOT

CADENERA

FAGO

GURRIÓ

GAVINA

◀ Ⓐ (2km) & Alcúdia

N

0   200 m

▲ Port de Pollença beach

Anglada Camarasa and **Passeig Voramar** – has been pedestrianized. When – or if – you get bored by the beach, you can also hire a bike and **cycle** out into the surrounding countryside, make the enjoyable hike across to Cala Bóquer (see pp.158–159), or head off to the wondrous mountain scenery of the neighbouring Península de Formentor.

Arrival and information

Buses to Port de Pollença stop beside the marina bang in the centre of the resort and metres from the **tourist office** (May–Sept Mon–Fri 8am–8pm & Sat 10am–5pm; Oct–April Mon–Fri 8am–3pm, Sat 9am–1pm; ☎971 86 54 67, ⓦwww.pollensa.com), which has lots of local information, including accommodation lists, bus and boat-trip timetables and details of car rental companies.

Boat trips of various descriptions are extremely popular in Port de Pollença and they all leave from the west side of the marina. There are regular excursions out into the Badía de Pollença (June–Sept 1 daily except Sun; 2.5hr; €18.50), to Cap de Formentor (June–Sept 4 weekly; 2.5hr; €18.50), and round the coast to Cala Sant Vicenç (June–Sept 2 weekly; 1.5hr each way; €23), but the most popular trip is the quick, twenty-minute hop over to the golden sands of the Platja de Formentor (3–5 daily; €5.30 each way, €10 return), for more on which see p.161.

Local cycling and hiking

The rusticated flatlands edging the Badía de Pollença and stretching inland as far as Pollença make for easy, scenic cycling, and **mountain bikes** as well as ordinary **bicycles** can be rented from *Rent March*, in the centre of Port de Pollença at c/Joan XXIII, 89 (Mon–Sat 9am–1pm & 4–8pm, Sun 9am–12.30pm; ☎971 86 47 84, ⓦwww.rentmarch.com). Ordinary bikes cost in the region of €6 per day or €30 per week. Alternatively, the most obvious **hike** is the delightful jaunt north over to Cala Bóquer, a route that is described in detail on pp.158–159, but for longer excursions contact **Mallorcan Walking Tours – MWT** (℡609 70 08 26, Ⓦ www.mallorcanwalkingtours.puertopollensa.com). This small, independent and local company operates an outstanding range of day-long hikes throughout the year, with the exception of July and August when it's too hot. There is something to suit most levels of fitness and they cover the whole of the Serra de Tramuntana mountains as well as the hilly uplands north of Artà (see p.188). Naturally enough, costs vary depending on the hike but begin at about €27 per person including transport to the trailhead where appropriate, though walkers need to take their own food and water. MWT also do a week-long traverse of the Serra de Tramuntana from Valldemossa to Pollença at a cost of around €480 per person. Potential hikers need to **book** (by phone or internet only) a minimum of 24 hours beforehand, much more for the longer hikes.

Accommodation

Port de Pollença has around a dozen **hotels** and not quite as many **hostales**. Needless to say, most of the rooms are block-booked by tour operators, but there's a reasonably good chance of finding a vacancy in the places listed below, especially in the shoulder season. The part of town you want is the pedestrianized Passeig Anglada Camarasa; try to avoid Passeig Saralegui unless you're indifferent to traffic.

A valley hike from Port de Pollença to Cala Bóquer

6km; 101m of ascent; 2hr return. Easy.

The walk through the sheltered **Vall de Bóquer** is an attractive, easy stroll over the gently undulating ground that lies across the neck of the Península de Formentor. The headland at the end of the walk offers splendid views of the severe sea-cliffs that mark the northern coast with the cove and beach below. Return is by the same route, about 3km each way. The walk is suitable for most ages and abilities – though the last leg down to the beach is uneven and can be difficult for young children. The peninsula is also favoured by ornithologists for the variety of resident and migrant bird life and by feral goats whose acrobatics can be entertaining.

The route

Start by heading north along the seafront from Port de Pollença's marina and then turn left up **Avinguda Bochoris**. Continue across the Carretera Formentor into the Area Publica Bóquer, a green and leafy space with c/Bóquer to either side. Proceed up the green area with the seafront behind you to a triple carriageway road. The footpath starts on the opposite side of the roundabout.

On the far side of the roundabout, keep straight along the path with the ridge of the Serra del Cavall Bernat straight ahead. Approximately 300m further on, the path passes through an iron gate. The **Bóquer farmhouse** is ahead on the right, while on the left, before you get to the farmhouse, is an interesting but neglected **terraced garden** shaped like a ship with its prow facing out to sea: the terraces were watered from stone irrigation channels fed from holding tanks, but these are now all dry. There's a splendid view of the Badía de Pollença from here and some fine examples of the *Agave americana*, a succulent whose flower spikes reach heights of three metres.

Beyond the farmhouse, the path turns round to the right, heading north through a small iron gate, then ascends steadily for about 500m, passing between large rocks. Niches in the rocks are occupied by clumps of dwarf fan palms, and you'll probably see the blue rock thrushes that inhabit the area. Here and further along the walk, you may also spot wheatears, black-eared wheatears, black redstarts, rock sparrows and wrynecks, as well as buzzards, peregrines, kestrels, booted eagles, the occasional

Hostal Bahía Passeig Voramar 31 ☏ 971 86 65 62, 🌐 www.hoposa.es. In a great location a few minutes' walk north of the marina along the seashore, this unassuming *hostal* offers thirty fairly frugal rooms in one of the port's older villas. Closed Nov–March. ❷, ❹ with sea view.

🏃 **Hotel Can Llenaire** Camí de Llenaire s/n ☏ 971 53 52 51, 🌐 www.hotelllenaire .com. Just outside town, this imposing Mallorcan manor house sits on the brow of a hill with wide views over the Badía de Pollença. The owner still operates a farm here, with sheep munching away and groves of almond and olive trees, but the house itself has been turned into a charming country hotel with most of the original features, which date back to the eighteenth century, sympathetically revamped. There are just eleven guest rooms, each decked out in lavish period style. The hotel is signposted down a byroad – the Avinguda de Llenaire – that cuts off from the main coastal road just south of the centre of Port de Pollença. ❾

Hotel Daina c/Atilio Boveri 2 ☏ 971 86 62 50, 🌐 www.hoposa.es. Straightforward, tower-block hotel with three stars, sixty-odd rooms and an excellent bayshore location beside Passeig Anglada Camarasa. The public areas are slick and modern as are the bedrooms beyond with shades of white and grey to the fore. Closed Nov–Feb. ❺, ❻ with sea view.

Hotel Illa d'Or Passeig Colom 265 ☏ 971 86 51 00, 🌐 www.hotelillador.com. Well-equipped, four-star hotel by the waterfront on the northern edge of the resort. Set in its own grounds with its own jetty and beach, the hotel is built in traditional Spanish style and dates back to the 1920s, but the interior is ultra modern – pleasant enough but without much character. Good facilities including saunas, pools and a gym. Closed Dec–Jan. ❽

osprey, Eleonora's falcons in spring and in summer, stonechats and goldfinches. Various warblers pass through this area during migration too, but the big ornithological thrill is the **black vulture**, with a wingspan of around two metres, which glides the air currents of the north coast. There's a fairly good chance of spotting one from the Vall de Bóquer and if you're really lucky you'll get a close view, its large, black body contrasting with a brownish head, beak and ruff.

Beyond the boulders the path descends, becoming less rocky, then passes through a gap in a dry-stone wall before ascending gently for about 150m – a scattering of pine trees 50m to the left offers a shady spot for a picnic. The valley's semi-wild goats have heavily grazed the area, leaving the vegetation sparse and scrubby. The most noticeable plant is *Asphodelus microcarpus*, which grows up to two metres high, bearing tall spikes of white flowers with a reddish brown vein on each petal. Not even the goats like it. Other common shrubs are the *Hypericum balearicum*, a St John's wort whose yellow flowers are at their best in spring and early summer, and the narrow-leaved cistus and spurges, whose hemispherical bushes bear bright yellow glands.

At the top of the next incline the path passes through another wall. About 50m off to the right of the junction of wall and path, more or less due south, is a 1.5m high **tunnel**, inside which is a spring. Be careful, however, if you venture in, as it's popular with goats, who like the water and shade. They'll sometimes panic and charge out if they see you coming.

You then pass through a third wall beyond which the **path splits**. At this point you will notice some stone seats with an appearance of carved wood to the right of the path. To descend to the sea take the path which bears to the left and then runs down alongside a dried-up watercourse amidst the cries of sea birds and the whispering of the tall carritx grass. Patches of aromatic blue-flowered rosemary line the path. The **beach** at the end of the walk at **Cala Bóquer** is disappointing, being predominantly shingle and it can also be littered, although the water is clean and is a good place for a swim. Alternatively, take the right fork to reach the headland, from which there are stupendous views of the sea-cliffs and the cove below. Narrow goat tracks will take you to this headland.

To return to Port de Pollença retrace your steps along the same route.

Hotel Miramar Passeig Anglada Camarasa 39
☎971 86 64 00, ⓦwww.hotel-miramar.net.
Pleasant, three-star hotel in an elegant building –
all iron grilles and stone lintels – that dates back to
1912, when it must have been pretty much the
only building on the beach. The rooms are
standard-issue modern affairs, but it's still worth
paying the extra €25 or so for a room with a sea
view and a balcony – or you might be plonked at
the back looking out over Carretera Formentor.
Closed Nov–March. ❹

Eating and drinking

Port de Pollença heaves with **cafés and restaurants**. Most of them offer
run-of-the-mill tourist fodder, but others serve the freshest of seafood and skill-
fully blend Catalan and Castilian cuisines. As a general rule, competition keeps
prices down to readily affordable levels, with around €12–15 covering a main
course at all but the ritziest establishments.

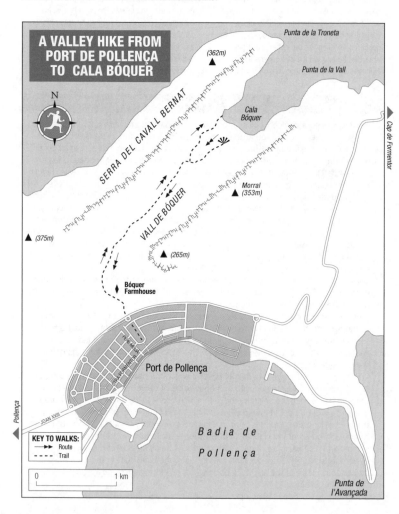

La Balada del Agua del Mar Passeig Voramar 5. Pleasant beachside café occupying an old villa, whose tiny terrace is shaded by an ancient fig tree. Good salads and snacks. Salads €11–13.

Little Italy Passeig Voramar 57 ☎ 971 86 67 49. Amenable, low-key restaurant metres from the beach where the pizzas are large, authentically Italian and very, very good. Pizzas from €8.

Na Ruixa c/Mendez Nunez 3 ☎ 971 86 66 55. On a pedestrianized side street just off the beach, this attractive restaurant, with its traditional Spanish décor and expansive terrace, is especially strong on seafood. Mains average €16. Open mid-March to mid-Oct daily except Tues 1.30–3.30pm & 7–10.30pm.

Restaurant Stay on the Moll Nou jetty ☎ 971 86 40 13. Recently refitted, this long-established restaurant is renowned for a wide-ranging menu in general, and the quality of its seafood in particular – though the main courses tend towards the small size. Décor is crisp and modern, and prices a bit above average, if well worth it for the setting out on the pier; top-notch wine list too. It's a popular spot, so reservations are advised in the evening when mains are anywhere between €16 and €50, but prices are much lower in the daytime. Open daily noon–10.30pm.

The Península de Formentor

Port de Pollença has been popular with middle-class Brits for decades – witness Agatha Christie's crime story *Problem at Pollensa Bay* – but the hoi polloi were kept away from the adjoining **Península de Formentor** by an Argentine swank called Adan Diehl. In 1928, Diehl bought the whole peninsula – a final, twenty-kilometre-long spur of the Serra de Tramuntana – and then built himself the *Hotel Formentor* (see p.162) to cater for his friends and contacts. Since then, the Diehl family and then the government have permitted almost no development and you can now drive to the cape on the final headland and savour the peninsula's stupendous mountain scenery without a villa in view. There may be no development, but you certainly won't have the road to yourself: in the summertime, the road can heave with cars and buses and you're best off going either early (before 10am) or late (after 6pm). There's no public transport to the far end of the peninsula, but there are **buses** (see below) **and boats** (see p.157) from Port de Pollença to the Platja de Formentor.

To the Mirador de la Creueta

Heading northeast out of Port de Pollença, Carretera Formentor clears the military zone at the far end of the resort before weaving up into the hills at the start of the peninsula. At first, the road travels inland, offering grand views back over Pollença, but then, after about 3.5km, it reaches a wonderful viewpoint, the **Mirador de la Creueta**, where a string of lookout points perch on the edge of plunging, north-facing sea-cliffs. There are further stunning views over the southern shore from the **Talaia d'Albercuix** watchtower, but in this case you'll have to brave the wiggly side road that climbs the ridge opposite the Mirador de la Creueta.

The Platja de Formentor

Beyond the Mirador, the road cuts a handsome route as it threads its way along the peninsula, somehow negotiating the sheerest of cliffs before slipping down to a fork in the road, where it's straight on for the cape (see p.162) and right for the *Hotel Formentor* (see p.162). The fork is a couple of hundred metres from the start of the **Platja de Formentor**, a narrow strip of golden sand that stretches east for about 1km beneath a low, pine-clad ridge. It's a beautiful spot, with views over to the mountains on the far side of the bay, though it can get a tad crowded in the height of the season. Most visitors drive here, using the large car park beside the fork in the road, but it's possible to arrive by **boat** from Port de Pollença (see p.157) and by **bus** from Alcúdia and Port de Pollença (May–Oct Mon–Sat 4 daily); buses terminate beside the car park. As you would expect, there is a seashore **café–bar** here, but it really is rather routine and it's well worth stumping up the extra to eat at the beachside *Restaurant Platja Mar* (daily: April–Oct; ☎971 89 91 00), an outpost of the *Hotel Formentor*; the restaurant, which occupies a brisk, modern, two-storey building, serves up delicious grilled fish and a tasty paella.

The Hotel Formentor

Turn right at the fork in the road and it's about 900km to the **Hotel Formentor** (☎971 89 91 00, ◍www.barceloformentor.com; ◉), one of the island's most prestigious hotels, with wonderful terraced gardens that stretch up the hillside behind the beach. Opened in 1930, the Formentor was once the haunt of the rich and fashionable – Charlie Chaplin and F. Scott Fitzgerald both stayed here – and although its socialite days are long gone, the hotel preserves an air of understated elegance befitting its hacienda-meets-Art-Deco architecture. The hotel, which is now owned by the Barceló chain, has every facility, and breakfast is taken on the splendid upper-floor loggia with spectacular views over the bay. The rooms are not quite as grand as you might expect, but are still charming – and it's well worth staying here if you have the cash.

The Cap de Formentor

Beyond the hotel turn-off, the main peninsula road runs along a wooded valley before climbing up to tunnel through Mont Fumat. Afterwards, it emerges on the rocky mass of **Cap de Formentor**, a tapered promontory of bleak sea-cliffs, which offers magnificent views and top-notch **birdwatching**. The silver-domed lighthouse stuck on the cape's windswept tip is out of bounds, but you can gaze at its rocky environs, where the sparse vegetation offers a perfect habitat for lizards and small birds, especially the deep-blue feathered rock thrush and the white-rumped rock dove. From the lighthouse, you can also spy the steep, eastward-facing sea-cliffs which shelter colonies of nesting Eleonora's falcons from April to October, whilst circling overhead there are often ravens, martins and swifts. During the spring and summer migrations, thousands of seabirds fly over the cape, Manx and Cory's shearwaters in particular. For a closer look at the cape, take the steep but clearly marked **footpath** leading along the east coast from the lighthouse to the **Moll des Patronet viewpoint**; allow 15min each way.

If you fancy a snack before heading back from the cape, there's a **coffee bar** next to the lighthouse.

The Badía d'Alcúdia

Moving south from Port de Pollença, it's just 10km round the bay to the pretty little town of **Alcúdia**, whose main claims to fame are its imitation medieval walls and the rubbly remains of the old Roman settlement of Pollentia. The place gets flooded with tourists on market days – Tuesdays and Sundays – but otherwise is really rather restrained and, with its clutch of smart hotels, can make a useful base for exploring this part of the island. The obvious draw is the rugged **Alcúdia peninsula** that juts east from the town, its further recesses holding a fine old chapel, the **Ermita de la Victòria**, and some handsome mountain scenery readily explored on the four-hour **hike** described on pp.168–169 (though you will need a car to get to the trailhead). Just south down the road from Alcúdia lies the mega-resort of **Port d'Alcúdia**, where glistening sky-rises sweep around the glorious sandy beach of the **Badía d'Alcúdia**. In summer the resort is packed to the gunnels but the shoulder seasons are more relaxing and the beach is comparatively uncrowded. In the wintertime you'll barely see a soul, but then most of the hotels and many of the restaurants are closed.

Port d'Alcúdia's assorted hotels, villas and apartment blocks stretch round the bay to the resort of **Ca'n Picafort**, 10km to the south, almost without interruption. The developers drained the swampland that once extended behind this coastal strip years ago, but one small area of wetland has been protected as the **Parc Natural de S'Albufera**, a real birdwatchers' delight. Further behind the coast lies a tract of fertile farmland dotted with country towns, amongst which **Muro**, with its imposing church and old stone mansions, is the most diverting.

Transport connections, particularly from April to October, are very good. Frequent **buses** run along the coast linking Pollença, Port de Pollença, Alcúdia, Port d'Alcúdia and Ca'n Picafort and there are regular buses to all of them from Palma. There is also a useful bus service from Port de Sóller and Sóller to Lluc, Pollença, Port de Pollença, Alcúdia and Port d'Alcúdia, but this only operates twice daily Monday through Saturday between April and October. There is, however, no bus service east from Alcúdia to the Ermita de la Victòria. Regular **trains** connect Palma and Inca with Muro – though Muro train station is a few kilometres out of town (with no bus connection) – and the rail line will eventually be pushed through to Alcúdia. For bus and rail frequencies and journey times, see p.173.

Alcúdia

To pull in the day-trippers, **ALCÚDIA** holds one of the largest open-air markets on the island, a sprawling, bustling affair held on Tuesdays and Sundays, its assorted tourist trinkets taking over the whole east end of the old centre. Otherwise, the town's salient feature is the **crenellated wall** that encircles its centre and although this is, in fact, a modern restoration of the original medieval defences, the sixteenth- to eighteenth-century stone houses within are the genuine item. Nowadays, it's all very neat and trim, but Alcúdia has had an especially troubled history. Situated on a neck of land separating two large and sheltered bays, the site's strategic value was first recognized by the Phoenicians, who settled here in around 700 BC and used it as a staging-post for the sea trade between northwest Africa and Spain. A few Phoenician baubles have been unearthed here – including several fine examples of their delicate, coloured-glass jewellery – but their town disappeared when the Romans razed the place and built their island capital, **Pollentia**, on top of the earlier settlement. In 426 AD, Pollentia was, in its turn, destroyed by the Vandals and lay neglected until the Moors built a fortress in about 800 AD, naming it Al Kudia (On the Hill). After the Reconquista, the Christians began again, demolishing much of the Moorish town and establishing Alcúdia as a major trading centre for the western Mediterranean, a role it performed well into the nineteenth century, when the town slipped into a long and impoverished decline – and what a decline it was: "There is no difficulty in finding a place for shelter in Alcúdia both for man and beast", wrote a certain E.G. Bartholomew in the 1860s, "for by far the greater number of houses are tenantless and doorless." This sorry state of affairs persisted until tourism eventually refloated the town's economy.

Arrival and information

Buses to Alcúdia stop on the south side of the centre beside the ring road, Avinguda del Prínceps d'Espanya. The **tourist office** is about five minutes' walk away, bang in the centre of the old town at c/Major 17 (May–Sept Mon–Fri 9.30am–8.30pm, Sat & Sun 9.30am–3pm; Oct-April Mon–Fri & Sun 9.30am–3pm; ☏971 89 71 13, ⓦwww.alcudia.net). Alcúdia also has its own ultra-modern

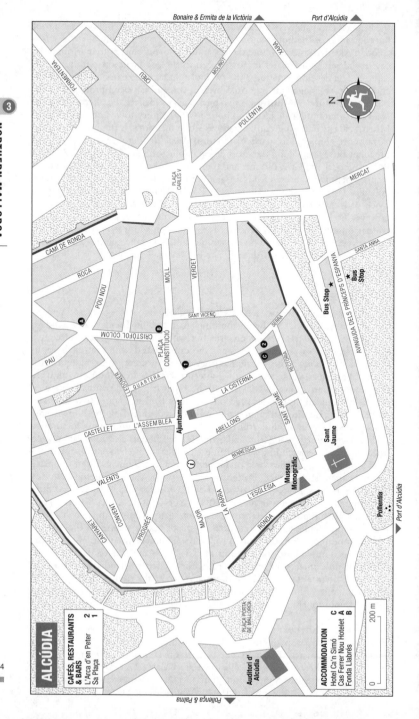

Bonaire & Ermita de la Victòria ▲

Port d'Alcúdia ▲

N

Pollença & Palma ▲

▲ Port d'Alcúdia

Pollentia ▲

FORMENTERA

CREU

MOLINOT

XARA

POLLENTIA

MERCAT

SANTA ANNA

PLAÇA CARLES V

CAMI DE RONDA

ROCA

POU NOU

MOLL

VERDET

SANT VICENÇ

SERRA

Bus Stop ★

★ Bus Stop

PAU

LLEDONER

QUARTERA

PLAÇA CONSTITUCIO

CRISTÓFOL COLOM

RECTORIA

A

B

1

2

C

AVINGUDA DELS PRÍNCEPS D'ESPANYA

CASTELLET

L'ASSEMBLEA

Ajuntament

LA CISTERNA

SANT JAUME

VALENTS

ABELLONS

i

BENNESSAR

Sant Jaume

CONVENT

CANYARET

PROGRÉS

MAJOR

LA PARRA

L'ESGLÉSIA

Museu Monogràfic

RONDA

PLAÇA PORTA DE MALLORCA

Auditori d' Alcúdia

0   200 m

ALCÚDIA

CAFÉS, RESTAURANTS & BARS
L'Arca d'en Peter   2
Sa Plaça   1

ACCOMMODATION
Hotel Ca'n Simó   C
Cas Ferrer Nou Hotelet A
Fonda Llabrés   B

cultural centre, the **Auditori d'Alcúdia** (☏971 89 71 85, Ⓦ www.auditorialcudia .net), which includes a library, theatre and arts centre; it's just outside – and to the west of – the city wall on Plaça de la Porta de Mallorca.

Accommodation

Alcúdia is light on accommodation, but it does possess a couple of smart, new **hotels** in tastefully modernized old premises as well as an inexpensive albeit rather frugal *fonda* (guesthouse).

③

Hotel Ca'n Simó c/Sant Jaume 1 ☏971 54 92 60, Ⓦ www.cansimo.com. Appealing hotel occupying a substantial, three-storey nineteenth-century stone town house that has been sympathetically refurbished; its seven double bedrooms are kitted out in a modern version of period style. ❸
Cas Ferrer Nou Hotelet c/Pou Nou 1 ☏971 89 75 42, Ⓦ www.nouhotelet.com. Self-consciously stylish hotel, with a mere half a dozen guest rooms, in a tall and slender former blacksmith's house dating back to the nineteenth century if not beyond. Wood decking and coffee-table books set the tone, minimalist/modern furnishings do the rest. ❹
Fonda Llabrés Plaça Constitució 6 ☏971 54 50 00, Ⓦ www.fondallabres.com. The cheapest place in town with a handful of sparse, modern rooms above a café-bar, in a nineteenth-century building on the main square. Rooms available both en suite and with shared facilities. ❶

The town centre

It only takes an hour or so to explore the antique lanes of **Alcúdia's compact centre** and to check out the town wall and its fortified gates. This pleasant stroll can be extended by a visit to a series of minor sights, which combine to make an enjoyable whole, although none of them are especially compelling in themselves.

Beginning at the old town's eastern entrance, on **Plaça Carles V**, walk through the gateway and keep to the main drag – here c/Moll – and you'll soon reach the slender **Plaça Constitució**, a pleasant square lined with pavement cafés. Just beyond, on c/Major, is Alcúdia's best-looking building, the **Ajuntament** (Town Hall), a handsome, largely seventeenth-century structure with an elegant balcony, a fancy bell tower and overhanging eaves. From c/Major, take any of the several side streets that lead to the southwest corner of the old town, where you'll find the most diverting of Alcúdia's several sights, the **Museu Monogràfic**, c/Sant Jaume 30 (Tues–Fri 10am–4pm, Sat & Sun 10am–2pm; €3, including admission to Pollentia – see below). The museum consists of just one large room, but it's stuffed with a satisfying collection of archeological bits and bobs, primarily Roman artefacts from Pollentia, including amulets, miniature devotional objects, tiny oil lamps and some elegant statuettes.

Across the street, dominating this portion of the old town, is the heavyweight and heavily reworked Gothic church of **Sant Jaume**, part of which holds a modest religious museum (May–Oct Tues–Fri 10am–1pm; €1). Amongst the museum's assorted vestments, chalices and crucifixes are a few medieval **panel-paintings** illustrative of the Mallorcan Primitives (see p.65). The paintings on display are of unknown provenance, but two sixteenth-century panels stand out – one depicting the Archangel Michael standing on a devil, who is painted red, the second of St John the Baptist, shown – as painterly fashion dictated – with almond-shaped eyes and full lips.

Pollentia and the Teatre Romà

Across the ring road from the church lie the broken pillars and mashed-up walls of Roman **Pollentia** (same times and ticket as the Museu Monogràfic), the disappointingly meagre remains of what was once the island capital. Nearly all the stone was looted by the locals years ago, so you'll need lots of imagination

▲ Teatre Romà

to picture the Roman town, though at least the ruins are clearly labelled and the site is partly redeemed by the substantial, open-air remains of the **Teatre Romà** (Roman Theatre). Dating from the first century BC, this is the smallest of the twenty Roman theatres to have survived in Spain. Nonetheless, despite its modest proportions, the builders were able to stick to the standard type of layout with eight tiers of seats carved out of the rocky hillside and divided by two gangways, though the stage area, which was constructed of earth and timber, has of course disappeared. It's a pleasant spot, set amidst fruit and olive trees, though you do have to put up with the rumble of the traffic from the main road nearby.

Eating and drinking

Alcúdia has more than its fair share of very average **cafés** and **restaurants**, but there are a couple of good places too – and both of them are right in the centre. Also, if you have your own transport, it's worth considering the 6km jaunt out to the *Restaurant Mirador de la Victòria* (see p.168).

L'Arca d'en Peter c/Serra 22 ☏ 971 53 91 78. An ambitious menu featuring local, seasonal ingredients is the hallmark of this attractive restaurant, which occupies a cleverly modernized old stone house and its terrace. The *menú del día* is a snip at €9, otherwise mains average €14. Open April–Sept daily 12.30–3.30pm & 6–11pm; Oct–Mar restricted opening hours.

Sa Plaça Plaça Constitució 1 ☏ 971 54 62 78. Slick and smart restaurant where they focus on traditional Mallorcan/Catalan cuisine – try the house speciality, salted fish (*bacalao*) or their excellent paella. Main courses average €15. Open daily except Wed 11am–4pm & 7–11pm.

The Alcúdia peninsula

The **Alcúdia peninsula**, a steep and rocky promontory to the east of Alcúdia town, pokes a wild finger out into the ocean, its **northern shore** traversed by a country road which begins at the easternmost intersection of Alcúdia's ring road. After about 2km, this promontory road runs past the turning for both the

Fundació Yannick i Ben Jakober (see p.169) and the day-hike trailhead and then weaves its way through the suburban villas of **Bonaire**. Thereafter, the road emerges into more scenic terrain, offering fine views of the Badía de Pollença as it rolls over the steep, pine-clad ridges that fringe the coast.

The Ermita de la Victòria

After about 5.5km, a signed turning on the right climbs 700m up the wooded hillside to the **Ermita de la Victòria**, a fortress-like church built in the seventeenth century to hold and protect a crude but much-venerated statue of the Virgin. It was a necessary precaution: this part of the coast was especially prone to attack and, even with these defences, pirates still stole the statue twice, though on both occasions the islanders managed to ransom it back. The Virgin is displayed in the simple, single-vaulted chapel on the ground floor of the Ermita, but this plays second fiddle to the panoramic views out across the bay. Even better, you can stay the night here as the old monastic quarters up above the chapel have been turned into a delightful *hostal*, the ⚒ *Hostatgeria Ermita de la Victòria* (☎971 54 99 12, Ⓦ www.lavictoriahotel.com; ❶), whose beamed ceilings, ancient stone arches

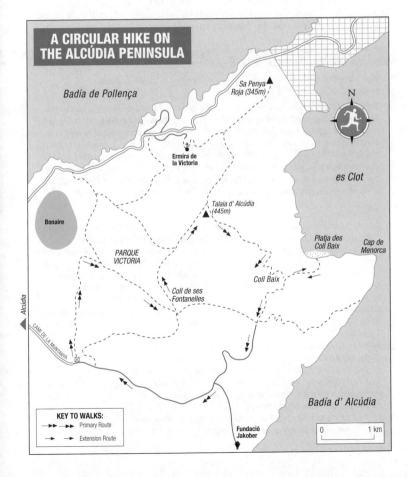

A CIRCULAR HIKE ON THE ALCÚDIA PENINSULA

Badía de Pollença

Sa Penya Roja (345m)

Ermira de la Victoria

es Clot

N

Talaia d' Alcúdia (445m)

Bonaire

PARQUE VICTORIA

Platja des Coll Baix

Cap de Menorca

Coll Baix

Coll de ses Fontanelles

Alcúdia

CAMÍ DE LA MUNTANYA

Badía d' Alcúdia

KEY TO WALKS:
➤➤ ➤➤ Primary Route
➤ ➤ Extension Route

Fundació Jakober

0   1 km

and exposed masonry walls hold twelve en-suite guest rooms decorated in a suitably frugal, but highly buffed and polished style. There's a first-rate **restaurant** here too, the *Mirador de la Victòria* (☎971 54 71 73; Feb to mid-April Tues–Sun 12.30–4pm; mid-April to Oct Tues–Sun 1–3.30pm & 7–11pm), which offers sweeping sea views from its wide terrace as well as delicious food. They specialize in traditional Mallorcan dishes – try the snails, the suckling pig or the guinea fowl – and do a good paella; main courses cost €14 and up.

The Ermita is also a popular starting point for **hikes** out along the promontory, whose severe peaks are dotted with ruined defensive installations, including a watchtower and an old gun emplacement. One of the most obvious targets is **Sa Penya Roja** (345m), from the top of which there are more great views. The outward part of the hike, leading up through woods and beneath steep cliffs, is quite strenuous; return is by the same route. Allow thirty to forty-five minutes each way. It begins on the wide and clearly signposted dirt road that climbs up behind the Ermita, but the later sections are on trails that require a proper hiking map.

The Fundació Yannick i Ben Jakober

Doubling back from the Ermita about 4km, turn sharp left at the *Bodega del Sol* bar onto **Camí de la Muntanya** and, after a couple of kilometres,

---

A circular hike on the Alcúdia peninsula

9km; 450m of ascent; 4hr round trip, plus 1hr for diversion to Platja des Coll Baix. Moderately difficult.

This walk through the heart of the **Alcúdia peninsula** offers stunning sea views, including a 360-degree panoramic vista from the **Talaia d'Alcúdia**, at 445m the peninsula's highest point. The first part of the walk has moderate ascents on tracks, changing to a more strenuous ascent over exposed ground and a rock scramble to reach the Talaia peak. The second half of the walk steadily descends to the Coll Baix and returns through pine woods to the starting point. If time permits, a diversion can be made from the Coll Baix to the **Platja des Coll Baix**, a small secluded and unspoilt beach, returning by the same route. There is parking at the trailhead.

The route

Leave Alcúdia on the road to El Mal Pas and Bonaire. After about 2km, turn sharp right at the *Bodega del Sol* bar onto **Camí de la Muntanya** and continue straight on until you reach, after another 2km or so, Parque Victoria, a nature reserve administered by ICONA (National Institute for Nature Conservation). Leave your car just inside the park near the **iron gates**. The walk starts at this point: take the path on the uphill side of the gates. It climbs gently upwards and then drops into a shallow valley dotted with pine trees. Walk in the direction of a new white house with columns, which appears on the skyline ahead. Pass by the house, which will be on your left, and descend for about 400m following the path until you reach a T-junction. Turn right at this point to begin your **ascent to Coll de ses Fontanelles**. After 2–3 minutes you will arrive at a stream, the upstream side of which has been dammed with a concrete wall. Do not take the obvious path, which continues ahead of you, but bear right to walk along a narrower track above the dam. Continue along this and wind your way up the stoned path to the valley head (Coll de ses Fontanelles). Beyond the stream crossing point, the valley is largely treeless but is densely vegetated with waist-high shrubs.

The **Coll de ses Fontanelles** is populated by a stand of trees including a large olive tree. These offer valuable shade on a hot day and make this a good spot to stop, rest,

continue along the dirt road beyond the trailhead for the circular walk described in the box on pp.168–169. From the trailhead, it's about 2.5km more to the **Fundació Yannick i Ben Jakober** (Tues 9.30am–12.30pm & 2.30–5.30pm; free; Wed–Sat prebooked guided tours only, €9; ☎971 54 98 80, ⓦwww.fundacionjakober.org), where the subterranean water cistern of a sprawling mansion has been turned into a bespoke art gallery. Dating from the 1970s, the **house**, Finca Sa Bassa Blanca, has wide views over the ocean and was built in the manner of a Moroccan fortified palace to a design by the Egyptian architect Hassan Fathy. The owners, the eponymous Jakobers, are art-loving sculptors and the house's **gardens** are dotted with large, modern sculptures. The gallery itself is entirely devoted to **children's portraits** dating from the seventeenth to the nineteenth century. It was Yannick who began the collection in the 1970s, when she picked up a striking *Girl with Cherries* by the nineteenth-century Mallorcan artist Joan Mestre i Bosch. None of the artists represented is particularly well known – and neither are the children – but together they provide an intriguing insight into the way the aristocracy of early modern Spain saw their children as miniature adults. Indeed, many of the portraits were hawked around the courts of Europe in search of a suitable bride or groom. Only from the 1750s onwards, do the children seem more childlike, innocent and relaxed.

take a drink and get your bearings. Moving on, you should take the path to the left of the olive tree (this runs in a northwesterly direction) and ascend through a boulder strewn area. The path continues to ascend over open, rocky terrain and soon affords excellent sea views. Ahead and above you is the **Talaia** on which you will see a stone building. This ground is now exposed and rocky on what is the most arduous part of the walk. Aim for the left of this stone building as the ridge on which it stands is too steep to tackle. Nevertheless, to gain access to the peak you will still need to negotiate a steep although short rock face. This involves an energetic and exhilarating rock scramble. Once on the top you can climb up to the **Trig Point** (stone column) and be rewarded with a panoramic view of the peninsula with sea views in every direction.

To descend, take the path at the other side of the Trig Point, which drops down to a signpost. Here **turn right for Platja des Coll Baix**. The path bears right again and then sharp left. You will now be walking with a deep valley below to your right. Take care here as the path is subject to falling rocks from the left. Upon reaching the ridge, traverse it straight ahead, noting that there are now two valleys: one left and one right of you. Eventually a large pine tree overlooking the sea looms in front of you and the path ascends to the right. When the path zigzags, descend again and at a sharp right turn look below to see a lovely secluded beach, **Platja des Coll Baix**, tucked in tight against the coastal cliffs. Continue your descent until at the bottom you reach a sparsely wooded area, beyond which are picnic tables, a welcome water fountain and shelter. These are provided by ICONA. The sign for Platja des Coll Baix is also here and if you have time, visit to see its lovely turquoise waters. Be aware, however, that **swimming is not recommended** due to the strong undertows.

Return to Coll Baix by the same route and then follow the easily graded **dirt road** to the walk's starting point by the gates. En route you will pass through pine woods, which have an undergrowth of lentiscs, narrow-leaved cistus, carritx, dwarf fan palms, euphorbias, asphodels and the occasional giant orchid; there are also almond and carob groves.

Port d'Alcúdia

PORT D'ALCÚDIA, 2km south of Alcúdia, is easily the biggest and busiest of the resorts in the north of the island, a seemingly interminable string of high-rise hotels and apartment buildings serviced by myriad restaurants and café bars. Despite the superficial resemblance, however, Port d'Alcúdia is a world away from the seamy resorts on the Badía de Palma. The tower blocks are relatively well distributed, the streets are neat and tidy and there's a prosperous and easygoing air, with families particularly well catered for. Predictably, the daytime focus is the **beach**, a superb arc of pine-studded golden sand that stretches south for 10km from the jetties of Port d'Alcúdia's combined marina, cruise boat and fishing harbour. About 500m east of the marina along the headland lies the **commercial and ferry port**, Mallorca's largest container terminal after Palma and the departure point for car ferries and catamarans over to Ciutadella, on Menorca (see box, p.256).

Arrival, information and getting around

Port d'Alcúdia acts as northern Mallorca's summertime transport hub, with fast and frequent **buses** up and down the coast between Ca'n Picafort and Port de Pollença as well as regular buses to and from Palma. There's no bus station as such, but instead most local and long-distance buses travel the length of the **Carretera d'Artà**, the main drag, dropping off passengers at clearly signed stops along the way. The main **tourist office** occupies a distinctive kiosk in what is the effective centre of the resort on Passeig Marítim, just behind the marina (May–Oct Mon–Fri 10am–1.30pm & 3–5.30pm, Sat 9am–1pm; ☎971 54 72 57, ⓦwww.alcudia.net). They have all sorts of local information, including useful free maps marked with all the resort's hotels and apartments.

There's a super-abundance of **car**, **moped** and **bike rental** companies strung out along the Carretera d'Artà. Summer boat trips, leaving from the marina, explore the rocky, mountainous coastline of the neighbouring Alcúdia peninsula: the shorter excursions travel as far as its tip, Cap des Pinar, without venturing into the Badía de Pollença (May–Oct 3 daily; 2hr; €16); the longer

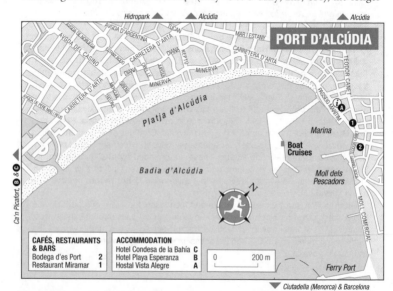

CAFÉS, RESTAURANTS & BARS		ACCOMMODATION	
Bodega d'es Port	2	Hotel Condesa de la Bahía	C
Restaurant Miramar	1	Hotel Playa Esperanza	B
		Hostal Vista Alegre	A

0   200 m

Ciutadella (Menorca) & Barcelona

versions continue round this headland and cross the bay to the Platja de Formentor (April–Oct 1–3 daily; 4–6hr; €21, €26 or €35).

Accommodation

In season, vacant **rooms** are few and far between in Port d'Alcúdia, but there's still a vague chance of finding something amongst the budget *hostales* clustered behind the marina in the oldest – and tattiest – part of the resort. In winter, most of the **hotels and hostales** close down, but in the shoulder seasons it's sometimes possible to get a good deal at one of the plusher chain hotels.

Hotel Condesa de la Bahía c/Rossellas 4 ☎971 89 01 19, ⓦwww.marhotels.com. Mammoth, three-star hotel occupying an L-shaped complex beside the beach about 3km south of the marina. Every facility, from a kiddies' playground to outside pools. ❷ in shoulder season.

Hotel Playa Esperanza Avgda S'Albufera 4 ☎971 89 05 68, ⓦwww.esperanzahoteles.com. Whopping, four-star hotel on the seashore about

5km south of the marina. Has a full range of facilities and splendid, well-tended gardens. ❹ in shoulder season

Hostal Vista Alegre Passeig Marítim 10 ☎971 54 73 47, ⓦwww.hvista-alegre.com. Family-owned, all-year hostal in a plain modern block on the seafront. There are 29 frugal rooms here, both en suite and with shared facilities. ❶

The Town

Port d'Alcúdia marks the start of an intensively developed tourist zone, which was built to take advantage of the great swath of pine-studded sandy beach stretching around the Badía d'Alcúdia. Some lessons have been learnt from earlier developments – there are more recreational facilities and at least some of the coast has been left unscathed – but first impressions are primarily of concrete and glass. The beach and the sky-rises end on the outskirts of **CA'N PICAFORT**, once an important fishing port; its harbour-marina still preserves vestiges of its earlier function but today the town is an uninteresting suburban sprawl.

From June to September, a tourist "**train**" (on wheels, with clearly marked roadside stops) runs up and down Port d'Alcúdia every hour or so during the daytime, transporting sunbaked bodies from one part of the beach to another. Not that there's very much to distinguish anywhere from anywhere else – the palm-thatched *balnearios* (beach bars) are a great help in actually remembering where you are. A boardwalk runs along the back of the beach, which is usually more crowded to the north. Just as crowded, and located a kilometre or so inland along Avinguda del Tucán, is the much-hyped **Hidropark**, a gigantic pool complex with all sorts of flumes and chutes (May–Oct daily 10.30am–6pm; ⓦwww.hidropark.com; €17 for 12-year-olds plus, €8 for 3–11-year-olds).

Eating and drinking

There are dozens of **cafés and restaurants** in Port d'Alcúdia, and although many of them are identikit pizzerias and tourist-style places serving mediocre versions of Spanish food, there are a few distinctive exceptions, two of which stand out.

Bodega d'es Port c/Teodor Canet 8 ☎971 54 96 33. Set on the waterfront, between the marina and the commercial port, and decked out in an appealing version of traditional *bodega* style with wide windows, wooden chairs and a stone façade, this is one of the resort's best restaurants. The prime

offering here is the first-rate selection of tapas from as little as €5. Open daily 8am–11.30pm.

Restaurant Miramar Passeig Marítim 2 ☎971 54 52 93. Well-established seafront restaurant serving a fine range of seafood. A full meal with wine will set you back about €40.

The Parc Natural de S'Albufera

Given all the high-rise development along the Badía d'Alcúdia, the pristine wetland that makes up the 2000-acre **Parc Natural de S'Albufera** (daily: April–Sept 9am–6pm; Oct–March 9am–5pm; free), on the west side of Ca'n Picafort, is a welcome relief. Swampland once extended round most of the bay, but large-scale reclamation began in the nineteenth century, when a British company dug a network of channels and installed a steam engine to pump the water out. These endeavours were prompted by a desire to eradicate malaria – then the scourge of the local population – as much as by the need for more farmland. Further drainage schemes accompanied the frantic tourist boom of the 1960s, and only in the last decade or two has the Balearic government recognized the ecological importance of the wetland and organized a park to protect what little remains.

The park

The **park entrance** is clearly signposted on the Ma-12, about 6km round the bay from Port d'Alcúdia's marina. From the entrance, a country lane leads just over 1km inland to the **reception** centre, **Sa Roca**. Visitors are not allowed to drive down the lane, but there's a small **car park** beside the Ma-12 just east of the park entrance, and **buses** from Port d'Alcúdia to Ca'n Picafort stop close to the entrance too. During the summertime, there's (usually) a **bike rental** kiosk at the start of the lane (€10 per day). At Sa Roca, you can pick up a **free map** and introductory leaflet and visit a small wildlife display in an adjacent building. Note, however, that the map is not especially accurate and, although it's perfectly adequate for short, circular walks, anything more ambitious – say, walking to Can'n Picafort – is not advised as you would almost certainly get lost.

Footpaths and **cycle trails** head out from Sa Roca into the reedy, watery tract beyond, where a dozen or so well-appointed **hides** and observation decks allow excellent **birdwatching** – the best on the island. Over two hundred different types of bird have been spotted here, including resident wetland-loving birds from the crake, warbler and tern families; autumn and/or springtime migrants such as grebes, herons, cranes, plovers and godwits; and wintering egrets and sandpipers. Such rich pickings attract birds of prey in their scores, especially kestrels and harriers. The open ground edging the reed beds supports many different wild flowers, the most striking of which are the orchids that bloom during April and May.

Muro

From the Ma-12 on the west side of Ca'n Picafort, an easy country road heads west across a pancake-flat, windmill-studded hinterland to reach the hilltop town of **MURO**, a sleepy little place dotted with old stone town houses. Muro is at its liveliest on January 16 during the **Revetlla de Sant Antoni Abat** (Eve of St Antony's Day), when locals gather round bonfires to drink and dance, tucking into specialities like sausages and eel pies (*espinagades*), made with eels from the nearby marshes of S'Albufera. Quite what St Antony – an Egyptian hermit and ascetic who spent most of his long life in the desert – would have made of these high jinks it's hard to say, but there again he certainly wouldn't have been overwhelmed by temptation if he had stuck around Muro for the rest of the year.

The Town

Muro's main square, **Plaça Constitució**, is an attractive, airy piazza flanked by old stone houses and overseen by the domineering church of **St Joan Baptista**, a real hotchpotch of architectural styles, its monumental Gothic lines uneasily modified by the sweeping sixteenth-century arcades above the aisles. A slender arch connects the church to the adjacent **belfry**, an imposing seven-storey construction partly designed as a watchtower; it's sometimes possible to go to the top, where the views out over the coast are superb. The church's cavernous interior holds a mighty vaulted roof and an immense altarpiece, a flashy extravaganza of columns, parapets and tiers in a folksy rendition of the Baroque.

From the main square, it's a short walk south to the **Museu Etnològic**, c/Major 15 (Wed, Fri & Sat 10am–3pm, Thurs 5–8pm & Sun 10am–2pm; closed Aug; €3). This is one of the least-visited museums on the island, and the custodians seem positively amazed when a visitor shows up. It occupies a rambling old mansion and showcases a motley assortment of local bygones, from old agricultural implements, pottery and apothecary jars through to Mallorcan bagpipes and traditional costumes. Amongst the agricultural equipment there's a broken-down example of a mule- or donkey-driven water wheel, a *noria*. Introduced by the Moors, these were common features of the Mallorcan landscape for hundreds of years, though there are few of them left today. Among the pottery, look out for the **siurells**, miniature white-, green- and red-painted figurines created in a naive style. Once given as presents, but now debased as a mass-produced tourist trinket, these are whistles – hence the spout with the hole – shaped in the form of animals, humans and mythological or imaginary figures.

That's just about it for Muro, though on a hot summer's day you'll be glad of a drink at one of the **cafés** around the main square. Best of the bunch is *Los Arcos*, a neat modern little place with a good range of inexpensive tapas; it's located at the back of a mini-square, just off Plaça Constitució and across from the church. Muro has a **train station** with regular connections from Palma and the main towns of the central plain, but it's 4km or so away to the west. **Buses** pull in close to the main square.

Travel details

Buses

For further information, call ☎971 17 77 77, or check out ⊛http://tib.caib.es/.

Alcúdia to: Cala Sant Vicenç (April–Oct Mon–Sat 2 daily; 25min); Ca'n Picafort (May–Oct every 15min; Nov–April hourly; 1hr); Palma (Mon–Sat hourly, 5 on Sun; 1hr); Platja de Formentor (May–Oct Mon–Sat 2 daily; 35min); Pollença (April–Oct 3 daily; 20min); Port d'Alcúdia (May–Oct every 15min; Nov–April hourly; 10min); Port de Pollença (May–Oct every 15min; Nov–April hourly;15min); Port de Sóller (April–Oct Mon–Sat 2 daily; 2hr 15min); Sóller (April–Oct Mon-Sat 2 daily; 2hr).

Cala Sant Vicenç to: Alcúdia (April–Oct Mon–Sat 2 daily; 25min); Lluc (April–Oct Mon–Sat 2 daily; 35min); Pollença (5 daily; 25min); Port de Pollença (April–Oct Mon–Sat 2 daily; 30min); Port de Sóller (April–Oct Mon–Sat 2 daily; 1hr 50min).

Ca'n Picafort to: Alcúdia (May–Oct every 15min; Nov–April hourly; 1hr); Muro (Mon–Sat 5 daily, 2 on Sun; 25min); Palma (4–6 daily; 1hr 30min); Port d'Alcúdia (May–Oct every 15min; Nov–April hourly; 45min); Port de Pollença (May–Oct every 15min; Nov–April hourly; 1hr 15min).

Lluc to: Cala Sant Vicenç (April–Oct Mon–Sat 2 daily; 35min); Palma: bus from Lluc to Inca (Mon–Fri every 1–2 hours, 1 on Sat & Sun; 35min), then train to Palma (see below); Pollença (April–Oct Mon–Sat 2 daily; 40min); Port de Pollença (April–Oct Mon–Sat 2 daily; 45min); Port de Sóller (April–Oct Mon–Sat 2 daily; 1hr 20min); Sa Calobra (April–Oct Mon–Sat 1 daily; 1hr); Sóller (April–Oct Mon–Sat 2 daily; 1hr).

Muro to: Ca'n Picafort (Mon–Sat 5 daily, 2 on Sun; 25min).

Palma to: Alcúdia (Mon–Sat hourly, 5 on Sun; 1hr); Ca'n Picafort (4–6 daily; 1hr 30min); Lluc: train to Inca (see below), then bus from Inca to Lluc (Mon–Fri every 1–2 hours, 1 on Sat & Sun; 35min); Platja de Formentor (May–Oct Mon–Sat 1 daily; 1hr 30min); Pollença (Mon–Fri hourly, 7 on Sat & Sun; 1hr 10min); Port d'Alcúdia (Mon–Sat hourly, 5 on

Sun; 1hr 15min); Port de Pollença (Mon–Fri hourly, 7 on Sat & Sun; 1hr 15min).

Platja de Formentor to: Alcúdia (May–Oct Mon–Sat 2 daily; 35min); Palma (May–Oct Mon–Sat 1 daily; 1hr 30min); Port d'Alcúdia (May–Oct Mon–Sat 2 daily; 50min); Port de Pollença (May–Oct Mon–Sat 2 daily; 20min).

Pollença to: Alcúdia (April–Oct 3 daily; 20min); Cala Sant Vicenç (5 daily; 25min); Lluc (April–Oct Mon–Sat 2 daily; 40min); Palma (Mon–Fri hourly, 7 on Sat & Sun; 1hr 10min); Port d'Alcúdia (April–Oct 3 daily; 20min); Port de Pollença (May–Oct every 15min to 1hr, Nov–April hourly; 15min); Port de Sóller (April–Oct Mon–Sat 2 daily; 1hr 50min); Sóller (April–Oct Mon–Sat 2 daily; 1hr 40min).

Port d'Alcúdia to: Alcúdia (May–Oct every 15min; Nov–April hourly; 10min); Ca'n Picafort (May–Oct every 15min; Nov–April hourly; 45min); Palma (Mon–Sat hourly, 5 on Sun; 1hr 15min); Platja de Formentor (May–Oct Mon–Sat 2 daily; 50min); Pollença (April–Oct 3 daily; 20min); Port de Pollença (May–Oct every 15min; Nov–April hourly; 30min); Port de Sóller (April–Oct Mon–Sat

2 daily; 2hr 30min); Sóller (April–Oct Mon–Sat 2 daily; 2hr 20min).

Port de Pollença to: Alcúdia (May–Oct every 15min; Nov–April hourly; 15min); Cala Sant Vicenç (April–Oct Mon–Sat 2 daily; 30min); Ca'n Picafort (May–Oct every 15min; Nov–April hourly; 1hr 15min); Lluc (April–Oct Mon–Sat 2 daily; 45min); Palma (Mon–Fri hourly, 7 on Sat & Sun; 1hr 15min); Platja de Formentor (May–Oct Mon–Sat 2 daily; 20min); Pollença (May–Oct every 15min to 1hr, Nov–April hourly; 15min); Port d'Alcúdia (May–Oct every 15min; Nov–April hourly; 30min); Port de Sóller (April–Oct Mon–Sat 2 daily; 2hr); Sóller (April–Oct Mon–Sat 2 daily; 1hr 50min).

Trains

For further information, call ☎971 17 77 77, or check out ⊛http://tib.caib.es/.

Palma to: Binissalem (every 20min; 30min); Inca (every 20min; 40min); Lloseta (every 20min; 35min); Manacor (hourly; 1hr); Muro (hourly; 50min); Petra (hourly; 55min); Sineu (hourly; 50min).

Southern Mallorca

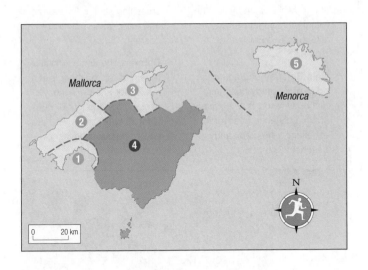

CHAPTER 4 # Highlights

✳ Sineu The most attractive of the ancient agricultural towns of central Mallorca, home to the island's finest parish church and a bustling Wednesday market.
See p.182

✳ Artà Handsome old town, whose honey-stone mansions clamber up the hillside to a much venerated chapel-shrine, while close by lies the remarkably intact prehistoric village of Ses Paisses.
See p.188

✳ Cala Rajada Perched on the edge of a bumpy headland, this busy resort is within easy striking distance of several excellent, pine-clad sandy beaches. See p.194

✳ Coves del Drac Perhaps the finest of eastern Mallorca's numerous cave systems, with fantastically shaped stalactites and stalagmites, as well as one of the world's largest subterranean lakes.
See p.200

✳ Colònia de Sant Jordi Charming low-key resort with several sandy beaches, smashing seafood restaurants and easy-going hotels and *hostales*. See p.207

✳ Cabrera The fiercely hostile terrain of this offshore islet makes for an unusual day's excursion – and lots of rare Lilford's wall lizards will help you with your sandwiches. See p.210

▲ Artà

Southern Mallorca

M ost of **southern Mallorca** comprises the island's central plain, **Es Pla**, a fertile tract bounded to the west by the mountainous Serra de Tramuntana and to the east by the hilly range that shadows the coast, the **Serres de Llevant**. For many visitors the region is no more than a monotonous interlude between airport and resort, and although it may now seem like a sleepy backwater, it was Es Pla that pretty much defined Mallorca until the twentieth century: the majority of the island's inhabitants lived here, it produced enough food to meet almost every domestic requirement, and Palma's gentry were reliant on Es Pla estates for their income. Indeed, Mallorca's medieval kings constructed hilltop fortresses along the Serres de Llevant simply to defend the plain from marauding pirates, leaving the eastern shoreline's smattering of insignificant fishing villages and tiny ports unprotected. This situation persisted until the 1960s, when the tourist boom stood everything on its head and the developers simply bypassed Es Pla to focus on the picturesque coves of the east coast.

The **towns of Es Pla** have largely chosen to ignore the tourist industry and, although things are beginning to change, few put themselves out to attract visitors: accommodation is thin on the ground, good restaurants are unusual and tourist offices rare. Nevertheless, it's here that you can get the full flavour of an older, agricultural Mallorca, whose softly hued landscapes are patterned with olive orchards, chunky farmhouses and country towns of low, whitewashed houses huddled beneath outsized churches. Admittedly, there's precious little to distinguish one settlement from another, but there are exceptions, most notably wine-growing **Binissalem**, with its streets of handsome old houses; **Sineu**, once the site of a royal palace and now one of the plain's prettiest towns; and **Petra**, with its clutch of sights celebrating the life and times of the eighteenth-century Franciscan monk and explorer Junipero Serra. Other sights worth making a beeline for are the impressive monastery perched on the summit of **Puig Randa** and, in the Serres de Llevant, the hilltop shrine at **Artà** plus the delightful medieval castle at **Capdepera**. All these destinations are readily accessible from either the Ma-13, the fast road from Palma to Alcúdia, or the Ma-15, which runs the 70km from Palma to Artà, as are the region's two biggest towns, **Manacor**, noted for its artificial pearl factories, and **Inca**, where the big industrial deal is shoes.

The ancient fishing villages of the **east coast** have mostly been swallowed up within mega-resorts, whose endless high-rises and villa complexes blemish the land for miles. There are, however, a couple of enjoyable seaside towns which have avoided the worst excesses of concrete and glass: **Cala Rajada**, a lively holiday spot bordered by fine beaches and a beautiful pine-shrouded coastline,

SOUTHERN MALLORCA

CABRERA

0   1 km

PARC NACIONAL
DE CABRERA

Cova Blava

Boat dock

French
Memorial

Es Port

Sa Plageta

Colònia de
Sant Jordi
(18 km)

MEDITERRANEAN SEA

N

Port d'Alcúdia

Badia d'Alcúdia

Cala Agulla

Cala Rajada

Capdepera

Coves
d'Artà

Platja de Canyamel

Costa des Pins

Cala Bona

Cala Millor

Sa Coma

S'Illot

Porto Cristo

Coves
del Drac

Coves
d'es Hams

Cala Magraner

Cales de Mallorca

Cala d'Or

Porto Petro

Cala Mondragó

Cala Figuera

Cala Santanyí

Cala Llombards

MASSÍS D'ARTÀ

Ermita de
Betlem

Colònia de
Sant Pere

Ca'n Picafort

Ses
Païsses

Artà

Son
Servera

Manacor

SERRES DE LLEVANT

Santuari
de Sant
Salvador

Cala
Murada

Porto
Colom

MONDRAGÓ
PARC
NATURAL

Santa Margalida

Muro

Sa Pobla

Campanet

Binibona

Selva

Inca

Petra

Ermita de
Bonany

Vilafranca
de Bonany

Felanitx

Castell de Santueri

Santanyí

Ses
Salines

Cap de
Ses Salines

Sant Joan

Els
Calderers

ES PLA

Montuïri

Sineu

Porreres

Campos

Sa
Ràpita

Salines de
Llevant

Es Trenc

Colònia de Sant Jordi

Cala Pi

Santuari
de Cura

Puig
Randa

Randa

Algaida

Pina

Llucmajor

Ses
Covetes

Lluc

SERRA DE TRAMUNTANA

Fornalutx

Port de Sóller

Sóller

Llucalcari

Deià

Son Marroig

Miramar

Valldemossa

La Granja

Esporles

Establiments

Raixa

Bunyola

Alaró

Castell
d'Alaró

Orient

Mancor
de la Vall

Caimari

Lloseta

Binissalem

Consell

Gordiola
Glassworks

Capocorb
Vell

Capocorb

Cap
Blanc

Illetes

PALMA

Badia
de Palma

Ca'n
Picafort

MA-12

MA-15

MA-3

MA-13

MA-15

MA-15

MA-19

MA-19

MA-19A

MA-14

MA-4014

MA-4020

MA-4040

Cabrera (18km, see inset)

0   10 km

and **Cala Figuera**, which surrounds a lovely, steep-sided cove. The former fishing village of **Porto Petro** has also managed to retain much of its original charm, as has the ramshackle old port of **Porto Cristo**. Different again is tiny Cala **Mondragó**, where a slice of coast has been belatedly protected by the creation of a park. The east coast also boasts the cave systems of **Coves del Drac**, justifiably famous for their extravagant stalactites and stalagmites. On the **south coast**, the scenery changes again, with hills and coves giving way to sparse flatlands, whose only star turn is the port-cum-resort of **Colònia de Sant Jordi**, from where boat trips leave for the bleached remoteness of **Cabrera** island.

Given the difficulty of finding a room in the coastal package resorts on spec and the general dearth of **accommodation** in the interior, **advance reservations** are a good idea – and pretty much essential in the height of the season. Potential bases, each of which has a healthy supply of non-package hotels and *hostales*, include Artà, Cala Rajada, Porto Cristo and Colònia de Sant Jordi, though towns like Binissalem and Sineu chip in with excellent hotels too. In addition, three of the region's former **monasteries** offer simple, inexpensive lodgings and usually have space at any time of year. These are the Santuari de Nostra Senyora de Cura, on Puig Randa near Algaida (see p.186); the Ermita de Nostra Senyora de Bonany, near Petra (see p.184); and, best of the lot, the Santuari de Sant Salvador outside Felanitx (see p.202).

Direct **buses** link Palma with almost every resort and town in the region, but services between the towns of Es Pla and along the east coast are patchy. More positively, there are fast and frequent **trains** north and east from Palma to Binissalem, Inca, Sineu, Petra and Manacor with **connecting bus services** leaving Inca and Manacor train stations for surrounding towns and villages.

Binissalem, Inca, Sineu and Petra

The busiest and fastest road on the island, the **Ma-13** motorway, linking Palma with Alcúdia, cuts an ugly swathe through the landscape as it sweeps round the towns on the northern edge of Es Pla, with the old main road, the **Ma-13A**, running parallel to it as far as Inca. The key targets here are **Binissalem**, long the centre of Mallorca's prime wine-growing area and a town of some architectural distinction, and sprawling **Inca**, formerly a grimy industrial town but now a pleasant enough place with a re-energized and revamped old centre. Southeast of Inca, you're into the rural heart of **Es Pla**, whose easy landscapes hold two especially interesting towns: **Sineu**, with its imposing church, and **Petra**, the hometown of the energetic, self-flagellating missionary-monk, Junipero Serra.

Binissalem

BINISSALEM, about 25km east of Palma, may look dull and ugly from the old Palma–Inca road (the Ma-13A), but the tatty, semi-industrial sprawl that straddles the highway camouflages an antique town centre, whose narrow streets hold a proud ensemble of old stone mansions dating from the seventeenth and eighteenth centuries. The Romans settled here, and so did the Moors – Binissalem could be derived from the Arabic "Bani Salaam", meaning Sons of Peace – but the town's commercial heyday began in the sixteenth century, boosted by its vineyards and stone quarries.

Binissalem's main square, the **Plaça Església**, is a pretty, stone-flagged piazza lined with benches where old-timers shoot the breeze in the shade of the plane trees. The northeast side of the square is dominated by the **Església Nostra**

Senyora de Robines, whose clumpy, medieval nave is attached to a soaring neo-Gothic bell tower added in 1908. Inside, the single-vaulted nave is dark and gloomy, its most distinctive features being its glitzy Baroque altarpiece and the grooved stonework that appears above and beyond the high altar. This grooved stonework pops up all over town, representing the cockle-shell emblem of **St James the Greater**. One of the apostles, James witnessed the Transfiguration and the capture of Jesus in the Garden of Gethsemane and was the first of the apostles to be martyred, at the hands of Herod in 44 AD. Despite his early demise, however, Spanish legend insists that he visited Spain and preached here; tradition also claims that James's body was brought from Jerusalem to Spain and buried at Santiago de Compostela in the far northwest of Spain. Although these tales verge on the ridiculous, they made St James one of Spain's most venerated saints. An especially good time to visit Binissalem is in the third week of July, during the week-long **festivities** that precede the saint's feast day on July 25. A second calendar highlight is the **Festa d'es Vermar** (Festival of the Grape Harvest) at the back end of September, when the town's cordoned-off streets are lined with trestle tables weighed down with all sorts of local wines and foods, proudly presented by their makers.

The **Ajuntament** (Town Hall) is metres from the southwest corner of Plaça Església and from here it's a five-minute walk via c/Concepció to **Can Sabater**, c/Bonaire 25, one of the town's most distinguished patrician mansions. This was once the home of the writer Llorenç Villalonga (1897–1980), whose most successful novel was *The Dolls' Room*, an ambiguous portrait of Mallorca's nineteenth-century landed gentry in moral decline. In his honour, the house has been turned into the **Casa Museu Llorenç Villalonga** (Mon–Sat 10am–2pm; also Tues & Thurs 4–8pm; free), with detailed (Catalan) explanations of his life and times as well as his library and study. The house is typical of its type, with elegant stone arches and high-ceilinged rooms redolent of oligarchic comfort. It also has its own chapel: the island's richer families usually had their own live-in priests.

From the museum, it's a five-minute walk south along c/Bonaire to the Ma-13A, which doubles as c/Conquistador, and another five minutes or so west (towards Palma) for the **Bodega José Luis Ferrer**, c/Conquistador 103 (☎971 51 10 50, ⓦwww.vinosferrer.com), which produces the best reds on the island. If you book ahead, you can tour parts of the winery during the

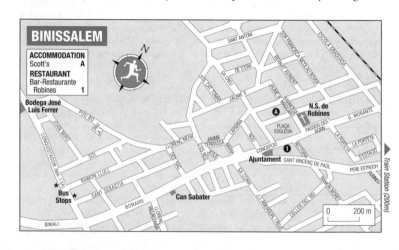

working week (Mon–Fri 2 daily; €6), but most visitors are content to visit the **shop** (Mon–Fri 9am–7pm & Sat 10am–2pm), which stocks the full range of the company's wines.

Practicalities

Buses pull in beside the Ma-13A (c/Conquistador), a few metres to the west of c/Bonaire, which leads straight up towards Plaça Església. Binissalem is also on the **train** line from Palma to Manacor, and regular trains from both directions stop at the station on the northern edge of the town centre. From the train station, it's a five- to ten- minute walk to Plaça Església: head straight down c/S'Estació, turn right at the end and then left at the end of this second street. There's no tourist office.

Binissalem boasts one of Mallorca's most distinctive **hotels**, ⅞ *Scott's*, right in the centre of town beside the main square at Plaça Església 12 (☎971 87 01 00, ⓦwww.scottshotel.com; ❼). The house, which was originally owned by an almond grower, has been tastefully restored, the sweeping stone arches and high ceilings of its public rooms leading to a series of elegantly decorated guest rooms in broadly nineteenth-century style. At the back, the old stone outbuildings surround a leafy courtyard and hold more recent rooms, each air-conditioned and decorated in crisp modern style. Breakfast is served on a sunny terrace at the back of the hotel, and there's a non-chlorinated spa pool. The owner, George Scott, is familiar with every nook and cranny of the island and has put his knowledge to good use in his crime novels, including *The Bloody Bokhara* and *The Chewed Caucasian* (see p.302).

The town lacks a good **restaurant** and the best you'll do is the *Bar-Restaurante Robines*, Plaça Església 25 (closed Tues), an old-fashioned place serving all the Spanish classics with mains averaging about €16.

Inca and around

Poor old **INCA**, Mallorca's third city, just 8km east of Binissalem, has long had a bad press as an industrial eyesore. In medieval times, one of the few ways to keep out of the clutches of the island's landowners was to practise a craft and then join the appropriate guild. As early as the fifteenth century, Inca had attracted enough **shoemakers** to become the centre of a flourishing shoemaking industry – and so it remains today with Camper's HQ and main factory-warehouse firmly ensconced here. This may not sound too enticing, but the town centre has recently been spruced up and the **walk** across its pedestrianized core, from the **train station** in the west to Plaça Orient in the east, is an agreeable way to spend an hour or so. Along the way, you'll spy a scattering of immaculate *Modernista* buildings and the town's main church, **Santa Maria la Major**, an imposing sandstone pile with all sorts of Baroque flourishes.

As you might expect, Inca has oodles of cafés and restaurants with one of the best being the long-established *Ca'n Amer*, a wonderfully old-fashioned cellar restaurant a short walk west of the main church at c/Pau 39 (May–Sept Mon–Fri 1–4pm & 7.30–11pm; Oct–April Mon–Sat same hours, but closed for hols most of Jan; ☎971 50 12 61).

There's no real reason to overnight here, but one of the island's best **finca-hotels** is close at hand near the hamlet of **BINIBONA**, about 8km north of Inca amidst the foothills of the Serra de Tramuntana. ⅞ *Es Castell*, c/Binibona s/n (mid-Feb to mid-Dec; ☎971 87 51 54, ⓦwww.fincaescastell.com; ❺), is a tastefully and sympathetically restored old stone *finca*, parts of which date back to the sixteenth and seventeenth centuries. Accessed by a wonderfully antique gateway-courtyard, with the mountains on one side and the plain on the other, the *finca* occupies a superb vantage point, flanked by olive groves as well as carob, almond, orange and lemon trees. There's an outside pool, books galore and twelve smart and unfussy guest rooms, each of which makes the most of its rustic stonework. Add to this an excellent **restaurant** where they highlight homegrown ingredients – oranges, lemons, honey, figs and a superb olive oil – and Binibona's geographical proximity to Lluc, just a short drive (or 5hr hike) away, and you could stay here for days. To get to *Es Castell* from Inca, drive north on the Ma-2130 to the hamlet of **Selva** and then follow the signs along country lanes for the next 6.5km.

Sineu

Without doubt, **SINEU**, 14km southeast of Inca, is one of the most interesting of the ancient agricultural towns of Es Pla. Glued to a hill at the geographical centre of the island, the town had obvious strategic advantages for the independent kings of fourteenth-century Mallorca. Jaume II built a royal palace here; his asthmatic successor, Sancho, liked the place for its upland air; and the last of the dynasty, Jaume III, slept in Sineu the night before he was defeated and killed at the battle of Llucmajor by Pedro of Aragón. The new Aragonese monarchs had no need of the Sineu palace, which disappeared long ago, but former pretensions survive in the severe stone facade of **Nostra Senyora de los Angeles**, the grandest parish church on the island. Built in the thirteenth century, the church was extensively remodelled three hundred years later, but the majestic simplicity of the original Gothic design is still plain to see. At the side, a single-span arch connects with the colossal freestanding **bell tower**, and close by, at the top of the steps, a big, modern and aggressive **statue** of a winged lion – the emblem of the town's patron, St Mark – stands guard, courtesy of Franco's cronies.

The church overlooks the main square, **Sa Plaça**, a charming medley of old stone buildings that slides into a string of narrow side streets with more of the same. The best time to visit is on **Wednesdays**, when the town fizzes with one of Mallorca's liveliest fresh produce and clothes **markets** (the only one still licensed to sell large livestock), and the cafés round the main square are filled to the gunnels.

Practicalities

There are regular **trains** to Sineu from Palma and several other towns to the east and west. From Sineu **train station**, it's about 500m west up the hill to Sa Plaça, the main square; there are no signs, you just follow your nose. There is no tourist office, but there are a couple of central **hotels**, the more agreeable of which is the *Hotel Son Cleda*, Plaça Es Fossar 7 (☎971 52 10 38, ⓦwww.hotelsoncleda .com; ❷), in a handsome old mansion about 100m from Sa Plaça. The hotel has just eight bedrooms, each of which is kitted out in an attractive modern version of traditional Spanish style. Alternatively, try the less expensive but rather more basic *Ca'n Font* (☎971 52 02 95, ⓦwww.canfont.com ❶), located right on the main square and offering a mere seven rooms. Just outside of Sineu, around 6km to the southeast, there's also *Sa Rota d'en Palerm* (☎971 52 11 00, ⓦwww.sa-rota .com; ❺), a charming rural retreat, set in a tastefully restored, eighteenth-century country mansion with a pool and period(ish) guest rooms. Breakfast features homemade products and, although there's no restaurant, you can reserve dinner beforehand and it will be delivered to your room. To reach the hotel from Sineu, take the road towards Lloret de Vista Alegre. About 500m before you reach that village, take the left turn towards Montuïri and after about 800m there's a sign to the hotel on the left; continue for 2.5km to reach the hotel.

The **best place to eat** in Sineu is the *Celler Es Grop*, a few metres from Sa Plaça at c/Major 18. This friendly place, whose cavernous interior doubles as a wine vault, hence the wooden barrels, serves first-rate Mallorcan meals, with main courses averaging around €12–17 (closed Mon).

Petra and around

Nothing very exciting happens in **PETRA**, 11km southeast of Sineu and 10km northwest of Manacor (see p.188), but it was the birthplace of **Junipero Serra**, the eighteenth-century Franciscan friar who played an important role in the settlement of Spanish North America. Serra's missionary endeavours began in 1749 when he landed at Veracruz on the Gulf of Mexico. For eighteen years, Serra thrashed around the remoter parts of Mexico until, entirely by chance, political machinations back in Europe saved him from obscurity. In 1768, King Carlos III claimed the west coast of the North American continent for Spain and, to substantiate his claim, dispatched a small expeditionary force of soldiers and monks north from Mexico. Serra happened to be in the right place at the right time, and was made the leader of the priests. Even by Serra's standards, the walk from Mexico City to California was pretty daunting, but almost all of them survived to reach the Pacific Ocean somewhere near the present US–Mexico border in early 1769. Over the next decade, Serra and his small band of priests set about converting the Native Americans of coastal California to the Catholic faith, and established a string of nine missions along the Pacific coast, including San Diego, Los Angeles and San Francisco. Pope John Paul II beatified Serra in 1988.

Petra makes a reasonable hand of its connection with **Serra**. In the upper (southerly) part of town, on c/Major, is the chunky church of **Sant Bernat**, behind which – down a narrow side street – lies a modest sequence of majolica panels honouring Serra's life and missionary work. This simple tribute is backed up by a self-effacing **museum** in a pleasant old house at the end of this same side street (Mon–Fri 9am–7pm; donation requested), with several rooms devoted to Serra's cult: the honours paid to him, the books written about him, and the paintings of him. Another room focuses on Serra's work in California, with photos and models of his foundations. Two doors up the street, at no. 6, is the humble stone **house** where he was born (same hours). The museum and house are sometimes locked, but there are instructions posted outside explaining how to collect the key from the custodian.

Finally, Petra is home to one of the star turns of the Pla i Llevant DO (Denominació d'Origen, see p.32), **Miquel Oliver**, who operates a **bodega** in the centre of town at c/Font 26 (Mon–Fri 9am–1pm & 2.30–6pm; ☎971 56 11 17). Oliver is perhaps best known for a dry white, *Muscat Original*, which has garnered a cupboardful of awards.

Practicalities

Petra **train station** is on the northern edge of town, about 700m from Sant Pere, the large church at the north end of c/Major – and a further 500m or so from the church of Sant Bernat. There's no tourist office. Aside from the Bonany monastery (see p.184), **accommodation** is limited to the *Hotel Sa Plaça* (☎971 56 16 46; ❸), which has just three double rooms with big, old furniture and a mix of whitewashed and rough-stone walls. Plaça Ramon Llull is the main square and it's located one block east of c/Major – take either c/Ciutat or c/Sol just a couple of blocks south of Sant Pere. Petra's best **restaurant** is in the *Hotel Sa Plaça;* it's an attractively old-fashioned place, where you can eat traditional Mallorcan cuisine either in the antique-filled interior or on the terrace outside; main courses average around €18. Alternatively, try the (comparatively) funky *Miratar*, a bar-cum-restaurant with lounge sofas, a cellar bar and a huge garden next to Sant Pere at Plaça des Caparrot 7 (March–June daily except Tues 11am–4pm & 7pm–late; July–Dec daily except Tues 7pm–late). Caparrot runs east-west from the church at the north end of c/Major.

Ermita de Nostra Senyora de Bonany

The hilltop **Ermita de Nostra Senyora de Bonany**, about 5km southwest of Petra, offers extensive views over Es Pla. To get there, take the Felanitx road out of Petra and look out for the sign on the edge of the village. The monastery is at the end of a bumpy, four-kilometre-long country lane, and takes its name from events in 1609 when desperate locals gathered here at the chapel to pray for rain. Shortly afterwards, the drought broke and the ensuing harvest was a good one – hence *bon any* ("good year"). The prettiest feature of the complex is the **chapel**, which is approached along an avenue of cypress and palm trees and comes complete with a rose window, twin towers and a little cupola. The monastery's conspicuous stone cross was erected in honour of Junipero Serra, who left here bound for the Americas in 1749. There are five simple double **rooms** (☎971 82 65 68; €24 per double, ❶), one shared bathroom with hot water, and cooking facilities, but you'll have to bring your own food and bedding.

East from Palma to Artà

The fast and busy **Ma-15** whizzes through the agricultural landscape due east of Palma, passing a string of roadside tourist attractions. The most successful of these is the **Can Gordiola glassworks**, which houses a first-rate glassware museum, and **Els Calderers**, a big old country house which is now a museum illustrating *hacienda* life in the nineteenth century. Further east, the highway skirts workaday **Manacor**, the island's second biggest town – albeit a distant rival to Palma with a population of just 36,000 – before proceeding onto pint-sized **Artà**, an attractive little place tucked away amongst the hills of the Serres de Llevant. Artà boasts **Ses Paisses**, one of Mallorca's most complete Talayotic settlements, and is within easy striking distance of the laid-back mini-resort of **Colònia de Sant Pere**, not to mention the assorted coves of the east coast (see pp.193–206). By far the most interesting detour from the Ma-15 is south from near the glassworks to the monastery on top of **Puig Randa**, but the road also passes near Sineu (see p.182) and Petra (see p.183), two particularly appealing country towns.

Buses from Palma to Montuïri, Manacor and Artà are fast and frequent and Manacor can also be reached by **train**. As for **accommodation**, Artà has an excellent hotel, and there are monastery rooms on Puig Randa and near Montuïri.

The Gordiola glassworks

Heading east from Palma on the Ma-15, it's about 20km to the roadside **Can Gordiola glassworks** (June–Sept Mon–Sat 9am–7pm, Sun 9am–1.30pm; Oct–May Mon–Sat 9am–6pm, Sun 9am–1.30pm; free; ⓦwww.gordiola.com), which occupies a conspicuous castle-like building, whose crenellated walls and clumsy loggias date from the 1960s. Don't be put off by its appearance, however, or by the herd of tourist coaches parked outside, for here you can watch highly skilled **glassblowers** in action, practising their precise art in a gloomy hall designed to resemble a medieval church and illuminated by glowing furnaces. Staff are usually on hand to explain the techniques involved – the fusion of silica, soda and lime at a temperature of 1100°C – though this is really part of a public relations exercise intended to push you towards the adjacent **gift shops**. These hold a massive assortment of glass and ceramic wares, everything from the most abysmal tourist tat to works of great delicacy, notably green-tinted **chandeliers** of traditional Mallorcan design costing anything from €2000 to a whopping €20,000 for a fanciful chandelier with coloured glass flowers; more affordably, a single simple goblet will rush you about €25.

The Museum

The gift shops are one thing, but the **Museu del Vidre**, on the top floor, is quite another. The owners of the glassworks, the Gordiola family, have been in business in Mallorca since the early eighteenth century, when the first of the line, Gordiola Rigal, arrived from the Spanish mainland. Since then, successive generations have accumulated an extraordinary collection of glassware, now exhibited in thirty-odd cabinets, each devoted to a particular theme or country, and although the museum is dusty and neglected, there's no gainsaying the quality of the items on display. Unfortunately, the labelling is abysmal and so, to make much sense of what you see, you'll need to invest in a guidebook (€7; on sale at the gift shops).

The **earliest Gordiola pieces** are transparent jugs, whose frothy consistency – provided by trapped air bubbles – was unwanted. Heated by wood and coal, the original hoop-shaped furnaces had windows through which works in progress could be rotated. With such limited technology, it was impossible to maintain a consistently high temperature, so the glass could not be clarified or cleared of its imperfections. Aware of these deficiencies, the next of the line, Bernardo Gordiola (1720–91), spent years in Venice gaining knowledge from the leading glassmakers of the day, and the results of what he learnt can be seen in the same display case. He greatly improved the quality of the glass and also developed a style of Mallorcan-made jugs decorated with *laticinos*, glass strips wrapped round the object in the Venetian manner. Amongst **later Gordiola work**, kitchen- and tableware predominate – bottles, vases, jugs and glasses – in a variety of shades, of which green remains the most distinctive. There's also a tendency to extrapolate functional designs into imaginative, ornamental pieces, ranging from hideous fish-shaped receptacles designed for someone's mantel-piece to the most poetic of vases.

Yet Gordiola glassware is just a fraction of the collection. Other cabinets feature pieces from **every corner of the globe**, beginning with finds from Classical Greece, the Nile and the Euphrates. There's also an exquisite sample of early Islamic glassware, Spanish and Chinese opalescents, and superb Venetian vases dating from the seventeenth and eighteenth centuries. More modern items include goblets from Germany and Poland, traditional Caithness crystal from Scotland, and a striking melange of Swedish Art Nouveau glasswork. The museum also exhibits decorative items from cultures where glass was unknown – an eclectic ensemble of pre-Columbian pieces worked in clay, quartz and obsidian, along with the zoomorphic and anthropomorphic basalt figures characteristic of the Sahara.

Algaida and Randa

ALGAIDA, just off the main highway 2km or so east of the glassworks, is typical of the small agricultural towns that dot Mallorca's central plain – low, whitewashed houses fanning out from an old Gothic-Baroque church. There's nothing remarkable about the place, but it's a veritable metropolis compared with some of its neighbours: as late as the 1980s, a young British anthropologist, who was here to research rural communities, spent several months living in the hamlet of **Pina**, just north of Algaida. It was an eye-opener: she was criticized for having her light on late at night (she should have been sleeping) and for wanting to live on the edge of the village (she must have something to hide), but the final straw was the anonymous letters she received suggesting that she was only there to entice a young man back to the UK.

From Algaida it's about 4km south to the turning for **Puig Randa**, at 540m the highest of a slim band of hills that lies between Algaida and Llucmajor. The road to the summit – a well-surfaced but serpentine affair, some 5km long – starts by climbing through **RANDA**, a tiny little place of old stone houses harbouring a comfortable three-star **hotel**, ⚲ *Es Reco de Randa*, at c/Font 21 (☎971 66 09 97, Ⓦ www.esrecoderanda.com; ❻). The hotel has just fourteen guest rooms decorated in traditional Spanish style and comes complete with an outdoor swimming pool on a balustraded terrace that offers panoramic views over the plain below. The place is usually booked up months in advance during the summer, but there are often vacancies out of season, and there's also a delightful ⚲ **restaurant**, where the specialities include roast lamb and suckling pig.

Puig Randa

The top of **Puig Randa** is flat enough to accommodate a substantial walled complex, the **Santuari de Nostra Senyora de Cura** (Hermitage of Our Lady of Cura), with Cura being the name of the upper part of the mountain. Entry is through a seventeenth-century portal, but most of the buildings beyond are plain and modern, the work of the last incumbents, Franciscan monks who arrived in 1913 after the site had lain abandoned for decades. The scholar and missionary **Ramon Llull** (see p.75) founded the original hermitage in the thirteenth century, and it was here that he prepared his acolytes for their missions to Asia and Africa. Succeeding generations of Franciscans turned the site into a centre of religious learning, and the scholastic tradition was maintained by a grammar school, which finally fizzled out in 1826. The Llull connection makes the monastery an important place of pilgrimage, especially for the **Benedicció del Fruita** (Blessing of the Crops), held on the fourth Sunday after Easter.

Nothing remains of Llull's foundation. The oldest surviving building is the quaintly gabled **chapel**, parts of which date from the 1660s. Situated to the right of the entrance, the chapel is homely and familiar, its narrow, truncated nave spanned by a barrel-vaulted roof. Next door, in the old school, there's a modest **museum** (daily 10.30am–1.30pm & 3–6pm; donation requested) with a collection of ecclesiastical bric-a-brac and a few interesting old photos taken by the Franciscans before they rebuilt the place.

The Santuari de Sant Honorat and the Santuari de Gràcia

There are two other, less significant sanctuaries on the lower slopes of Puig Randa. Heading back down the hill, past the radio masts, it's a couple of kilometres to the easily missable sharp left turn for the **Santuari de Sant Honorat**, which comprises a tiny church and a few conventual buildings of medieval provenance. Back on the main summit road, a further 1.2km down the hill, is the more appealing third and final monastery, the **Santuari de Gràcia**, which is approached through a signposted gateway on the left and along a short asphalt road. Founded in the fifteenth century, the whitewashed walls of this tiny sanctuary are tucked underneath a severe cliff face, which throngs with nesting birds. The simple barrel-vaulted church boasts some handsome majolica tiles, but it's the panoramic view of Es Pla's rolling farmland that holds the eye.

Practicalities

If you decide to stay the night, head for the **information office** by the sanctuary's main entrance, where you can fix yourself up with a **room** in the guest quarters (℡971 12 02 60, ⓦwww.santuariodecura.com; ❶). These 35 en-suite rooms, which have recently been refurbished in plain but pleasant modern style, occupy a self-contained block. An extra €20 per person per night is charged for one of the four rooms with a balcony. The sanctuary's terrace **café** offers average food, good coffee and superb views out across the island.

Els Calderers

East of Algaida, tucked away at the end of a country lane 2km north of – and clearly signposted from – the Ma-15 between Montuïri and Vilafranca de Bonany is **Els Calderers** (daily: April–Oct 10am–6pm; Nov–March 10am–5pm; €8; ⓦwww.elscalderers.com). Dating mostly from the eighteenth century, this charming country house bears witness to the wealth and influence once enjoyed by the island's landed gentry – in this case the **Veri family**. The house was the focus of a large estate that produced a mixed bag of agricultural produce. The main cash crop was originally grapes, but the phylloxera aphid destroyed the vineyards and the Veris switched to cereals, before subsequently experimenting with a variety of other crops. Indeed, at the beginning of the twentieth century the Veris were at the forefront of efforts to modernize Mallorcan agriculture, much to the consternation of some of their more stick-in-the-mud neighbours, and to the horror of a workforce used to more traditional methods.

The house

Flanked by a pair of crumpled-looking lions, the entrance to the **house** leads to a sequence of handsome rooms surrounding a cool courtyard with a well. All are kitted out with antique furniture, *objets d'art* and family portraits, and each has a clearly defined function, from the dainty music room to the hunting room, with assorted stuffed animal heads, and the **master's office**, with big armchairs and a polished desk. You can also see the family's tiny chapel (like every landowning family on the island, the Veris had a live-in priest), and there's more religious material upstairs in the assorted prints which line the walls. They're neither original nor of good quality, but they give the flavour of the mawkish piety that characterized the island's landed class in the late nineteenth century. Attached to, but separate from, the family house are the living quarters of the *missatge* (farm manager), the barn and the farmworkers' kitchen and eating area. To complete your visit, take a stroll round the **animal pens**, though don't expect to see much farmyard activity in the heat of the day. The animals are breeds traditionally used on Mallorcan farms, though they're here to illustrate the past rather than to be of any practical use.

It takes an hour or so to wander round the house and the adjacent animal pens, more if you stop at the simple little **café**, where they serve traditional Mallorcan snacks: the *pa amb oli* (bread rubbed with olive oil) with ham and cheese is delicious.

Manacor

Hometown of the tennis star Rafael Nadal, industrial **MANACOR** declares its business long before you arrive, with vast roadside hoardings promoting its furniture, wrought-iron and artificial pearl factories. On the strength of these, Manacor has risen to become Mallorca's second city, much smaller than Palma, but large enough to have spawned unappetizing suburbs on all sides. More positively, Manacor's **old centre** has been attractively restored, with a string of bustling squares, pretty churches and an impressive convent.

Manacor's prinicipal attraction is the **Església Nostra Senyora Verge dels Dolors** (daily 8.30am–12.45pm & 5.30–7.30pm; free), a sprawling stone church built on the site of the Moors' main mosque in the thirteenth century, though what you see today is mostly neo-Gothic. The church abuts **Plaça Rector Rubí**, a busy square that is home to the *Palau Café* (closed Sun), at no. 8, where you can sample a local speciality, spicy pork sausage made from black pig (*sobrasada de cerdo negro*). From the square, it's a short walk northwest to Manacor's other main sight, the **Convent de Sant Vicenç Ferrer** (Mon–Fri 8am–2pm & 5–8pm; free), on Plaça Convent, a good-looking Baroque complex dating from the late sixteenth century.

Despite these two ecclesiastical attractions, most visitors skip the centre. Instead they stick to the ring road, close to which, on the north side of town on c/Pedro Riche, is the **Perlas Majorica artificial pearl factory**, signposted as the Pearl Centre (Mon–Fri 9am–7pm, Sat & Sun 10am–1pm; July–Sept Mon–Sat 10am–8pm, Sun 10am–7pm; free), which offers a somewhat perfunctory **free factory tour** and a general insight into the manufacturing process. The core of the imitation pearl is a glass globule onto which are painted many layers of a glutinous liquid primarily composed of fish scales. Artificial pearls last longer than, and are virtually indistinguishable from, the real thing and are consequently expensive - as you will discover if you visit the showroom. Also located just outside the city centre, in a medieval stone enclosure on the road to Cales de Mallorca, is the **Museu d'Història de Manacor** (mid-June to mid-Sept Mon & Wed–Sat 9.30am–2.30pm & 6–8.30pm; mid-Sept to mid-June Mon & Wed–Sat 10am–2pm & 5–7.30pm, Sun 10.30am–1pm; free), which holds a small but interesting collection of archeological finds, especially ceramics. In particular, look out for the well-preserved sixth-century mosaics.

Practicalities

Manacor **train and bus station** are located on the northwest edge of the old centre, about 1km from Plaça Rector Rubí. The **tourist office** is about 300m south of Plaça Rector Rubí on Plaça Ramon Llull (Mon–Fri 9.30am–1.30pm; ☎971 84 72 41, ⓦwww.manacor.org); they have a useful selection of local information, including a map marking the town's architectural high points. There's no obvious reason to overnight here, but nearby, just 4km or so north of town, is *La Reserva Rotana* (☎971 84 56 85, ⓦwww.reservarotana .com; ❾), a luxury resort in a much extended and tastefully modernized old manor house. Facilities include a pool and spa and the place even has its own nine-hole golf course. Suites are decorated with unusual antiques and there's also a top-notch restaurant where the menu is firmly Mediterranean; count on around €60 a head for a full dinner. If this all sounds much too expensive, then it's a five-minute drive through pastureland to the more secluded – and much more affordable – *Mayolet Agriturismo* (☎971 84 56 85, ⓦwww.mayolet .com; ❺), which has just eight rooms kitted out in a modern rendition of traditional Spanish style plus a pool and a small terrace overlooking the vineyards.

Artà and around

Beyond Manacor, the Ma-15 veers northeast to run parallel to the coast, with the flatlands soon left behind for the easy peaks of the **Serres de Llevant**. The top end of this mountain range bunches to fill out Mallorca's eastern corner, providing a dramatic backdrop to **ARTÀ**, an ancient hill-town of sun-bleached roofs clustered beneath a castellated chapel-shrine. It's a delightful scene, even though at close quarters the town's cobweb of cramped and twisted alleys doesn't quite match the setting until you clamber up to the **Santuari de Sant Salvador**, long a place of pilgrimage and offering wonderous views back over the central plain, Es Pla.

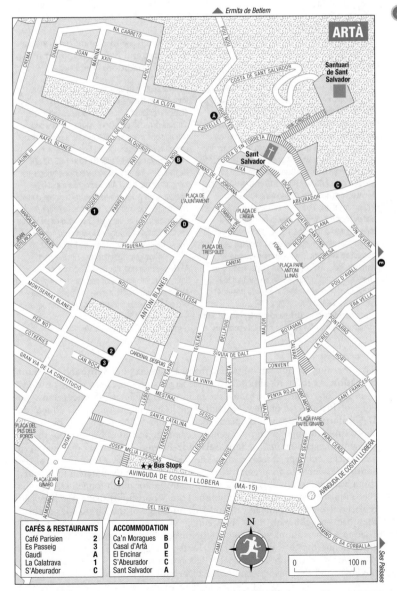

Arrival and information

Buses to Artà stop beside the Ma-15 on the southern edge of the town centre. From the bus stops, it's a couple of hundred metres west to the foot of the short main street, **c/Ciutat**. The town **tourist office** (Mon–Fri 10am–2pm; ☎971 83 69 81) is in the old train station on the western reaches of the Ma-15. They have a useful selection of local information, including a free town map and an illustrated heritage trail leaflet. There's a **market** on Plaça del Conqueridor every Tuesday.

Accommodation

Artà has four small, good-quality **hotels**, all of which are in elegant town houses in the old centre between Plaça de L'Ajuntament and Sant Salvador. You can also opt for a rural stay just 5km out of town in a traditional *finca*.

Ca'n Moragues Pou Nou 12 ☎971 82 95 09, Ⓦwww.canmoragues.com. Decorated in calming shades of yellow and cream, some of this hotel's eight comfortable rooms oversee a courtyard garden with a small swimming pool and sauna – the two ground-floor rooms give directly onto the garden, the others are upstairs. Watch out for the two pet turtles, who are very willing to share your breakfast. ❹

Casal d'Artà c/Rafael Blanes 19 ☎971 82 91 63, Ⓦwww.casaldarta.de. Overlooking Plaça de L'Ajuntament, the *Casal d'Artà* occupies an immaculately restored, three-storey former grandee's mansion dating from the 1930s. It still has much of the original decor – stained glass, wooden ceilings, decorative ironwork, tiled walls and antique furniture, including several four-poster beds. There's a charming sun terrace on the roof too. ❸

El Encinar Carretera Artà-Son Servera (Ma-4041) ☎971 18 38 60 or 639 38 59 74, Ⓦwww .elencinardearta.com. This handsomely restored and immaculately maintained country estate occupies

an ideal spot 'twixt town and beach, about 5km from Artà on the Ma-4041 road to Son Servera. The eleven traditionally decorated rooms, sited in the airily modernized old manor house, breathe oodles of atmosphere and facilities include a pool, restaurant and lush garden. Closed Nov–Feb. ❹

S'Abeurador c/Abeurador 21 ☎971 83 52 30. Named after the ancient stone drinking trough just along the road, the *S'Abeurador* has a lushly planted, multi-level roof garden, its terraces dotted with ponds and arbours. Decorated in both rustic and modern styles, the well-appointed guest rooms are distributed in several different buildings. ❷

Sant Salvador c/Castellet 7 ☎971 82 95 55, Ⓦwww.santsalvador.com. Once a grand *Modernista* mansion, the *Sant Salvador* is now a luxury hotel with an interior decorated in vibrant Almodóvar colours. Six of the eight rooms – each decorated in a different style and some with Jacuzzis – have balconies. Their top-notch restaurant is an added bonus. ❻

The Town

The ten-minute trek up to Artà's main attraction, the **Santuari de Sant Salvador**, is a must. It's almost impossible to get lost – just keep going upwards: from the foot of the town, follow the main street, c/Ciutat, as it slices across the edge of Plaça del Conqueridor, and then head straight on up to **Plaça de L'Ajuntament**, a leafy little piazza that is home to the town hall. Beyond, a short stroll through streets of gently decaying mansions brings you to the gargantuan parish church of **Sant Salvador**. From this unremarkable pile, steep stone steps and cypress trees lead up the **Via Crucis** (Way of the Cross) to the **santuari**, which, in its present form, dates from the early nineteenth century, though the hilltop has been a place of pilgrimage for much longer. During the Reconquista, Catalan soldiers demolished the Moorish fort that stood here and replaced it with a shrine accommodating an image of the Virgin Mary, which they had brought with them. This edifice was, in its turn, knocked down in 1820 in a superstitious – and ultimately fruitless – attempt to stop the spread of an epidemic that was decimating the local population. Built a few years later, the interior of the present chapel is hardly awe-inspiring – the paintings are mediocre and the curious statue of Jesus behind the altar has him smiling as if he has lost his mind – but the views are exquisite, with the picturesque town below and Es Pla stretching away to distant hills.

Ses Països

On the southern peripheries of Artà, about 800m from the ring road, lie the substantial and elegiacally rustic remains of the Talayotic village of **Ses Països** (April–Oct Mon–Sat 10am–12.30pm & 2.30–6pm; Nov–March Mon–Sat 9am–1pm & 2.30–5pm; €2). To get there, walk east from c/Ciutat along the main through-road and watch for the signposted – and well-surfaced – country lane on the right. A clear footpath explores every nook and cranny of the site, and its numbered markers are thoroughly explained in the English-language **leaflet** available at the entrance.

Tucked away in a grove of olive, carob and holm-oak trees, the prehistoric village is entered through a **monolithic gateway**, whose heavyweight jambs and lintels interrupt the Cyclopean walls that still encircle the site. These outer remains date from the second phase of the Talayotic culture (c.1000–800 BC), when the emphasis was on consolidation and defence; in places, the walls still stand at their original size, around 3.5m high and 3m thick. Beside the gate, there's also a modern plinth erected in honour of Miquel Llobera, a local writer who penned romantic verses about the place. Beyond the gateway, the central **talayot** is from the first Talayotic phase (c.1300–1000 BC), its shattered ruins flanked by the foundations of several rooms of later date and uncertain purpose. Experts believe the horseshoe-shaped room was used, at least towards the end of the Talayotic period, for cremations, whilst the three rectangular rooms were probably living quarters. In the rooms, archeologists discovered iron objects and ceramics imported from elsewhere in the Mediterranean. Some of them were perhaps brought back from the Punic Wars (264–146 BC) by mercenaries – the skills of Balearic stone slingers were highly prized by the Carthaginians, and it's known that several hundred accompanied Hannibal and his elephants over the Alps in 218 BC.

Eating and drinking

There are several **café–restaurants** dotted along c/Ciutat, the main commercial drag. A couple of hotels chip in with quality restaurants too.

Café Parisien c/Ciutat 18 ☎971 83 54 40. A chic little place with a shaded courtyard garden at the back. Their tasty and reasonably priced soups, salads and Italian-influenced dishes are based on what is freshly available in the market. Closed Sun.

Es Passeig c/Ciutat 22 ☎971 82 92 75. Quality restaurant with a traditional menu emphasizing Mallorcan cooking in an up-to-the-minute setting. Mains hover around €15.

Gaudi c/Castellet 7 ☎971 82 95 55. Stylish place located in the *Hotel Sant Salvador* (see p.190), and featuring great Mediterranean cuisine with a modern twist; you can eat indoors or outside on the terrace overlooking the swimming pool and gardens. Daily 1–3pm & 7.30–10pm.

La Calatrava c/de los Roques 13 ☎971 83 66 63. The most luxurious option in town with a lovely inner courtyard and a menu comprising delicacies such as red tuna tartar or lobster with wild asparagus. Closed Sun.

S'Abeurador c/Abeurador 21 ☎971 83 52 30. Located in the hotel of the same name, this decent restaurant is run by a German family and specializes in fresh food bought daily from the market. Wed–Sun 7.30–11pm.

Around Artà: the Ermita de Betlem

Hidden away in the hills 10km northwest of Artà, the **Ermita de Betlem** is a remote and minuscule hermitage founded in 1805. In itself, the *ermita* is not a major pull, but the scenery hereabouts is lovely. The route begins on the north side of Artà, but the start is poorly signed and tricky to find: aim for c/Figueretes, go past the *Hotel Sant Salvador* and then follow the signs. The

▲ Ermita de Betlem

road's rough surface and snaking course also make for a difficult drive, so an alternative is to **walk** – reckon on five or six hours for the return trip. The first portion is an easy stroll up along the wooded valley of the **Torrent des Cocons**, but then – after about 3km – the road squeezes through the narrowest of defiles, with the hills rising steeply on either side. Beyond, the road begins to climb into the hills of the Serra de Llevant – here the **Massís d'Artà** – until, some 3km after the defile, a signposted turn signals the start of the strenuous part of the journey. Here, the track wriggles for 4km up and down the steep hillside before finally reaching the *ermita* at the end of a cypress-lined path.

Amongst the huddle of old stone buildings that comprise the hermitage, the **church** is perhaps the most interesting structure, its ponderous frame holding crude religious paintings on the walls and a poor-quality fresco on the ceiling. The *ermita*'s only facility is a small shop (with uncertain opening hours) that sells religious trinkets and postcards, but there's more than enough compensation in the panoramic views down along the coast and across the Badía d'Alcúdia. A hiking trail leads down from the *ermita* to the bay, ending up on the road just to the east of Colònia de Sant Pere (see below), but this is a difficult hike and you'll need to be properly equipped. Incidentally, if you haven't taken your own picnic, then you can make a pit-stop at the **restaurant** *Sa Tafona de Son Fang* (☏971 82 95 91; closed Wed), just 3km or so out from Artà. In this galleried *finca*, which once housed an ancient oil press (*tafona*), you'll find a good range of Mallorcan dishes – they're particularly proud of their charcoal-grilled specialities.

Colònia de Sant Pere

West of Artà, the **Ma-12** ploughs through the hills on its way to Ca'n Picafort and Port d'Alcúdia. On the way, it passes the turning for **COLÒNIA DE SANT PERE**, a downbeat resort and one-time fishing village nestled beside the Badía d'Alcúdia, with the stern escarpments of the Massís d'Artà for a backdrop. Founded in 1881, Colònia de Sant Pere is no more than a few blocks wide, its plain, low-rise modern buildings set behind a pocket-sized sandy beach, and although a flurry of recent building work has festooned the village with villa complexes, at least local planning laws prohibit the construction of houses over two storeys high. It's all very low-key and laid-back – perfect for families with young children – and this, along with the setting, is its charm as a day-trip destination or for a longer stay, though accommodation is light on the ground unless you've booked a villa.

Practicalities

Colònia de Sant Pere is light on **accommodation**, the only appealing central choice being the recently opened *Hotel Rocamar* (℡971 82 85 03, Ⓦwww .hotelrocamar.net; ❹), a bright, homely sort of place with a rooftop terrace just in from the seashore at c/Sant Mateu 9. For fresh fish you can pick any of the first-rate **restaurants** along the boulevard or at the harbour. On the seafront, one of the best choices is the *Blau Mari* (℡971 58 94 07; closed Nov–Feb), which specializes in seafood and paellas – and there's even a tank from which you can select your own live lobster. Further along the seafront, and with its terrace overlooking the harbour, stands the *Café & Restaurant Club Nautic* (℡971 58 90 09), which serves excellent paellas and *bacalao al ajo confitado* (salt cod with garlic confit), or you can enjoy good-value salads, pastas and fresh seafood at *Es Vivers* (℡971 58 94 78) whilst sitting in the shade of the tamarisks; *Es Vivers* is also *the* place to go in the afternoons to sample their home-made fruit flans (apple, lemon, apricot, strawberry) and cheesecakes.

The east coast

Stretching south for about 60km from Cala Rajada to Cala Santanyí, **Mallorca's east coast** is fretted by narrow coves, the remnants of prehistoric river valleys created when the level of the Mediterranean was much lower. All of these inlets have accrued at least some development, ranging from a mild scattering of second homes to intensive chains of tower blocks, but everywhere it's tourism – and the tourist economy – that holds sway. An attractive minor road links the resorts, running for the most part a few kilometres inland along the edge of the **Serres de Llevant**, a slim band of grassy hills which rises to over 500m at its two extremities, south outside Felanitx and north around Artà. If you have your own transport, this coastal route enables you to pick and choose destinations with the greatest of ease, dodging the crassest examples of over-development – principally Cala Millor, Calas de Mallorca and Cala d'Or – altogether.

Amongst the larger resorts, boisterous **Cala Rajada** is easily the most enticing, especially as it is within easy reach of excellent sandy beaches, and the lovely medieval fortress of **Capdepera**. South of here, the old port of **Porto Cristo** has a dishevelled charm, which is much more than can be said for the burgeoning bargain-basement resort of nearby **Porto Colom**. By contrast, **Porto Petro** is small and really rather demure, whilst **Cala Figuera** is a lively, medium-sized resort, which possesses some fine restaurants. At the southern end of the east coast are the relatively untouched beaches of **Cala Mondragó**, now protected as **Mondragó Parc Natural**. The east coast is also famous for its limestone cave systems, with the most impressive formations found at the **Coves d'Artà** in the north, and the **Coves del Drac** at Porto Cristo.

It would be lovely to work your way down the coast, stopping for a couple of nights here and there, but the problem is **accommodation**. In the height of the season, locating a vacant room in one of the more attractive resorts can be a real tribulation – if you do find somewhere reasonable, you'll probably want to stay put. An alternative is to select a less popular spot, primarily Porto Cristo, where there's far more chance of a bed. Things ease up in the shoulder season, but in winter many hotels and *hostales* are closed.

With a bit of patience, you can explore the bulk of the east coast by **bus** from May to October, though in winter you'll need your own transport. There are regular buses from Palma to most of the resorts and one of these services links Felanitx, Cala d'Or and Porto Petro; another connects the **train station** at Manacor with Artà, Capdepera and Cala Rajada. Otherwise, bus services up and down the coast are sketchy, though there is a reasonably frequent bus connecting Cala d'Or, Porto Petro and Cala Mondragó.

Capdepera

Spied across the valley from the west or south, the crenellated walls dominating **CAPDEPERA**, a tiny village 8km east of Artà and 3km west of Cala Rajada, look too pristine to be true. Yet the triangular fortifications are genuine enough, built in the fourteenth century by the Mallorcan king Sancho to protect the coast from pirates. The village, snuggled below the walls, contains a pleasant medley of old houses, its slender main square, Plaça de L'Orient, acting as a prelude to the steep steps up to the **Castell de Capdepera** (daily: April–Sept 9am–7.30pm; Oct–March 9am–4.45pm; €2). The steps are the most pleasant way to reach the castle, but you can also follow the signs and drive up narrow c/Major. Flowering cactuses give the fortress a special allure in late May and June, but it's a beguiling place at any time, with over 400m of walls equipped with a parapet walkway and sheltering attractive terraced gardens. At the top of the fortress, **Nostra Senyora de la Esperança** (Our Lady of Good Hope) is the quaintest of Gothic churches, its aisle-less, vaulted frame furnished with outside steps that lead up behind the bell gable to a flat roof, from where the views are simply superb.

Practicalities

The small but helpful **tourist office** is in the centre of town at Cuitat 22 (Mon–Fri 8am–3pm; ☎971 55 64 79). There's nowhere to **stay** in Capdepera itself, but it's only about 3.5km north on the Cala Mesquida road to a first-rate *finca*, ⚵ *Son Barbassa* (☎971 56 57 76, ⓦ www.sonbarbassa.com; ❽), a carefully restored sixteenth-century rural estate complete with watchtower. There are twelve stylish rooms here as well as a pool with beautiful views over the valley and back across to Capdepera. They also have a very recommendable restaurant using fresh vegetables from their own garden. The best time to visit is during the three-day **medieval market**, held in the third week of May. The locals dress up in medieval costumes and the entire town is jam-packed with people sampling local food, crafts and music.

Back in town, run-of-the-mill **cafés** line up on Plaça de L'Orient – the best is *Pizzeria Kikinda* (closed Mon), with good pizzas, pastas and salads. Capdepera also has several excellent **restaurants**, the best being *La Fragua*, c/Es Pla d'en Coset 3 (☎971 56 50 50; closed Tues), an intimate, romantic spot where they serve steak and other grilled specialities. It's located just off Plaça de L'Orient, on the way up towards the castle steps.

Cala Rajada

Awash with cafés, bars and hotels, vibrant **CALA RAJADA** lies on the southerly side of a stubby headland in the northeast corner of Mallorca. The town centre, an unassuming patchwork of low-rise modern buildings, is hardly prepossessing, but it is neat and trim, and around the town is a wild and rocky coastline, all backed by pine-clad hills and sheltering a series of delightful **beaches**.

Arrival, information and getting around

Most **buses** to Cala Rajada stop in the town centre, near the intersection of c/Juan Sebastian Elcano and c/Castellet. From here, it's a good five-minute walk southwest along the Via Mallorca to the **tourist office** at no. 36 (Mon–Fri 9am–1.30pm & 2.30–5.30pm, Sat 9.30am–1.30pm; March–Oct also Sun 10am–1.30pm; ☎971 56 30 33). The office can supply an excellent range of local information including restaurant lists, bus schedules, details of car and bicycle rental firms, and free town maps marked with all accommodation. They also sell a popular, though not very detailed, pamphlet on local **hiking routes**.

The town centre is easy to explore on foot, but for the outlying beaches you'll probably want a **local bus**. Among several summertime services from the bus stops along c/Castellet, a short distance north of Plaça dels Pins, three of the most useful are to Cala Agulla, Platja de Canyamel and the Coves d'Artà. In addition, **Cruceros Creuers** (☎971 81 06 00, ⓦwww.cruceroscreuers.com) offers a wide range of summer **boat trips** along the east coast, linking Cala Rajada with several resorts, but principally Porto Cristo (1–2 daily; €22 return).

Accommodation

The only real problem with Cala Rajada is finding **accommodation**. The town is a favourite German package resort and in high season you'll be lucky to find a vacant room: the best place to try is among the *hostales* and hotels dotted around the busy commercial streets just up from the harbour. In the shoulder season, things ease up and it's worth trying one of the popular hotels on the seafront. All the places listed here are **closed** between November and March.

Hotel Cala Gat Cala Gat s/n ☎971 56 31 66, ⓦwww.hotelcalagat.com. Unassuming, fairly traditional hotel in a secluded location in the pine woods above Cala Gat. Many rooms have sea-facing balconies and the dining room and bar have recently had a facelift. ❹

Hostal Cala Ratjada Corner of c/Monges at c/Elíonor Servera 79 ☎971 56 32 02, ⓦwww .hostalcalaratjada.com. Good-value hostal, close to the port, set in a pleasant white-stucco building with rustic touches. ❶

Hostal Ca's Bombu c/Elíonor Servera 86 ☎971 56 32 03, ⓦwww.casbombu.com.

Homely place kitted out in a rustic style with lots of dark wood, a pool and large bar. Breakfast included; great value. ❶

Hotel Ses Rotges c/Rafael Blanes 21 ☎971 56 31 08, ⓦwww.sesrotges.com. Delightful three-star establishment in an elegantly restored antique villa just out of earshot of the main square, comprising just 23 rooms. ❸

Hotel Vista Pinar c/Reis Catòlics 11 ☎971 56 37 51, ⓦwww.hotelvistapinar.com. Large, adequate two-star hotel with ninety rooms – most with balconies – and its own swimming pool. ❶

The town and its beaches

Cala Rajada was once a fishing village, but there's little evidence of this today, and the **harbour** is now used by pleasure boats and overlooked by restaurants. From the harbour, **walkways** extend along the headland's south coast. To the southwest, past the busiest part of town, it takes about ten to fifteen minutes to stroll round to **Platja Son Moll**, a slender arc of sand overlooked by Goliath-like hotels. More rewarding is the ten-minute stroll east from the harbour to **Cala Gat**, a narrow cove beach tucked tight up against the steep, wooded coastline. The beach is far from undiscovered – there's a beach bar and at times it gets decidedly crowded – but it's an attractive spot all the same.

Up above the footpath to Cala Gat you can glimpse the gardens of the **Palau Joan March** (no public access), a lavish mansion built in 1916 for the eponymous tobacco merchant (see p.69), who was to become the richest man in Franco's Spain. On the landward side of the gardens, c/Elíonor Servera, which begins in the town centre, twists steeply up through the pine woods to reach,

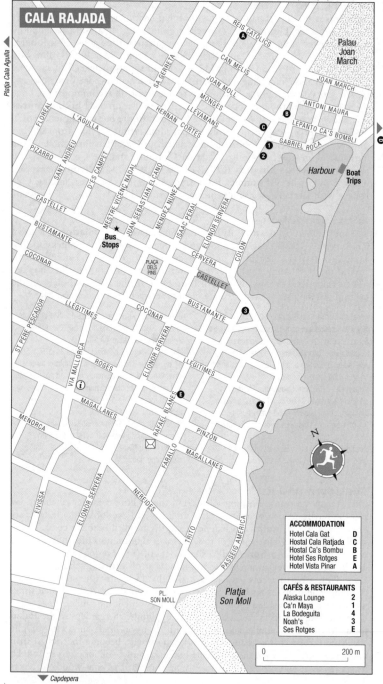

CALA RAJADA

Cala Gat & Cap de Capdepera ▲

Platja Cala Agulla ◀

REIS CATÓLICS
Ⓐ

Palau
Joan
March

CAN MELIS

SA GERRETA

JOAN MOLL

JOAN MARCH

MONGES

ANTONI MAURA

LLEVAMANS

Ⓑ

LEPANTO CA'S BOMBLI

HERNAN CORTES

Ⓒ

GABRIEL ROCA

FLORAL

L'AGULLA

❶
❷

Ⓓ

PIZARRO

SANT ANDREU

DES CAMPET

MESTRE VICENÇ NADAL

Harbour

Boat
Trips

CASTELLET

JUAN SEBASTIAN ELCANO

MENDEZ NUÑEZ

ISAAC PERAL

ELIONOR SERVERA

COLON

BUSTAMANTE

★
Bus
Stops

COCONAR

PLAÇA
DELS
PINS

CERVERA

CASTELLET

ST PERE PESCADOR

LLEGITIMES

COCONAR

BUSTAMANTE

❸

ELIONOR SERVERA

VIA MALLORCA

ROGES

LLEGITIMES

ⓘ

MAGALLANES

RAFAEL BLANES

Ⓔ

❹

MENORCA

FARALLO

PINZÓN

EIVISSA

ELIONOR SERVERA

NEREIDES

MAGALLANES

TRITO

PASSEIG AMERICA

N

PL.
SON MOLL

Platja
Son Moll

ACCOMMODATION
Hotel Cala Gat   D
Hostal Cala Ratjada   C
Hostal Ca's Bombu   B
Hotel Ses Rotges   E
Hotel Vista Pinar   A

CAFÉS & RESTAURANTS
Alaska Lounge   2
Ca'n Maya   1
La Bodeguita   4
Noah's   3
Ses Rotges   E

0   200 m

▼ Capdepera

after about 1km, the bony headlands and lighthouse of the **Cap de Capdepera**, Mallorca's most easterly point. The views out along the coast are a treat.

Heading north from Cala Rajada, c/L'Agulla crosses the promontory to hit the north coast at **Platja Cala Agulla**. The approach road, some 2km of tourist tackiness, is of little appeal, but the beach, a vast curve of bright golden sand, is big enough to accommodate hundreds of bronzing pectorals with plenty of space to spare. The further you walk – and there are signed and shaded footpaths through the pine woods to assist you – the more privacy you'll get.

Eating and drinking

Cala Rajada heaves with **restaurants, cafés and bars** and there's a particular concentration on and around the seafront and c/Elíonor Servera, the main boulevard. Competition is fierce, which keeps prices down, but don't expect too much culinary variation: most restaurants have almost identical menus with something for the Germans – sauerkraut and sausages, for instance – plus a range of traditional Spanish dishes.

Alaska Lounge c/Elíonor Servera 74 ☏ 971 81 96 14. Right on the harbourfront, this modern restaurant-cum-bar offers great views from its terrace. Mains, with mainly organic ingredients, come in at around €18.

Ca'n Maya c/Elíonor Servera 80 ☏ 971 56 40 35. An upmarket place serving superb seafood with main courses around €20. Try their first-rate paella.

La Bodeguita Passeig America 14 ☏ 971 81 90 62. Inviting restaurant located in an old villa near the seashore on the southern side of the resort.

Huge plates piled with meats, pastas and salads for around €15. Leafy garden too.

Noah's Passeig America 2 ☏ 971 81 81 25. Just past the main tourist traps, this café-bar serves up very decent tapas platters and is good for fresh salads; also has the occasional DJ on the weekend.

Ses Rotges c/Rafael Blanes 21 ☏ 971 56 31 08. The finest restaurant in town, serving from a broadly French menu in immaculate surroundings; with main courses averaging about €30, though, it's very pricey. Closed Sun.

The Coves d'Artà

The succession of coves, caves and beaches notching the seashore between Cala Rajada and Cala Millor begins promisingly with the memorable **Coves d'Artà** (often in Castilian "Cuevas de Artà"), reached along the first major turning off the main coastal road (here the Ma-4040) just south of Capdepera (**tours** every half-hour; daily: May, June, Sept & Oct 10am–6pm; July & Aug 10am–7pm; Nov–April 10am–5pm; Ⓦ €10; Ⓦ www.cuevasdearta.com). This is the pick of the numerous cave systems of eastern Mallorca, its sequence of cavernous chambers, studded with stalagmites and stalactites, extending 450m into the rock face. Artificial lighting exaggerates the bizarre shapes of the caverns and their accretions, especially in the **Hall of Flags**, where stalactites up to 50m long hang in the shape of partly unfurled flags. Exiting the caves, you're greeted with a stunning view, courtesy of a majestic stairway straight out of a horror movie, which leads up to a yawning hole, beckoning like the mouth of hell high in the cliffs above the bay. The place has had a chequered history. During the Reconquista, a thousand Moorish refugees from Artà were literally smoked out of the caves to be slaughtered by Catalan soldiers waiting outside. In the nineteenth century, touring the caves for their scientific interest became fashionable amongst the rich and famous – Jules Verne was particularly impressed – and visits now feature prominently on many a package-tour itinerary. The tour guides give a complete geological description of the cave in several languages (including English) as you wander the illuminated abyss. Allow about an hour for the visit – more if there's a queue, as there sometimes is.

From May to October, Monday through Saturday, there are **buses** to the caves (8 daily) from Cala Rajada and Capdepera; there are also daily **boat trips** here from Cala Rajada (April–Oct; €12 not including admission).

Platja de Canyamel

PLATJA DE CANYAMEL – not to be confused with the tedious Costa de Canyamel *urbanització* immediately to the south – is a cove resort whose smart modern villas are draped around a pine-backed sandy **beach** in sight of a pair of rocky headlands. The *platja* is situated about 1km south of the Coves d'Artà, though there's no connecting road: you have to return to the Ma-4040 coastal road, running a few kilometres inland, to make the journey. The *platja* makes an agreeable spot for a few hours sunbathing, and there are several inviting **restaurants** plus a number of **hotels**, though they're usually block-booked by German tour operators. Indeed, the only vague chance of a room on spec is at the freshly painted *Laguna* (☎971 84 11 50; ❸; closed Nov–April), an attractive two-star hotel plonked right on the beach. A more deluxe option is the rural hotel *Can Simoneta* (☎971 81 61 10, ⓦwww.cansimoneta.com; ❾), in between the *platja* and the *urbanització* – just follow the signs from the main roundabout. Attractively located on a cliff and divided between two nineteenth-century buildings, this luxurious hotel is elegantly decorated in white and beige tints and has all the mod-cons one could ask for.

From May to October, local **buses** link Platja de Canyamel with Cala Rajada and Capdepera (Mon–Sat 10 daily) as well as Artà (Mon–Sat 1–3 daily).

Cala Millor and around

Continuing south along the main coastal road towards Porto Cristo, you'll soon pass the turning for the well-heeled villas of **COSTA DES PINS**, the most northerly and prosperous portion of a gigantic resort conurbation centred on **CALA BONA** and **CALA MILLOR**. This is development gone quite mad, a swath of apartment buildings, sky-rise hotels and villa-villages overwhelming the contours of the coast as far as the eye can see. The only redeeming feature – and the reason for all this frantic construction in the first place – is the **beach**, a magnificent two-kilometre stretch of sand fringed by what remains of the old pine woods.

To avoid this visual assault, stay on the main coastal road, which remains just inland, cutting a rustic route through vineyards and almond groves as it clips past the turnings for a long string of resorts culminating in **SA COMA** and **S'ILLOT**. Thereafter, the main road encounters the multi-coloured billboards that announce the cave systems of Porto Cristo.

Porto Cristo

PORTO CRISTO prospered in the early days of the tourist boom, sprouting a string of hotels and *hostales*, but it's fared badly since mega-resorts like Cala Millor and Cala d'Or came on the scene. Don't be deceived by the jam of tourist buses clogging the town's streets; they're usually on their way to the nearby **Coves del Drac** (see p.200) – and few of their occupants will actually be staying here. Consequently, this is one of the very few places on the east coast where you're likely to find a room in July and August, and it's not too bad a spot to spend a night in a low-key, small-town sort of way.

Porto Cristo has one major claim to historical fame: in August 1936, it was the site of a **Republican landing** designed to capture Mallorca from the Falangists. The campaign was a fiasco: the Republicans disembarked over seven thousand men and quickly established a long and deep bridgehead, but their commanders, completely surprised by their initial success, quite literally

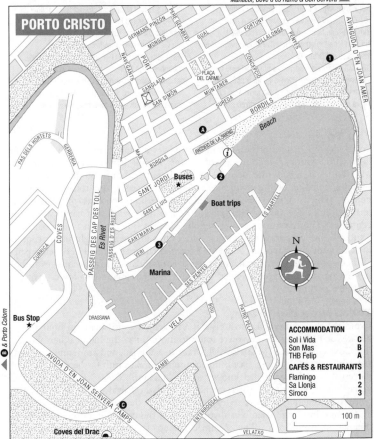

PORTO CRISTO

ACCOMMODATION

Sol i Vida	C
Son Mas	B
THB Felip	A

CAFÉS & RESTAURANTS

Flamingo	1
Sa Llonja	2
Siroco	3

0   100 m

didn't know what to do next. The Nationalists did: they counterattacked and, supported by the Italian air force, soon had the Republicans dashing back to the coast. Barcelona Radio put on a brave face, announcing, "The heroic Catalan columns have returned from Mallorca after a magnificent action. Not a single man suffered from the effects of the embarkation."

Arrival and information

The main coastal road passes along Porto Cristo's seafront, and several long-distance **buses**, principally from Palma, terminate in the centre close to the harbour and the beach. The **tourist office** is also close to the beach on c/Moll (Mon–Fri 9am–3pm; ☎971 81 51 03, ⓦ www.manacor.org). They can provide useful maps of the town and neighbouring resorts.

Accommodation

Porto Cristo has half-a-dozen **hotels and hostales** and there's a good chance of a vacancy here at any time of the year. The town is also close to a first-class rural hotel.

Sol i Vida Avgda d'en Joan Servera Camps 11 ☎971 82 10 74, ⓦwww.solivida.es. A neat and trim two-star, family-run hotel in a pleasant wooded location on a residential street metres from the Coves del Drac. ❶

Son Mas Camí de Son Mas s/n ☎971 55 87 55, ⓦwww.sonmas.com. Owned by an architect and located in a cleverly recycled old farm, this *finca* offers sixteen stylish suites, a climatized pool,

sauna, spa and restaurant. To get there, follow the Ma-4014 towards Porto Colom for 5km and turn right into the Camí de Son Mas de la Marina; the hotel is signposted from here. ❾

THB Felip c/Bordils 41 ☎971 82 07 50, ⓦwww.thbhotels.com. Four-star chain hotel in a big old balconied building overlooking the beach. The interior has been revamped in modern style and the rooms are neat and trim – ask for a harbour view. ❸

The Town

Porto Cristo's origins are uncertain, but it was definitely in existence by the thirteenth century, when it served as the fishing harbour and seaport of Manacor – it boasts one of the most sheltered harbours on the east coast. Nothing remains of the medieval settlement, however, and today the **town centre**, which climbs the hill behind the harbour, consists of high-sided terraced buildings mostly dating from the late nineteenth and early twentieth centuries. The town has its own **beach**, which is fine enough for sunbathing – though the swimming isn't great – and it's handily located right in the centre tucked inside the **harbour**, a narrow V-shaped channel entered between a pair of rocky promontories. The harbour also accommodates a marina and lies at the mouth of the oily-green River Es Rivet, which forms the town centre's southern perimeter.

The Coves del Drac

Exploring the centre of Porto Cristo is a pleasant way to spend an hour or so, but it won't be long before you're ready to move on to the big deal hereabouts, the **Coves del Drac** ("Cuevas del Drac" in Castilian, and sometimes spelled "Drach"), across the river, about fifteen minutes' walk south of the centre along the coastal road. Locals had known of the "Dragon's Caves" for hundreds of years, but it was the Austrian archduke Ludwig Salvator (see p.124) who recruited French geologists to explore and map them in 1896. The French discovered four huge chambers that penetrated the coast's limestone cliffs for a distance of around 2km. The eccentric shapes of the myriad **stalactites and stalagmites** adorning each chamber immediately invited comparison with more familiar objects. As the leader of the French team, Edouard Martel, wrote, "On all sides, everywhere, in front and behind, as far as the eye can see, marble cascades, organ pipes, lace draperies, pendants of multi-faceted gems hang suspended from the walls and roof." Since the French exploration, the caves have been thoroughly **commercialized**. The present complex accommodates a giant car park, ticket office and restaurant, behind which lurk the gardens that lead to the flight of steps down to the caves. You may come to know each step well, as you can wait in line for ages, especially on the weekend. Hour-long **guided tours** every hour or hour and a half (daily: April–Oct 10am–5pm; Nov–March 10.45am–4.30pm; €10.50; ⓦwww.cuevasdeldrac.com).

Boat trips from Porto Cristo

Cruceros Creuers (☎971 81 06 00, ⓦwww.cruceroscreuers.com) organizes a wide range of summer boat trips along the east coast, linking Porto Cristo with a string of resorts, including Cala Rajada (2 daily; €22 return). They also offer ninety-minute scoots round Porto Cristo harbour in glass-bottomed boats from May to Oct (7 daily; €16).

Inside the caves, rainwater has dripped and drizzled through the soft limestone to create innumerable concretions of calcium carbonate – many of which are illuminated. Shunting you through the multilingual tour, the guides invite you to gawp and gush at formations such as "the Buddha", "the Pagoda" and "the Snowy Mountain" as well as magnificent icicle-like stalactites, some of which are snowy white, whilst others have picked up hints of orange and red from the rocks they hang off. The *tour de force* is the larger of the two **subterranean lakes**, at 177m long, 40m wide and 30m deep one of the largest underground lakes in the world. The lake's translucent waters flicker with reflected colours, the mysterious atmosphere further enhanced by a small group of musicians drifting by in boats (performances usually begin on the hour). At the end of the tour, some visitors leave on foot, but you can also take a brief boat ride (included in the admission price) across part of the lake.

Eating

Many of Porto Cristo's **restaurants and cafés** are geared up for the passing tourist trade, which doesn't augur well, but there are nonetheless several good places amongst the mediocre. A very recommendable and inexpensive spot is the *Siroco* (℡971 82 24 44; closed Mon), whose cosy terrace abuts the harbour a few metres south from the beach on c/Veri. A second good choice, right on the harbourfront near the tourist office, is *Sa Llonja* (℡971 82 28 59), which specializes in chargrilled seafood. But cream of the gastronomic crop is the *Flamingo*, c/Bordils s/n (℡971 82 22 59), which offers enjoyable views over the town and port and serves up delicious home-made paellas – or try the steamed mussels.

South to Porto Colom

The modern resorts disfiguring the pint-sized coves to the south of Porto Cristo reach their nadir at the **CALES DE MALLORCA**, the collective name for a band of tourist settlements extending from Cala Magraner to Cala Murada. This part of the shoreline didn't have much charm in the first place – the coves are mostly scrawny and shadeless – and it's even less compelling now. Inland, however, the main coast road – now the **Ma-4014** – gives few hints of these scenic disasters as it wends its pastoral way past honey-coloured dry-stone walls and a smattering of ancient farmhouses in the lee of the Serres de Llevant.

The Ma-4014 becomes the **Ma-4012** at the point where the main road meets the turning for **PORTO COLOM**, a burgeoning resort which straggles round a long and irregular bay some 20km south of Porto Cristo. Originally a fishing village supplying the needs of the neighbouring town of Felanitx, the port boomed throughout most of the nineteenth century from the export trade in wine to France. The good times, however, came to an abrupt end when the phylloxera aphid wiped out the island's vines in the 1870s and the villagers returned to fishing – until, that is, the developers turned up in force during the 1990s. Now, Porto Colom is doomed to spawn villas by the street load.

Felanitx and around

The town of **FELANITX**, located some 13km inland from Porto Colom, is an industrious place, producing wine, ceramics and pearls, and although hardly beautiful, it does have more than a modicum of charm, its tangle of narrow streets lined by handsome old houses mostly dating from the eighteenth and nineteenth centuries. The finest building is the church of **Sant Miquel**, whose mighty, soaring, honey-gold facade boasts a dramatic statue of St Michael, shown triumphant with a cringing devil at his feet. The church overlooks one of the town's main squares, **Plaça Sa Font**, where, in an unusual arrangement, a wide and really rather grand flight of stone steps digs down below street level to reach **Font de Santa Margalida**, once the municipal well and now a water fountain. More recently, the square has also picked up a modern **statue** of a Balearic slinger (see box in Contexts, p.273), which – no matter what sort of gloss you put on it – is dispiritingly macho: in classical times, the islanders were hired as slingers by any number of armies, but it's almost certain they didn't look like this muscular brute in his loin cloth.

The church stands on a hillock and its easterly supporting wall shadows **c/Major**. Everything looks secure today, but in 1844 the wall collapsed, killing over four hundred people in the worst disaster to hit the town since the days of pirate attack: a **plaque** on c/Major commemorates the dead. The best time to visit Felanitx is on Sunday morning, when a lively fresh produce and craft **market** takes over much of the town centre; there's also a very good covered market, the **mercat municipal** (Tues–Sun), just behind **Sant Miquel** on c/Esglesia. In particular, look out for the capers (Catalan *tapèras*; Castilian *alcaparras*), produced locally and sold by size; the smallest are the most flavoursome, either as *nonpareilles* (up to 7mm) or *surfines* (7–8mm).

Felanitx is on several **bus** routes, including Palma to Porto Colom; buses stop near the main square. There is no tourist office, and neither is there anywhere **to stay** except the nearby Santuari de Sant Salvador.

Around Felanitx: the Santuari de Sant Salvador

Within easy striking distance of Felanitx is one of the more scenic portions of the Serres de Llevant. The best and most obvious atttraction is the **Santuari de Sant Salvador**, whose assorted buildings stretch along a slender ridge at the top of the 509m-high Puig de Sant Salvador. The drive to the monastery is easy enough and takes about fifteen minutes: head east out of Felanitx on the road to Porto Colom and after about 2km take the signposted, five-kilometre-long side road that weaves its way up the mountain. The Santuari was founded in the fourteenth century in an attempt to stave off a further visitation of the Black Death, which had mauled Felanitx in 1348. It worked, but the original buildings were demolished long ago and the present structure, a strikingly handsome fortress-like complex perched on the edge of the ridge, dates from the early eighteenth century. Inside, beyond the strongly fortified gatehouse, ancient vaulted corridors lead to the **church**, which shelters a much-venerated image of the Virgin Mary. The other end of the ridge is dominated by a gargantuan **statue of Christ the King** stuck on top of a massive plinth. The statue was erected in 1934 and is visible for miles around, though it may well be the island's ugliest landmark. As compensation, the views down across Mallorca from the ridge are simply fabulous.

Sant Salvador was the last of Mallorca's monasteries to lose its monks – the last ones moved out in the early 1990s. Thereafter, visitors were initially lodged in the old cells, but a new wing has been added and this holds 24 really rather comfortable, modern 🛉 **guest rooms** (☎971 51 52 60, Ⓦwww.santsalvadorhotel .com; ❶), all of which are en suite and most with absolutely stunning views. Breakfast in served in an ancient vaulted room. The monastery also has a **café** and a **restaurant**, but confirm their opening times if you're going to arrive hungry. If you've got a car, you could make the sanctuary an unusual and useful base for exploring the locality. It's certainly a very quiet place to stay.

The Castell de Santueri

The custodians at the Santuari de Sant Salvador should be able to point you towards the **footpath** to the **Castell de Santueri**, about 4km away across the hills to the south. The route is fairly easy to follow and the going isn't difficult, although it's still advisable to have a walking map and stout shoes. The path meanders through a pretty landscape of dry-stone walls, flowering shrubs and copses of almond and carob trees, bringing you to the castle after about an hour and a half. Plastered onto to a rocky hilltop, the battered ramparts date from the fourteenth century, though it was the Moors who built the first stronghold here. Getting inside the ruins is pot luck: sometimes you can (in which case a small entry fee is levied at the main gate), but mostly you can't. If you don't fancy the walk, you can **drive** to a point below the castle along a five-kilometre country lane, signed off the Felanitx–Santanyí road about 2km south of Felanitx. Curiously enough, one strong local legend insists that **Christopher Columbus** was conceived here in the castle, the result of a coupling between a local servant girl, one Margalida Colom, and an imprisoned baron, Prince Carl of Viana.

Cala d'Or

South along the coast from Porto Colom, the pretty little fishing villages that once studded the quiet coves as far as Porto Petro have been blasted by development. The interconnected resorts that now stand in their place are largely indistinguishable, a homogeneous strip of whitewashed, low-rise villas, hotels, restaurants and bars, mostly designed in a sort of *pueblo* style. Confusingly, this long string of resorts is now usually lumped together under the title "**Cala d'Or**", though this name in fact refers to one particular cove, which is also one of the smallest. The "Cala d'Or" we refer to in this account is the original cove and not the whole development.

To be fair, the pseudo-Andalucian style of the new resorts blends well with the ritzy *haciendas* left by a previous generation of sun-seekers. The latter are largely concentrated on the humpy little headland that separates **CALA D'OR** from its northerly neighbour, **CALA GRAN**. These two fetching little coves, tucked between the cliffs and edged by narrow golden beaches, are the highlights of the area. The beaches are jam-packed throughout the season, but the swimming is perfect and the wooded coastline here is far preferable to the more concentrated development all around.

Arrival and information

Buses stop on Cala d'Or's crowded and charmless main drag, Avinguda Fernando Tarrago, two minutes' walk from the beach. Under various designations, this same street links the main cove resorts, from Cala Esmeralda in the north to Cala Llonga in the south – about a twenty-minute walk from one end to the other. From May to September, a tourist "train" on wheels, the **mini tren** (May–Sept 9–11 times daily; ⓦ www.minitren.net), shuttles along the coast, linking Cala Esmerelda, Cala d'Or, Cala Llonga and Porto Petro (see p.204), stopping along the main street and beside all the beaches.

The Cala d'Or **tourist office** (Mon–Fri 8.30am–2pm; May–Sept also Sat 9am–1pm; ⓣ 971 65 74 63) is situated a few metres up from the Cala Llonga waterside at c/Perico Pomar 10. They can provide resort maps marked with all the hotels and *hostales*, though finding a place to stay is well-nigh impossible in the summer.

Accommodation

One of Cala d'Or's most appealing **hotels** – where you'll almost certainly need an advance reservation – is the four-star *Hotel Cala d'Or*, right above the beach on Avinguda Bélgica (ⓣ 971 65 72 49, ⓦ www.hotelcalador.com; ❻). The hotel has ninety-odd balconied bedrooms, each furnished in a straightforward modern style and mostly with sea views. If your wallet's lighter, try the *Hostal La Ceiba*, Avinguda de Calonge 2 (☎971 65 75 07, ⓦwww.la-ceiba.com; ❶), with thirteen basic rooms and a rooftop terrace.

Porto Petro

PORTO PETRO rambles round a twin-pronged cove a couple of kilometres south of Cala Llonga, its old and tiny centre perched on the headland above the marina, with a cluster of whitewashed houses recalling the days when it served as Santanyí's seaport. Although it's now all but swallowed up by the Cala d'Or conurbation, Porto Petro still manages to hang onto something of its original character: aside from a small artificial strip close to the *Blau* hotel, there's no beach, so development has been fairly restrained, and even though the old fishing harbour has been turned into a marina and villas dot the gentle, wooded hillsides, it remains a quiet and tranquil spot. Indeed, the only real activity is the promenade round the crystal-watered cove. Altogether, Porto Petro can make a pleasant base for exploring this part of the island.

Practicalities

Buses – from Palma, Felanitx and Cala d'Or – pull in right beside the harbour, and an electric *mini-tren* (May–Sept Mon–Sat 5 daily; ⓦwww.minitren.net) links it with the resorts to the north and Cala Mondragó to the south. Furthermore, there's a reasonable chance of getting a **room** on spec at the two-star *Hostal Nereida* (☎971 65 72 23, ⓦwww.hostalnereida.com; ❶; closed Nov–April), a comfortable and neat little place occupying a three-storey modern block just above the main dock; the *hostal* also has its own outside pool, garden and rooftop sun terraces. Porto Petro has several very good, moderately priced, harbourside **restaurants**: the *Ca'n Martina* (☎971 65 75 17), by the main dock, serves up a delicious paella (€13 per person), whilst the multi-level *Varadero* (☎971 65 74 28) has the prettiest terrace with comfortable lounge sofas, a decent cocktail list and tasty seafood. This place is popular, so be sure to reserve ahead.

Mondragó Parc Natural

Beginning about 3km south of Porto Petro, **Mondragó Parc Natural** protects a small but diverse slice of the east coast, around two thousand acres of wetland, farmland, beach, pine and scrub. The park's road signs are a tad confusing, but there are two **car parks** to aim for, both signposted from the Ma-19 between Porto Petro and Santanyí. The better target is the **Fonts de n'Alis** car park, 100m from the tiny resort of Cala Mondragó (see below), and this can also be reached direct from Porto Petro along a country road – just follow the signs. The other car park, **S'Amarador**, is on the low-lying headland south across the cove from Cala Mondragó. The park is latticed with footpaths and country lanes, and you can pick up a (rather poor) **map** from the Fonts de n'Alis **visitor centre** (daily 9am–4pm; ☎971 18 10 22), at the Fonts de n'Alis car park. This shows the park's four hiking trails: all are easy loops, two of forty minutes, two of thirty, though the signposting is very patchy. Amongst them, the blue route is a pleasant enough loop giving good views of the bay and access to a small secluded beach. If you can't spot a sign, just keep the ocean on your right-hand side and you shouldn't go far wrong.

Cala Mondragó

CALA MONDRAGÓ is one of Mallorca's prettiest resorts. There was some development here before the creation of the park in 1990, but it's all very low key and barely disturbs the cove's beauty, with low, pine-clad cliffs framing a pair

▲ Cala Mondragó beach

of sandy beaches beside crystal-clear waters. Predictably, the cove's "unspoilt" reputation and safe bathing acts as a magnet for sun-lovers from miles around, but you can escape the crowds by staying the night (if there's space) at either of two beachside **hotels**. Choose between the *Hotel Playa Mondragó*, a straightforward, modern block with plain but perfectly adequate rooms (℡971 65 77 52, Ⓦwww.playamondrago.com; ❷; closed Nov–March), or the slightly more enticing *Hostal Condemar*, about 200m from the beach, where most of the rooms have sea-view balconies and there's an outside pool (℡971 65 77 56, Ⓦwww .hostalcondemar.com; ❷; closed Nov–April).

From May to October, there are **buses** to Cala Mondragó from Porto Petro and Cala d'Or (8 daily); Cala Mondragó is also the southern terminus of the summertime **mini tren**, which runs north as far as Cala Esmerelda (May–Oct Mon–Sat 5 daily).

Santanyí and around

Taking its name from a shortened version of 'Santi Annini' (the Lamb of God), the crossroads town of **SANTANYÍ**, about 10km west of Porto Petro, has long guarded the island's southeastern approaches, a role that has cost it dear. Corsairs ransacked the place time and time again, prompting a medieval German traveller to bemoan their fate – "The Saracens constantly arrive in their ships, carry away prisoners, torment them and use them as slaves or sell them for money." In hope, rather more than belief, the townsfolk attempted to protect themselves by fortifying the town on several occasions and, although it didn't do them much good, one of the medieval gates, **Sa Porta**, has survived in good condition. Nonetheless, it's Santanyí's narrow alleys, squeezed between high-sided sandstone houses, that are the town's main appeal along with **Sant Andreu Apòstol**, a bulky, eighteenth-century pile which incorporates a finely worked, early Gothic chapel, the **Capella del Roser**, a thirteenth-century survivor from the first church built on the site.

Practicalities

Santanyí's main square, Plaça Major, is flanked by **cafés** and bars, amongst which the pick is *Sa Cova*, at no. 31, a groovy little place painted in cheerful colours and with a tiny stage hosting regular live music (Wed & Sat). While you're here, you could also drop by the chic, German-run jewellery and accessory shop, *Reina Rana*, at Plaça Major 15. You can explore Santanyí in an afternoon, but if you do decide to **stay**, the *Hotel Santanyí* (☎971 64 22 14, Ⓦwww.hotel-santanyi.com; ❹), in an old stone town house near the main square on Plaça Constitució, has seven pleasantly modern rooms.

④

SOUTHERN MALLORCA | The south coast

Cala Figuera and Cala Santanyí

Travelling southeast from Santanyí, a five-kilometre-long byroad (the Ma-6102) cuts a pretty, rustic route through to **CALA FIGUERA**, whose antique harbour sits beside a fjord-like inlet below the steepest of coastal cliffs. Local fishermen still land their catches and mend their nets here, but nowadays it's to the accompaniment of scores of photo-snapping tourists. Up above, the pine-covered shoreline heaves with villas, hotels and *hostales*, although the absence of high-rise buildings means the development is never overbearing. What you won't get is a **beach**. The nearest is 4km west at **CALA SANTANYÍ**, a busy little resort with a medium-sized (and frequently crowded) beach at the end of a steep-sided, heavily wooded gulch. To get there, head back towards Santanyí for about 1.5km and follow the signs.

Practicalities

Cala Figuera is popular and there are precious few vacant **rooms** at its dozen or so hotels and *hostales*, even in the shoulder season. If you do decide to chance your arm, the obvious place to start is on the steep pedestrianized ramp – c/Verge del Carmen – which leads up from the harbour. In this prime location, at no. 50, is the unassuming *Hostal Cala*, with twenty rooms stashed above a restaurant (☎971 64 50 18; ❶; closed Nov–March). Moving up a notch, the two-star *Hotel Villa Sirena*, c/Virgen del Carmen 37 (☎971 64 53 03, Ⓦwww .hotelvillasirena.com; ❷), is a proficient modern hotel with its own swimming platforms above the water; it's located at the end of the promontory above the end of the cove. Of Cala Figuera's many **restaurants**, the most distinguished are the seafood places lining c/Verge del Carmen. It's difficult to select – and hard to go wrong – but *La Marina*, at no. 64, is first-rate, with good views and a decent selection of seafood.

From May to October, there are regular **buses** to Cala Figuera from Palma, Santanyí and Colònia de Sant Jordi (see opposite).

The south coast

Mallorca's **south coast** – stretching from the Cap de Ses Salines, the island's most southerly point, to the Bay of Palma – has hardly been developed at all, but the reasons for this lack of interest are pretty obvious when you come here: most of the shoreline is unenticingly spartan, a long and low rocky shelf with barely a decent beach in sight. That said, there are moments when the landscape has an eerie sense of desolation – especially at wind-buffeted **Cap de Ses Salines** – and some visitors find this barrenness strangely fascinating. A smattering of modern resorts have gamely made the most of these disheartening surroundings and the pick of them is undoubtedly **Colònia de Sant Jordi**, a curious and most enjoyable amalgamation of tourist settlement and old seaport, which thoroughly deserves an overnight visit. Even better, the resort is also the main departure point for boat trips to the remote islet of **Cabrera**, now a

national park. Colònia is also near a wide skirt of saltflats that attracts birds by the thousand – and backs onto the region's longest beach, **Es Trenc**, though this is a somewhat forlorn stretch of seashores. In between Colònia de Sant Jordi and the Badia de Palma, however, things are pretty dismal with the grim and untidy resorts of Valgornera, S'Estanyol and Sa Ràpita no more than clumps, where mundane second homes blotch the treeless shoreline it's best to keep straight ahead.

Planning an itinerary is straightforward. The best advice is to use the **Ma-19** road, which runs from Santanyí northwest to S'Arenal on the Bay of Palma, as your baseline, branching off as you wish. As ever, **accommodation** is at a premium. Throughout the season, your best chance by a long chalk is in Colònia de Sant Jordi, but from November to March nearly everything is closed and you'll almost certainly have to visit on a day trip. **Bus** services are adequate if you're heading somewhere specific from Palma, but are dreadful when you attempt to move between the resorts themselves.

Cap de Ses Salines

Heading southwest from Santanyí (see p.205), a fast and easy country road drifts through a landscape of old dry-stone walls, broken-down windmills, ochre-flecked farmhouses and straggling fields bound for Colònia de Sant Jordi. After about 4km, you pass through tiny **Es Llombards** and shortly afterwards you reach the turning for the **Cap de Ses Salines**, a bleak, brush-covered headland 10km to the south through coastal pine woods. The lighthouse here is closed to the public, but there are fine views out to sea. Thekla larks and stone curlews are often to be seen on the cape, whilst gulls, terns and shearwaters glide about offshore, benefiting from the winds which, when they're up, can make the place intolerable. If the cape takes your fancy, then walk northwest along the seashore to the wide, shallow bay and deserted sandy beach of the **Platja des Caragol**. It's easy walking; allow thirty minutes each way.

Colònia de Sant Jordi

The wide streets of **COLÒNIA DE SANT JORDI**, about 13km west of Santanyí, pattern a substantial and irregularly shaped headland that pokes its knobbly head out into the ocean. The main approach road is **Avinguda Marquès del Palmer**, at the end of which – roughly in the middle of the headland – lies the principal square, the unremarkable **Plaça Constitució**. From here, c/Sa Solta and then *Avinguda Primavera* lead west to the *Hotel Marquès del Palmer*, which sits tight against the **Platja d'Estanys**, whose gleaming sands curve round a dune-edged cove. South of Avinguda Primavera is the surprisingly pleasant main tourist zone, whose domineering lines of flashy hotels are broken by low-rise villas and landscaped side streets. To the north are the **Salines de S'Avall**, the saltpans which once provided the town with its principal source of income.

Arrival and information

Buses to Colònia de Sant Jordi stop at several central locations, including the bus stop at the north end of the old harbour beside Plaça Es Dolç and again at the south end on c/Gabriel Roca. During the season, a toy-town **mini-tren** shuttles around town every hour or two, but if all else fails call a **taxi** (☎971 65 52 78).

The **tourist office** is located next to the Cabrera kiosk right on the harbourfront (Mon–Fri 8am–2pm; ☎971 65 60 73, ⊛www.mallorcainfo.com).

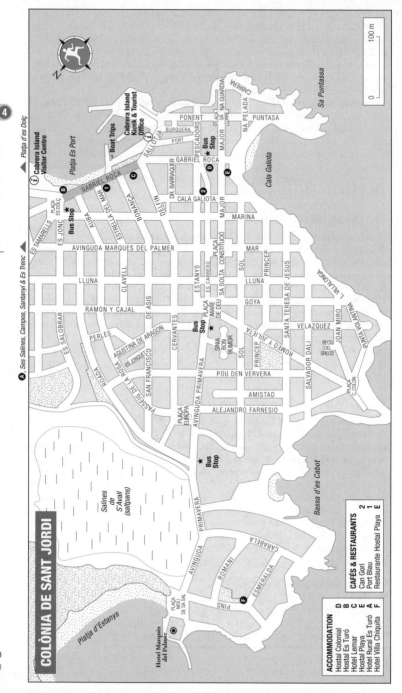

COLÒNIA DE SANT JORDI

ACCOMMODATION
Hostal Colonial — D
Hostal Es Turó — B
Hotel Lemar — C
Hostal Playa — E
Hotel Rural Es Turó — A
Hotel Villa Chiquita — F

CAFÉS & RESTAURANTS
Can Gori — 2
Port Blau — 1
Restaurante Hostal Playa — E

Salines de S'Avall (saltpans)

Bassa d'es Cabot

Platja d'Estanys

Hotel Marquès del Palmer

Platja d'es Dolç

Platja Es Port

Cabrera Island Visitor Centre

Cabrera Island Kiosk & Tourist Office

Boat Trips

Sa Puntassa

Cala Galiota

Platja d'es Dolç

Ses Salines, Campos, Santanyi & Es Trenc

Island hiking

Most visitors to Mallorca and Menorca make a beeline for the beach, but an increasing number arrive here to hike the islands' breathtaking trails, especially in the relative cool of the spring and autumn. There are paths to suit all aptitudes and levels of fitness, from the easiest of strolls to lung-wrenching hauls up to the top of mountain peaks, trails which are now better signposted than they ever have been, though admittedly signage is still very patchy.

The Serra de Tramuntana

As you struggle through Mallorca's massive international airport, it seems incredible that you're just thirty kilometres or so away from some of the Mediterranean's most magnificent **mountain scenery**. Mallorca may have an unenviable reputation for untrammelled development, but the island's northern coast is banded by the wild and wonderful Serra de Tramuntana mountains, whose rearing peaks crash down to the sea, interrupted by the occasional rocky cove and inhabited by such distinctive birds as the black vulture. This is Mallorca at its scenic best and today these mountains attract hundreds of hikers, though until the late nineteenth century they were home only to a motley crew of monks and bandits, renegades and peasants, who eked out a living from the thin upland soils. Some locals still tend the olive and almond groves that dot the *serra*, but other mountain trades disappeared long ago, notably the hunters and charcoal burners who took meat and charcoal to the villages below.

The trails

Until the early 1990s, the assorted foot, mule and cart tracks that lattice the **Serra de Tramuntana** were often poorly signed and difficult to navigate. Things aren't perfect yet – far from it – but the island's ruling council has begun to take matters in hand and today the mountains boast a dense network of clearly signposted **hiking trails**. As part of the process, the council have created – or almost created – a clearly signed, long-distance hiking trail, the Ruta de Pedra en Sec (Dry-stone Route), the **GR221**, which will ultimately run right across the mountains from Sant Elm in the west to Sóller and

Dry stone wall construction ▲

Hiking near Sant Elm ▼

Black vulture ▼

then Pollença – ultimately because long-term and hard-to-unpick access disputes with local landowners mean that a section of the GR221 between Banyalbufar and Estellencs is presently inaccessible. The GR221 is also equipped with five strategically placed **hikers' hostels** (*refugis*; see p.28, for the full list) with another under construction near Sant Elm.

Menorca's trails

Very different from its larger neighbour, Menorca has no high mountains, but it does possess deep wooded gorges and a wild and windswept northern coast, whose craggy capes and headlands shelter a clutch of beautiful cove beaches. For hikers, the island's pride and joy is the Camí de Cavalls, a **long-distance footpath** that circumnavigates the whole of the island, bringing together a network of old mule and military trails.

▲ Hiking in the Serra de Tramuntana

▼ Donkey, Serra de Tramuntana

Hiking essentials

On both Mallorca and Menorca, the prime **hiking seasons** are spring – March, April and May – and autumn, from early October to mid-November. The islands are also warm enough to allow for pleasant hiking in the depths of winter, though there's more rain at this time of year, temperatures can drop dramatically, snow is fairly common on the high peaks of Mallorca, and the number of daylight hours is restricted. In summer, the heat makes all but the shorter hikes unpleasant and very tiring plus you'll have to haul a large quantity of water around with you. Bear in mind also that the mountains are prone to mists, though they usually lift at some point in the day. For obvious safety reasons, lone mountain walking is not recommended.

Hiking from Deià to Port de Sóller ▲

Sa Torreta, Menorca ▼

Seven island hikes

We have described seven day-hikes in detail in this Guide. They are:

Mallorca

▶▶ A coastal hike from Deià to Port de Sóller. Linear; 12km; 4hr–4hr 30min. Mainly easy; difficult in parts. See pp.122–123.

▶▶ A circular hike from Valldemossa to Puig d'es Teix. 12.5km; 674m of ascent; 4hr 30min–5hr. Medium difficulty. See pp.132–133.

▶▶ A valley hike from Port de Pollença to Cala Bóquer. Circular; 6km; 101m of ascent; 2hr return. Easy. See pp.158–159.

▶▶ A circular hike on the Alcúdia peninsula. 9 km; 450m of ascent; 4hr, plus 1hr for diversion to Platja des Coll Baix. Moderately difficult. See pp.168–169.

Menorca

▶▶ A coastal hike from Maó to Punta Prima. Linear; 16km; 100m ascent; 5hr–6hr. Easy. See pp.232–233.

▶▶ A day's hike: Es Grau to Sa Torreta. Circular; 9km; 150m ascent; 3hr–3hr 30min. Easy. See pp.240–241.

▶▶ A day's hike: Es Migjorn Gran to the coast, via the Barranc de Binigaus. Circular; 8km; 150m ascent; 3hr–3hr 30min. Moderate. See pp.252–253.

Hiking checklist

▶▶ Pair of good boots
▶▶ Waterproof jacket
▶▶ Whistle
▶▶ Spare warm clothing
▶▶ Food and plenty of drinking water
▶▶ Compass (on remoter hikes)
▶▶ Sunhat
▶▶ Sunblock
▶▶ Editorial Alpina maps (Ⓦwww.editorialalpina.com) for the Serra de Tramuntana or for Menorca, **Menorca Tour & Trail Map** produced by Discovery Walking Guides (Ⓦwww.walking.demon.co.uk).

They issue free town maps, supply a comprehensive list of local accommodation and have information on local **bike rental** shops – cycling in the flatlands around the resort is a popular pastime.

Accommodation

The glossy modern hotels at the west end of the resort are very much package territory, but there is a good chance of a spare room on spec amongst the reasonably priced hotels and *hostales* in the vicinity of the old harbour.

Hostal Colonial c/Gabriel Roca 9 ☎971 65 61 82, ⓦwww.hostal-colonial.com. Very agreeable, family-run, one-star *hostal* with eight frugal but entirely adequate modern rooms, each of which has a small terrace or balcony. Also a great ice-cream parlour downstairs. Closed Dec–Feb. ❶

Hostal Es Turó Plaça Es Dolç s/n ☎971 65 50 57, ⓦwww.hostalesturo.com. Unassuming, recently revamped one-star *hostal* in a solid three-storey building plonked right on Es Port beach. There's a rooftop swimming pool and eighteen guest rooms – those at the back look out over the beach. Closed Nov–April. ❶

Hotel Lemar c/Gabriel Roca 55 ☎971 65 51 78, ⓦwww.hotellemar.com. Old but well-equipped, high-sided, balconied building overlooking the harbour. Some of the ninety-odd rooms give onto a side street – c/Bonança – so specify you want a room at the front. Three stars. Closed Nov to mid-April. ❷

Hostal Playa c/Major 25 ☎971 65 52 56, ⓦwww.restauranteplaya.com. About a 5-minute walk from the main harbour, this eminently appealing little place has seven double rooms, four of which – and these are the ones you want – look out over the sea as it laps against the beach to the rear of the *hostal*. The rooms are pretty basic, but they are quite large and each of the sea-facing rooms has a balcony. The public area is delightfully old-fashioned with lots of wood, old photos and plates stuck on the walls. Breakfast is served on a pretty, sea-facing patio terrace, which doubles as a restaurant (see p.210). ❸

Hotel Rural Es Turó Camí de Cas Perets s/n ☎663 80 85 26, ⓦwww.esturo.com. Classic *finca*, which has been tastefully converted into an immaculate, modern hotel, all bright-white walls, wood-beam ceilings and tiled floors. The hotel is located on a gentle hill 2.5km to the east of (and signposted from) the hamlet of Ses Salines, which is on the approach road to Colònia de Sant Jordi. ❻

Hotel Villa Chiquita c/Esmeralda 14 ☎971 65 51 21, ⓦwww.hotelvillachiquita.com. This smart and well-tended hotel occupies a rambling, *pueblo*-style modern villa in the tourist zone at the west end of Avinguda Primavera. It has a good-looking garden, with lots of exotic cactuses, and eighteen smartly decorated en-suite rooms. Closed Nov–Jan. ❼

The Town

East from Plaça Constitució along c/Major, and then left (north) down c/Gabriel Roca, is the old **harbour**, the most diverting part of town. Framed by an attractive, early twentieth-century ensemble of balconied houses, the port makes the most of a handsome, horseshoe-shaped bay. There's nothing special to look at, but it's a relaxing spot with a handful of restaurants, fishing smacks, a marina and a pocket-sized beach, the **Platja Es Port**. Here also is the **kiosk** where you book the boat to Cabrera (see p.211), whose island delights you can sample at the brand new **Cabrera island visitor centre** (daily 10am–2.30pm & 3.30–6pm; free), housed in a watchtower-like building at the north end of the harbour. The centre welcomes visitors with a short introductory film, after which you can view the impressive aquarium, displaying many species you're likely to find on local menus, as well as small sharks and rays. Upstairs is a less interesting section devoted to the island's terrestrial species.

From the centre, it's a five-minute walk along the footpath north round the bay to the slender, low-lying headland that accommodates the extensive sands of the **Platja d'es Dolç**.

Eating

A string of first-rate **restaurants** line up along the harbour and although they are all geared up for the tourists, everything is pleasantly low-key and small-scale. The big gastronomic deal is the seafood, but here, in a town with its own fishing fleet, portions are substantial and often as not you get the whole fish rather than a slice. Things get busy from around 8pm, but close down early – by about 10.30pm.

Can Gori c/Estanys 21 ☎ 971 65 64 69. A favourite local hangout with cheap beer, tasty tapas – fried squid, green pepper and spicy sausages and so forth – plus very pleasant service. Not the place for an intimate dinner perhaps, but still a great spot for a quick bite and a lively slice of island life. Daily 8am–1am.

Port Blau c/Gabriel Roca 67 ☎ 971 65 65 55. This smart restaurant lives up to its smashing harbourside location with some of the town's top food, including big, beautifully presented portions of the freshest fish, plus heaped salads and great bread. Mains hover around €25. Closed Tues and Dec & Jan.

Restaurante Hostal Playa c/Major 25 ☎ 971 65 52 56. The restaurant of the *Hostal Playa* (see p.209) may lack a few frills, but there's no complaining about the food – fish and more fish prepared in the traditional Mallorcan manner. The restaurant occupies a very pleasant, sea-facing patio-terrace. Main courses average around €20. Tues–Sun noon–3.30pm & 7.30–10pm, Mon 7.30–10pm.

Around Colònia de Sant Jordi: Es Trenc

One of Colònia de Sant Jordi's attractions is its proximity to **Es Trenc**, a 4km strip of sandy beach that extends as far as the eye can see. It's neither unknown nor unspoilt, but the crowds are easily absorbed except at the height of the season, and development is virtually non-existent. To drive there, head north from Colònia de Sant Jordi and, about 0.5km out of town, turn left at the roundabout towards Campos; after another 2.8km, take the signed left turn and follow the country lane leading across the salt pans and wetlands to the large car park (€6) at the east end of the beach – a total distance of around 6km. This end of the beach is far more appealing than the other, at **Ses Covetes**, which is blotched by improvised shacks and drinks stalls.

The saltpans backing onto the beach – the **Salines de Llevant** – and the surrounding farm and scrubland support a wide variety of **birdlife**. Residents such as marsh harriers, kestrels, spotted crakes, fan-tailed warblers and hoopoes make a visit enjoyable at any time of year, but the best time to come is in the spring when hundreds of migrants arrive from Africa. Commonly seen in the springtime are avocets, little ringed plovers, little egrets, common sandpipers, little stints, black-tailed godwits, collared pratincoles and black terns. Several **footpaths** lead from Es Trenc beach into the saltpans, but it's not a good area to explore on foot: the scenery is boring, it's smelly and for much of the year insects are a menace. It's much better to drive or cycle round using the maze-like network of narrow country lanes that traverse the saltpans, stopping anywhere that looks promising.

Cabrera National Park

The **Illa de Cabrera** ("Goat Island") is a bumpy, scrub- and tree-covered chunk of rock lying 18km offshore from Colònia de Sant Jordi. Largely bare, almost entirely uninhabited and no more than 7km wide and 5km long, it is nonetheless easily the largest of a cluster of tiny islets that comprise the Cabrera archipelago. The only significant hint of Cabrera's eventful past is the protective **castle** above its supremely sheltered harbour. Pliny claimed the island to have been the birthplace of Hannibal; medieval pirates hunkered down here to plan future raids; and during the Napoleonic Wars, the Spanish stuck nine thousand French prisoners of war out on the island and promptly forgot about them – two-thirds died from hunger and disease during their four-year captivity. More recently, the island was taken over by Franco's armed forces, subsequently winning protected status as the **Parc Nacional de l'Arxipèlag de Cabrera**.

In Colònia de Sant Jordi, the **harbourfront kiosk** (℡971 64 90 34, 🆆www
.excursionsacabrera.com) has information on, and takes reservations for once
daily Cabrera island **boat trips** (March–Oct; 7–8hr; €38). There's only one **café**
on Cabrera, just where the ferry docks, and it sells sandwiches and drinks, but
you can also opt for the boat company's buffet (€7.50 with drinks an added
extra). If you don't want to spend the entire day venturing out to the island, a
speedboat excursion (March–Oct 6 daily; ℡622 57 48 06, 🆆www.marcabrera
.com; €38) will whisk you around all the highlights in two hours; Marcabrera,
the company concerned, have their offices just back from the harbour at
Gabriel Roca 20 (daily 9am–1pm & 4–8pm).

The island
The longer, seven- to eight-hour boat trip starts with a one-hour voyage to the
island. On the final stretch, the boat nudges round a hostile-looking headland
to enter the harbour, **Es Port** – a narrow finger of calm water edged by hills
and equipped with a tiny jetty. National Park personnel meet the boat to advise
about what visitors can do and where – some parts of Cabrera are out of bounds
– and there's a small park **information office** by the jetty too. The most
popular excursion is the stiff, thirty-minute hoof up the path to the ruins of the
fourteenth-century **castle**, which perches high up on Cabrera's west coast. The
views from the fortress back to Mallorca are magnificent, and all sorts of **birds**
can be seen gliding round the sea-cliffs, including Manx and Cory's shearwaters
and the rare Audouin's gulls, as well as peregrine falcons and shags. It is, however,
the blue-underbellied **Lilford's wall lizard** that really steals the show: after
you've completed the walk to the castle, take time to have a drink down by the
jetty, where you can tempt the Lilford's lizards out from the scrub with pieces
of fruit.

As an alternative to the castle, it's an easy fifteen-minute walk round the
harbour to **Sa Plageta beach**, or you can head inland to the sombre
memorial commemorating the dead French prisoners of war: the path to the
memorial begins at Sa Plageta and takes about twenty minutes to walk. Along
the way you'll pass the **museum** (limited opening hours – park staff will
advise), in a former wine cellar and grain warehouse, which traces the history
of Cabrera illustrated by a ragbag of archeological finds recovered from the
island and its surrounding waters. On the return journey, the boat bobs across
the bay to visit **Sa Cova Blava** (Blue Grotto), sailing right into the cave
through the fifty-metre-wide entrance and on into the yawning chamber
beyond. The grotto reaches a height of 160m and is suffused by the bluish light
from which it gets its name; you can swim here too.

Campos and Llucmajor
Plonked down amongst the sun-baked flatlands of Es Pla, modest **CAMPOS**,
13km north of Colònia de Sant Jordi, isn't much to look at, but it does have two
surprises up its sleeve: it's home to what many consider to be the best **patisserie**
on the island, *Pastisserie Pomar*, in the main square at Plaça 20, while its church, Sant
Julià, holds an especially fine painting of Christ by Bartolomé Esteban Murillo
(1617–82), the first Spanish painter to achieve a Europe-wide reputation.

Pushing on, **LLUCMAJOR**, the next settlement to the west, has little to
detain you, despite its medieval origins as a market town and its long association
with the island's shoemakers. It was here, just outside the old city walls, that
Jaume III, the last of the independent kings of Mallorca, was defeated and killed
by Pedro IV of Aragon. Llucmajor is just 27km from central Palma.

Travel details

Buses

For further details, call ☎971 17 77 77, or check out ⊕http://tib.caib.es/.

Artà to: Cala Rajada (Mon–Sat 8–18 daily, Sun 6–8 daily; 15min); Capdepera (Mon–Sat 8–17 daily, Sun 6–8 daily; 10min); Manacor train station (6–8 daily; 30min); Palma (Mon–Sat 4–5 daily, Sun 2 daily; 1hr 20min); Platja de Canyamel (May–Oct Mon–Sat 1–3 daily; 20min).

Cala Figuera to: Palma (May–Oct Mon–Sat 2 daily; 1hr 30min); Santanyí (May–Oct Mon–Sat 2 daily; 15min).

Cala Mondragó to: Cala d'Or (May–Oct Mon–Fri 9 daily; 25min); Porto Petro (May–Oct Mon–Fri 9 daily; 10min).

Cala Rajada to: Artà (Mon–Sat 8–18 daily, Sun 6–8 daily; 15min); Capdepera (Mon–Sat 8–17 daily, Sun 6–8 daily; 5min); Coves d'Artà (May–Oct Mon–Sat 8 daily; 30min); Manacor train station (6–8 daily; 50min); Palma (2–6 daily; 1hr 35min); Platja de Canyamel (May–Oct Mon–Sat 12 daily; 15min).

Capdepera to: Cala Rajada (Mon–Sat 8–17 daily, Sun 6–8 daily; 5min); Manacor train station (6–8 daily; 45min); Palma (2–6 daily; 1hr 30min).

Colònia de Sant Jordi to: Manacor (2–4 daily; 1hr); Palma (May–Oct Mon–Sat 5–9 daily, Sun 3 daily; 1hr); Santanyí (May–Oct Mon–Sat 6–7 daily, Sun 3 daily; 10min).

Coves d'Artà to: Cala Rajada (May–Oct Mon–Sat 8 daily; 30min).

Coves del Drac to: Palma (Mon–Sat 3 daily, Sun 2 daily; 1hr).

Felanitx to: Palma (May–Oct Mon–Sat every 1–2hr, Sun 5 daily; 1hr); Porto Colom (May–Oct 5–7 daily; 30min); Santanyí (May–Oct 1 daily; 1hr).

Manacor to: Colònia de Sant Jordi (2–4 daily; 1hr); Palma (Mon–Sat 10 daily, Sun 5 daily; 45min); Santanyí (2–4 daily; 50min).

Manacor train station to: Artà (6–8 daily; 30min); Cala Rajada (6–8 daily; 50min); Capdepera (6–8 daily; 45min); Porto Cristo (6–8 daily; 30min).

Palma to: Algaida (Mon–Sat every 1–2hr, Sun 5 daily; 25min); Artà (Mon–Sat 4–5 daily, Sun 2 daily; 1hr 20min); Binissalem (3–6 daily; 20min); Cala d'Or (Mon–Sat 6 daily, Sun 3 daily; 1hr 10min); Cala Figuera (May–Oct Mon–Sat 2 daily; 1hr 30min; Cala Millor (Mon–Sat 10 daily, Sun 3 daily; 1hr 15min); Cala Rajada (2–6 daily; 1hr 35min); Campos (Mon–Sat 6 daily, Sun 3 daily; 35min); Capdepera (2–6 daily; 1hr 30min); Colònia de Sant Jordi (May–Oct Mon–Sat 5–9 daily, Sun 3 daily; 1hr); Coves del Drac (Mon–Sat 3 daily, Sun 2 daily; 1hr); Felanitx (May–Oct Mon–Sat every 1–2hr, Sun 5 daily; 1hr); Inca (Mon–Sat hourly, Sat & Sun 3–5 daily; 30min); Manacor (Mon–Sat 10 daily, Sun 5 daily; 45min); Montuiri (Mon–Sat every 1–2hr, Sun 5 daily; 35min); Porto Colom (May–Oct 3–6 daily; 1hr 30min); Porto Cristo (May–Oct Mon–Sat 8 daily, Sun 3 daily; 1hr 10min); Porto Petro (May–Oct 3–6 daily; 1hr 35min); Santanyí (May–Oct Mon–Sat 6 daily, Sun 3 daily; 1hr).

Porto Colom to: Felanitx (May–Oct 5–7 daily; 30min); Palma (May–Oct 3–6 daily; 1hr 30min).

Porto Cristo to: Manacor train station (6–8 daily; 30min); Palma (May–Oct Mon–Sat 8 daily, Sun 3 daily; 1hr 10min).

Porto Petro to: Cala d'Or (May–Oct 9 daily; 25min); Cala Mondragó (May–Oct Mon–Fri 9 daily; 10min); Santanyí (3–6 daily; 35min).

Santanyí to: Cala Figuera (May–Oct Mon–Sat 2 daily; 15min); Cala Santanyí (May–Oct Mon–Sat 1 daily; 10min); Colònia de Sant Jordi (May–Oct Mon–Sat 6–7 daily, Sun 3 daily; 25min); Felanitx (May–Oct 1 daily; 1hr); Manacor (2–4 daily; 50min); Palma (May–Oct Mon–Sat 6 daily, Sun 3 daily; 1hr); Porto Petro (3–6 daily; 35min).

Trains

For further information, call ☎971 17 77 77, or check out ⊕http://tib.caib.es/.

Palma to: Binissalem (every 20min; 30min); Inca (every 20min; 40min); Lloseta (every 20min; 35min); Manacor (hourly; 1hr); Petra (hourly; 55min); Sineu (hourly; 50min).

Menorca

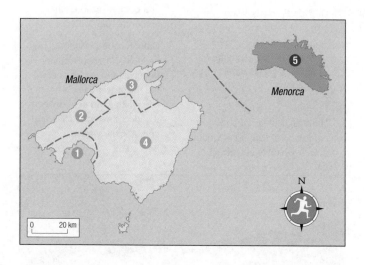

Mallorca

Menorca

0   20 km

N

CHAPTER 5 # Highlights

* **Maó** The labyrinthine lanes and alleys of Menorca's engaging capital ramble along the top of a ridge, high above its deep and long harbour. See p.219

* **Talatí de Dalt** One of the most satisfying of Menorca's many prehistoric remains, in a charming rustic setting just outside Maó. See p.230

* **Cap de Favàritx** Wind-stripped headland where a solitary lighthouse shines out over a lunar-like landscape of tightly layered slate. See p.241

* **Fornells** This attractive little resort is famous for its *caldereta de llagosta* – lobster stew – which is served up at a batch of fine seafood restaurants. See p.243

* **Monte Toro** Menorca's highest point, offering wonderful views over the whole of the island. See p.250

* **Ciutadella** The island's prettiest town, its compact centre an inordinately appealing maze of handsome stone buildings culminating in a pocket–sized Gothic cathedral. See p.256

* **Cala Turqueta** Menorca has a clutch of unspoilt cove beaches and this is one of the finest, with a band of fine white sand set between wooded limestone cliffs and crystal-clear waters. See p.266

▲ Cap de Favàritx

Menorca

S econd largest of the Balearic islands, boomerang-shaped **MENORCA** stretches west from the enormous natural harbour of **Maó** to the smaller port of **Ciutadella**, a distance of just 45km. Each of these two small towns, which together boast around seventy percent of the population, has preserved much of its eighteenth- and early nineteenth-century appearance, though Ciutadella's labyrinthine centre, with its princely mansions and Gothic cathedral, has the aesthetic edge over Maó's plainer, more mercantile architecture. Running through the rustic interior between the two, the main **Me-1** highway forms the island's backbone, linking a trio of pocket-sized market towns – **Alaior**, **Es Mercadal** and **Ferreries** – and succouring what little industry Menorca enjoys, a few shoe factories and cheese-making plants. Branching off the highway, a sequence of asphalted side roads cut along to the **resorts** that notch the north and south coasts. Mercifully, however, the tourist development is largely confined to individual coves and bays, and only amongst the sprawling villa-villages of the southeast has it become at all overpowering. What's more, there are still many remote cove **beaches** with not a speck of concrete in sight, though access to them is usually along rough and dusty lanes. Neither is the development likely to spread: determined to protect their island from the worst excesses of the tourist industry, the Menorcans have clearly demarcated **development zones** and have also created a chain of **conservation areas** that will eventually protect around forty percent of the island, a far-sighted plan that prompted UNESCO to declare Menorca a **Biosphere Reserve** in 1993. The islanders are especially keen to protect their undeveloped beaches, bringing both them and their immediate hinterland into public ownership as speedily as possible. To this end, the old mule and military track that encircles the entire island has been turned into a long-distance footpath, the **Camí de Cavalls**.

Topography and landscapes

The Me-1 acts as a rough dividing line between Menorca's two distinct **geological areas**. In the north, sandstone predominates, giving a red tint to the low hills which roll out towards the bare, surf-battered coastline, one of whose many coves and inlets shelters the lovely fishing village and mini-resort of **Fornells**. To the south all is limestone, with low-lying flatlands punctuated by bulging hills and fringed by a cove-studded coastline. Wooded ravines gash this southern zone, becoming deeper and more dramatic as you travel west – especially around **Cala Galdana**, a popular resort set beneath severe, pine-clad seacliffs. Straddling the two zones, **Monte Toro**, Menorca's highest peak and the site of a quaint little church, offers panoramic views that reveal the topography of the island to dramatic effect.

This varied terrain is sprinkled with farmsteads, present witnesses to an **agriculture** that had become, before much of it was killed off by urbanization/modernization, highly advanced. **A dry-stone wall** (*tanca*) protected every field – the island has no less than fifteen thousand kilometres of stone wall – and prevented the **Tramuntana**, the vicious north wind, from tearing away the topsoil. Even olive trees had their roots individually protected in little stone wells, while compact stone **ziggurats** sheltered cattle from both the wind and the blazing sun. Nowadays, apart from a few acres of rape and corn, many of the fields are barren, but the walls and ziggurats survive, as do many of the old twisted **gates** made from olive branches. The landscape is further cluttered by scores of **prehistoric stone monuments**, mostly dating from the second millennium BC. Perhaps surprisingly, considering this widespread physical evidence, little is known of the island's early settlers and there has been endless academic debate about exactly what means what. The most common remains are **talayots**, cone-shaped mounds made of stone that may or may not have been watchtowers. It's from these *talayots* that the prehistoric **Talayotic Period** is named, running from 1500 to 123 BC, when the Romans arrived. Four of the finest sites are **Talatí de Dalt**, just outside Maó; **Torre d'en Gaumés**, near Alaior; **Torrellafuda**, just off the Me-1; and the **Naveta d'es Tudons**, near Ciutadella.

British rule and the growth of tourism

In more recent times, Maó's long, deep-water port, the **Port de Maó**, promoted Menorca to an important position in European affairs. The **British** saw its potential as a **naval base** and captured the island in 1708 during the War of the Spanish Succession, confirming their conquest five years later under the terms of the Treaty of Utrecht. Spain regained possession in 1783, but with the threat of Napoleon in the Mediterranean, a new British base was temporarily established under admirals Nelson and Collingwood until Britain finally relinquished all claims to the island in 1802. The **British influence** on Menorca, especially its architecture, is still manifest: the sash windows so popular in Georgian design are even now sometimes referred to as *winders*, and locals often part with a fond *bye-bye*. The British also introduced the art of distilling juniper berries, and **Menorcan gin** (Xoriguer, Beltran or Nelson) is now world-renowned.

Today, Menorca's economy is dependent on the **tourist industry**, but this is mainly a niche affair focused on holiday homes and package tours with a strong sideline in activity holidays, from walking through to diving. As such, it's a much quieter, less rumbustious affair than in neighbouring Mallorca and the independent traveller is not especially well catered for: only in Maó, Ciutadella and Fornells, for instance, is there much chance of finding a **room on spec**. Other peculiarities are the dominance of the British, who account for no less than sixty percent of the island's visitors, and the seasonal nature of the tourist industry: outside of the season, which runs from May to October,

Website

Menorca's official **website** will soon be Ⓦwww.menorca.es, replacing Ⓦwww.e-menorca.org.

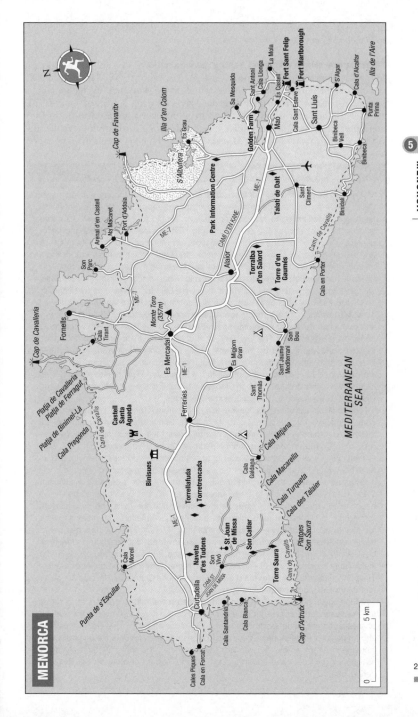

MENORCA

many restaurants, cafés and hotels are closed and the **bus** network is reduced to a skeleton service.

Menorca airport and ferry terminals

Menorca **international airport**, just 5km southwest of Maó, is a smart, compact affair with a handful of car-rental outlets, currency-exchange facilities and a **tourist information desk** (May–Oct daily 7.30am–10pm; ☎971 15 71 15). The latter issues free island maps and has a good selection of free literature, including *Menorca Weekly*, a leaflet detailing forthcoming events, and a general information booklet, *Menorca Explorer*, which contains maps of every

Menorca's Talayotic sites

Menorca's **Talayotic sites** conform to a common pattern, though as you might expect there are marked differences in their state of repair. The tallest structure on each site is generally the *talayot* (from *atalaya*, Arabic for "watchtower"), a cone-shaped mound between 5m and 10m high, built of stone but without mortar or cement. There are dozens of ruined **talayots** on Menorca and the detail of their original design varies from site to site: some are solid, others contain one or more chambers. Most are found in settlements, but there are solitary examples too. This diversity has generated considerable academic debate about their original purpose, with scholars suggesting variously that they were built for defence, as dwellings for chieftains, as burial sites or as storehouses. Popular belief has it that they functioned as **watchtowers**, but it's a theory few experts accept: they have no interior stairway and only a handful are found on the coast. Even so, no one has come up with a more convincing explanation. The mystery of the *talayots*, which are also found on Mallorca, is compounded by their unusualness. The only Mediterranean structures they resemble are the Nuragh towers found on Sardinia. A Sardinian connection would support the view that this phase in the Balearics' development resulted from contact with other cultures, though Sardinia is but one of several options, with Egypt, Crete and Greece also touted as possible influences.

These *talayots* are often positioned a few metres from a **taula**, a T-shaped structure comprising two huge stones up to 4.5m high. Some sites may contain several *talayots*, but there's rarely more than one *taula*, and this almost always sits in the middle of a **circular enclosure** whose perimeter is (or was) marked by a low wall. Archeologists have unearthed objects in these enclosures and the remains of firepits have been found against the perimeter wall. These discoveries would seem to imply a **religious function**, though this is only conjecture – there's certainly insufficient evidence to justify referring to these enclosures as "shrines", as they've sometimes been called. There's general agreement, however, that the *taula* and its enclosure formed the public part of the settlement, and – as confirmation – on many sites the remains of family dwellings surround them. Finally, Menorca also holds a number of **navetas**, stone-slab constructions shaped like inverted loaf tins and dating from between 1400 and 800 BC. Many have false ceilings, and although you can stand up inside, they were clearly not living spaces, but rather communal tombs, or ossuaries. The prime example is the **Naveta d'es Tudons**, outside Ciutadella. *Navetas* are never found in the same place as the *talayots* and *taulas*.

Archeologists divide the **Talayotic period** into several different eras, but as far as the nonspecialist is concerned, the only significant difference between the various phases is the encircling, **perimeter wall**, a dry-stone affair often several metres high and made up of large stones. These Cyclopean walls were for defence and reflect an increase in piracy across the western Mediterranean: the earlier settlements don't have them, the later ones – from around 1000 BC – do. For more on the Talayotic period, see p.271.

town on the island as well as all sorts of listings. There are regular buses from the airport to Maó bus station, which is handily located near the main square (May–Oct every 30min, Nov–April every 30min to 1hr; €1.60). A taxi will set you back €10–12.

Most **ferries and catamarans** from Barcelona and Palma dock at **Maó ferry terminal**, a five-minute walk from the town centre, but there's also a second ferry terminal at the other end of the island in Ciutadella (see p.257). For further details of ferries and catamarans to Menorca, see Basics pp.20–21.

Maó

Despite its status as island capital, **MAÓ** (in Castilian, Mahón) has a comfortable, small-town feel – the population is just 27,000 – and wandering around its ancient centre, with its long-established cafés and old-fashioned shops, is a relaxing and enjoyable way to pass a few hours. Nowadays, most visitors approach Maó from its landward side, but this gives the wrong impression. Thanks to its position beside the largest natural harbour in the Mediterranean, the town has always been a port and it's only from the water that the logic of the place becomes apparent, its centre crowding the crest of a steep ridge that stands tall against the south side of the harbour. From this angle, Maó is beautiful, its well-worn houses stacked up high on the ridge interrupted by fragments of the old city walls and the occasional church. The town centre possesses two highlights, the Churrigueresque chapel in the church of **St Francesc** and the historical paintings of the **Museu Hernández Sanz, Hernández Mora**, but really it's the general flavour of the place that appeals rather than any individual sight. The icing on the cake is the town's striking and unusual hybrid architecture: tall, monumental Spanish mansions stand cheek-by-jowl with classical Georgian sash-windowed town houses, elegant reminders of the British occupation. Outside the centre, you might also enjoy visiting both the harbourside **Xoriguer gin distillery**, where you can sample as many of the island's liquors as you can brave, and the substantial Talayotic remains of **Talatí de Dalt**, just west of town along the Me-1.

Port it may be, but there's no seamy side to Maó. **Nightlife** is limited to a few bars and clubs near the ferry terminal, and the harbourfront's main draw is its long string of **restaurants and cafés** which attract tourists in their droves, though few stay the night, preferring the purpose-built resorts close by. As a result, Maó has surprisingly few *hostales* and hotels, which means that you can base yourself here and – if you avoid the waterfront – escape the tourist throngs with the greatest of ease. The lack of places to stay, however, means that **rooms** are in short supply in July and August, and **reserving** in advance during this period is strongly recommended.

Arrival

Torres Autocars (☎902 07 50 66, ⊛www.e-torres.net) operates regular **local buses** to Maó from Menorca's international **airport** (see p.218), just 5km southwest of town. These buses run on a circular route, but they all drop by the **bus station**, off Avinguda Josep Anselm Clavé, a couple of minutes' walk from Mao's main square, Plaça S'Esplanada. Torres Autocars also runs two other local bus services, both of which stop at the bus station before looping round Maó and travelling along the harbourfront past the ferry terminal. All island-wide buses arrive at – and depart from – the bus station too.

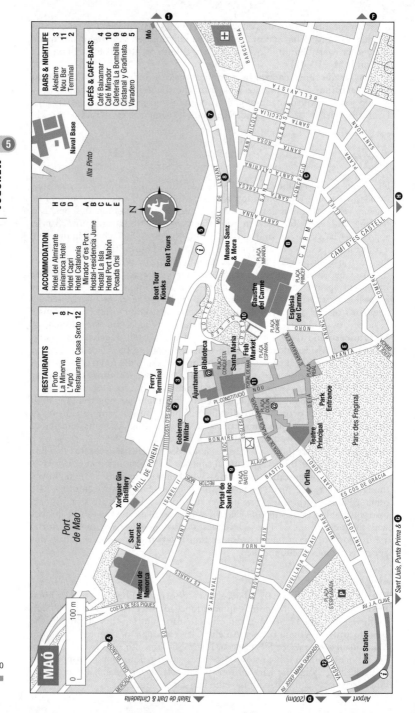

MAÓ

0   100 m

Port
de Maó

Illa Pinto

Naval Base

BARS & NIGHTLIFE
Akelarre   3
Nou Bar   11
Terminal   2

CAFÉS & CAFÉ-BARS
Café Baixamar   4
Café Mirador   10
Cafetería La Bombilla   9
Cristanal y Gradinata   6
Varadero   5

RESTAURANTS
Il Porto   1
La Minerva   8
L'Arpó   7
Restaurante Casa Sexto   12

ACCOMMODATION
Hotel del Almirante   H
Biniarroca Hotel   G
Hotel Capri   D
Hotel Catalonia   A
Mirador d'es Port   B
Hostal-residencia Jume   C
Hostal La Isla   F
Hotel Port Mahón   E
Posada Orsi

Boat Tours

Boat Tour
Kiosks

Ferry
Terminal

N

Museu Sanz
& Mora

PLAÇA
MIRANDA

PLAÇA
PRINCEP

Claustre
del Carme

PLAÇA
CARME

Església
del Carme

Biblioteca

Santa Maria

Fish
Market

PLAÇA
CONQUISTA

PLAÇA
ESPANYA

PLAÇA
DEL MAR

Ajuntament

Gobierno
Militar

Xoriguer Gin
Distillery

Sant
Francesc

PL. CONSTITUCIÓ

NOU

PLAÇA
COLÓN

Park
Entrance

Teatre
Principal

Parc des Freginal

BONAIRE

ESGLÉSIA

ST. ROC

Portal de
Sant Roc

PLAÇA
BASTIÓ

Orfila

BASTIÓ

ALAIOR

FORN

PLAÇA
S'ESPLANADA

P

Bus Station

AV. J.A. CLAVE

Museu de Menorca

COSTA DE SES PIQUES

Port
de Maó

MOLL DE PONENT

MOLL DE LLEVANT

BARCELONA

BELLAVISTA

SANTA CECILIA

SANTA NICOLAU

ROSA

SEBA

SANTA CATARINA

CONCEPCIÓ

CARME

CAMI D'ES CASTELL

COMERÇ

PLANA

SANT JOAN

ANUNCIVAY

INFANTA

ES CÓS DE GRÀCIA

SANT JOSEP

SANT JORDI

MORERES

ROVELLADA DE DALT

SA ROVELLADA DE BAIX

COSTA DE SA PLAÇA

S ARRAVAL

ES FRARES

SOLS

ISABEL II

SANT JAUME

MORÍ

RECTOR MORÍ

COSTA DES GENERAL

DES VOLTES

Sant Lluís, Punta Prima & G

Airport

Talatí de Dalt & Cintadella

Ferries from Barcelona and Palma sail right up the Port de Maó to Maó harbour. They usually moor next to the **ferry terminal**, which is located directly beneath the town centre, though sometimes – when all the berths are taken – they have to moor on the other side of the harbour, a ten- to fifteen-minute walk away. From the ferry terminal, it's a brief walk up the wide stone stairway of Costa de Ses Voltes to Plaça Espanya and the oldest part of town.

Driving through the labyrinthine lanes of central Maó is well-nigh impossible and you're better off **parking** on the periphery. The obvious – and easiest – spot is the **underground car park** (Mon–Sat 8am–10pm) below Plaça S'Esplanada, though this is (at €2.40–2.60 per hour) a good deal more expensive than on-street parking – assuming you can find a place. **On-street parking** is metered during shopping hours (Mon–Fri 9am–2pm & 5.30–8.30pm, Sat 9am–2pm) and there's a maximum stay of two hours (€1.35). At other times, it's free – and there's more chance of a space. Note that if the time you've paid for overlaps into a free period, your ticket will be valid for the time you've got left when the next restricted period begins.

Information

There is a **tourist information desk** at the airport (see p.218), but the main tourist office is down on Maó harbourfront, metres from the ferry terminal at Moll de Llevant 2 (May–Oct daily 8am–8.30pm; Nov–April Mon–Fri 10am–1pm & 5–7.30pm, Sat 10am–1pm; ☎971 35 59 52). Both will provide a free map of the island and free leaflets giving the lowdown on almost everything you can think of, from archeological sites and beaches to bus timetables, car rental, taxis, accommodation and banks. They also sell the best **Menorca road map** on the market – the Mapa Menorca (1:60,000; €4.50), but they won't help you find accommodation. There's also a **public transport information desk** at the bus station.

Accommodation

Maó has a limited supply of hotels and *hostales*, but at least none of them are block booked by tour operators. Amongst them, there are a handful of inexpensive **hostales** close to the town centre and, although they are not especially inspiring, they're reasonable enough and convenient – unlike Maó's smartest **hotels**, which are stuck out on the edge of town. **Prices** vary considerably according to season, with rates in July and August about thirty percent more than in winter; **advance reservations** are advised from June to October and are pretty much essential in July and August.

Hotel del Almirante Carretera Maó ☎971 36 27 00, ⓦ www.hoteldelalmirante.com. Located about 2km east of Maó beside the coastal road to Es Castell, this maroon and cream Georgian house was once the residence of British admiral Lord Collingwood. The delightful lobby is crammed with ancient bygones, and although the modern bedrooms beyond are quite modest, they are all perfectly adequate. The garden terrace, meanwhile, is especially attractive and there's also an outside pool. Package-tour operators use the place, but there are often vacancies. To get there from the town centre, take a taxi or the Es Castell bus and ask to be dropped off. Closed Nov–April. ❸

Biniarroca Hotel Camí Vell 57, Sant Lluís ☎971 15 00 59, ⓦ www.biniarroca.com. A lavishly renovated old *finca* about 5km from the centre of Maó, just to the northeast of the little town of Sant Lluís (see p.237), this deluxe hotel comes with eighteen plush guest rooms decorated in pleasant retro style. There's also an outside pool, lovely gardens and a first-rate restaurant (reservations required), where the menu features home- and island-grown ingredients. Closed Dec–March. ❻

Hotel Capri c/Sant Esteve 8 ☎971 36 14 00, ⓦwww.artiemhotels.com. Proficient three-star hotel in a modern block that's handily located near the old centre of Maó, just a couple of minutes' walk west of Plaça S'Esplanada. The rooms are decorated in standard-issue chain style, but they are pleasant enough, comparatively large and most have balconies. The hotel also has a rooftop spa and pool. ❹

🏃 **Hotel Catalonia Mirador d'es Port** c/Dalt Vilanova 1 ☎971 36 00 16, ⓦwww.hoteles-catalonia.com. This well-equipped, three-star chain hotel, with its own pool and gardens, occupies a modern block perched on a hill, about 10 minutes' walk west of Plaça Bastió. The interior is kitted out in brisk minimalist style and many of the bedrooms have balconies with wide harbour views. ❸

Hostal-residencia Jume c/Concepció 6 ☎971 36 32 66. Centrally located on a narrow side street, this large, old-fashioned, one-star *hostal* occupies a five-storey modern block and has 35 frugal, en-suite rooms. ❶

Hostal La Isla c/Santa Caterina 4 ☎971 36 64 92. Rooms at this amenable one-star *hostal* may be on the small side, but they are reasonably attractive and comfortable, and all have private bathroom and TV. There's a bar and restaurant downstairs. ❶

Hotel Port Mahón Avgda Port de Maó s/n ☎971 36 26 00, ⓦwww.sethotels.com. Attractive, colonial-style, four-star hotel in a superb location overlooking the portside, with grand views down along the Maó inlet. There's an outside swimming pool and a patio café, plus each of the eighty-odd rooms is kitted out in smart, modern style with air conditioning. It takes about 20 minutes to walk to the hotel from the town centre, but you can also get here by local city bus (see p.219); a flight of steps leads up to the hotel from the harbour. Room prices vary enormously, but start at ❹

Posada Orsi c/Infanta 19 ☎971 36 47 51. In a large, old terrace house a couple of minutes' walk from Plaça Reial, this one-star, budget *hostal* has seventeen rooms (nine doubles, three singles and five triples), mostly with shared facilities. The rooms are quite small, but you couldn't possibly complain about the colour scheme – bright pinks, reds, oranges and blues throughout. ❶

The Town

With its high-sided mansions and handsome churches, the oldest and most diverting part of **Maó** rolls along the clifftop above the harbour for roughly 1km. Behind, immediately to the south, the predominantly nineteenth-century town clambers upwards, its complicated pattern of tiny squares and short lanes bisected by the principal shopping street and pedestrianized main drag, which goes under various names, with **Costa de Sa Plaça** and **c/Moreres** being the longest individual strips. It takes five to ten minutes to walk from one end of the main street to the other and you emerge at **Plaça S'Esplanada**, the humdrum main square.

Plaça Espanya

From behind the ferry terminal, a graceful stone **stairway** and a narrow, twisting street – the Costa de Ses Voltes – tangle together as they climb up the hill to emerge in the middle of the old town at **Plaça Espanya**. On the north side of the square, a sociable little **fish market** is plonked on top of a sturdy bastion that was originally part of the **Renaissance city wall**. This mighty zigzag of fortifications, bridges and gates once encased the whole city and replaced the city's medieval walls, sections of which also survive. Work on the new Renaissance walls started under the Habsburgs in the middle of the sixteenth century, though the chain of bastions took over one hundred years to complete. On the right-hand side of the fish market a narrow, dead-end alley offers fine views down over the port and is home to the *Café Mirador* (see p.228).

Plaça Carme

Plaça Carme, just to the east of the fish market, is overshadowed by the massive facade of the eighteenth-century **Església del Carme**, a Carmelite church whose barn-like interior is almost entirely devoid of embellishment. The adjoining cloisters, the **Claustre del Carme**, have, after long service as the municipal courts, been refurbished to house the town's fresh meat, fruit and vegetable **market**, with the stalls up against a set of vaulted arches. The cloisters were taken from the Carmelites in 1837 under the terms of a national edict that confiscated church property, passing vast estates and buildings to the state in what was the largest redistribution of land since the Reconquista. For the liberals, who pushed the edict through, the Church was the acme of reaction, and its monks and priests, who usually opposed progressive reform, the representatives of arcane medievalism. Their legislation was, as might be expected, bitterly resented by the Church, but it caught the popular mood, a volatile mix of anti-clericalism and self-interest, with many small farmers hoping to buy the confiscated land from the state at knock-down prices. The confiscation was just one aspect of the prolonged struggle between conservatives and liberals that destabilized Spain throughout the nineteenth century, but it had permanent effects: later conservative administrations did return some of the ecclesiastical property, but most of the land was lost to the Church for good.

Museu Hernández Sanz, Hernández Mora

In the northeast corner of the Claustre del Carme, one upper floor has been given over to the **Museu Hernández Sanz**, **Hernández Mora** (Mon–Sat 10am–1pm; free), which comprises an idiosyncratic connoisseur's collection gathered together by the historian Hernández Sanz and gifted to the city by his son, **Joan Hernández Mora** (1902–84). It's not a large collection – it only fills half a dozen small rooms – but it begins smartly enough in the entrance hall with portraits of many of the leading figures from Menorca's history, including **Sir Richard Kane** (see p.246) and two pictures of **Admiral Byng** (see p.242), one plump and bewigged, the other of his execution, by which time he seems to have lost a few pounds. The first room proper holds several sketches of islanders in traditional costume as well as paintings of Hernández Sanz in his pomp. Then come two rooms stuffed with nineteenth-century paintings, marine-scapes for the most part, both oils and watercolours. The highlight here are **Joan Chiesa**'s five historical paintings recording, in precise detail, the comings and goings of the British army, including the final evacuation of Maó in 1802. Little is known of this Chiesa, but he was related to **Giuseppe Chiesa** (1720–89), one-time Spanish governor of the island and himself an artist with a penchant for painting historical scenes. The next room displays some rather dull canvases by one of the Mora family and then it's upstairs for a whole set of island maps. Here also, and this is much more unusual, is a vitriolic British cartoon entitled *The English Lion Dismember'd*: Menorca had been returned to Spain by the Treaty of Amiens in 1802 and this clearly infuriated the cartoonist, who shows the English lion with one of his paws chopped off – and the offending paw is shaped like Menorca.

Plaça Conquesta

North of Plaça Espanya lies slender **Plaça Conquesta**, whose attractive Georgian facades are ill-served by a poorly crafted **statue of Alfonso III**, which was placed here by Franco in a typically nationalist gesture – this was the Aragonese king who expelled the Menorcan Moors. At the far end of the square, turn left along the cobbled lane – c/Alfons III – and you'll soon spy the genteel arcades, bull's-eye upper windows and wrought-iron grilles of the seventeenth-century **Ajuntament** (Town Hall). This was built by the Spanish, but subsequently occupied by the island's colonial governors, including Richard Kane (see box, p.246), who donated its distinctive clock. Kane also had portraits of King George III and Queen Charlotte hung in the entrance hall, but these were replaced long ago by portraits of three Spanish kings – Alfonso XIII (1886–1941), Carlos III (1716–88) and Carlos IV (1748–1819), the last two having the flamingo-like noses which centuries of inbreeding accentuated amongst the Spanish Habsburgs.

Església de Santa Maria

The Ajuntament is on the northern edge of **Plaça Constitució**, a narrow piazza overshadowed by the **Església de Santa Maria** (daily 7.30am–1pm & 6–8.30pm; free), a heavy-duty pile founded in 1287 by Alfonso III to celebrate the island's reconquest. Rebuilt in the middle of the eighteenth century and remodelled on several subsequent occasions, the church's exterior is an enjoyable architectural hybrid, its Gothic features encased within later Neoclassical accretions. Inside, the **nave** is all Catalan Gothic, a hangar-like, aisle-less, single-vaulted construction designed to make the **high altar** visible to the entire congregation – and indeed there's no missing it, its larger-than-life Baroque excesses featuring the Virgin Triumphant with a flock of helpful cherubs. Unfortunately, the nave is also dark and gloomy, as most of the windows are bricked up in flat contradiction to the original design in which kaleidoscopic floods of light would have poured in through soaring, stained-glass windows.

In contrast to the clean lines of the nave, the truncated **transepts** sport intricate stuccowork, with another flock of cherubs peering out from a swirling, decorative undergrowth, but the church's pride and joy is really its **organ**, a monumental piece of woodwork filling out the elevated gallery above the south entrance. The instrument, with its trumpeting angels, four keyboards and three thousand pipes, was made in Austria in 1810 and lugged across half of Europe at the height of the Napoleonic Wars. Britain's Admiral Collingwood helped with the move, probably as a crafty piece of appeasement: defiance of their new Protestant masters had played a large part in the locals' decision to rebuild the church during the British occupation.

Carrer Isabel II

Running west from Plaça Constitució, long and slender **c/Isabel II** is distinguished by its Georgian architecture, all handsome wooden doors and fancy fanlights, sash windows, bay windows and ornate ironwork. This street was once the heart of the British administration as recalled by today's military governor's house, the eighteenth-century Gobierno Militar, about halfway along, with its elaborate paintwork and shaded, colonial-style arcades.

There's a useful – and extremely pleasant – shortcut down to the harbour from c/Isabel II: head down **Costa d'es General**, an alley at the foot of c/Rector Mort, which tunnels through the old city wall before snaking its way down the cliff to the waterside below.

The Església de St Francesc

At the end of c/Isabel II, the Baroque facade of the **Església de St Francesc** (daily 10am–12.30pm & 5–7pm; free) appears as a cliff-face of pale stone rising above the rounded, Romanesque-style arches of its doorway. The church was a long time in the making, its construction spread over the late seventeenth and eighteenth centuries following the razing of the town by the piratical Barbarossa in 1535. The son of an Ottoman soldier, **Hizir Barbarossa** (c.1473–1547) had established a series of fortified bases in today's Algeria and Tunisia by about 1505. He then proceeded to attack Christian shipping, ransoming his prisoners or selling them into slavery, until the protracted struggle for control of the

Mediterranean between the Ottomans and the Habsburgs gave him another business opportunity: the Sultan paid him handsomely for lending a helping hand and the sacking of Maó was a prime result. Barbarossa died in 1547, but the war lasted for another twenty-odd years until the Turkish fleet was destroyed at the Battle of Lepanto in 1571.

Inside the church, the strong lines of the Gothic **nave** are disturbed by some clumsy concrete panelling round the shallow side chapels, but there's aesthetic compensation in the pinkish tint of much of the stone and the unusual spiral decoration of the pillars. The roof vaulting is also very impressive and the flamboyant **high altar** is flanked by paintings depicting scenes from the lives of the Virgin Mary and St Francis, each and every one of them designed to edify the (illiterate) congregation. Tucked away off the north side of the nave, there's also the **Chapel of the Immaculate Conception**, an octagonal wonderland of clear white stone decorated with garlanded vines and roses in the full flourish of the Churrigueresque style. Completed in 1752, the chapel is attributed to Francesc Herrara, the painter, engraver and architect who trained in Rome and worked in Menorca before moving on to Palma in Mallorca.

The Museu de Menorca

The old monastic buildings adjacent to the Església de St Francesc now house the **Museu de Menorca** (April–Oct Tues–Sat 10am–2pm & 6–8.30pm, Sun 10am–2pm; Nov–March Mon–Fri 9.30am–2pm, Sat & Sun 10am–2pm; €2.40), easily the island's largest museum, with multilingual labels to explain many of the exhibits. The collection is spread over **three floors** with temporary exhibitions on the ground floor and the permanent collection up above. Entry is through the old Franciscan **cloister**, whose sturdy pillars and vaulted aisles, dating back to the early eighteenth century, illustrate the high point of the Menorcan Baroque.

The **first floor** holds a wide range of prehistoric artefacts, beginning with bits and pieces left by the Neolithic pastoralists who were well established here by

▲ Old town, Maó

about 4000 BC. Then it's on to the **Talayotic period** (1500–123 BC), where the earlier items – household objects and the like – are pretty crude, unlike the later pieces, which exhibit considerable sophistication both in home-made goods and in the use of imported items. In particular, look out for the dainty, rather quizzical-looking **bronze bull**, probably of fifth-century Phoenician manufacture and found at Torralba d'en Salord (see p.248), and a small Egyptian bronze of **Imhotep** unearthed at Torre d'en Gaumés (see p.248). These key exhibits reflect the final flourishing of Talayotic culture when Menorca became a major port of call for ships sailing through the Mediterranean, particularly between Italy and Spain. The first floor is rounded off by an enjoyable sample of Roman pottery, including a number of noticeably large amphorae.

The permanent collection continues on the **second floor**, where a series of displays gallops unconvincingly through the Moorish period and carries on all the way up to 1900. Amongst the assorted aristocratic portraits and paintings of Maó harbour, the only item of much interest is the collection of majolica pottery, though there is also a medieval stone cross retrieved from the Castell Santa Àgueda and three small displays on island crafts – costume jewellery, silver purses and shoes. You might also spare a moment for the whimsical wooden figurines (*vellons*) carved in the likeness of various island notables by two local carpenters, the scurrilous Monjo brothers, in the late nineteenth century.

Plaça Bastió
From the Museu de Menorca, it's a brief walk southeast to **Plaça Bastió**, an attractive square that holds Maó's one remaining medieval gateway, the **Portal de Sant Roc**, a sturdy affair of roughly hewn stone comprising two turrets, a connecting arch and a projecting parapet. The gateway is named after Saint Roch, a fourteenth-century hermit who was popular hereabouts as a talisman to ward off the plague: Christian legend asserted that he both recovered from a bout of the plague and cured fellow sufferers, a good recommendation at a time when every city in Europe feared an outbreak.

Costa de Sa Plaça and Plaça S'Esplanada
From Plaça Bastió, it's a few paces through to Maó's steeply sloping main street, here known as **Costa de Sa Plaça** (also signed as c/Hannover), whose old-fashioned shops and tiny piazzas form the town's commercial centre. Stroll up the hill, along c/Moreres, another portion of the main drag, and you'll soon spy a dinky bust-on-a-plinth of Maó's **Mateu Josep Orfila** (1787–1853), to all intents and purposes the founder of modern toxicology. Carrer Moreres then brings you to the flowerbeds, cafés, bars and benches of the principal square, leafy Plaça S'Esplanada, liveliest at weekends, when it fills up with crowds converging on its ice-cream vendors and kiddies' swings.

The quayside
Below the town centre stretches the three-kilometre-long **quayside**, in the middle of which is Maó's ferry terminal. To the west of the terminal, beyond a few bars and restaurants, the waterfront is occupied by the town's small fishing fleet and a mini-marina, and then comes an industrial area, which extends round the murky waters at the head of the inlet. To the east, it's a couple of hundred metres to the departure point for **boat tours** of Port de Maó (see box opposite) and another short stroll to **Mô**, the pint-sized mermaid statue that has recently appeared here – no points, then, for originality given that Copenhagen got their harbourfront mermaid ages ago. Mô looks out at the town's

main marina, an elongated affair where flashy chrome yachts face a string of restaurants, bars and cafés. By day, the half-hour stroll east along the quayside is tame verging on boring; at night, with tourists converging on the restaurants, it's slightly more animated, but not by much.

There is, however, one enjoyable daytime attraction a couple of minutes' walk west of the ferry terminal beside the fishing boats. This is the showroom of the **Xoriguer gin distillery** (June–Sept Mon–Fri 8am–7pm, Sat 9am–1pm; Oct–May Mon–Fri 9am–1pm & 4–7pm; free), where you can help yourself to free samples of gin, various liqueurs and other spirits. Multilingual labels give details of all the different types, and there are some pretty obscure examples, such as **calent**, a sweet, brown liqueur with aniseed, wine, saffron and cinnamon; and **palo**, a liquorice-flavoured spirit supposedly of Phoenician provenance. The lime-green **hierbas**, a favourite local tipple, is a sweet and sticky liqueur, partly made from camomile collected on the headlands of La Mola (see p.235). In all

Boat trips from Maó – and the islands of Port de Maó

Departing from the dock near the foot of Costa de Ses Voltes, various companies run regular **boat trips** along the **Port de Maó**, with an hour-long scoot down and around the inlet costing €10 per person. Frequency depends on the season: in summer there are departures every hour or so, whereas in January there are only a handful of sailings every week, if any at all. Almost all of the boats have glass bottoms for underwater viewing. Of the three main companies, each of which has a harbourside ticket kiosk, **Yellow Cats** (☎639 67 63 51, ⓦwww.yellowcatamarans.com) is as good as any. If this doesn't appeal, there is also a **water taxi** service down the inlet from Maó to the massive La Mola fortress (mid-May to mid-June Mon, Wed & Fri 2 daily; mid-June to mid-Sept Mon–Sat 2 daily; €17 return, including admission to La Mola). Reservations need to be made at least 24 hours before departure at the kiosk down at the bottom of Costa de Ses Voltes; for more on La Mola, see p.235.

These Port de Maó boat trips are the easiest way to get close to **the three islets** that dot the inlet – four if you count tiny **Illa Pinto**, just opposite the dock, which is used by the navy and attached to the north shore by a causeway. The first of the islands to the east of Illa Pinto is the **Illa del Rei**, whose dilapidated buildings once accommodated a military hospital. This was also where Alfonso III landed at the start of his successful invasion of Muslim Menorca in 1287. Next comes pocket-sized **Illa Quarentena**, a pancake-flat islet that has been used variously as a quarantine station and a naval base. Finally, the larger **Illa del Llatzeret** is the site of a former hospital for infectious diseases, which remained in service until 1917. This islet is surrounded by imposing walls built of stone retrieved from Fort Sant Felip (see p.234): the Menorcans were convinced that contagion could be carried into town by the wind, so they built the walls to keep the germs inside. Internal walls separated patients suffering different diseases for precisely the same reason. Llatzeret was only separated from the mainland in 1900 when a canal was cut on its landward side to provide a more sheltered route to the daunting **La Mola** fortress (see p.235).

During the summer, there are also longer **boat trips** north and south along the coast with the most popular target being Es Grau (see p.239). One company offering these longer trips is Rutas Marítimas de la Cruz (☎971 35 07 78, ⓦwww.rutasmaritimasdelacruz.com); a second is Charter Menorca (☎655 75 38 08, ⓦwww.chartermenorca.com). Prices vary enormously, but a day-long trip to Es Grau should cost around €80 per adult, including a stop for swimming and snorkelling. Finally, the decaying buildings of the Illa del Rei have attracted the attention of a **conservation society**, which organizes once-weekly guided tours of the island beginning in Es Castell (see p.232); for more details, check out ⓦwww.islahospitalmenorca.org or ask at the tourist office (see p.221).

its various guises, the main liquor is **gin** with *pomada*, a gin cocktail with lemonade, pretty much Menorca's national drink. British sailors first brought gin to Menorca in the late eighteenth century, but a local businessman, a certain Beltran, obtained the recipe in obscure circumstances and started making the stuff himself. Nowadays, Xoriguer is the most popular island brand, mostly sold in modern versions of the earthenware bottles once used by British sailors and known locally as *canecas*. Here at the showroom, a litre of Xoriguer gin costs about €12.

⑤ Eating, drinking and nightlife

Maó has a place in culinary history as the birthplace of **mayonnaise** (*mahonesa*). Various legends, all of them involving the French, claim to identify its eighteenth-century inventor: take your pick from the chef of the French commander besieging Maó; a peasant woman dressing a salad for another French general; or a housekeeper disguising rancid meat from the taste buds of a French officer. The French also changed the way the Menorcans bake their bread, while the British started the dairy industry and encouraged the roasting of meat. Traditional Menorcan food is, however, not very much in evidence these days, as most of Maó's **restaurants** specialize in Spanish, Catalan or Italian dishes. These tourist-oriented establishments are mainly spread out along the quayside – the Moll de Ponent west of the main stairway, the Moll de Llevant to the east. There's also a smattering of more economical **cafés** and **café-bars** in the town centre. As far as **opening hours** are concerned, almost all the town's cafés and restaurants open daily during high season, though restaurants usually take a siesta between 4pm and 7pm or 8pm, and things can get eerily quiet on Sundays. Out of season, many places shut completely, while others close early depending on trade.

Nightlife isn't Maó's forte, but there are some fairly lively **bars** dotted along the harbourfront with one cluster just up from the ferry terminal and another towards the east end of the harbour on Moll de Llevant. Places come and go with remarkable speed, so the best advice is to follow the crowds, though we have made a handful of recommendations below. These harbourfront bars open late – some not until midnight – and keep going until well into the small hours, until dawn at weekends, though they sometimes don't open at all in the winter.

Cafés and café-bars

Café Baixamar Moll de Ponent 17. An attractively decorated little café-bar, with old-fashioned mirrors and pastel paintwork, serving tasty traditional Menorcan snacks and tapas – island cheese and sausage, for example, at very reasonable prices. Open daily: May–Oct 8am–2am, Nov–April noon–11.30pm.

Café Mirador Plaça Espanya 2. Located a few steps from the fish market – and just off the main stairway leading from the harbour to the town centre – this appealing little café-bar offers a good range of snacks and tapas, and has great views over the harbour from its terrace. Jazz is the favoured background music. Open Mon–Sat noon–1am.

Cafetería La Bombilla c/Sant Roc 31. This pleasant little café, in the town centre on Plaça

Bastió, offers a tasty range of *racion* from €7 per portion. Has a relaxing outside terrace too. Open Mon–Sat 10am–4pm & 7–11.30pm.

Cristanal y Gradinata c/Isabel II, 1. Amenable little café in the midst of the old town whose modern décor is enlivened by miscellaneous bygones, including several ancient radios. Good for drinks and snacks. Open Mon–Fri 8.30am–3pm & 8–11pm, Sat 10am–3pm.

Varadero Moll de Llevant 4. Close to the ferry terminal – and adjacent to the Yellow Cats boat dock – this modern place has a restaurant on one side and a café-bar on the other. The café-bar is the place to aim for – a pleasant spot to nurse a drink and sample a small and inexpensive range of tapas. Café-bar: Mon–Sat 9.30am–11pm, evenings only on Sun, and from noon in winter.

Restaurants

Il Porto Moll de Llevant 225 ⓣ971 35 44 26. The cooks perform in full view here at this large and popular spot, turning out tasty fish and meat dishes from a wide-ranging menu that features Italian dishes – the pizzas are particularly good (from €9.50). Popular with families. Open July & Aug daily 6.30pm–1am; Sept–Nov & Feb–June daily except Wed 1–3.30pm & 7–11.30pm.

La Minerva Moll de Llevant 87 ⓣ971 35 19 95. This is one of the more polished restaurants in town, with smart furnishings and fittings, a pontoon-terrace, and a menu focused on seafood. It's also one of the most popular spots in town, which can be a bit of a problem – sometimes it feels more like a canteen than a restaurant. Nonetheless, many regular visitors swear by the paella and the main courses average a very afford-able €15. Save room for the desserts – the vanilla custard boats in syrup speak (or even shout) for themselves. Reservations well-nigh essential at the height of the season. Open daily 1.30–3.30pm & 8–11pm.

L'Arpó Moll de Llevant 124 ⓣ971 36 98 44. Unlike many of its quayside neighbours, this well-established restaurant has not jazzed itself up, but although the décor may be routinely modern, they serve an outstanding range of seafood – probably the widest selection in town. Attentive service too. Mains from €17. Open daily noon–3pm & 7–10pm.

Restaurante Casa Sexto c/Vassallo 2 ⓣ971 36 84 07. First-rate Galician restaurant just off the main square. The interior is a little too dark for comfort, but there's a pavement gazebo and the food is reliably delicious, especially the seafood and the beef. Good wine cellar too. Mains average €18, whereas the *menu del dia* is a snip at €15. Open daily Mon–Sat 12.30–4 & 8–11pm, Sun 12.30–4pm.

Bars and nightclubs

Akelarre Moll de Ponent 41 ⓣ971 36 85 20. Set down on the waterfront near the ferry terminal, this is probably the best – and certainly the most fashionable – bar in town, occupying an attractively renovated ground-floor vault with stone walls and a miniature garden-cum-terrace at the back, right at the foot of the old city walls. Jazz and smooth modern sounds form the backcloth, with occasional live acts. Open daily from 8pm, though sometimes closed in winter.

Nou Bar c/Nou 1. The ground-floor café, with its leather armchairs and gloomy lighting, is a dog-eared sort of place much favoured by locals. Standing-room only whenever there's a major festival – as there often is.

Terminal Costa des General 10. Head up the ramped lane across from the ferry terminal to find this late-night bar; there are several other tiny places close by, all of which come to life after midnight and groove on till dawn.

Listings

Banks Banks and ATMs are dotted along the main street between Plaça Espanya and Plaça S'Esplanada.

Beaches For a sandy beach, head south to either Punta Prima (see p.233) or Cala d'Alcalfar (see p.237). There are fast and frequent buses to both from Maó bus station; see p.219 for details.

Bicycle rental Bike Menorca, out on the ring road to the southeast of the centre at Avgda Francesc Femenies 44 (ⓣ971 35 37 98, ⓦwww .bikemenorca.com), rents out ordinary and mountain bikes from €12 per day.

Car rental Amongst many, there are branches of Europcar (ⓣ971 36 64 00) and Centauro (ⓣ971 35 58 88) at the airport. There are also lots of other, smaller downtown companies – the tourist office has the complete list.

Email and internet access The public library, the Biblioteca Pública, on Plaça Conquesta, allows visitors one hour's free PC access (mid-June to mid-Sept Mon–Fri 9.30am–1.30pm; mid-Sept to mid-June Mon–Sat 9.30am–1.30pm & Mon–Fri 5–8.30pm). There's also internet and

email access at the VIC Menorca Internet Centre, just off the main street on Plaça Colon (daily 10am–2am).

Ferries and catamarans Three companies offer car ferry and/or catamaran services between Maó and the Spanish mainland and/or Mallorca. They are Balearia (ⓣ902 16 01 80, ⓦwww.balearia .com); Acciona-Trasmediterranea (ⓣ902 45 46 45, ⓦwww.trasmediterranea.es); and Iscomar (ⓣ902 11 91 28, ⓦwww.iscomar.ferries.org). Schedules, tariffs and tickets are available direct from the operators down at the ferry terminal. Note that Menorca's car rental firms do not allow their vehicles to leave the island. For further details of ferry and catamaran routes as well as prices, see Basics, pp.20–21.

Maps & books Llibrería Fundació, facing Plaça Colón at Costa de Sa Plaça 14 (Mon–Fri 9am–2pm & 5.30–8.30pm, Sat 9.30am–1.30pm), stocks a few English-language guidebooks and island birdwatching guides. It also sells Menorca road maps, though the main tourist office (see p.221) has much the better range.

Market On Tuesdays and Saturdays (9am–2pm), there's a large open-air food and more especially clothes market on Plaça S'Esplanada.

Parks Maó's main park, the Parc des Freginal (daily 8am–8pm; free), occupies a shallow gorge in the centre of town. The main entrance is on c/Deià.

Pharmacies Amongst several downtown pharmacies, there's one at c/S'Arravaleta 5 and another at c/Moreres 28 (Mon–Fri 9am–2pm & 5–8.30pm, Sat 9am–2pm).

Post Office The central *correu* is at c/Bonaire 15, just east of Plaça Bastió (Mon–Fri 8.30am–8.30pm & Sat 9.30am–2pm).

Taxis There are taxi ranks on Plaça S'Esplanada and Plaça d'Espanya; alternatively, phone Radio Taxi Menorca on ☎971 36 71 11. Advance booking is recommended.

Around Maó: Talatí de Dalt

Of the several Talayotic sites in the vicinity of Maó, easily the pick is **Talatí de Dalt** (May–Oct daily 10am–sunset, €3; Nov–April open access; free), whose rusticated remains lie about 4km from the centre of Maó, just south off the Me-1 highway. If you're driving along the Me-1, watch for the sign

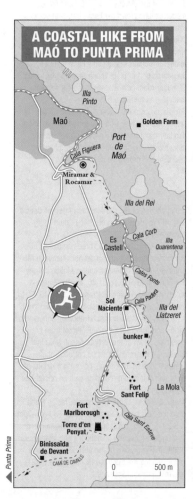

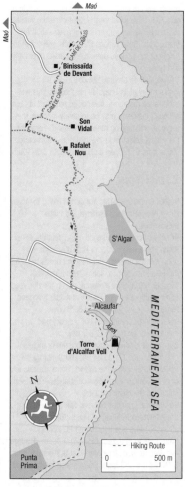

and then follow the dusty track that reaches the site after 300m; there is no public transport.

Partly enclosed by a Cyclopean wall, **Talatí de Dalt** features an imposing *taula* set within a circular precinct. The *taula* here appears to be propped up by a second T-shaped pillar, though it's generally agreed that this is the result of an accidental fall, rather than by prehistoric design. Next to the *taula* are the heaped stones of the main **talayot** and just beyond are three **subterranean chambers** with columns and flagstones forming a rough roof. These three chambers, which date from the very end of the Talayotic period, abut an inner courtyard and are much more sophisticated in construction than the earlier prehistoric dwellings that dot the rest of the site. Their exact function is not known, but there's no doubt that the *taula* was the village centrepiece, and probably the focus of religious ceremonies too. The site's rural setting is also charming – olive and carob trees abound and a tribe of hogs roots around the undergrowth.

Port de Maó

Port de Maó, as Menorcans term the whole of the extended inlet that links Maó with the Mediterranean, is one of the finest natural harbours in the world. Over 5km long and up to a kilometre wide, the channel boasts the narrowest of deep-sea entrances, strategic blessings that have long made it an object of nautical desire. The high admiral of the Holy Roman Emperor Charles V quipped that "June, July, August and Mahon are the best ports in the Mediterranean", and after Barbarossa's destruction of Maó in 1535, the emperor finally took the hint and had the harbour fortified. Later, the British eyed up the port as both a forward base for Gibraltar and a lookout against the French naval squadron in Toulon. Using the War of the Spanish Succession as an excuse, they occupied Menorca in 1708 and, give or take the occasional French and Spanish intervention, stayed in control until 1802. They poured vast resources into the harbour defences and, since their departure, the Spaniards have updated and remodelled the **fortifications** on several occasions.

Both shores – as well as a trio of mid-channel islets (see box, p.227) – bear witness to all this military activity and are pockmarked by ruined fortifications, thick-walled affairs hugging the contours of the coast. The two highlights of Port de Maó's **south shore** are the unusual subterranean fortress of **Fort Marlborough** and Cala **Sant Esteve**, the pretty fishing village where it is located. Of lesser interest is the former garrison town of **Es Castell**, purpose-built by the English in the 1770s. The **north shore** comprises a hilly promontory that nudges out into the ocean, protecting the channel from the insistent northerly wind, the Tramuntana. The promontory's steep terrain has deterred the islanders from settling here, and although recent development has spawned a pair of ritzy suburbs – Sant Antoni and Cala Llonga – the north shore's key feature is the nineteenth-century fortress of **La Mola**, which sprawls over the headland at its very tip, some 7km from Maó.

To explore either shore thoroughly you'll need your own transport, though there is a frequent **bus** service from Maó to Es Castell and you can get to La Mola by **water taxi or bus**. The walk on pp.232–233 offers a good introduction to Port de Maó's southern shore.

A coastal hike from Maó to Punta Prima

16km; 100m ascent; 5–6 hr. Easy.

Starting in the centre of **Maó**, this long but very varied walk winds around the south-eastern corner of the island, initially following the **Port de Maó**, then detouring inland before rejoining the coast to finish at the resort of **Punta Prima**, from where there are regular buses back to Maó (May–Oct hourly; 30min). The coastal scenery is magnificent throughout, while the walk also gives a good impression of the successive layers of fortification that grew up to protect Maó's seaward approaches, as well as more recent tourist development. The going is easy throughout.

The hike

Beginning in Maó's **Plaça Espanya**, descend Costa de Ses Voltes and turn right along the waterfront, walking around the headland and the narrow inlet of **Cala Figuera** to reach, after 1.5km, the *Miramar* and *Rocamar hostales* (both shut-up and abandoned). About 200m past here, shortly before the road turns into a slipway and disappears under water, a flight of steps (leading up to no. 14) ascends to the right. Climb these and go through the gap in the wall at the top to reach an area of overgrown cliff-top scrub, divided into tiny fields by a lattice of stone walls. Follow the cliff-top path, from where there are expansive views across the Port de Maó: to the **Illa dei Rei** and its hospital buildings in the middle of the channel, with the striking salmon-pink Palladian villa known as the **Golden Farm** (see p.235) perched on a hilltop on the estuary's northern shore behind. Ahead in the distance, stacked up above the mouth of the port, are the sombre-looking bastions of **La Mola** (see p.235).

Continue along the cliffs to reach the edge of **Es Castell** (for more on which, see p.232). You should come out at a large, dark-red apartment block. Keep left of this building, then continue straight on down c/Stuart for 150m to the junction with c/Cala Corb. Turn left here and walk down to the boat-filled *cala*, then up the steep flight of steps on your right. Carry on ahead down c/Cales Fonts to Es Castell's main square, also named **Plaça S'Esplanada**, then continue straight on to rejoin the waterfront above the cove of Cales Fonts. Head right here for 50m; go straight past the *Restaurante Irene* and take the second left (opposite the *Cafeteria Can Omi*) onto c/Llevant. Follow this road for 300m (straight ahead and over a crossroads) to reach the top of **Cala Padera**. Continue along this road and turn left down the paved steps which run in front of the *Sol Naciente* restaurant. These lead up to the Passeig Maritím, where you turn left and pass a block of memorably kitsch *pueblo*-style development. About 50m further on – just past a (nameless) *supermercat* and the *peublo*-style Sunrise Village apartment block – a narrow and indistinct path heads left off the road. Take this path to walk along low cliff tops, with a line of holiday villas on the landward side to reach open country.

Proceed along the waterfront, passing a walled enclosure containing a Civil War-era bunker. Beyond here, the path zigzags through the scattered outer remains of **Fort Sant Felip** (see p.234), Port de Maó's main defensive emplacement until Carlos III obligingly had it demolished, allowing the British to retake the island in 1798 without a single casualty. Continue 50m along the cliff top until you reach the high perimeter fence of the Fort Sant Felip army camp, part of the Es Castell complex. Then follow the path inland as it makes its way around the fence before bearing right across a field to reach the road leading to the army camp entrance, over which flies the

Port de Maó's south shore

Tucked in tight against the shore just 3km from Maó, the gridiron streets of **ES CASTELL** have a militaristic and very English air. Originally called Georgetown, the town is ranged around **Plaça S'Esplanada**, the old parade ground-cum-plaza,

Spanish flag. Turn right for 10m, then go left down the road with the dead-end sign for 400m to reach a second dead-end sign, where a track heads off right – the solid-looking cobbles here are reputedly of Roman provenance, part of a road that once stretched back to Maó. Follow this track down to reach the sequestered inlet of **Cala Sant Esteve** (see p.234), then rejoin the road and turn right, heading round the *cala* for 300m and past the subterranean entrance to **Fort Marlborough** (see p.234).

When the road ends, head up through a tiny gap in the clump of trees on your left in front of house number 128 and scramble up to the top to reach a huge well. Then continue around the cliff top through further decaying military remains and innumerable crumbling dry-stone walls, aiming for the fort's most notable surviving structure, the imposing **Torre d'en Penyat** ("The Hanging Tower"). Built by the British in 1798 at the beginning of their third and final occupation of the island, the tower subsequently acquired a rather lurid reputation as a place in which local miscreants were executed – you can climb a small ladder up into the tower to enjoy its eerily echoing acoustics.

The route now heads inland. From here, go round the right-hand side of the tower, following the small path which heads inland to reach an old donkey trail between high stone walls – the **Camí de Cavalls** – for many centuries a major agricultural and military thoroughfare that ran right round Menorca's coast. Recently restored, the *camí* is open to hikers once more, but this particular stretch is distinctly overgrown. Turn left onto the *camí* and after about 400m you will reach the entranceway to Villa Eugenia. Continue over this and after a further 750m you will emerge onto a large track. Turn right here and follow the track as it curves round to the left until it meets a tarmac road. This road leads to the nearby **Binissaida de Devant** farm with its handsome farm buildings. The word *bini* is a Moorish legacy, meaning "sons" in Arabic and a common component of many place names hereabouts. If you wish to view the farm, turn right along the tarmac road. If not, turn left along the tarmac road where after about 30m a path signed Camí de Cavalls turns off to the right.

Follow this path until you reach the entrance to Son Vidal farm, where the path meets a much larger farm access road. Continue on this larger road for 300m to a T-junction and the gate to **Rafalet Nou** farm which is to your left. If the gate is locked, circumnavigate it by carefully climbing onto the stone wall which flanks the farm access road. Then head on to the farmhouse a further 750m beyond and continue straight on through another gate. After 150m there's a gateway (currently minus its gate) where a small path heads off to the right. Follow this path for 200m to a T-junction. Turn right and continue along it for 400m where you cross a cattle grid. Go on past the drab outlying buildings of **S'Algar** for a further 600m (ignoring all side roads off on the left) until you reach a tarmac road. Head straight across for 500m to reach a second road. Turn left, then right, following the signs down to tiny **Xuroy beach**, where there's a bar in summer – you'll probably feel you've earned a drink by now .

Walk to the top of the beach, then go left through the gap in the wall and up around the cliff top, heading to the right of the large **Torre d'Alcalfar Vell** (tower), constructed by the Spanish in 1787 and restored in the 1990s. The final 2km to Punta Prima is along magnificently unspoilt coast. The path here is waymarked by wooden posts denoting the "Camí de Cavalls" and clearly visible is the Illa de l'Aire lighthouse just offshore.

In Punta Prima, **buses** back to Maó can be picked up from the bus stop just west of the beach on c/Xaloc, beside the *Hotel Xaloc*.

whose elongated barracks and Georgian-style town hall, with its stumpy, toy-town clock tower, bear witness to the British influence. Elsewhere, sash windows, doors with glass fanlights, and wrought-iron grilles adorn many of the older houses, though nowadays the centre looks somewhat bedraggled: as a garrison town, the fortunes of Es Castell have always been tied to those of the military, and, with Franco gone, the army no longer has the same prestige.

Nevertheless, Es Castell is still worth a brief wander, beginning on the Plaça S'Esplanada, where one of the old barracks is home to a modest **military museum**, equipped with a motley collection of old rifles and uniforms (June–Aug Mon–Fri & first Sun in the month 10am–1pm; Sept–May Mon, Wed, Fri & first Sun in the month 10am–1pm; €3). From the plaza, it's a couple of minutes' walk east down c/Stuart to the harbour, a pleasant spot occupying the thumb-shaped cove of **Cales Fonts**. Stroll north along the waterside from here and you'll pass a string of **restaurants** before you reach the sullen **bastion** at the end of the harbour that is all that remains of the town's fortifications. Beyond, c/Bellavista leads west back towards the main square – hang a left at either c/Sant Ignasi or c/Victori.

Buses from Maó stop on c/Gran, just steps away from the main square along c/Victori.

Fort Sant Felip

Beyond Es Castell, the main coastal road continues down towards the mouth of the Port de Maó before veering right for Sant Lluís (see p.237). Keeping straight, you soon pass the turning for Cala Sant Esteve (see below), from where it's a further 300m or so to the gates of a *zona militar*. This restricted military area sprawls over the inlet's most southerly headland, where the Emperor Charles V built an imposing star-shaped fortress in the 1550s, naming it **Fort Sant Felip** (guided tours only: June Thurs at 5pm & Sun at 10am; July–Sept Thurs & Sun at 10am; Oct, Nov & March–May Sat at 10am; €5; ☎971 36 21 00) after his son, later Philip II. Once Menorca's greatest stronghold, the fort was adapted by the British, who controlled the seaway from the multitude of subterranean gun batteries they and their predecessors had carved in the soft sandstone. Unfortunately, this irritated the Spanish so much that when Menorca was returned to them in 1782 they promptly destroyed the fort in a fit of pique – a rather misguided move since the lack of defences allowed the British to recapture the island with the greatest of ease just a few years later. Today, nothing survives except the most fragmentary of ruins above ground with several old Spanish and British gun galleries and tunnels down below.

Cala Sant Esteve and Fort Marlborough

From Fort Sant Felip, it's a short hop along a narrow country lane to **CALA SANT ESTEVE**, an extraordinarily picturesque little village, where old fishermen's houses necklace a slender cove with a turquoise sea lapping against crumbly cliffs. On the far side of the cove, near the end of the village, a tunnel burrows into the hillside to enter what was once **Fort Marlborough** (June–Sept Tues–Sat 9.30am–7pm, Sun & Mon 9.30am–2.30pm; April–May & Oct–Nov Tues–Sun 9.30am–2.30pm; closed Dec–March; €3), an intricate, largely subterranean stronghold built by the British to guard the southern approach to Fort Sant Felip between 1710 and 1726 and substantially reinforced sixty years later. The fort, which was named after one of Britain's most talented generals, Sir John Churchill, the Duke of Marlborough, is a complicated affair, beginning with a long gallery dug into the soft rock with counter-galleries cut at right angles to detect enemy attempts to mine into the fortress. In addition, the main gallery encircles an interior moat – dry now, but once filled with water – and comes complete with gun slits that would have been used to fire on the moat from every angle imaginable. In turn, the moat encircles a small fortified hillock, the most protected part of the fortress and once the site of an artillery battery that had this stretch of the coast in its sights. Fort Marlborough was besieged twice – by the French in 1756 and the Spanish in 1781 – and although it was captured on both occasions, it was only after a prolonged siege. One of the advantages of this type of fortress was that it could tie up a large enemy force for weeks and yet require a minuscule garrison – the British put just sixty men here. The self-guided tour round the fort takes about fifty minutes; note also that the **official car park** is at the beginning of Cala Sant Esteve, a ten-minute walk from the fort.

Port de Maó's north shore

From the traffic island at the west end of Maó's harbour, a byroad soon leaves the city behind, threading its way over leafy hills to pass, after 3.2km, the **Golden Farm** (no public access), a fine old mansion in the British colonial style, perched on the hillside overlooking the Port de Maó. The house is actually seen to best advantage when approached from the east and only then can you spy its grand portico, whose two arcaded galleries dominate the south (Maó) side of the house. The upper gallery – the balcony – is equipped with a delicate balustrade and classical deities decorate the tympanum, a trio of languorous figures in vaguely erotic poses. The mansion may well have been **Admiral Nelson**'s headquarters, albeit briefly, during the island's third British occupation (1798–1802), and there's all sorts of folkloric tittle-tattle alluding to romantic trysts here between Nelson and his mistress, **Emma Hamilton**. In fact, Nelson was much too concerned with events in Naples, where the Hamiltons were ensconced and where he was involved in supporting the Neapolitan king, the Bourbon Ferdinand, against the incursions of the French. Indeed, Nelson did his best to avoid visiting Menorca at all – he only came here once or twice for a couple of days apiece – despite it being crucial for Britain's naval control of the Mediterranean. In July 1799, his superior, Lord Keith, mustered his fleet at Port de Maó to resist a possible French attack and ordered Nelson to join him. Nelson refused point blank, writing to the Admiralty, "I am fully aware of the act I have committed, but, sensible of my loyal intentions, I am prepared for any fate which may await my disobedience." The Admiralty let it go – a good job considering Trafalgar was just round the corner – and Keith ranted and raved in vain.

East to La Mola

Moving on from the Golden Farm, the road skirts the well-heeled suburbs of **Sant Antoni** and **Cala Llonga**, where a scattering of modern villas tumble down the hillside to the water's edge way down below. Beyond, the road weaves over a stretch of wind-raked heathland before passing close to the severe stone walls of the **Illa del Llatzeret** (see box, p.227) as it approaches the causeway over to the imposing fortifications of **La Mola** (May–Sept daily 10am–8pm; Oct daily 10am–6pm & Nov–April Tues–Sun 10am–2pm; €7; Ⓦwww.fortalesamola.com). Visitors proceed over the causeway, carrying on for another 600m or so until they reach the **car park** in sight of the main gate, the **Porta de la Reina** (Queen's Gate), named after **Queen Isabel II** of Spain, during whose turbulent reign the fortress was constructed. If you haven't got your own transport, you can reach La Mola by **bus** (mid-May to mid-June Mon, Wed & Fri 1 daily; mid-June to mid-Sept Mon–Sat 1 daily) and **water taxi** (mid-May to mid-June Tues, Thurs & Sat 1 daily; mid-June to mid-Sept 1 daily; €17 including fortress admission fee), departing from the **ticket office** on Maó's waterfront, at the foot of Costa de Ses Voltes. Reservations (which can also be made at the ticket office) are advised for the bus and are essential for the water taxi at least 24 hours in advance.

Isabel II (1830–1904) was proclaimed queen on the death of her father, King Fernando VII, when she was just three years old. The first years of her reign were dogged by civil war between the queens' regents and Fernando VII's brother, Don Carlos – and his Carlist troops – who disputed the (female) succession. The Carlists surrendered in 1839, but there followed another period of chaos as the major power brokers – the army, the Church, the Crown, and two liberal political parties (confusingly, the Moderates and the Progressives) – played a brutal version of musical chairs with the government of the country. Emerging as queen in her own right in 1856, Isabel proved to be dim-witted and quite unable to deal with the competing forces that were destroying her country. The Progressives regarded her attachment to **Sor Patrocino**, a nun who professed to have received the marks of the stigmata, as inane if not insane, and the conservatives were much offended by both the sexual favours she was thought to have granted to a series of favourites and the conspicuous failure of her marriage (to her cousin). No less a figure than **Washington Irving** described her as being "rough and somewhat mealy", but it was Isabel's conservatism that did for her, not her appearance: her attempt to run the country by royal decree created an avalanche of opposition, which simply swept her into exile in 1868.

La Mola is one of the most imposing fortresses in the Mediterranean, its assorted stone walls and gun emplacements dominating the spatulate headland that rears up at the end of the Port de Maó. Given all the shenanigans of Queen Isabel's reign (see box above), it seems surprising that anyone had either the time or the money to build the stronghold, which was meant to protect Spain's Mediterranean coast from the French and the British. Work began on the fortress in 1850 and continued for 25 years with most of the effort going into the **landward defences**, whose tiers of complementary bastions, ditches and subterranean gun batteries were designed to resist the most intensive of artillery bombardments. The sheer scale of these defences is quite remarkable and can't help but impress, especially in the sophisticated design of the polygonal salient known as the **Coop**, but in the event it was all a waste of time. La Mola was built on the assumption that naval guns had a limited elevation, but when the British, amongst others, armed their ships with guns that could be elevated (and therefore lob shells over the walls) the fortress was immediately obsolete: consequently no one ever bothered to attack it – and hence its good state of repair. Allow at least a couple of hours for a thorough exploration.

Southeast Menorca

The southeast corner of Menorca, bounded by the road between Maó and Cala en Porter, consists of a low-lying limestone plateau fringed by a rocky shoreline with a string of craggy coves. In recent years this part of the island has been extensively developed. The coast has mushroomed resorts, not the high-rise resorts of the 1960s but low-rise villa-villages that have gobbled up large chunks of land. Many prefer this low-rise architecture to the sky-rises of before, but it's difficult to be enthusiastic, especially in **Cala en Porter**, the biggest and perhaps the ugliest *urbanització* of the lot. More appealing places include the attractive resort of **Cala d'Alcalfar**, one of the earliest developments, which fringes a particularly picturesque cove, and **Punta Prima**, a straightforward, medium-sized modern resort with few pretensions and a sizeable sandy beach.

Away from the coast, the interior is dotted with holiday homes, but it's all very discrete and for the most part this remains an agricultural landscape criss-crossed by country lanes and dotted with tiny villages, plus one town – mildly diverting **Sant Lluís**.

As for **accommodation**, holiday homes and package-tour operators rule the local roost, so there are only lean pickings for the independent traveller. Never-theless, there is a reasonable chance of finding a room here and there amongst the southeast's scattering of hotels and *hostales*, with Cala d'Alcalfar being the best bet. From May to October, getting around by bus is fairly straightforward. There are hourly services from Maó to Sant Lluís and Punta Prima, as well as regular services to Cala d'Alcalfar. In winter, there's a good bus service from Maó to Sant Lluís, but nothing much else (see p.268 for full details). Bear in mind also that, with the exception of compact Cala d'Alcalfar and Punta Prima, most of the resorts hereabouts spread for miles, and if you've rented a villa you could be facing a very long, hot and confusing trek from the nearest **bus** stop. You might prefer to ring for a **taxi** – try **Radio Taxis** on ☏971 36 71 11.

Sant Lluís

It's just 4km south from Maó along the Me-8 to **SANT LLUÍS**, a trim, one-square, one-church town of brightly whitewashed terraced houses. As at Es Castell, the town's gridiron street plan betrays its colonial origins: on this occasion, it was a French commander, the Duc de Richelieu, who built Sant Lluís to house his Breton sailors in the 1750s, naming the new settlement after the thirteenth-century King Louis IX, who was beatified for his part in the Crusades. The French connection is further recalled by the three coats of arms carved on the west front of the large, whitewashed **church** – those of the royal household and two French governors.

Buses from Maó stop at the north end of town beside Plaça Nova.

Southeast to Cala d'Alcalfar

At the south end of Sant Lluís, keep on the main road (the Me-8) and you'll soon reach the turning for Punta Prima (see below) and then the fork that leads to either **S'ALGAR**, where rank upon rank of suburban-looking villas sprawl along the coast, or – a far better option – the pretty little resort of **CALA D'ALCALFAR**. The development here is restrained, with just a smattering of holiday homes and old fishermen's cottages set beside an inlet of flat-topped cliffs beside a turquoise sea; you can enjoy the sandy beach and then stroll out across the surrounding headlands, one of which has its own Martello tower. The main footpath down to the beach runs through the family-run *Hostal Xuroy* (☏971 15 18 20, ⓦwww.xuroymenorca.com; ❹; closed Nov–April), a pleasant two-star establishment with forty-odd, spick-and-span modern rooms, the pick of which have sea-facing balconies; it's a popular spot, so advance reservations are advised.

Buses from Maó stop in the centre of the resort, about 200m from the *Hostal Xuroy*.

Punta Prima

From Sant Lluís, it's 6km south to **PUNTA PRIMA**, a standard-issue modern resort whose villas, restaurants and supermarkets back onto a wide and windy **cove beach** at the island's southeastern tip. The place doesn't have that much going for it, but there is safe swimming off the beach and pleasing views of the offshore **Illa de l'Aire**, a low-lying chunk of grass-covered rock that comes

The Cova d'en Xoroi

Sprawling **CALA EN PORTER** may be an unappetizing *urbanització*, but it does possess one of the island's most popular attractions, the **Cova d'en Xoroi**, a large cave set in the cliff-face high above the ocean with a dramatic stairway leading to the entrance from the clifftop up above. During the day, the cave is open to visitors (May–Oct daily 11.30am–7pm; €5, including one drink; ☎971 37 72 36, ⓦwww .covadenxoroi.com), but at night it really comes into its own as a **nightclub** (May–Oct Fri–Sun from 11pm) showcasing some big-name DJs; check the website or give them a call to see who is on when. A taxi from Maó to the *cova* should cost around €25.

The cave is also the subject of one of the island's best-known **folk tales**. Legend has it that a shipwrecked Moor named **Xoroi** (literally, "One Ear") hid out here, raiding local farms for food. Bored and lonely, he then kidnapped a local virgin – the so-called "Flower of Alaior" – and imprisoned her in his cave. Eventually, Xoroi's refuge was discovered when locals picked up his tracks back to the cave after a freak snowstorm. Cornered, Xoroi committed suicide by throwing himself into the ocean, while the girl (and her children) were taken back to Alaior, where they lived happily ever after.

---

equipped with an automatic lighthouse. Pedalos and sunbeds can be rented and windsurfing is popular too, but you can't swim out to the island as the currents are too strong.

Punta Prima is at the end of the coastal walk from Maó described on pp.232–233. The handiest **bus stop**, with fast and frequent services to and from Maó (May–Oct only), is located just west of the beach on c/Xaloc, beside the *Hotel Xaloc*.

Fornells and the northeast coast

Stretching out between Es Grau and the Cap de Cavalleria, Menorca's **northeast coast** holds some of the island's prettiest scenery, its craggy coves, islets and headlands rarely rattled by the developer as the harsh prevailing wind – the Tramuntana – makes life a tad too blustery for sun-seeking packagers. There are developed coves for sure – and four of them contain substantial villa resorts – but these are the exception rather than the rule, and for the most part this stretch of coast remains delightfully pristine.

Most of the northeast coast is readily reached via the enjoyable, 25km-long minor road, the **Me-7**, linking Maó and Fornells. This runs alongside cultivated fields protected by great stands of trees, with the low hills that form the backbone of the interior bumping away into the distance. At regular intervals you can turn off towards the seashore with the first turning taking you to **Es Grau**, the starting point for a delightful two- to three-hour hike along the coast or a shorter stroll along the marshy shores of **S'Albufera**, a freshwater lake noted for its birdlife. The next major turning – just beyond the Camí d'en Kane (see p.246) – clips north to the windy bleakness of the **Cap de Favàritx**, and the two turnings after that head north again for the four big resorts hereabouts – **Port d'Addaia**, **Na Macaret**, **Arenal d'en Castell** and **Son Parc**. Much more rewarding than this quartet, however, is **Fornells**, whose delightful bayside location and more measured development makes it one of the most appealing resorts on the island. Fornells is renowned for its excellent restaurants and, unlike all of its near neighbours, none of its *hostales*, of which there are three, is block-booked by package-tour operators, so you've a reasonable chance of a room even in the height of the season. There's no **beach** at Fornells itself, but the resort does make a good base for visiting some of the more remote cove beaches nearby, such as **Platja de Cavalleria** and Platja de Ferragut, to name but two.

From mid-June to mid-September, there's a good **bus service** from Maó to both Fornells and Es Grau, but nothing to Cap de Favàritx. In the same months, there is also a good-ish bus service from Maó to Arenal d'en Castell and Son Parc. Out of season, there's a skeleton service from Maó to Fornells, but nothing much else. All these buses are operated by Autos Fornells (Ⓦ www.autosfornells.com).

Es Grau

The first right turn off the Maó–Fornells road threads its way up through wooded hills on its way to **ES GRAU**, a neat and trim little village overlooking a horseshoe-shaped bay, where scrub and sand dunes fringe an unenticing arc of greyish sand. The shallow waters here are, however, ideal for children, and on weekends the handful of bars and restaurants that dot the main street are crowded with holidaying Mahonese. The most popular place is the *Bar Es Grau*, whose shaded terrace perches on the water's edge at the start of the village, though you'd be well advised to stick to their salads rather than the pizzas. Alternatively, you could aim for the *Tamarindos* (daily noon–4pm & 7–10.30pm; ☎ 971 35 94 20), a slightly smarter place just a few metres further into the village along the waterfront, where they serve a good range of seafood with main courses averaging €15–20.

Parc Natural S'Albufera des Grau

The scrub-covered dunes behind Es Grau's beach form the eastern periphery of an expanse of dunes encircling the freshwater lagoon of S'Albufera des Grau. Only 2km from east to west and a couple of hundred metres wide, the lagoon has just one outlet, the faint stream – La Gola – that trickles out into the bay beside

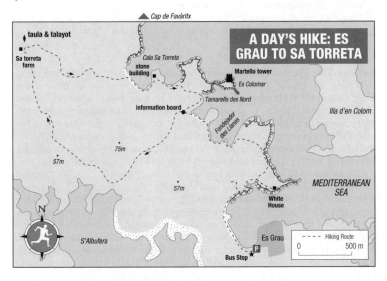

▲ Cap de Favàritx

A DAY'S HIKE: ES GRAU TO SA TORRETA

taula & talayot

Sa torreta farm

Cala Sa Torreta

stone building

Martello tower

Es Colomar

Tamarells des Nord

information board

Illa d'en Colom

Fondejador des Llanes

75m

57m

57m

MEDITERRANEAN SEA

White House

N

S'Albufera

Es Grau

Bus Stop

- - - Hiking Route

0   500 m

A day's hike: Es Grau to Sa Torreta

Circular. 9km; 150m ascent; 3hr–3hr 30min. Easy.

This **coastal walk** takes you from the small resort of Es Grau along one of the wildest sections of the Menorcan seaboard, with a circular detour inland past the S'Albufera lagoon to visit the Talayotic complex of Sa Torreta, one of the remotest prehistoric sites on the island. The going is mainly easy and largely along well-marked tracks, with only one modest ascent towards the highest point of the walk at Sa Torreta farm. There's also about 2km of backtracking at the end of the walk, though this is no hardship given the splendour of the coastal scenery. Note that some of the gates on the route are inscribed "Propriedad Privato" (Private Property). You can safely ignore these signs and go through but make sure that you keep to the tracks.

The hike

Starting at the tarmac car park (and bus stop) at the entrance to **Es Grau**, walk round the large sandy beach and follow the path on the far side as it climbs up onto the low cliffs. At the top, ignore the well-defined track that heads off left and continue straight on, descending very sharply, then follow the path as it bears right until you see a solitary white house ahead.

About 50m before you reach the house, a path branches off uphill to the left. Follow this to the top of the hill, with the low-slung **Illa d'en Colom** (island) off the coast directly ahead, after which the path swings left, giving expansive views of the rugged coast beyond, without a single sign of human habitation to be seen until, about 50m further on, the **lighthouse** on Cap de Favàritx hoves into view. As soon as you see the lighthouse, watch out for the path that descends to your right. Clamber down this path, past a curious little stone shelter built into the cliff side, then continue leftwards along the coast, which is clothed in wild maquis, comprising low, convoluted clumps of mastic and wild olive dotted with spiky pin-cushions of *Launaea cervicornis* (try not to sit on them). Aim about 45 degrees left of the Martello tower ahead, keeping left of the bare, rocky headland to your right and avoiding any of the various paths which cross the maquis to reach the small bay of **Fondejador des Llanes**, a tiny, driftwood-covered cove, plus a longer, sandier inlet immediately beyond.

Follow the path directly above the beach, which is waymarked with posts inscribed "Camí de Cavalls", to a wall with a gap. Twenty metres beyond this is a small sandy clearing that accommodates a large information board relating to Cala Tamarells, a

Es Grau. The lake was once fished for bass, grey mullet and eels – a real island delicacy – but fishing and hunting have been banned since the creation of the **Parc Natural S'Albufera** in the 1990s. The park boasts a varied terrain, including dunes (which are glued together by a combination of Aleppo pine, marram grass and beach thistle), and wetland, concentrated at the west end of the lake and containing patches of saltworts and rushes. Not surprisingly, therefore, the lagoon and its surroundings are rich in birdlife, attracting thousands of migrant birds in spring and autumn; for more on Menorca's birds, see pp.292–294.

The **access road** into the park begins 2.5km back from Es Grau on the road to Maó. Just 1.5km long, this side road skims past a scattering of villas before it reaches the **park information centre** (May–Sept Tues 9am–2.30pm, Wed–Fri 9am–7pm, Sat & Sun 9am–2.30pm; Oct–April daily 9am–2pm), which is good for maps and general stuff about local flora and fauna. Just after the information centre, veer left at the fork and keep going until you reach the dirt **car park**, from where clearly marked paths run (in either direction) along the lake's southern shore. It's easy walking and the scenery is gentle on the eye, with the

neighbouring beach. Bear left at the end of the clearing, following a path for a few more metres to reach a wide track (remember this point carefully for later on). Turn left and follow the track inland as it climbs up and then downhill through a beautifully secluded valley. After 750m the track gradually swings right and you have your first proper view of the **S'Albufera lagoon** (see p.239) to your left, one of Menorca's richest ornithological sites (with binoculars you may be able to see some of its bird life). The track slaloms right and gradually ascends for a further 1km, climbing steadily uphill (ignore the couple of subsidiary paths which head off to the left). The island's highest point, **Monte Toro**, now becomes visible in the distance as you ascend, while near the top to your left there's an overgrown and impassable walled track, typical of many of the island's abandoned donkey trails.

Go through a Menorcan-style gate to reach a T-junction, then go left to arrive at the farmhouse of **Sa Torreta**. Go through another gate, then turn right and walk 100m to a second T-junction. Go left here through a third gate. After 25m you'll pass a large circular threshing floor on your left, with the Sa Torreta's **taula and talayot** now visible ahead. Just past the threshing floor, go through the gap in the wall on your right and cross the field to reach the walled Talayotic enclosure, one of the least-visited prehistoric sites on Menorca, and one of the few on the northern side of the island. The fine four-metre *taula* and partly collapsed *talayot* here are proof of the longevity of Menorca's megalithic culture, postdating earlier examples by as much as a thousand years.

You're now at the highest point of the walk, with grand views down to the coast below. Retrace your steps past the threshing floor and back to the (third) gate, then turn left, continuing on along the main track for 1km downhill (ignoring a prominent left turn just before you rejoin the seafront) through a Menorcan style gate to reach **Cala Sa Torreta**, a remote, scrub-covered beach littered with dried seaweed and sea-borne rubbish – not much good for swimming, though the clump of Aleppo pines behind the beach is a pleasant spot for a picnic and some birdwatching.

The track continues behind the beach to reach a fork. Go left here and past a small stone building, then across a small headland back towards the small bay of **Tamarells des Nord** and the Martello tower which you saw earlier. Here the path swings away from the shore. Walk inland on the track and continue for about 500m until you reach the narrow path on your left leading back to the sandy clearing with the Cala Tamarells information board. You will (or should) remember this from earlier. From this point retrace your steps back to Es Grau.

blue of the lake set against the rolling greens and yellows of the dunes. Birders – both casual and enthusiasts – should aim for **Es Prat**, the large patch of wetland at the west end of the lake, and should be sure to pack binoculars.

Cap de Favàritx

Back on the Maó–Fornells road, heading northwest from the Es Grau turning, it's about 7km to the right turn that weaves its way over to **Cap de Favàritx**. This eight-kilometre-long side road cuts along a wide valley and slips through dumpy little hills before the landscape becomes barer – and the grass gives way to succulents – as it approaches the cape. At the cape itself, even the succulents can't survive and the solitary **lighthouse** shines out over a bare lunar-like landscape of tightly layered, crumbly slate. The lighthouse is closed to the public, but the views out over the coast are dramatic and you can pick your way along the adjacent rocks, though if the wind is up (as it often is) this isn't much fun.

▲ Sa Torreta

In 1756, Cap de Favàritx witnessed one of the British navy's more embarrassing moments when **Admiral John Byng** (1704–57) anchored his fleet off here for no particular reason. The French had besieged the British garrison at Fort Sant Felip (see p.234) at the start of the Seven Years' War and Byng had been dispatched to Menorca to relieve them. Instead, he dillied and he dallied, allegedly reading and re-reading the Admiralty's instruction book, and managed to get caught with his nautical trousers down when the French fleet turned up off Cap de Favàritx too. The resulting battle was an inconclusive affair, but Byng faint-heartedly withdrew to Gibraltar, abandoning the British garrison to its fate. Back in London, the prime minister, the Duke of Newcastle, fumed: "He shall be tried immediately; he shall be hanged directly" – and proceeded to carry out his threat, if not exactly to the letter. On his return, Byng was court-martialled and shot by firing squad on his own flagship in Portsmouth harbour, an event which famously prompted **Voltaire** to remark in *Candide* that the British needed to shoot an admiral now and again "pour encourager les autres".

Port d'Addaia and Son Parc

"I shall ever think of Adaia, and of the company I enjoyed at that charming little Retirement, with the utmost Complacency and Satisfaction," wrote John Armstrong, an engineer in the British army, in the 1740s. If only he could see it now. The old **PORT D'ADDAIA**, at the mouth of a long, wooded inlet, has mushroomed dreary holiday homes, supermarkets and a marina, and as if that weren't bad enough, the neighbouring headlands now heave with the villas and apartment buildings of two oversized resorts – low-key **NA MACARET** and **ARENAL D'EN CASTELL**, which at least boasts a wide and sandy beach set within a circular cove.

The next turning along the Maó–Fornells road leads to **SON PARC**, a workaday grid of coastal holiday homes and apartment blocks flanking a golf course.

Fornells

FORNELLS may be expanding in some haste, with villas starting to trail over its immediate surroundings, but in essence it remains a classically pretty fishing village at the mouth of a long and chubby bay. The place has been popular with tourists for years, above all for its **seafood restaurants**, whose speciality, *caldereta de llagosta* (langosta in Castilian), is a fabulously tasty – and often wincingly expensive – lobster stew. Beyond the village and across the bay lie austere rocky headlands, where winter storms and ocean spray keep vegetation to a minimum. This bleak terrain envelops various fortifications – evidence of the harbour's past importance – of which two are easy to reach: the battered remains of **Castell de Sant Antoni** (open access; free), in Fornells itself, and a circular watchtower, the **Torre de Fornells** (April–Oct Tues–Fri 10am–3.30pm, Sat & Sun 10am–3pm; €2.40), which is approached up a wide walkway at the northern end of the village. The short haul up to the watchtower is well worth the effort as the views over the coast are simply fantastic.

Fornells picked up its first **fortifications** in the late seventeenth century to ward against the threat of Arab and Turkish corsairs, but the British went further, constructing a string of mini-forts here, including the Torre de Fornells, and then posting a garrison. In a controversial piece of early tourist development, one of the British commanders also exceeded his military brief, turning a local chapel into a tavern and thereby incurring the disapproval of fellow officer John Armstrong: "In the Temple of Bacchus, no bounds are set to their [the soldiers'] Debauches and such a quantity of Wine is daily swallowed down, as would stagger Credulity itself." Quite – but there again, there wasn't much else for the squaddies to do.

Watersports and beaches

The village's sweeping inlet provides ideal conditions for **scuba diving and windsurfing** – you'll see flocks of windsurfers scooting across the calm waters at the southern end of the bay as you approach Fornells. The **Diving Center Fornells** (☎971 37 64 31, ⓦwww.divingfornells.com), on the waterfront at the south end of the village, rents out equipment and organizes diving courses for both novice and experienced divers. Advance reservations for courses and equipment are strongly advised, though 24 hours is usually enough except in the height of the season. As for windsurfing, **Wind Fornells** (☎971 18 81 50, ⓦwww.windfornells.com), located just beyond the southern edge of the village, offers tuition to both novices and more experienced hands, and they teach **sailing** skills too. Alternatively, **Aventura Náutica**, just south of the centre along the waterfront at Passeig Marítim 68 (☎689 02 28 86, ⓦwww.aventuranauticamenorca.com), organizes speedboat excursions round the north coast with snorkelling and swimming part of the deal.

Fornells does not have a **beach**, but there are several attractive beaches in the vicinity – try the Platja de Farragut (see p.245) and the Platja de Cavalleria (see p.245) for starters, though you will need your own transport to get there.

Arrival and accommodation

Buses to Fornells stop right on the waterfront in front of the main restaurant strip and metres from the minuscule main square, Plaça S'Algaret. The **tourist office** (May–Oct daily 9am–2pm & 4.30–7pm; ☎902 92 90 15) is a couple of minutes' walk away to the north, also on the waterfront. Fornells has three reasonably priced and comfortable **hostales** and there's a fair chance of a vacancy in one or other of them even in the high season – but it's best to book ahead just in case. **Parking** can be a pain: the long approach road leading into Fornells is often jam packed, but there's nearly always space on the waste ground just behind – and west of – the main square.

🏃 **Hostal Fornells** c/Major 17 ☎971 37 66 76, ⓦwww.hostalfornells.com. Located half a block from the village's central square, Plaça S'Algaret, Fornells' smartest hostal is a pleasant three-star establishment spreading west from c/ Major with the original building, which now houses reception and a bar, at the front, and a modern three-storey extension at the back. In between is a particularly pleasant outside pool. All the rooms are in the extension and although the décor is fairly simple and straightforward, they are spotlessly clean and the marble floors fairly glisten. Avoid the rooms right at the back as they overlook waste ground, but plump instead for a balconied room overlooking the pool. Closed Nov–April. ❷

Hostal La Palma Plaça S'Algaret 3 ☎971 37 64 87, ⓦwww.hostallapalma.com. Bang in the centre of Fornells on the main square, this two-star *hostal* is a neat little place, with simple but cheerfully bright and colourful, en suite rooms. There's also an outside pool. Closed Nov–March. ❷

Hostal S'Algaret Plaça S'Algaret 7 ☎971 37 65 52, ⓦwww.hostal-salgaret.com. Straightforward two-star *hostal* with some thirty guest rooms, all en suite and decorated in brisk modern style, plus a small outside pool. Closed Jan. ❸

Eating

Nightlife in Fornells is confined to the **restaurants** that populate the centre of the village: such is their reputation that many islanders phone up days in advance to book a table or place an order.

Es Cranc c/Escoles 31 ☎971 37 64 42. A 5-minute walk north of Plaça S'Algaret, along the pedestrianized main street and just past the church, this popular and very informal restaurant offers a wide variety of fish dishes, with the signature *caldereta de llagosta* going for €70. Closed Wed and Nov–March.

Es Port c/Riera 5 ☎971 37 64 03. On the waterfront, just south of Plaça S'Algaret, this relaxed and easygoing restaurant concentrates on a magnificent *caldereta de llagosta* (€70).

🏃 **Sa Llagosta** c/Gabriel Gelabert 12 ☎971 37 65 66. This cosy little restaurant in a sympathetically converted old fisherman's house just along the waterfront from Plaça S'Algarete, has a small but select menu with the emphasis on local dishes and ingredients. The portions may be petite, but the flavours are delicious with each dish carefully prepared and presented. Main courses average €19, though the *caldereta de llagosta* will cost you €72. Open daily.

Sa Nansa c/Vivers 5. Just out of the main restaurant scrum, a short walk north along the waterfront from the centre of the village, this café-restaurant may be short on decorative charm, but its menu is competitively priced and it covers all the Menorcan classics as well as pizzas and *bocadillos*. Eat inside or on the small pavement terrace. Mains from €15, pizzas from €10.

Beyond Fornells

The wild and rocky coastline west of Fornells boasts several **cove beaches** of outstanding beauty, most memorably the **Platja de Cavalleria**. The developers have barely touched this portion of the island, but nonetheless access to this *platja* is straightforward, even if there are no facilities – so be sure to take your own food and drink. There's also dramatic coastal scenery hereabouts at the **Cap de Cavalleria**, whose louring seacliffs rise precipitously from the ocean.

Public transport is, as you might expect, non-existent on this stretch of the coast and neither is there anywhere to stay.

Cap de Cavalleria

About 3km south of Fornells, the roads from Maó and Es Mercadal meet at a staggered crossroads. From here, a signposted turning leads west down a pretty country lane through a charming landscape of old stone walls and scattered farmsteads. After about 3km, keep straight on at the intersection and proceed for another kilometre or so to the signposted right turning that leads north (along an asphalted byroad) to the **Cap de Cavalleria**, Menorca's northernmost point, named after the *cavalleries* – baronial estates – into which the island was divided after the Reconquista. This is easy driving, and 1.9km later, at the bend in the road, there is roadside parking at the start of the seven hundred-metre-long footpath that leads across the dunes to **Platja de Ferragut**, an arc of sand sheltered to the west by a jutting promontory. Back on the road, it's another 1km to the car park for the delightful **Platja de Cavalleria**, a slightly longer and wider beach next door to the Platja de Ferragut, only on this occasion the walk to the beach only takes a few minutes. Other more secluded coves can be reached from these two beaches westwards along the Camí de Cavalls coastal footpath, the two obvious targets being the **Platja de Binimel-Là**, a shale beach where the waters are clear and good for swimming and snorkelling, though seaweed can be a problem, and, further to the west, **Cala Pregonda**, a seastack-studded bay with a wide sandy beach.

The Ecomuseu, the Port de Sanitja and the lighthouse

Pushing on past the **Platja de Cavalleria car park**, it's about 1km more to the short side road that leads up to the **Ecomuseu Cap de Cavalleria** (daily: April, May, June & Oct 10am–7pm; July, Aug & Sept 10am–8pm; €3), an odd little museum located in an old farmstead perched on a hillock with wide views over the cape beyond. This area was settled by the Romans in 123 BC, a connection which convinced the European Union to fund the Ecomuseu, but it's hard not to think it was more of a job-creation scheme – an impression the museum's paltry if gallant collection of Roman and Talayotic bits and pieces does little to dispel. Clearly visible from the Ecomuseu is the **Port de Sanitja**, the long and sheltered inlet just to the north of the museum, where the Romans built the town and port of **Sanisera** on the ruins of an earlier Phoenician settlement, though almost nothing survives from either period. Archeologists have explored the site of the Roman settlement, which begins about 500m north of the museum turning, and you can spot the scant results of their endeavours beside the road, but the main historical artefact hereabouts is the **Martello tower** – the **Torre de Sanitja** – built at the very mouth of the inlet by the British at the end of the eighteenth century.

Beyond the museum, the road clips across a bare and rocky plateau nibbled by scores of goats before shelving up towards the **Cap de Cavalleria** itself, a bleak and wind-buffeted hunk of rock with mighty seacliffs, 90m high, and a lonely **lighthouse** (*far*; no access). If you're lucky you'll glimpse some of the Balearic shearwaters that congregate here – a recent environmental project to restore their habitat has boosted their numbers.

The Martello tower

Popular with the British military in the late eighteenth and early nineteenth centuries, the design of the **Martello tower**, a combined barracks, gun battery and storehouse, was copied from a Corsican tower (at Martello Point) that had proved particularly troublesome to the Royal Navy when they had tried to capture it. These self-contained, semi-self-sufficient defensive fortifications, equipped with thick walls and a protected entrance, proved so successful and easy to build that they were erected in every corner of the empire, only becoming militarily obsolete in the 1870s.

Central Menorca

Central Menorca is the agricultural heart of the island, its rippling hills and rolling plains dotted with scores of whitewashed farmsteads. Admittedly, the tourist boom has knocked some of the stuffing out of the island's agriculture – witness the many unkempt fields – but it's still surprising, considering Menorca's package popularity, just how traditional things are here. Furthermore, the land still carries the myriad marks of past agrarian endeavours in its dry-stone walls and stone **ziggurats** (*barraques*), which were built to shelter cattle from wind and sun, and then there are scores of **Talayotic sites** in various states of repair and interest. By accident or design, neither have the four little towns of the interior – Alaior, Es Mercadal, Ferreries and Es Migjorn Gran – been much modernized, and each contains a comely ensemble of old houses dating back to the eighteenth century, sometimes further. All four towns are readily reached via the Me-1, which runs the 45km across the island from Maó to Ciutadella.

Heading west from Maó, the **Me–1** begins by traversing a flattish agricultural district before looping round the hilltop town of **Alaior**, which boasts a pretty little centre of mazy cobbled streets. From Maó, Alaior (and ultimately Es Mercadal) can also be reached on the **Camí d'en Kane**, the old island road, which bears the name of a British governor (see below) and follows a rusticated route just to the north of the Me-1: to get to the start, take the Fornells road out of Maó and, 1.2km after the Es Grau turning, watch for the sign on the left. Alaior is also close to two of the island's most extensive prehistoric sites,

---

Richard Kane and the Camí d'en Kane

Born in Ulster, **Sir Richard Kane** (1662–1736) was the quintessential military man, his long career in the British army including service in Canada and campaigns with the Duke of Marlborough. In 1712, during the first British occupation of the island, Kane was appointed **Lieutenant-Governor of Menorca**, a post he held – with one or two brief interruptions – until the year of his death.

When Kane arrived in Menorca, he found a dispirited and impoverished population, governed from Ciutadella by a reactionary oligarchy. Kane's initial preoccupation was with the island's **food supply**, which was woefully inadequate. He promptly set about draining swampland near Maó and introduced new and improved strains of seed corn. The governor also had livestock imported from England – hence the Friesian cattle that remain the mainstay of the island's cheese-making industry. Meanwhile, a tax on alcohol provided the cash to develop Menorca's infrastructure, resulting in improved port facilities at Maó and the construction of the first **road** right across the island. Much of this road, the **Camí d'en Kane** (see above), has since disappeared beneath newer versions, but part of it – from just north of Maó to Es Mercadal – has survived and now serves as a scenic alternative to the Me-1.

Kane's innovations were not at all to the taste of the Menorcan aristocracy, who, holed up in Ciutadella, were further offended when Kane arranged for the capital to be moved to Maó. They bombarded London with complaints, eventually inducing a formal governmental response in an open letter to the islanders entitled "A Vindication of Colonel Kane". Most Menorcans, however, seem to have welcomed Kane's benevolent administration, except in **religious matters**, where the governor caused offence by holding Protestant services for his troops in Catholic churches. That apart, there's little doubt that, by the time of his death, Kane was a widely respected figure, whose endeavours were ill served by the colonial indifference of some of his successors.

Cheese and cheese-making

Known generically as **Queso Mahon**, after the island capital, from where it was traditionally exported, **Menorcan cheese** is a richly textured, white, semi-fat cheese made from pasteurized cow's milk with a touch of ewe's milk added for extra flavour. The cheese is sold at four different stages of maturity, either *tierno* (young), *semi-curado* (semi-mature), *curado* (mature) or *añejo* (very mature), and central Menorca is dotted with **cheese-making plants**, several of which encourage visitors. The most enjoyable by a long chalk is the Hort Sant Patrici, near Ferreries (see p.254), but the tourist office has the complete list.

Torralba d'en Salord and **Torre d'en Gaumés**, which is itself close to **Son Bou**, a large and unenticing resort partly redeemed by its long sandy beach. Further west, the Me-1 slips into the village of Es Mercadal, overlooked by Monte Toro, the island's highest peak, its summit occupied by a cute little church. The road to the mountaintop is excellent and the views superb, revealing the geological make-up of the whole island.

From Es Mercadal, it's a short journey southwest to **Es Migjorn Gran**, a pleasant if unremarkable little town that is the starting point for an excellent two- to three-hour hike down the **Barranc de Binigaus** (see box, pp.252–253), while nearby lurks another big resort, **Sant Tomàs**. Back on the Me-1, you'll soon reach **Ferreries**, the fourth of the towns of the interior, from where it's a short hop south to **Cala Galdana**, an attractive resort of manageable proportions that's within easy hiking distance of several isolated cove beaches.

Fast and frequent **buses** ply the Me-1, with supplementary summertime services running from Maó to Sant Tomàs, Son Bou, and Cala Galdana plus destinations in between. Es Migjorn Gran and Cala Galdana are also reachable by bus from both Maó and Ciutadella (for more details on bus travel, see p.268). **Accommodation**, on the other hand, is more troublesome, at least for the independent traveller. The resorts are dominated by the package-tourist industry, though you can, of course, take pot luck, and of the four inland towns, only Es Mercadal and Es Migjorn Gran have recommendable hotels or *hostales* – though only one each.

Alaior

ALAIOR, an old market town some 12km from Maó, has long been a nucleus of the island's dairy industry, but in recent years it has also become something of a manufacturing centre, its tangle of new – and newish – buildings spreading formlessly across the flat land just to the north of the Me-1. This modern part of town is not at all prepossessing, but beyond, about 1km up a steep hill, is the more appealing **old centre**, whose rabbit-warren of narrow lanes and alleys surround the imposing parish church of **Santa Eulàlia**, a magnificent edifice of fortress-like proportions built between 1674 and 1690. The church's main doorway is a Baroque extravagance, its exuberant scrollwork dripping with fruits and fronds, while the facade above accommodates a rose window and a pair of balustrades. Beyond the church – just up the hill to the northwest along the L-shaped c/Moli de l'Angel – a mini-watchtower is plonked on top of the **Munt de l'Angel**, a hill from where you can look out over the countryside. From the end of c/Moli de l'Angel, it's a few metres north to the old town's main square, **Plaça Nova**, an attractive piazza flanked by pastel-painted civic buildings of considerable age.

Buses to Alaior pull in on c/St Joan Baptista, from where it's a steep 500m haul northwest to the old centre – and the church of Santa Eulàlia. There's nowhere to stay. The best time to be in Alaior is the second weekend of August, when the town lets loose with the **Festa de Sant Llorenç**, a drunken knees-up with displays of horsemanship. As its climax, a procession of horses tears through the packed town square, bucking and rearing, with their riders clinging on for dear life. Although no one seems to get hurt, you might prefer to enjoy the spectacle from the safety of a balcony.

Southeast of Alaior: the Torralba d'en Salord

One of the island's more extensive Talayotic settlements, **Torralba d'en Salord** (June–Sept daily 10am–8pm; Oct–May Mon–Sat 10am–1pm & 3–6pm; €3.50) lies about 3km southeast of Alaior beside the road to Cala en Porter. The site is muddled by the old (and disused) Cala en Porter road, which slices right through the site, and by the modern stone walls built alongside both the old and new roads. Nevertheless, it doesn't take too long to figure things out. From the car park, signs direct you round the remains of a **talayot** just beyond which is the **taula**, one of the best preserved on the island. The rectangular enclosure surrounding it is also in good condition, and has been the subject of much conjecture by archeologists, who discovered that several of the recesses contained large fire pits, which may well have been used for the ritual slaughter of animals. It was, however, the unearthing of a tiny **bronze bull** (now in Maó's Museu de Menorca, see p.225) that really got the experts going. The theory was that the Menorcans (in common with several other prehistoric Mediterranean peoples) venerated the bull, with the *taula* being a stylized representation of a bull's head. The argument continues to this day. Beyond the *taula*, the signed trail circumnavigates the remainder of the site, which contains a confusion of stone remains, none of them especially revealing. The most noteworthy are the battered remains of a second **talayot** just next to the *taula* and an underground chamber roofed with stone slabs.

Southwest of Alaior: Torre d'en Gaumés

On the western edge of Alaior, the Me-1 clips past the **Son Bou turning**, which leads to both the beaches of the south coast and the rambling Talayotic settlement of **Torre d'en Gaumés** (May–Sept Tues–Sat 9.30am–8pm, Sun & Mon 9.30am–3pm; April & Oct Tues–Sun 10am–2.30pm, €3; Nov–March open access; free). For Son Bou (see p.249) keep straight, for the ruins go left at the signposted fork about 2.3km south of the Me-1. As you near the ruins, you'll pass a small **visitor information centre**, where two short films provide some background on Talayotic life, but this is eminently missable and you're better off keeping going the extra 1km to the site itself. The higher part of Torre d'en Gaumés – the part near the entrance – possesses no fewer than three **talayots**, the largest of which is next to a broken-down **taula** in the centre of a walled, horseshoe-shaped enclosure. Together, the *taula* and the enclosure form what is presumed to have been the public part of the village, and it was here that archeologists unearthed a little bronze figure of the Egyptian god of knowledge, **Imhotep** (now in the Museu de Menorca in Maó, see p.225), a discovery which reinforced the theory that these enclosures possessed religious significance. In the lower part of the settlement, there are the scant remains of several more houses, another walled enclosure and a comparatively sophisticated storage chamber – the subterranean *Sala Hipostila*. Here also are the clearly discernible remains of a **water collection system** in which rainwater was channelled down the hillside between a series of shallow, artificial indentations to end up in underground cisterns and a cave, which had previously served as a funerary chamber – the site was inhabited and continually modified well into Roman times.

Son Bou and Sant Jaume Mediterrani

Down on the coast at **SON BOU**, 7km southwest of Alaior, the antiquarian interest is maintained by an extensive **cave complex**, cut into the cliff-face above the final part of the approach road. There are also the foundations of an early **Christian basilica**, set behind the beach at the east end of the resort, but these are hardly popular attractions when compared with the **beach**, a whopping pale-gold strand some 3km long and 40m wide. This is Menorca's longest beach, and behind it has mushroomed a massive tourist complex of skyscraper hotels and villa-villages that spreads west into the twin resort of **SANT JAUME MEDITERRANI**. The sand shelves gently into the sea, but the bathing isn't quite as safe as it appears: ocean currents are hazardous, particularly when the wind picks up, and you should watch for the green and red flags. The beach accommodates several bars, and **watersports equipment** is widely available – everything from jet-skis, snorkels and windsurfing boards to sunloungers and pedalos.

Accommodation and camping

The development is at its crassest – and the crowds at their worst – towards the east end of the beach, where the foreshore is dominated by several huge sky-rise **hotels**, principally the *Sol Milanos* (☏971 37 12 00, ⦿www.solmelia.com; ❺; closed Nov–April) and the *Sol Pinguinos* (same details). These two hotels share facilities, including sun terraces, outside pools, bars and restaurants, and have spruce modern balconied bedrooms. A little to the west, a strip of dune-fringed, marshy scrubland runs behind the beach, providing the shoreline with some much needed protection and pushing the villa developments a kilometre or so inland. As a result, the bathing along this stretch of coast is much more secluded. More economically, one of Menorca's rare **campsites**, the *Son Bou* (☏971 37 27 27, ⦿www.campingsonbou.com; closed Oct to March), is located 3.5km inland on the more westerly access road linking the Me-1 with Sant Jaume Mediterrani. This well-equipped campsite has several hundred pitches in amongst the pine woods, as well as its own swimming pool, sports area, laundry, supermarket and restaurant. In high season (July & Aug), adult campers pay €7.75 each, plus €4.40–14 per tent, depending on size; cars (€5.25) further add to the bill, and there is a small supplementary charge for electrical hook-ups. Shoulder-season rates are around ten percent less.

Es Mercadal

ES MERCADAL, 9km northwest of Alaior along the Me-1, sits amongst the hills at the very centre of the island. Another old market town, it's an amiable little place whose antique centre of whitewashed houses and trim allotments is now flanked by modern houses of a neat and trim demeanour. At the heart of the town, the minuscule main square, **Plaça Constitució**, has a couple of sleepy cafés and is a few paces from the Ruritanian **Ajuntament** (Town Hall), at c/Major 16. That's just about it for sights unless, that is, you count the rain-catching, water reservoir – the **Aljub** – which was built on the orders of Richard Kane (see p.246); it's located on the edge of town, a short walk northwest of c/Major off c/Sol.

Buses to Es Mercadal pull in on Avinguda Mestre Gari, just off the Me-1 on the southern edge of town, a five-minute walk from Plaça Constitució: to get there, walk straight down Avinguda Mestre Gari and its continuation c/Nou. There's no tourist office, but there is somewhere **to stay**, the *Hostal Jeni*, in a brightly decorated modern building at c/Mirada del Toro 81 (☎971 37 50 59, ⓦwww.hostaljeni.com; ❷). The *hostal* has fifty-odd, en-suite bedrooms decorated in spick-and-span modern style as well as a swimming pool and sauna; it's situated on the south side of town – c/Mirada del Toro runs parallel to, and one block east of, Avinguda Mestre Gari.

Monte Toro

Es Mercadal is the starting point for the ascent of **MONTE TORO**, a steep 3.2km climb along a serpentine but easily driveable road. At 357m, the summit is the island's highest point and offers wonderful views: on a good day you can see almost the whole island; on a bad one, you can still see at least as far as Fornells. From this lofty vantage point, Menorca's **geological division** becomes apparent: to the north, Devonian rock (mostly reddish sandstone) supports a hilly, sparsely populated landscape edged by a fretted coastline; to the south, limestone predominates in a rippling, wooded plain that boasts the island's best farmland and, as it approaches the south coast, its deepest wooded gorges (*barrancs*).

It's likely that the **name of the hill** is derived from the Moorish Al Thor ("high point"), but medieval Christians invented an alternative etymology. In predictable fashion, this involves villagers (or monks) spotting a mysterious light on the mountain and, on closer investigation, being confronted by a bull (*toro*), which, lo and behold, obligingly leads them to a miracle-making statue of the Virgin. Whatever the truth, a statue of the Virgin – the Verge del Toro – was installed in a crude but long departed shrine in the thirteenth century and Monte Toro has been a place of pilgrimage ever since. The ceremonial highlight is on the first Sunday of May, when the **Festa de la Verge del Toro** (Festival of the Virgin of

▲ Monte Toro

the Bull) begins with a special mass at the Monte Toro church and continues with a knees-up down in Es Mercadal.

The hilltop

The Augustinians plonked a monastery on the summit in the seventeenth century, but fearful islanders soon interrupted their monkish reveries by building a small fortress here against the threat of an Ottoman invasion. Bits of both the monastery and the fort survive, the former incorporated within the present **monastery** – though the monks left long ago – the latter in a square stone **tower** that now stands forlorn and neglected. High above both stands a **statue of Christ** erected in honour of those Menorcans who died in a grubby colonial war launched by Spain in Morocco in the 1920s.

The tower and much of the monastery is out of bounds, but the **public area**, approached across a handsome courtyard with a dinky little well, is still large enough to accommodate a couple of gift shops, a terrace café, a restaurant, and a charming **church**, entered through a low and deep stone porch that is decorated with flowers and shrubs. Inside, the barrel-vaulted nave is a modest, truncated affair dating from 1595, its gloominess partly dispelled by a central dome. The most prominent feature is the gaudy, 1940s high altarpiece, whose fancy woodwork swarms with cherubs and frames the much-venerated **Verge del Toro**, depicting the crowned Virgin holding Jesus in her arms with the enterprising bull of folkloric fame at her feet. The statue is typical of the so-called black Catalan Madonnas, made either from black-stained wood or dark stone.

Es Migjorn Gran

Heading southwest from Es Mercadal, the road weaves a rustic route on its way to **ES MIGJORN GRAN**, a sleepy little town that trails along a low ridge amidst intricate terraced fields. Of the several towns founded on the island in the eighteenth century, this is the only one not to have been laid out by foreigners. Consequently, the gridiron streets of the likes of Es Castell are replaced by a more organic layout, the houses of the old agricultural workers straggling along the elongated main street, **c/Major**, as it curves through town.

Buses pull in beside the bypass on the southeast side of Es Migjorn Gran, a short walk from c/Major. The village hardly sets the pulse racing, but it is the starting point for an excellent hike (see pp.252–253) and it does have two **places to stay**, the more agreeable of which is *Fonda S'Engolidor*, c/Major 3 (☎971 37 01 93, ⓦwww.sengolidor.com; ❶; closed

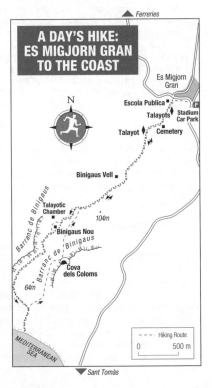

A DAY'S HIKE:
ES MIGJORN GRAN
TO THE COAST

▲ Ferreries

Es Migjorn Gran

Escola Publica

Talayots

Talayot

Stadium Car Park

P

Cemetery

N

Binigaus Vell

Talayotic Chamber

104m

Barranc de Binigaus

Binigaus Nou

Barranc de Binigaus

Cova dels Coloms

64m

MEDITERRANEAN SEA

- - - Hiking Route

0   500 m

▼ Sant Tomàs

A day's hike: Es Migjorn Gran to the coast, via the Barranc de Binigaus

Circular. 8km; 150m ascent; 3hr–3hr 30min. Moderate.

Despite its modest dimensions, Menorca packs a surprising diversity into its landscape. One of the island's most unexpected – and best hidden – topographical features are the dramatic limestone gorges, or *barrancs*, which score and scour the southern coast, running from the hills inland down to the sea. Starting in the inland village of **Es Migjorn Gran**, this walk follows one of these gorges, the **Barranc de Binigaus**, down to the coast near Sant Tomàs, passing through an area rich in **Talayotic** remains and impressive natural limestone formations.

The hike

The walk starts on the edge of Es Migjorn Gran at the **car park** outside the municipal sports stadium (Camp Municipal D'Esports), which is by the town's main roundabout. From the car park walk along the right-hand side of the main road (Avinguda de la Mar) in the direction of Sant Tomàs as far as the **Bar S'Auba**. Turn right up the hill along Avinguda David Russell and continue to the T-junction with Escola Publica in front of you and turn left; the distance from the car park to the Escola Publica is 450m.

The first half of the walk follows the road that you are now on, after a short while becoming a stony track, meandering slowly downhill towards the coast. The road starts by running picturesquely between limestone walls flanked by handsome old Aleppo pines, an old enclosure housing the substantial remains of two *talayots*, and a cemetery. Some 200m further on you'll pass another *talayot* on your right, followed by an attractive ensemble of white houses and Menorcan-style gates. Continue for a further 1km, passing enclosures littered with limestone boulders, until you reach the attractive old whitewashed farmstead of Binigaus Vell.

Just past here you'll have your first sight of the sea. The path continues for a further 750m, with the dramatic limestone formations of the **Barranc de Binigaus** coming into view on your left. Beyond here, the track passes through an intricate but overgrown system of terraces and enclosures before climbing past a potholed limestone outcrop to reach the brow of the hill. Two more *talayots* are now visible to your left – the land hereabouts holds an incredible jumble of natural, prehistoric and

Nov–April), with four extremely cosy guest rooms in a cheerfully restored eighteenth-century house towards the west (Ferreries) end of town. Beneath the *Fonda* is a smashing little **restaurant**, the *58 S'Engolidor* (same phone number; closed Mon), where the emphasis is on traditional Menorcan cuisine with mains around €17. The restaurant possesses a charming, summer-only garden courtyard with views over a wooded gorge; reservations are strongly advised.

Sant Tomàs

South of Es Migjorn Gran, the road shuttles along a wooded ravine that leads down to the south coast – and the crass hotel and apartment buildings of **SANT TOMÀS**. The resort's saving grace is its three-kilometre-long sandy **beach**, very similar to that of Son Bou, a couple of headlands away to the east, and very inviting it is too. The road reaches the shore halfway along the beach, which is called **Platja Sant Adeodat** to the west and **Platja Sant Tomàs** to the east. The latter is easily the more congested, and it's here you'll find the resort's high-rise hotels, among which the air-conditioned, ultra-modern Santo Tomàs is the most lavish (☎971 37 00 25, ⓦwww.sethotels.com; ❻ with half board; closed Nov–March), though the slightly less expensive Sol Menorca will do just as well (☎971 37 00 50,

more recent agricultural stone-working, with the Barranc de Binigaus, issuing into the sea via a narrow defile – your eventual goal – far ahead and below.

Descend through a Menorcan-style gate to the farmhouse of **Binigaus Nou**, a striking baronial-looking structure. About 50m before a second farm gate, turn right off the track onto a narrow path signed **Cova-y-Platja**. This leads to an unusual (but strangely unsigned) Talayotic **hypostyle chamber** and a fine view of the limestone cliffs of a secondary arm of the *barranc* behind. From the chamber continue along the path to rejoin the track. From here, the track hairpins down into the *barranc* beneath high walls of limestone and then proceeds past further wildly overgrown agricultural terracing before reaching the bottom of the hill at a Menorcan-style gate opposite a path signposted to the **Cova dels Coloms**.

The route continues along this path to the *cova* (cave). If you want to make the brief **detour to the coast**, walk through the gate ahead and continue straight on for 150m to reach the sea next to an old gun emplacement buried in the dunes and covered in windswept vegetation. If you're in need of food and drink, head left here and walk along the beach for 750m to reach the resort of **Sant Tomàs** (see p.252). Back on the main route, head along the path signposted to the **Cova dels Coloms**. This path gradually ascends back into the *barranc* for 1km through woodland before reaching a large dry stone wall and a fork. Head right here, along the narrowing gorge and beneath increasingly impressive limestone cliffs, scored with caves, until, after a further 750m, you reach a gap in another large wall marked with a splash of red paint. Pass through the gap and then bear left – ignoring the path going straight ahead – up a narrow path through thick woodland for about 500m, where you need to look out for a narrow side path joining acutely from the right. Take this side path and follow it uphill for 20m and then turn left up a zigzagging stone terrace to reach the Cova dels Coloms – a huge natural cave, impressive for its size if nothing else (though the copious graffiti and overpowering smell of guano are less appealing).

Retrace your steps to the main path and turn right. After a few metres the path climbs to the left and becomes boulder strewn. It then zigzags up out of the gorge and returns you to the original track that you came down on at a point between Binigaus Vell and Binigaus Nou. Turn right and retrace your steps uphill to **Es Migjorn Gran** (see p.251).

Ⓦwww.solmelia.com; Ⓔ; closed Nov–April). Both have pools, restaurants, night-time entertainment and many types of sports facility. Windsurfing boards, jet-skis and pedalos can all be rented on the Platja Sant Tomàs.

Ferreries

The old centre of **FERRERIES**, a modest little town on the Me-1 some 8km from Es Mercadal – and 6km from Es Migjorn Gran – is tucked into a hollow beneath a steep hill, its narrow, sloping streets framed by ancient whitewashed houses. A surprise here is the pagoda-like piece of modern sculpture in the main square, the **Plaça Espanya**, while just up the hill at the back of the *plaça* – along c/Fred – stands the neatly shuttered **Ajuntament**, primly facing the parish church of **Sant Bartomeu**, a largely eighteenth-century edifice with an 1884-vintage belfry tacked onto the top. The liveliest time to be here is on Saturday morning (9am–1pm), when a small food and crafts **market** is held on Plaça Espanya, but otherwise there's not much to detain you in the town itself, though there are a couple of neighbouring attractions. The more obvious of them is the large **Jaime Mascaró factory shoe and leather shop** (Mon–Sat 9.30am–8.30pm & Sun 10am–2pm), 1km or so east of town along the Me-1, but there's also the **Hort de Sant Patrici cheese** plant (May–Sept Mon–Sat 9am–1.30pm & 4.30–8pm; Oct–April Mon–Fri 9am–1pm & 4–6pm, Sat 9am–1pm; Ⓦwww.santpatrici.com), where an assortment of farm buildings surround a good-looking old *hacienda* with attractive gardens. You can watch cheese being made, buy it at the shop, stroll the gardens and visit the cheese museum, though this last activity will cost you €4.50, whereas all the rest is free. The plant has a pleasant rural setting just north of Ferreries: to get there, take the unsigned northern exit off the Me-1 roundabout on the eastern edge of Ferreries, by the Meubles allés store; follow this road across the industrial estate (*polígon industrial*) until it becomes a country lane and the cheese plant is a couple of minutes' drive further on. It's just 1.2km from the roundabout to the cheese plant.

One definite plus in Ferreries is the *Vimpi* café-bar, beside the Me-1 on Plaça Joan Carles, which serves tasty tapas for €3–8. You wouldn't choose to stay in Ferreries – it's just too quiet – which is just as well because there's no recommendable **accommodation**. **Buses** stop in front of the *Vimpi*, which is itself a four-minute walk from Plaça Espanya, straight up Avinguda Verge del Toro.

Cala Galdana

Just to the west of Ferreries, a fast, eight-kilometre road cuts south off the Me-1 to breeze through a pretty pastoral landscape on its way to the resort of **CALA GALDANA**. Once a much-loved beauty spot, the bay has experienced a rash of development since the building of the road and is now cluttered with high-rises and low-rises alike. But, despite the concrete, there's no denying the beauty of the setting, the curving sandy **beach** framed by wooded, limestone cliffs and flanked by a pint-sized rocky promontory, which is itself next to a narrow river. Early in the morning or out of season is the best time to appreciate the scene – or you can escape the crowds by hiking west or east along the coast to more secluded coves (see below). It's possible to hire out all sorts of **watersports** equipment in Cala Galdana, from pedalos and water scooters to windsurfing boards and snorkelling tackle, and there are a couple of **car hire** outlets too.

The resort has four large chain **hotels**, easily the pick of which is the four-star *Sol Gavilanes* (Ⓣ971 15 45 45, Ⓦwww.solmelia.com; ❼; closed Nov–March), set in its own verdant grounds and built against the cliffs that frame the beach. The hotel has every facility, from air-conditioning, swimming pools to satellite TV, and most of the attractive, modern guest rooms have sea-facing balconies. At the other end of the market, the **S'Atalaia campsite** is located about 3km back down the road towards Ferreries (Ⓣ971 37 42 32, Ⓦwww.campingsatalaia.com; April–Sept). Pine trees shade much of the site, which has an outdoor swimming pool, a supermarket and a restaurant–bar; it's not a large campsite and it is popular, so advance **reservations** are strongly advised. In high season (July & Aug), adult campers pay €6.90 each, plus €4–9 per tent, depending on size; cars (€2.15) further add to the bill, and there is a small supplementary charge for electrical hook-ups. Shoulder-season rates are around fifteen percent less.

From May to October, there are regular **buses** to Cala Galdana from Maó, Ferreries and Ciutadella; buses stop in the centre of the resort, a brief walk from the beach. There is also a bus stop outside the campsite, but be sure to let the driver know you want to get off here, otherwise you will go whizzing by.

Beaches east of Cala Galdana: Cala Mitjana

There are several exquisite **cove beaches** within easy reach of Cala Galdana, the most obvious choice being **CALA MITJANA**, just 1km to the east. The

footpath to Cala Mitjana begins at the Plaça Na Gran car park, near the main entrance to the *Hotel Sol Gavilanes* (see below): from the centre of the resort, proceed back up the main approach road, turn right at the roundabout and the (signed) car park is on the left. A gate at the back leads onto an easy-to-follow path, which weaves its way through coastal pine woods to reach Cala Mitjana in about thirty minutes. The **beach** itself is a broad strip of sand at the back of a chubby little cove with wooded cliffs to either side. A favourite sport here is jumping into the crystal-clear water from the surrounding cliffs. It's a lovely spot, though there's sometimes an unpleasant smell of seaweed and the beach can get a little crowded now that a dirt road connects it with the main road between Ferreries and Cala Galdana; there are no beach facilities, so bring a **picnic**.

Beaches west of Cala Galdana: Cala Macarella and Cala Macarelleta

The **footpath** leading to the **cove beaches** west of Cala Galdana begins with a set of steps beside – and slightly to the front of - the large and lumpy *Hotel Audax*, which stands near the beach at the west end of the resort. From the steps, it takes about fifty minutes to reach **CALA MACARELLA**, whose severe, partly wooded limestone cliffs surround a band of white sand that shelves gently into the Med. The swimming is ideal and, unlike several other beaches hereabouts, seaweed is never a problem. There's a touch of development in the form of a summertime beach bar, and sunloungers and pedalos for rent, but it's nothing excessive. Fron Cala Macarella, a clifftop path leads to neighbouring **CALA MACARELLETA**, an even more secluded and equally beautiful beach.

Heading west from Cala Macarella, it takes about two hours to walk to the next major beach, **Cala Turqueta** (see p.266), via the Camí de Cavalls long-distance footpath.

Torrellafuda, Naveta d'es Tudons and the Lithica Pedreres de S'hostal

Heading west out of Ferreries, the Me-1 soon leaves the central hills behind for the flatlands that precede Ciutadella. These flatlands are dotted with some of the island's more important prehistoric sites, the first one of real significance being **Torrellafuda** (open access; free), whose mini-car park is reached down a clearly signed, 800m-long dirt road on the south side of the Me-1. From the car park, it's a brief walk to the site, where a particularly well-preserved *talayot* stands close to the *taula*, which is hidden away in a little, wooded dell. The rustic setting is delightful – it's a perfect spot for a picnic.

Back on the Me-1, it's almost 3km from the Torrellafuda turning to the **Naveta d'es Tudons** (May–Sept Tues–Sat 9.30am–8pm, Sun & Mon 9.30am–3pm; April & Oct Tues–Sun 10am–2.30pm, €2; Nov–March open access; free), easily the best-preserved *naveta* on the island. Standing in a field a short stroll from the main road, the *naveta* is seven metres high and fourteen long, consisting of massive stone blocks slotted together using a sophisticated dry-stone technique. The narrow entrance on the west side leads into a small antechamber, which was once sealed off by a stone slab; beyond lies the main chamber where the bones of the dead were stashed away after the flesh had been removed. Folkloric memories of the *navetas'* original purpose survived into modern times – Menorcans were loathe to go near these odd-looking and solitary monuments until well into the nineteenth century.

From the *naveta*, it's a couple of minutes' drive west along the Me-1 to the signed turning that leads to one of the island's most unusual sights, the **Lithica**

Pedreres de S'hostal, just to the south of the main road at Camí Vell s/n (April to late Oct Mon–Sat 9.30am–5.30pm & Sun 9.30am–2.30pm; late Oct to March daily 9.30am–2.30pm; €4; ⓦwww.lithica.es). Stone has been quarried here for centuries and the old workings have recently been opened to the public. From the ticket office, you descend to the old quarry floor, where you can wander amongst a labyrinth of giant stone stacks cut to all sorts of fanciful shapes. It was long the custom for the quarry men to plant gardens in some of their old workings and there's a lovely verdant garden here today, shaded by orange and almond trees, as well as an open-air theatre, which is used for live performances, and a stone maze. From the quarry, it's a couple of kilometres to Ciutadella.

Ciutadella

Like Maó, **CIUTADELLA** sits high above its harbour, but here navigation is far more difficult, up a narrow channel too slender for all but the smallest of cargo ships. Nonetheless, despite this nautical inconvenience, Ciutadella was the island's capital until the eighteenth century: the Romans chose it, the Moors adopted it as Medina Minurka, and the Catalans of the Reconquista flattened the place and began all over again. In the event, the medieval Catalan town didn't last either: in 1558, **Turkish corsairs** razed the place and carted off three thousand captives – around eighty percent of the population – to the slave markets of Istanbul. As news spread of the disaster, the pope organized a European whip-round, and, with the money in his bag, an intrepid Menorcan doctor, one Marcos Martí, ventured east to buy the slaves back. Martí was remarkably successful – but there again, the Turks were raiding for the cash, not to fight a religious war – and the returning hostages, together with the survivors of the assault, determinedly **rebuilt Ciutadella** in grand style. They refortified the town's compact centre and then, reassured, set about adorning it with fine stone churches and sweeping mansions.

Throughout the seventeenth century, Menorca's leading **landowners** hung out in Ciutadella, confident of their position and power. They were, however, in for a shock: the colonial powers of the eighteenth century had little time for the town's feeble port when compared with Maó's magnificent inlet, and the **British** simply – and abruptly – moved the capital to Maó in 1722. Thereafter, Maó flourished as a trading centre, while Ciutadella stagnated – a long-lasting economic reverie that has, by coincidence, preserved the town's old and beautiful centre as if in aspic.

Despite the loss of its capital status, the bulk of the Menorcan aristocracy decided to stay put. The island's foreign rulers pretty much left them to stew in their own juice – an increasingly redundant, landowning class far from the wheels of mercantile power. Consequently, there's very little British or French influence in Ciutadella's **architecture**: instead, the narrow, cobbled streets boast fine old palaces, hidden away behind high walls, and a set of Baroque and Gothic churches very much in the Spanish tradition. Essentially, it's the whole ensemble, centred on stately **Plaça d'es Born**, that gives Ciutadella its appeal rather than any specific sight, though the mostly Gothic **cathedral** is a delight, as is the eclectic **Museu Diocesà de Menorca**. An ambitious renovation programme has further enhanced the town, restoring most of the old stone facades to their honey-coloured best. Added to this are some excellent **restaurants** and a reasonably adequate supply of *hostales* and **hotels**. All in all, it's a

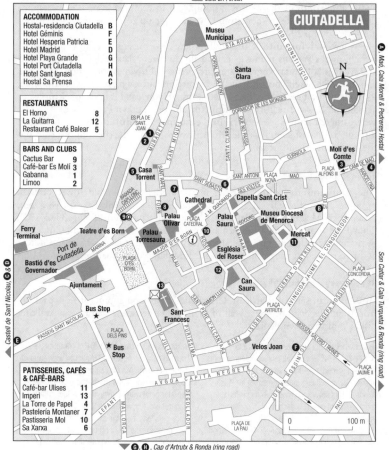

▲ *Cala En Forcat*

CIUTADELLA

ACCOMMODATION
Hostal-residencia Ciutadella	B
Hotel Géminis	F
Hotel Hesperia Patricia	E
Hotel Madrid	D
Hotel Playa Grande	G
Hotel Port Ciutadella	H
Hotel Sant Ignasi	A
Hostal Sa Prensa	C

RESTAURANTS
El Horno	8
La Guitarra	12
Restaurant Café Balear	5

BARS AND CLUBS
Cactus Bar	9
Café-bar Es Moli	3
Gabanna	1
Limoo	2

PATISSERIES, CAFÉS & CAFÉ-BARS
Café-bar Ulises	11
Imperi	13
La Torre de Papel	4
Pastelería Montaner	7
Pastisseria Mol	10
Sa Xarxa	6

N

0   100 m

▼ **G**, **H**, *Cap d'Artrutx & Ronda (ring road)*

lovely place to stay, and nothing else on Menorca rivals the evening *passeig* (promenade), when the townsfolk amble the narrow streets of the centre, dropping in on pavement cafés as the sun sets. Allow at least a couple of days, more if you seek out one of the beguiling **cove beaches** within easy striking distance of town. There are several wonderful spots to choose from, but **Cala Turqueta** is probably the pick of the bunch. Spare time also for the prehistoric sites hereabouts, most pertinently the **Naveta d'es Tudons** (see p.255) and **Son Catlar**.

Arrival

Buses from Maó and points east halt at the bus stops on the west side of Plaça dels Pins, whilst those from the tourist resorts of the west coast stop on the north side. From Plaça dels Pins, it's only a couple of minutes' walk into the town centre. **Car ferries** and catamarans dock beside the terminal building on the north side of the harbour, about five minutes' walk from the town centre. This may change, however, when the new harbour, located near the ring road about 4km south of the centre, is completed in the next couple of years. For details of bus services to and from Ciutadella, see p.268; principal ferry routes are given on pp.20–21.

If you're **driving into Ciutadella**, there's no missing the inner ring road, which, under various names – principally Avinguda Jaume I El Conqueridor and Avinguda Capità Negrete – encircles the old town. Approaching from the east, turn left when you hit it at the T-junction and keep going until you reach its conclusion beside the Plaça dels Pins. If you can't find a **parking** spot actually on this square, turn left at the top and drive down Passeig Sant Nicolau, where there's always space. **Driving east out of Ciutadella** is a tad more difficult as the last stretch of the Me-1 is westbound only; the solution is to use the outer ring road (*the ronda*).

Information

The main **tourist office** is bang in the middle of the old town, directly opposite the cathedral on Plaça Catedral (May–Oct daily 8.30am–8.30pm; Nov–April Mon–Fri 9am–1pm & 5–7pm, Sat 9am–1pm; ☎971 38 26 93). They have a good range of information on Menorca as a whole and Ciutadella in particular, including bus timetables, ferry schedules, lists of *hostales* and hotels, and free maps, but they don't help with finding accommodation.

Accommodation

By Menorcan standards at least, Ciutadella has a good supply of non-package **hotels** and *hostales*, and nearly all of them are either in or within easy walking distance of the town centre.

Hostal-residencia Ciutadella c/Sant Eloi 10 ☎971 38 34 62, ⓦwww.alojarseenmenorca.com. Well-maintained, two-star *hostal* in a pleasantly updated older building on a side street off Plaça Alfons III. Has seventeen modest but comfortable rooms, each of which is decorated in shades of yellow and brown. Open all year. ❶

Hotel Géminis c/Josepa Rossinyol 4 ☎971 38 46 44, ⓦwww.hotelgeminismenorca.com. Distinctively painted in pink and white, this well tended, comfortable two-star hotel has thirty rooms, each decorated in bright if somewhat frugal modern style. The rooms at the front have Art Deco-style balconies and overlook a quiet suburban street. To get there on foot, walk a few paces down c/Mossèn J. Salord i Farnés from the ring road and watch for the archway on the right; go through the arch and the hotel's on the right. Closed Oct–March. ❶

Hotel Hesperia Patricia Passeig Sant Nicolau 90 ☎971 38 55 11, ⓦwww.hesperia.com. Smart, modern hotel popular with business folk and in a great location, a few minutes' walk from the town centre. The comfortable, well-appointed rooms come with all facilities, the only downer being the lack of a sea view – though the best rooms have rooftop balconies with wide vistas over the town centre. There's also an outside swimming pool. Three stars. ❸

Hotel Madrid c/Madrid 60 ☎971 38 03 28. Located near the ocean, a 15-minute walk west of the town centre, *Madrid* comprises fourteen quite comfortable rooms in a run-of-the-mill, villa-style, two-star hotel with its own ground-floor café-bar. To get there, follow Passeig Sant Nicolau from the Plaça dels Pins, take the third turning on the left (c/Saragossa) and you'll hit c/Madrid just east of the hotel at the second intersection. There's an outside pool too. Closed Nov–April. ❶

Hotel Playa Grande c/Bisbe Juano 2 ☎971 48 08 64, ⓦwww.grupoandria.com. Straightforward one-star hotel with a brisk modern interior located about ten minutes' walk south of Plaça dels Pins, at the foot of c/Mallorca. At the front, its balconied rooms overlook a narrow cove and a busy road – ask for a room at the back if you're a light sleeper. ❷

Hotel Port Ciutadella Passeig Marítim 36 ☎971 48 25 20, ⓦwww.sethotels.com. A 15-minute walk southwest of Plaça dels Pins, this slick and ultra-modern four-star hotel flaunts a cleverly designed outside pool and 94 brightly decorated bedrooms with all mod cons – and wood floors. To get there head south on c/Mallorca and at the end turn left at the roundabout. ❺

Hotel Sant Ignasi Carretera Cala Morell s/n ☎971 38 55 75, ⓦwww.santignasi.com. This elegant nineteenth-century manor house – sited about 4km northeast of the centre of Ciutadella and clearly signposted (down a very narrow 1.5km-long lane) from the road to Cala Morell – has been tastefully converted into an immaculate hotel. Each of the twenty bedrooms is individually decorated in a style that blends with the original building, and there are gardens and an outside pool too. While the countryside location is peaceful, the surrounding farmland is nevertheless flat and dull. Closed Oct–March. ⑨

Hostal Sa Prensa c/Madrid 70 ☎971 38 26 98, ⓦ www.saprensa.com. Close to the rocky seashore at the end of c/Madrid, a 15-minute walk west of the centre, this neat and trim, villa-like, one-star *hostal* offers seven spartan bedrooms, three of which have balconies and sea views. To get there, follow Passeig Sant Nicolau from the Plaça dels Pins, take the fourth turning on the left (c/Joan Ramis i Ramis) and you'll hit c/Madrid just beside the *hostal* (sited above a café-bar) at the first major intersection. ❶

The town centre

All of Ciutadella's key attractions are clustered in the **town centre**, a dense cobweb of narrow lanes and alleys flanked by fine old mansions and handsome churches. Most of the centre is pedestrianized, but it only takes a few minutes to walk from one side to the other, and keeping your bearings is fairly straight-forward – the main square and harbour are on the west side of the centre, the inner ring road to the east.

Plaça d'es Born

Primarily a nineteenth-century creation, **Plaça d'es Born** is easily the finest main square in the Balearic islands. In the middle soars an **obelisk** commemo-rating the futile defence against the Turks in 1558, a brutal episode that was actually something of an accident. The Ottomans had dispatched 15,000 soldiers and 150 warships west to assist their French allies against the Habsburgs. With no particular place to go, the Turks rolled around the Mediterranean for a few weeks and, after deciding Maó wasn't worth the candle, they happened on Ciutadella, where the garrison numbered just forty. For the locals, the results were cataclysmic. The one-sided siege ended with the destruction of the town and the enslavement of its population – there was so much damage that when the new Spanish governor arrived, he was forced to live in a cave. The obelisk's original Latin inscription, penned by the mid-nineteenth-century politician and historian **Josep Quadrado**, reads, "Here we fought until death for our religion and our country in the year 1558." Such grandiose nationalism was typical of Quadrado, then the region's most prominent politician and leader of the reactionary Catholic Union, which bombarded Madrid with complaints and petitions whenever the local governor did anything progressive.

The Ajuntament and the Teatre d'es Born

On the western side of the Plaça d'es Born stands the **Ajuntament** (Town Hall), whose early nineteenth-century arches and crenellations mimic Moorish style, purposely recalling the time when the site was occupied by the Wali's *alcázar* (palace). Round the back, down the alley on the left-hand side of the Ajuntament, there's a more authentic reminder of early days in the **Bastió d'es Governador**, a massive stone-clad bastion that rises high above the harbour.

From the Ajuntament, it's a few paces along the north side of the square to the **Teatre d'es Born**, a neat, late nineteenth-century structure built to salvage some municipal pride: the merchants of Maó had just completed their opera house and, pricked into cultural action, the oligarchs of Ciutadella promptly followed suit – though they weren't quite as energetic when it came to actually getting people to perform here and the building lay neglected for years.

The Palau Torresaura and the Església de St Francesc

The northeast corner of the Plaça d'es Born is dominated by the sweeping lines of the **Palau Torresaura**, built in the nineteenth century but looking far older, and the grandest of several aristocratic mansions edging the plaza. Embellished by two handsome loggias, its frontage proclaims the family coat of arms above a large wooden door leading into a spacious coutryard. The antique interior, however, is off limits – like most of its neighbours, the house is still owner-occupied.

Metres away, tucked into the southeast corner of the square, the **Església de St Francesc** is a clean-lined, unpretentious structure, whose hybrid architecture reflects the island's ups and downs. The original church was constructed shortly after the Reconquista and it was here in 1301 that Jaume II met his nobles to parcel up the island into the feudal estates – the *Cavalleries* (from *cavaller*, the Catalan for knight) – that cemented his kingdom. In 1558, the Turks fired the church, but it was rebuilt to the original specifications in the 1590s, with further embellishments added later – the Baroque side door in the eighteenth century, the dome in the nineteenth. Like most of Ciutadella's churches, the Republicans ransacked the interior in the Civil War, but bits and pieces did survive, notably a motley crew of polychromatic saints.

The Cathedral

From beside the Palau Torresaura, c/Major d'es Born leads through to the **cathedral** (daily 9am–1pm & 6–9pm; free), a good-looking structure built by Jaume II at the beginning of the fourteenth century on the site of the chief mosque, but remodelled after the Turkish onslaught of 1558. During the rebuilding, the flying buttresses of the original were partly encased within a thick stone wall to guard against future attack, a modification which gives the cathedral its distinctive appearance. The Gothic **side door** – on the south side of the church – was, however, left intact, its arching columns decorated with strange-looking beasts and the coats of arms of Aragón and Ciutadella, all surmounted by a delicate carving of the Magi honouring the infant Christ. Another survivor was the set of fierce-looking **gargoyles** that decorates the buttresses at roof level. The principal (west) **entrance** was added much later, in 1813, its flashy Neoclassical portico contrasting with the rest of the church and the intricate rose window above.

Inside, light filters through the stained glass of the narrow, lofty windows to bathe the high altar in an ethereal glow. There's also a sequence of glitzy Baroque side chapels, though these look very mediocre when compared with the beautifully carved stonework of the chapel just off the top left-hand corner of the nave. The wall behind the high altar carries a medieval **panel painting**, *The Purification of the Virgin*, but most of the church's old furnishings and fittings were destroyed in a frenzy of **anti-clericalism** when the Republicans took control of Menorca during the Civil War. Although the British had made Maó the island's capital in 1722, Ciutadella remained Menorca's ecclesiastical centre and, almost without exception, its resident Catholic hierarchy were rich and reactionary in equal measure. The priesthood enthusiastically proclaimed its support for the officers of the Maó garrison when the latter declared for Franco in July 1936, but this turned out to be a major gaffe. The bulk of the garrison stayed loyal to the Republic, and, allied with local left-wing groups, they captured the rebels, shot their leaders and ransacked Ciutadella's main churches as retribution.

The Palau Olivar and the Església del Roser

Directly opposite the cathedral's main entrance is the **Palau Olivar** (no access), whose stern, eighteenth-century facade is partly relieved by a pair of miniature balconies fronted by wrought-iron grilles. In 1707, the house witnessed one of the town's crueller episodes, when a reclusive mother and daughter who worked and lived here were accused of witchcraft. Found guilty on palpably potty charges, the older woman was sent to prison for life, and the younger was executed – by any standard, a heavy price to pay for not joining in the town's social life.

From Plaça Catedral, head south along c/Roser and you'll soon reach the tiny **Església del Roser** (Mon–Sat 11am–1pm & 6–9pm; free), whose striking Churrigueresque facade, dating from the seventeenth century, boasts a quartet of pillars festooned with intricate tracery. The church was the subject of bitter controversy when the British governor Richard Kane (see p.246) commandeered it for Church of England services, which was not at all to the liking of the Dominican friars who owned the place. Now deconsecrated, the church's interior has been covered in oodles of cream paint and is now used for temporary exhibitions of contemporary, mostly local, art and crafts.

The Museu Diocesà de Menorca

Continuing down c/Roser, turn left past the palatial, seventeenth-century mansion of **Can Saura**, which is distinguished by its elegant stonework and overhanging eaves, and then left again onto c/Seminari, where you'll find the mildly enjoyable **Museu Diocesà de Menorca** (Diocesan Museum; Mon–Sat 10.30am–2pm; €3.50) occupying an old convent and its church. Before you go in, take a look at the convent's elongated **perimeter wall**, a sober affair interrupted by two doorways – one for the cloisters and the museum, the other for the church, though this is now closed off. This old church doorway is surmounted by the most bizarre of sculpted cameos, depicting the **Virgin Mary**, armed with a cudgel and standing menacingly over a cringing, cat-like dragon-devil.

Inside, the **museum collection** is distributed amongst the tiny rooms that flank the immaculately preserved Baroque **cloister**, whose vaulted aisles sport coats of arms and religious motifs. The first two rooms – to either side of the entrance – hold a hotchpotch of Talayotic and early classical archeological finds, notably a superbly crafted, miniature bull and a similarly exquisite little mermaid (*sirena*), almost certainly Greek bronzes dating from the fifth century BC. On the left-hand side of the cloister is the domed and single-aisled **Església dels Socors**, whose standard-issue Baroque decoration culminates in an extraordinarily artless high altar.

Moving on, the old, vaulted **refectory** displays some dreadful religious paintings, mostly dating from the eighteenth century, and then there is a room devoted to the artist **Pere Daura** (1896–1976), one-time Communist and Republican soldier, who fled Spain after Franco seized power. Both before and after his exile, Daura spent most of his time abroad, mostly in France or the USA, and although he was born in Ciutadella, this was more by accident than design – his family were travelling through here when he turned up. As for the paintings themselves, Daura is strongest when it comes to still lifes, done very much in the Impressionist manner, though his village scenes and landscapes can be engaging too.

The Capella del Sant Crist and the Estatua des Be

Strolling north from the **Museu Diocesà**, it's a few metres to the savings bank that occupies part of the **Palau Saura**, built in grand style by the British for a

Menorcan aristocrat, one Joan Miquel Saura, in return for his help in planning their successful invasion of 1708. From here, it's a few paces more to the flamboyant facade of the **Capella del Sant Crist**, a Baroque extravaganza with garlands of fruit and a pair of gargoyle-like faces. Inside, the intimate nave supports an octagonal stone dome and is also home to an unattributed medieval panel painting depicting three local saints of obscure significance. The skeletal crucified Christ above the high altar is supposed to have dripped with sweat in 1661 and remains a popular object of devotion.

From the chapel, it's a few metres north to **c/J.M. Quadrado**, one section of the narrow main street that cuts across the old town. Look to the left and you'll spy a perky bronze lamb – the **Estatua des Be** – stuck on a column. The lamb, symbolizing the Lamb of God, carries a flag bearing the cross of St John the Baptist and is a reminder of Ciutadella's biggest shindig, the Festa de Sant Joan (see p.36).

East from c/Seminari to Plaça Alfons III

From the top of c/Seminari, the pedestrianized main street of the old town runs east as **c/J.M. Quadrado**. The first stretch is crimped by a block of white-washed, vaulted arches, **Ses Voltes**, distinctly Moorish in inspiration and a suitable setting for a string of busy shops and cafés. Just beyond is **Plaça Nova**, an attractive little square edged by popular pavement cafés, and then it's on to **Plaça Alfons III**, where you leave the cramped alleys of the old town behind. The big old windmill on the far side of the square, the **Moli d'es Comte**, is the only landmark here, but it looks as if it should be in the countryside, its forlorn appearance not helped by its partial conversion into a bar.

The market

From Plaça Alfons III, it's a couple of minutes' walk southwest to the **market** (*mercat*; Mon–Sat 9am–2pm), which rambles over two miniature squares, Plaça Francesc Netto and Plaça Llibertat. This is another delightful corner of the old town, where fresh fruit, vegetable, meat and fish stalls mingle with lively and inexpensive cafés selling the freshest of *ensaimadas*. The fish stalls occupy a dinky little structure of 1895; the rest fill out a slender arcaded gallery that was constructed thirty years before as part of a municipal drive to clean up the town's food supply.

North of the centre: Santa Clara

Directly opposite the top of c/Seminari, a long, straight street – **c/Santa Clara** – shoots off north, hemmed in by the walls of old aristocratic palaces. At the top is the convent of **Santa Clara**, a mundanely modern incarnation of a centuries-old foundation. In 1749, this was the site of a scandal that had tongues clacking from Ciutadella to Maó. During the night, three young women hopped over the convent wall and placed themselves under the protection of their British boyfriends. Even worse, as far as the local clergy were concerned, they wanted to turn Protestant and marry their men. In this delicate situation, **Governor Blakeney** had the room where the women were staying sealed up by a priest every night. But he refused to send them back to the convent and allowed the weddings to go ahead, thereby compounding a religious animosity – Catholic subject against Protestant master – which had begun in the days of Richard Kane.

The Museu Municipal

Beyond Santa Clara, at the far end of c/Portal de Sa Font, the **Museu Municipal** (May–Sept Tues–Sat 10am–2pm & 6–9pm; Oct–April Tues–Sat 10am–2pm; €2.25, but free on Wed) occupies part of the old municipal fortifications, a

▲ Ciutadella

massive bastion overlooking a slender ravine that once had, until it was redirected, a river running along its base and on into the harbour. The museum consists of a long vaulted chamber that is mostly given over to a wide range of archeological artefacts, primarily a substantial collection of **Talayotic remains**, featuring finds garnered from all over the island. Each cabinet is clearly labelled, but the displays are not chronological, which is a tad confusing, and there's a small introductory section that attempts an overview, but only serves to confuse the chronology further. A leaflet detailing the exhibits in English is available free at reception.

The **earlier pieces**, dating from around 1500 to 700 BC, include many examples of crudely crafted beakers and tumblers as well as a set of **five skulls**, which appear to have been subjected to some form of brain surgery, though no one is sure quite how or why. **Later work** – from around 700 BC – reveals a far greater degree of sophistication, both in terms of kitchenware, with bowls and tumblers particularly common, and bronze weaponry. From this later period, which ended with the arrival of the Romans in 123 BC, comes most of the (imported) jewellery, whose fine detail and miniature size suggests a Carthaginian origin.

To the Baixada Capllonc and the Casa Museu Torrent

From the Museu Municipal, it's a five-minute stroll back to Plaça d'es Born along **c/Sa Muradeta** with pleasant views down the ravine to the harbour. As you near Plaça d'es Born, a wide flight of steps – the **Baixada Capllonc** – cuts down to the harbour, where yachts and fishing smacks bob around in front of a series of waterside restaurants, with the old town walls forming a scenic background.

From the steps, it's the briefest of walks east to the **Casa Museu Torrent**, Sant Rafel 11 (mid-May to Oct Mon–Sat 11am–1pm & 7.30–9.30pm & Sun 8–9.30pm; free), which displays around one hundred paintings in the old home of Ciutadella's own **José Roberto Torrent** (1904–90). The son of a cobbler, Torrent is usually regarded as the town's finest painter, a prolific and versatile artist who began with deftly coloured Menorcan landscapes in the Realist

Almost all of the time, Ciutadella's long and slender harbour is as flat as a mill-pond, but every so often, for reasons that remain obscure, it is subjected to a violent disturbance, the **Rissaga**. This begins with sudden changes to the water level and is followed by a dramatic rush of water into the harbour before normality returns. The last great Rissaga of 1984 submerged the harbourside beneath two metres of water, giving everyone down there a most unpleasant shock.

tradition. Later, in the 1960s, his paintings became more expressionistic, rendering island scenes in striking colours and shapes, but perhaps his most evocative work was produced in his old age with paintings of infirmity, loneliness and isolation.

Eating, drinking and nightlife

For an early **breakfast** the best place to go is the market (*mercat*) on Plaça Llibertat, where a couple of simple cafés serve coffee and fresh pastries. Later in the day, around **lunchtime**, aim for c/J.M. Quadrado, Plaça Nova and Plaça Alfons III, which together hold a good selection of inexpensive café-bars, offering tapas and light meals. In the **evening**, most tourists make a beeline for the **restaurants** that line up along the harbourside, but – with the odd exception – you're actually better off seeking out the better-value establishments amongst the side streets near Plaça d'es Born.

As regards **opening hours**, most cafés and bars open daily from approximately 9am to 10pm, whilst restaurants usually open from noon to 11pm with a siesta between 3/4pm and 7/8pm. Restaurants are more likely to close for one day a week and those down on the harbour mostly close altogether during the wintertime. Note also that, although the outside terraces on the harbourside restaurants look enticing, the nautical activity down along the waterfront can be deafening, especially when the ferries sail in and out.

People don't come to Ciutadella for the **nightlife**, but there is a small complement of **late-night bars** dotted round the old town with the liveliest places in the ravine at the head of the port, on Es Pla de Sant Joan. Ciutadella is also one of the few places in the Balearics where the evening **paseo** (promenade) has survived in fine fettle, with families wandering up and down the main street taking the evening air as they have done for generations.

Patisseries, cafés and café-bars

Café-bar Ulises Plaça Llibertat s/n. This amenable café-bar, in the heart of the city market, is popular with a youngish local clientele. Offers a tasty range of quiches and cakes during the day, tapas and (turned-down) house music/jazz at night. Open Mon–Sat from 8am till late.

Imperi Plaça d'es Born 6. Green-shuttered, neatly turned out café offering good (Illy) coffee, snacks and cakes. Giving onto the main square, its tiny terrace is a smashing spot to watch the milling crowd. Open daily 7am–1am.

La Torre de Papel Camí de Maó 46. The most urbane coffee house in town with a bookshop at

the front and a tiny, vaguely New Age terrace café at the back. Open Tues–Sat 10am–2pm & 6–9pm.

Pastelería Montaner c/Bisbe 11. Near the cathedral, this is the oldest pastry shop in town and they sell what many locals argue are the tastiest *ensaimadas* on the island, baked in their ancient ovens. Open Mon–Sat 9.30am–5pm.

Pastisseria Mol c/Roser 2. Across the square from the cathedral, this first-rate bakery sells excellent takeaway pizza slices, filled bread rolls and mouth-watering cakes. Open Mon–Sat 8.30am–2pm & 5.30–8pm.

Sa Xarxa c/Sebastià 1. Agreeable café serving a good line in tapas and snacks, all at inexpensive prices. Its terrace is just set off the main drag, which means it's a good place to watch the evening *paseo*. Open daily 10am–10pm.

Restaurants

El Horno c/Forn 12 ☎971 38 07 67. Neat and trim cellar restaurant near the northeast corner of Plaça d'es Born featuring a canny combination of Menorcan and French dishes. Try the rabbit or the mussels and don't miss out on the fish soup. Mains average €13. Open daily 7–11pm.

La Guitarra c/Nostra Senyora dels Dolors 1 ☎971 38 13 55. Located a short walk from the cathedral, this is arguably the best restaurant in town, a family-run affair featuring the very best of Menorcan cuisine with main courses – anything from seafood and lamb to rabbit and pigs' trotters – averaging an extremely reasonable €12–16. The restaurant occupies an old cellar, whose stone walls sport a scattering of agricultural antiques. Open Mon–Sat 12.30–3.30pm & 7.30–11pm.

Restaurant Café Balear Es Pla de Sant Joan 15 ☎971 38 00 05. Justifiably popular, this attractively decorated restaurant sits at the back of the harbour by the bridge – at a safe distance from the ferries and the moored boats. The terrace is the best place to eat, but there are tables inside too. The food is first rate, with shellfish and fish the big deals, and main courses average around €20. Open Mon–Sat 12.30–4pm & 7.30–11.30pm, but may operate more restricted hours in winter. Reservations advised.

Bars and clubs

Cactus Bar Baixada Capllonc s/n. At the foot of the steps leading down from the old town to the harbour, this busy bar has a large outside terrace and a cavernous interior, extending deep into the old city walls. The best cocktails in town plus free internet access. Starts to hop at about 11pm.

Café-bar Es Molí Camí de Maó 1. Housed in the Molí d'es Comte, the old windmill across the street from Plaça Alfons III, this is a noisy and gritty café-bar, with a (very) young Menorcan crowd at night, old timers during the day. Open till 1am.

Gabanna Es Pla de Sant Joan s/n ☎971 38 18 01. Cool and groovy bar-cum-club with a chill-out terrace and alternative jazz, house, rock and world music scene. Open from 11pm to 4am daily throughout the season.

Limoo Es Pla de Sant Joan s/n ⊕www.limoobar .com. Swishest place in town, a three-floor disco extravaganza with one floor devoted to house, a second to retro and a third holding a cocktail bar. Open nightly from 11pm throughout the season.

Listings

Banks ATMs are dotted all over the centre and there's one at the Banca March, Plaça d'es Born 10.

Bicycle and moped rental Velos Joan, c/Sant Isidre 34, near Plaça Artrutx (Mon–Fri 8am–1.30pm & 4–8.30pm, plus mid-May to mid-Oct Sat 10am–1pm & 7–8.30pm & Sun 10.30am–noon; ☎971 38 15 76, ⊕www.velosjoan.com).

Boat hire Menorca Boats, down on the harbour near the bridge, rent out all manner of speed boats (☎971 48 42 81, ⊕www.menorcaboats.com). Prices begin at a hefty €410 per day in high season, €280 in low.

Car rental One centrally located car rental company is Europcar Menorca, on the ring road at Avinguda Jaume I El Conqueridor 59 (☎971 38 29 98).

Diving Menorcatech, Pla de Sant Joan 10 (☎971 38 60 30, ⊕www.menorcatech.com) organizes a wide range of deep-sea diving trips out along the west coast.

Email and internet access Free internet access at the Cactus Bar (see above), down on the waterfront at the foot of the Baixada Capllonc stairway.

Ferries and catamarans Three companies offer car ferry and/or catamaran services between Ciutadella and the Spanish mainland and/or Mallorca. They are Balearia (☎902 16 01 80, ⊕www.balearia.com); Acciona-Trasmediterranea (☎902 45 46 45, ⊕www. trasmediterranea.es); and Iscomar (☎902 11 91 28, ⊕www.iscomar .com). Schedules, tariffs and tickets are available direct from the operators down at the ferry terminal in the city centre, though a new harbour facility is under construction by the ring road about 4km south of town. Note that Menorca's car rental firms do not allow their vehicles to leave the island. For further details of ferry and catamaran routes as well as prices, see Basics, pp.20–21.

Maps and books Libreria d'es Racó, c/J.M. Quadrado 40, stocks a limited range of island road maps.

Pharmacies Amongst several downtown options, there's a pharmacy at Plaça Nova 2.

Post Office The main *correu* is handily located at Plaça d'es Born 8 (Mon–Fri 8.30am–8.30pm, Sat 9.30am–1pm).

Taxis There's a taxi stand on Plaça dels Pins ☎971 48 22 22. The (regulated) fare from Ciutadella to Maó airport is €50.

Around Ciutadella

The diverse attractions of **west Menorca** are all within easy striking distance of Ciutadella, beginning with the pristine **cove beaches** that notch the island's southern shore just a few kilometres away. There are several delightful beaches to choose from – most memorably **Cala Turqueta** – and now that the island's ruling council has bought the rights from local landowners, access is free. On the other side of Ciutadella, the north coast is wild and almost completely undeveloped, but there is one resort here, the smart villa-village of **Cala Morell**, which occupies a bleak and barren cove with a gritty beach. Remember also that Ciutadella is only a few kilometres from two of the island's finest prehistoric sites, **Naveta d'es Tudons** (see p.255) and **Torrellafuda** (see p.255).

The **west coast** is different again with a flat and mostly treeless coastal plain slicing down to a string of resorts that dot the coast to either side of Ciutadella from **Cales Piques** in the north to **Cap d'Artrutx**, 15km away to the south. Some of these resorts have little to recommend them, comprising long lines of modern villas built in a sort of pan-Hispanic style, but here and there the villas bunch round narrow coves to form lovely little resorts, the pick of which is undoubtedly **Cala Santandria**.

From May to October, there are regular **buses** from Ciutadella's Plaça dels Pins to the tourist settlements of the west coast as well as Cala Morell. There are, however, no buses to the beaches southeast of town, including Cala Turqueta, and neither is there a bus service to the Naveta d'es Tudons because although Maó–Ciutadella buses pass by, they don't/won't stop. In winter time, from November to April, there is a limited bus service to most, but not all of the area's resorts; all these bus services are operated by **Torres Autocars** (T902 07 50 66, Wwww.e-torres.net).

Southeast of Ciutadella

Beginning on the ring road – the *ronda* – on the edge of town, the cross-country **Camí de Sant Joan de Missa** runs southeast from Ciutadella to the undeveloped coves of the south coast. After about 3km, you reach the farmhouse of **Son Vivó**, where the road branches into two, with each (signposted) **fork** leading to several south-coast beaches, the nearest of which are a further 6km away. Both roads are in fairly good condition, the signs are easy to follow, and if you opt for either **Cala Turqueta** or the **Platges Son Saura**, arguably the two most appealing beaches, you'll end up in a **parking lot** a five- to ten-minute walk from the seashore. There's only one **place to stay** hereabouts, the *Hotel Rural Morvedrà Nou*, a sympathetically converted stone farmhouse with seventeen air-conditioned guest rooms and a pool on the Camí Sant Joan de Misa, 7km from Ciutadella (April–Oct; T971 35 95 21, Wwww.morvedranou.es; 8).

South to Cala Turqueta

Taking the more easterly road from the Son Vivó fork, it's about 1.5km more to the **Ermita de St Joan de Missa**, a squat, brightly whitewashed church with a dinky little bell tower. There's a fork here too, but the signposting is clear and you keep straight, with the road slicing across the countryside, before you swing past the **Marjal Vella farmhouse**. Shortly afterwards, about 4.3km from the church, you turn at the sign, going through the gateway to cross the five hundred-metre-long dirt road which brings you to the car park for **Cala Turqueta**, a lovely cove flanked by wooded limestone cliffs. The beach consists of a sheltered horseshoe of white sand sloping gently into the sea, making it ideal for bathing, and because there are limited facilities it's unusual to find a crowd.

Son Catlar and the Platges Son Saura

Back at the Son Vivó fork, it's 3km along the more westerly road to **Son Catlar** (open access; free), the largest prehistoric settlement on Menorca and one which was still expanding when the Romans arrived in force in 123 BC. The most impressive feature of this sprawling Talayotic village is its extraordinary stone wall, originally three metres high and made of massive blocks – the square towers were added later. Inside the walls, however, all is confusion. The widely scattered remains are largely incomprehensible and only the *taula* compound and the five battered *talayots* make much sense.

Pushing on south, the asphalt peters out about 1.2km further down the road when you reach the ornate gateway of the **Torre Saura farmhouse**. To the left of the gateway, a two kilometre-long dirt road bumps its way down to the parking lot behind a wide horseshoe-shaped cove whose two beaches make up the **Platges Son Saura**. The west side of the cove is more exposed and is often sticky with seaweed, so aim for the more sheltered eastern side, where a wide arc of white sand is fringed by pines. There are more facilities here than at most of its neighbours, including a summer beach bar.

Northeast of Ciutadella

Signposted from the Me-1 on the eastern outskirts of Ciutadella, a well-surfaced country lane cuts northeast across a pastoral landscape bound for the smallish tourist settlement of **CALA MORELL**, just 8km from town. This is one of the island's more refined *urbanitzacions*, its *pueblo*-style villas – on streets named in Latin after the constellations – hugging a steep and rocky, dog-legged bay. There's swimming off the gritty beach here and you can also visit some of the old **caves** for which Cala Morell is noted, visible beside the road as you drive down into the resort. Dating from the late Bronze and Iron Ages, the caves form one of the largest prehistoric necropolises known in Europe, and are surprisingly sophisticated, with central pillars supporting the roofs, and, in some instances, windows cut into the rock and classical designs carved in relief. No one owns the caves, so there's unlimited access – just scramble up from the road. The sight of one or two is sufficient for most visitors, but if you're after more than a glimpse, bring a torch.

From the car park at the end of the main access road, a rough footpath leads north out along the bare and rocky promontory that protects the west side of the bay, but only the truly adventurous will attempt the very difficult hike west to the **Punta de S'Escullar** headland, the site of one of the largest colonies of Cory's shearwaters in the western Mediterranean with thousands of birds returning to their cliffside burrows in the late afternoon throughout the summer.

South to Cala Santandria

Heading south from Ciutadella, the main road stays within earshot of the coast, where a string of resorts cluster the dinky little coves that lie just beyond the edge of town. Perhaps the prettiest is **CALA SANTANDRIA**, where a narrow slit of a rocky cove backs onto a small sandy beach with safe swimming. The beach is flanked by hotels, villas and restaurants, but it's all very low-key and very manageable, and the beachside *Café del Sol* serves up the freshest of salads and snacks.

There is a good summer **bus** service from Ciutadella to Cala Santandria, and the bus stops just 200m from the beach.

Travel details

Island-wide bus timetables are available on Ⓦ www.tmsa.es, with the exception of the northeast coast (Ⓦ www.autosfornells.com) and the west coast resorts near Ciutadella (Ⓦ www .e-torres.net).

Buses (May–Oct)

Ciutadella to: Alaior (Mon–Fri hourly, 8 on Sat, 6 on Sun; 50min); Cala Galdana (hourly; 30min); Cala Morell (3 daily; 25min); Cala Santandria (every 30min to 1hr; 15min); Es Mercadal (Mon–Fri hourly, 8 on Sat, 6 on Sun; 35min); Es Migjorn Gran (4–6 daily; 40min); Ferreries (Mon–Fri hourly, 8 on Sat, 6 on Sun; 25min); Maó (Mon–Fri hourly, 8 on Sat, 6 on Sun; 1hr); Sant Tomàs (4–6 daily; 45min).

Es Mercadal to: Ciutadella (Mon–Fri hourly, 8 on Sat, 6 on Sun; 35min); Maó (Mon–Fri hourly, 8 on Sat, 6 on Sun; 25min).

Es Migjorn Gran to: Ciutadella (4–6 daily; 40min); Ferreries (4–6 daily; 10min); Maó (4–6 daily; 30min).

Ferreries to: Alaior (Mon–Fri hourly, 8 on Sat, 6 on Sun; 25min); Cala Galdana (hourly; 15min); Ciutadella (Mon–Fri hourly, 8 on Sat, 6 on Sun; 25min); Es Mercadal (Mon–Fri hourly, 8 on Sat, 6 on Sun; 10min); Es Migjorn Gran (4–6 daily; 10min); Maó (Mon–Fri hourly, 8 on Sat, 6 on Sun; 35min).

Fornells to: Maó (mid-June to mid-Sept Mon–Sat 8 daily, 3 on Sun; 35min).

Maó to: Alaior (Mon–Fri hourly, 8 on Sat, 6 on Sun; 10min); Cala Galdana (2 daily; 50min); Ciutadella (Mon–Fri hourly, 8 on Sat, 6 on Sun; 1hr); Es Castell (every 30min; 10min); Es Grau (mid-June to mid-Sept 6–7 daily; 15min); Es Mercadal (Mon–Fri hourly, 8 on Sat, 6 on Sun; 25min); Es Migjorn Gran (4–6 daily; 30min); Ferreries (Mon–Fri hourly, 8 on Sat, 6 on Sun; 35min); Fornells (mid-June to mid-Sept Mon–Sat 8 daily, 3 on Sun; 35min); Punta Prima (hourly; 30min); Sant Tomàs (4–6 daily; 45min); Son Bou (Mon–Sat hourly, 7 on Sun; 45min).

Buses (Nov–April)

Ciutadella to: Alaior (Mon–Fri hourly, 8 on Sat, 6 on Sun; 50min); Cala Santandria (2–4 daily; 15min); Es Mercadal (Mon–Fri hourly, 8 on Sat, 6 on Sun; 35min); Es Migjorn Gran (Mon–Fri 4 daily; 40min); Ferreries (Mon–Fri hourly, 8 on Sat, 6 on Sun; 25min); Maó (Mon–Fri hourly, 8 on Sat, 6 on Sun; 1hr).

Es Mercadal to: Ciutadella (Mon–Fri hourly, 8 on Sat, 6 on Sun; 35min); Maó (Mon–Fri hourly, 8 on Sat, 6 on Sun; 25min).

Es Migjorn Gran to: Ciutadella (Mon–Fri 4 daily; 40min); Ferreries (Mon–Sat 1 daily; 10min); Maó (Mon–Fri 6 daily, 1 on Sat; 30min).

Ferreries to: Alaior (Mon–Fri hourly, 8 on Sat, 6 on Sun; 25min); Ciutadella (Mon–Fri hourly, 8 on Sat, 6 on Sun; 25min); Es Mercadal (Mon–Fri hourly, 8 on Sat, 6 on Sun; 10min); Es Migjorn Gran (Mon–Sat 1 daily; 10min); Maó (Mon–Fri hourly, 8 on Sat, 6 on Sun; 35min).

Fornells to: Maó (2–4 daily; 35min).

Maó to: Alaior (Mon–Fri hourly, 8 on Sat, 6 on Sun; 10min); Ciutadella (Mon–Fri hourly, 8 on Sat, 6 on Sun; 1hr); Es Castell (hourly; 10min); Es Mercadal (Mon–Fri hourly, 8 on Sat, 6 on Sun; 25min); Es Migjorn Gran (Mon–Fri 6 daily, 1 on Sat; 30min); Ferreries (Mon–Fri hourly, 8 on Sat, 6 on Sun; 35min); Fornells (2–4 daily; 35min).

Contexts

Contexts

History

The earliest inhabitants of the Balearics seem to have reached the islands from the Iberian peninsula, and carbon-dating of remains indicates that human occupation was well established by 4000 BC. The discovery of pottery, flints and animal horns fashioned into tools suggests that these early people were **Neolithic pastoralists**, who supplemented their food supplies by hunting. A key part of their diet appears to have been *Myotragus balearicus*, a species of diminutive mountain goat unique to the islands and now extinct. Hundreds of these animals' skulls have been discovered and several are exhibited in the islands' larger museums. The frequency of these finds has encouraged some experts to assert that the *Myotragus* was actually domesticated, the principal evidence being the supposed remains of crude corrals on the coast of Mallorca near Deià, though this assertion is strongly contested.

Why, or how, these Neolithic peoples moved to the Balearic islands is unknown. Indeed, the first landfall may have been accidental, made by early seafarers travelling along the shores of the Mediterranean – and part of a great wave of migration that is known to have taken place in the Neolithic period. Many of the oldest archeological finds have been discovered in natural **caves**, where it seems likely that these early settlers first sought shelter. Later, cave complexes were dug out of the soft limestone that occurs on both islands, comprising living quarters, usually circular and sometimes with a domed ceiling, as well as longer, straighter funerary chambers. These complexes represent the flourishing of what is commonly called the **Balearic cave culture** – one good (and readily accessible) example is at the resort of **Cala Morell**, on Menorca (see p.267).

The archeological evidence indicates that Balearic cave dwellers soon came into regular contact with other cultures: the Mediterranean, with its relatively calm and tide-free waters, has always acted as a conduit of civilization. One of the earliest of these outside influences was the **Beaker people**, whose artefacts have been found right across Western Europe. Named after their practice of burying their dead with pottery beakers, their presence on the Balearics has been indicated by the discovery of Beaker ware at Deià. The Beaker people also had knowledge of the use of **bronze**, an alloy of copper and tin, and they exported their bronze-working skills into the Balearics around 1500 BC. This technological revolution marked the end of the cave culture and the beginning of the Talayotic period.

The Talayotic period

The megalithic remains of the **Talayotic period**, which lasted until the arrival of the Romans in 123 BC, are strewn all over Mallorca and Menorca – though, surprisingly, there's no evidence of them on Ibiza. The structure that gives its name to the period is the **talayot**, a cone-shaped tower with a circular base between five and ten metres in height. These *talayots* are commonly thought of as watchtowers, but this is unlikely and their actual function is unknown. What is clear is that by 1000 BC a relatively sophisticated, largely pastoral society had developed on both Mallorca and Menorca, with at least some of the islanders occupying the walled settlements that still dot the interior: the three best examples are **Torre d'en Gaumés** (see p.248), near Alaior on Menorca, where you can still inspect 3 *talayots* and the remains of several houses; **Ses Païsses** (see p.191), a well-protected settlement of impressive proportions outside Artà; and Menorca's **Son Catlar** (see p.267), not far from Ciutadella. All three were occupied well into the Roman period.

Talayotic culture reached dizzying heights on Menorca, and it's here you'll find the most enigmatic remains of the period. These are the **taulas** ("tables" in Catalan), T-shaped structures standing as high as four metres and consisting of two massive dressed stones. Their purpose is unknown, though many theories have been advanced. One early nineteenth-century writer believed that they were altars used for human sacrifice, but the height of most *taulas* makes this very unlikely – unless the islanders were on stilts. More intriguingly, some academics have argued that the "T" was a **stylized head of a bull**, an animal that was much venerated in many parts of the ancient Mediterranean, most notably in Minoan Crete. True or not, it seems probable that the enclosures which surround every *taula* had religious significance. This was confirmed during excavations at **Torralba d'en Salord** (see p.248), where archeologists discovered animal remains and pottery in side recesses of fireplaces, and concluded that these must have been ritual offerings. They also found a bronze sculpture of a bull, suggesting that cattle were, indeed, worshipped. Torralba d'en Salord is one of the many places where *taulas* and *talayots* stand cheek by jowl. Often the remains are too broken down to be of much interest, but three other good spots are **Torrellafuda** (see p.255), **Torre d'en Gaumés** (see p.248) and **Talatí de Dalt** (see p.230), which incorporates a *talayot*, a *taula* and several columned chambers or **hypostyles**. Partly dug out of the ground and roofed with massive slabs of stone, these hypostyles must have taken considerable effort to build, and may have been used for important gatherings, possibly of communal leaders.

The other distinctive structure to be found on Menorca is the **naveta**, made of roughly dressed dry-stone blocks and looking like an inverted bread tin. Dating from the beginning of the Talayotic period, the **Naveta d'es Tudons**, near Ciutadella (see p.255), is the finest example, but there are around 35 others sprinkled across the island. They were collective tombs, or, more correctly, ossuaries, where, after the flesh had been removed, the bones of the dead were placed along with some personal possessions such as jewellery, pottery and bone buttons.

Phoenicians and Greeks

Fearful of attack from the sea, the Talayotic people built their walled settlements a few kilometres inland. This pattern was, however, modified from around 900 BC, when the Balearics became a staging post for the **Phoenicians**, maritime traders from the eastern Mediterranean whose long voyages reached as far as Cornwall in southwest England: the Phoenicians made the islands safer and more secure and the Talayotic peoples were able to venture out from their walled settlements. According to the Roman historian Pliny, the Phoenicians established a large settlement at **Sanisera** on Menorca's north coast (see p.245), and archeologists have also discovered Phoenician artefacts at **Alcúdia** on Mallorca (see p.163). In general, however, very few Phoenician remains have been found on the Balearics – just a handful of bronze items, jewellery and pieces of coloured glass.

The **Greeks** displaced the Phoenicians around 800 BC, as several city-states explored the western Mediterranean in search of trade and potential colonies. Like the Phoenicians, the Greeks appear to have used the Balearics primarily as a staging post, for no Greek buildings have survived on either

Mallorca or Menorca. The absence of metal apparently made the islands unsuitable for long-term colonization, and the belligerence of the native population may have played a part too: the Greeks coined the islands' name, the **"Balearics"**, which they derived from *ballein*, meaning "to throw from a sling". The islanders were adept at this form of warfare, and many early visitors were repelled with showers of polished sling-stones – though some historians dispute this theory, claiming rather that the name comes from the Baleri tribe of Sardinia.

The Carthaginian Empire

The Greeks were also discouraged from colonization by the growth of the **Carthaginian Empire** across the western Mediterranean. The Phoenicians had established Carthage on the North African coast in 814 BC, and from this base they gradually extended their authority across the western Mediterranean. They began to colonize the Balearics in the seventh century BC and the islands were firmly under their control by the beginning of the third century BC, if not earlier. Little is known of the Carthaginian occupation except that they established several new settlements. It is also claimed that the Carthaginian general, **Hannibal**, was born on Cabrera island off Mallorca, though Ibiza and Malta claim this honour too.

In the third century BC, the expansion of the Carthaginian Empire up into the Iberian Peninsula triggered two **Punic Wars** with Rome. In both of these wars the Balearics proved extremely valuable, first as stepping stones from the North African coast to the European mainland and second as a source of mercenaries. **Balearic slingers** (see box below) were highly valued and accompanied Hannibal and his elephants across the Alps in the Second Punic War, when (for reasons that remain obscure) the islanders refused gold and demanded payment in wine and women instead. After Hannibal's defeat by the Romans at the battle of Zama in 202 BC, Carthaginian power began to wane and they withdrew from Mallorca and Menorca, although they continued to have some influence over Ibiza for at least another seventy years.

Balearic slingers

Quintus Metellus, the Roman commander who invaded Mallorca in 123 BC, had a healthy respect for the warlike qualities of the islanders in general and their skill with the **stone-throwing sling** in particular. He had good reason. The Carthaginians had been using Balearic mercenaries for many decades and the islanders had inflicted heavy casualties on the Roman legions throughout the Punic Wars. Consequently, Metellus went to great trouble to protect his men by erecting mammoth shields of hide along the decks of all his ships – a stratagem which worked extremely well.

Male islanders were trained to use the sling in childhood and they could propel a stone with great accuracy and force sufficient to crush most shields and helmets. The slinger had three slings of different lengths, one held in his hand, another wrapped round his stomach and a third tied round his head. According to the historian **Diodorus Siculus** (90–30 BC) these slingers were a particularly disagreeable bunch. They often went naked, covering their bodies in a mixture of pig fat and olive oil; were inordinately fond of wine; were keen on female slaves; and rounded off their weddings with all the male guests having congress with the bride in descending order of age – before passing her over to the groom.

The Romans

As the Carthaginians retreated so the **Romans** advanced, incorporating Ibiza within their empire after the final victory over Carthage in 146 BC. On Mallorca and Menorca, the islanders took advantage of the prolonged military chaos to profit from piracy, until finally, in 123 BC, the Romans, led by the consul Quintus Metellus, restored maritime order by occupying both islands. These victories earned Metellus the title "Balearico" from the Roman senate and two of the islands were given new names, Balearis Major (Mallorca) and Balearis Minor (Menorca).

For the next five hundred years all of the Balearic islands were part of the Roman Empire. Amongst many developments, Roman colonists introduced viticulture, turning the Balearics into a wine-exporting area, and initiated olive-oil production from newly planted groves. As was their custom, the Romans consolidated their control of the islands by building roads and establishing towns. On Mallorca, they founded Pollentia (Alcúdia) in the north and Palmaria on the south coast, near the site of modern Palma, whilst on Menorca they developed Port Magonum (Maó) as an administrative centre with Sanisera – previously the site of a Phoenician trading post – becoming an important port. Initially, the Balearics were part of the Roman province of Tarraconensis (Tarragona), but in 404 AD the islands became a province in their own right with the name **Balearica**.

The Vandals and Byzantines

By the fifth century the Roman Empire was in decline, its defences unable to resist the westward-moving tribes of central Asia. The **Vandals**, one of these tribes, moved in on the Balearics in around 425 AD, ending Roman rule at a stroke. So thoroughgoing was the destruction they wrought that Roman remains are at a premium, the only significant ruins being those of Pollentia at **Alcúdia** (see p.165). One of the reasons for the ferocity of the attack was religious. The Vandals had been Christianized long before they reached the Mediterranean, but they were followers of the **Arian sect**. This interpretation of Christianity, founded by Arius, an Alexandrian priest, insisted that Christ the Son and God the Father were two distinct figures, not elements of the Trinity. To orthodox Christians, this seemed dangerously close to the pagan belief in a multiplicity of gods and, by the end of the fourth century AD, Arianism had been forcibly extirpated within the Roman Empire. However, the sect continued to flourish amongst the Germanic peoples of the Rhine, including the Vandals, who, armed with their "heretical" beliefs, had no religious truck with their new Balearic subjects, persecuting them with vim and gusto.

In 533 the Vandals were defeated in North Africa by the Byzantine general Count Belisarius – who was later to be the subject of a novel by one of Mallorca's adopted sons, Robert Graves. This brought the Balearics under **Byzantine** rule and, for a time, restored prosperity and stability. Nonetheless, the islands were too far removed from Constantinople to be of much imperial importance and, when the empire was threatened from the east at the end of the seventh century, they were abandoned in all but name.

The Moors

As the influence of Byzantium receded, so militarized Islam moved in to fill the vacuum. In 707–8 the **Moors** of North Africa conducted an extended raid against Mallorca, destroying its entire fleet and carrying away slaves and booty, and by 716 the Balearics' position had become even more vulnerable with the completion of the Moorish conquest of Spain. In 798 the Balearics were again sacked by the Moors – who were still more interested in plunder than settlement – and in desperation the islanders appealed for help to **Charlemagne**, the Frankish Holy Roman Emperor. As emperor, **Charlemagne** was the military leader of Western Christendom (the pope was the spiritual leader), so the appeal signified the final severance of the Balearics' links with Byzantium and the East.

Charlemagne's attempt to protect the islands from the Moors met with some success, but the respite was only temporary. By the middle of the ninth century, the Christian position had deteriorated so badly that the Balearics were compelled to enter a non-aggression pact with the Moors, and, to add to the islanders' woes, the Balearics suffered a full-scale **Viking** raid in 859. Finally, at the beginning of the tenth century, the **emir of Córdoba** conquered both Menorca and Mallorca. Moorish rule lasted over three hundred years, though internal political divisions among the Muslims meant that the islands experienced several different regimes. In the early eleventh century, the emirate of Córdoba collapsed and control passed to the *wali* (governor) of Denia, on the Spanish mainland. This administration allowed the Christians – who were known as **Mozarabs** – to practise their faith, and the islands prospered from their position at the heart of the trade routes between North Africa and Islamic Spain.

In 1085 the Balearics became an independent emirate with a new dynasty of *walis*, from **Amortadha** in North Africa. They pursued a more aggressive foreign and domestic policy, raiding the towns of Catalonia and persecuting their Christian citizens. These actions blighted trade and thereby enraged the emergent city-states of Italy at a time when Christendom was fired by crusading zeal. Anticipating retaliation, the Amortadhas fortified Palma, which was known at this time as Medina Mayurka, and several mountain strongholds. The Christian attack came in 1114 when a grand Italian fleet – led by the ships of Pisa and supported by the pope as a mini-crusade – landed an army of 70,000 Catalan and Italian soldiers on Ibiza. The island was soon captured, but Mallorca, the crusaders' next target, proved a much more difficult proposition. Palma's coastal defences proved impregnable, so the Christians assaulted the landward defences instead, the concentric lines of the fortifications forcing them into a long series of bloody engagements. When the city finally fell, the invaders took a bitter revenge, slaughtering most of the surviving Muslim population. Yet, despite their victory, the Christians had neither the will nor the resources to consolidate their position and, loading their vessels with freed slaves and loot, they returned home.

It took the Moors just two years to re-establish themselves on the islands, this time under the leadership of the **Almoravides**, a North African Berber tribe who had previously controlled southern Spain. The Almoravides proved to be tolerant and progressive rulers, and the Balearics prospered: agriculture improved, particularly through the development of irrigation, and trade expanded as commercial agreements were struck with the Italian cities of Genoa and Pisa. The Pisans – crusaders earlier in the century – defied a papal ban on trade with Muslims to finalize the deal; consciences could, it seems, be flexible even in the "devout" Middle Ages when access to the precious goods of the east (silks, carpets and spices) was the prize.

Jaume I and the Reconquista

In 1203 the Almoravides were supplanted by the **Almohad** dynasty, who attempted to forcibly convert the islands' Christian population to Islam. They also started raiding the mainland, but this was an extraordinary miscalculation as the kingdoms of Aragón and Catalunya had recently been united, thereby strengthening the Christian position in this part of Spain. The unification was a major step in the changing balance of power: with their forces combined, the Christians were able to launch the **Reconquista**, which was eventually to drive the Moors from the entire peninsula. Part of the Christian jigsaw was the Balearics and, in 1228, the emir of Mallorca imprudently antagonized the young **King Jaume I of Aragón and Catalunya** by seizing a couple of his ships. The king's advisers, with their eyes firmly fixed on the islands' wealth, determined to capitalize on the offence. They organized the first Balearic publicity evening, a feast at which the king was presented with a multitude of island delicacies and Catalan sailors told of the archipelago's prosperity. And so, insulted by the emir and persuaded by his nobility, Jaume I committed himself to a full-scale invasion.

Jaume's expedition of 150 ships, 16,000 men and 1500 horses set sail for **Mallorca** in September 1229. The king had originally planned to land at Pollença, but adverse weather conditions forced the fleet further south and it eventually anchored off Sant Elm, where it must have given the solitary shepherd who lived there a terrific shock. The following day, the Catalans defeated the Moorish forces sent to oppose the landing and Jaume promptly pushed east, laying siege to Medina Mayurka. It took three months to breach the walls, but on December 31 the city finally fell and Jaume was hailed as "**El Conqueridor**".

The cost of launching an invasion on this scale placed an enormous strain on the resources of a medieval monarch. With this in mind, Jaume subcontracted the capture of **Ibiza**, entering into an agreement in 1231 with the Crown Prince of Portugal, Don Pedro, and the count of Roussillon. In return for the capture of the island, the count and the prince were to be allowed to divide Ibiza between themselves, provided they acknowledged the suzerainty of Jaume. This project initially faltered, but was revived with the addition of the archbishop of Tarragona. The three allies captured Ibiza in 1235 and divided the spoils, although Don Pedro waived his rights and his share passed to Jaume.

In the meantime, Jaume had acquired the overlordship of **Menorca**. Unable to afford another full-scale invasion, the king devised a cunning ruse. In 1232 he returned to Mallorca with just three galleys, which he dispatched to Menorca carrying envoys, while he camped out in the mountains above Capdepera on Mallorca. As night fell and his envoys negotiated with the enemy, Jaume ordered the lighting of as many bonfires as possible to illuminate the sky and give the impression of a vast army. The stratagem worked and the next day, mindful of the bloodbath following the invasion of Mallorca, the Menorcan Moors capitulated. According to the king's own account, they informed his envoys that "they gave great thanks to God and to me for the message I had sent them for they knew well they could not long defend themselves against me".

The terms of the Reconquista

In Menorca, Jaume's terms were generous: the Moors handed over Ciutadella, their principal settlement, and a number of other strongpoints, but the new king acknowledged the Muslims as his subjects and appointed one of their leaders as his *rais* (governor). The retention of Moorish government in Menorca, albeit under the suzerainty of the king, was, however, in marked contrast to events on Mallorca. Here, the land was divided into eight blocs, with four passing to the king and the rest to his most trusted followers, who leased their holdings in the feudal fashion, granting land to tenants in return for military service. In 1230 Jaume consolidated his position by issuing the **Carta de Població** (People's Charter), guaranteeing equality before the law, an extremely progressive precept for the period. Further-more, Mallorca was exempted from taxation to encourage Catalan immigration, and special rights were given to Jews resident on the island, a measure designed to stimulate trade. Twenty years later, Jaume also initiated a distinctive form of government for Mallorca, with a governing body of six **jurats** (adjudicators) – one from the nobility, two knights, two merchants and one peasant. At the end of each year the *jurats* elected their successors. This form of government remained in place until the sixteenth century.

The Balearic Kingdom in the thirteenth century

Jaume I died at Valencia in 1276. In his will he divided his kingdom between his two sons: **Pedro** received Catalunya, Aragón and Valencia, whilst **Jaume II** was bequeathed Montpellier, Roussillon and the Balearics. Jaume II was crowned in Mallorca on September 12, 1276, but the division infuriated **Pedro**, as the Balearics stood astride the shipping route between Barcelona and Sicily, where his wife was queen. He forced his brother to become his vassal, but in response Jaume II secretly schemed with the French. Predictably enough, Pedro soon discovered his brother's treachery and promptly set about planning a full-blooded invasion. However, Pedro died before the assault could begin and it was left to his son, **Alfonso III**, to carry out his father's plans. Late in 1285, Alfonso's army captured Palma without too much trouble, which was just as well for its inhabitants: wherever Alfonso met with resistance – as he did later in the campaign at the castle of Alaró – he extracted a brutal revenge. Indeed, even by the standards of thirteenth-century Spain, Alfonso was considered excessively violent and the pope excommunicated him for his atrocities – but not for long.

With Mallorca secured and Jaume deposed, Alfonso turned his attention to Menorca, where he suspected the loyalty of the Moorish governor – the *rais* was allegedly in conspiratorial contact with the Moors of North Africa. Alfonso's army landed on Menorca in January 1287 and decisively defeated the Moors just outside Maó. The Moors retreated to the hilltop fortress of Santa Agueda, but their resistance didn't amount to much and the whole island was Alfonso's within a few days. The king's treatment of the vanquished islanders was savage: those Muslims who were unable to buy their freedom were enslaved, and those who couldn't work as slaves – the old, the sick and the very young – were taken to sea and thrown overboard. Alfonso rewarded the nobles who had accompanied him with grants of land and brought in hundreds of Catalan settlers. The capital, Medina Minurka, was renamed **Ciutadella**, and the island's mosques were temporarily converted to Christian usage, before being demolished and replaced.

The Balearic Kingdom in the fourteenth century

Alfonso's violent career was cut short by his death in 1291 at the age of 25. His successor was his brother, Jaume, also the king of Sicily. A more temperate man, Jaume conducted negotiations through the papacy that eventually led, in 1298, to the restoration of the partition envisaged by Jaume I: he himself presided over Catalunya, Aragón and Valencia, while his exiled uncle, **Jaume II**, ruled as king of Mallorca and Menorca, and Montpellier and Roussillon. Restored to the Crown, Jaume II devoted a great deal of time to improving the commerce and administration of the Balearics. To stimulate trade, he established a weekly market in Palma, reissued the currency in gold and silver, and founded a string of inland towns, including Manacor, Felanitx, Llucmajor and Binissalem on Mallorca and Alaior and Es Mercadal on Menorca. Jaume II attended to God as well as Mammon, and his reign saw the building of many churches and monasteries. In the same vein, the king also patronized **Ramon Llull** (see p.75), the Mallorcan poet, scholar and Franciscan friar, providing him with the finance to establish a monastic school near Valldemossa. Perhaps his most important act, though, was to grant Menorca its own **Carta de Població**, which bestowed the same legal rights as the Mallorcans already enjoyed.

On his death in 1311, Jaume was succeeded by **Sancho**, his asthmatic son, who spent most of his time in his palace at Valldemossa, where the mountain air was to his liking. Nonetheless, Sancho did his job well, continuing the successful economic policies of his father and strengthening his fleet to protect his territories from North African pirates. Mallorca and Menorca boomed: Mallorca in particular had long served as the entrepôt between North Africa and Europe, its warehouses crammed with iron, figs, salt, oil and slaves, but in the early fourteenth century its industries also flourished, primarily shipbuilding and textiles. In 1325, the traveller Ramón Muntaner praised Palma as an "honoured city of greater wealth than any with the most businesslike inhabitants...of any city in the world". He may have been exaggerating, but not by much, and Palma's merchants were certainly inventive: spotting a gap in the market they went into **crossbow-making** and by 1380 they were exporting them by the boat load.

The end of independence

Internationally, Sancho worked hard to avoid entanglement in the growing antagonism between Aragón and France, but the islands' future still looked decidedly shaky when he died without issue in 1324. Theoretically, the islands should have passed to Aragón, but the local nobility moved fast to crown Sancho's ten-year-old nephew as **Jaume III**. Hoping to forestall Aragonese hostility, they then had him betrothed to the king of Aragón's five-year-old daughter, though in the long term this marriage did the new king little good. After he came of age, Jaume III's relations with his brother-in-law, **Pedro IV of Aragón**, soon soured and Pedro successfully invaded the Balearics in response to an alleged plot against him. Jaume fled to his mainland possessions and sold Montpellier to the French to raise money for an invasion. He landed on Mallorca in 1349, but was no match for Pedro, who defeated and killed him on the outskirts of Llucmajor. His son, the uncrowned **Jaume IV**, was also captured and although he eventually escaped, he was never able to drum up sufficient support to threaten the Aragonese.

Unification with Spain

For a diversity of reasons the **unification** of the Balearics with Aragón – and their subsequent incorporation within Spain – proved a disaster for the islanders. In particular, the mainland connection meant the islands' nobility soon gravitated towards the Aragonese court, regarding their local estates as little more than sources of income to sustain their expensive lifestyles. More fundamentally, general economic trends moved firmly against the Balearics. After the fall of Constantinople to the Turks in 1453, the lucrative overland trade routes from the Mediterranean to the Far East were blocked and, just as bad, the Portuguese discovered the nautical route round the Cape of Good Hope to the Indies. In 1479, **Fernando V of Aragón** married **Isabella I of Castile**, thereby uniting the two largest kingdoms in Spain, but yet again this was bad news for the islanders. The union brought mainland preoccupations and a centralized bureaucracy, which rendered the islands a provincial

Mallorca's Jews

For several centuries, Mallorca's large **Jewish** community, concentrated in Palma and Inca, played a crucial role in maintaining the island's money supply and sustaining trade with North Africa. In return, they were treated in that strangely contradictory manner which was common across much of medieval Europe, alternately courted and discriminated against. They were, for instance, expected to live in their own ghettos and wear a distinctive type of dress, but were also allowed (unlike their Christian neighbours) to divorce and re-marry. Predictably, they were often blamed for things over which they had no control, from famine to plague, and were intermittently subjected to pogroms like the ones in Palma in 1391 and again in 1435 (see p.74). They were also subject to the attentions of the **Holy Office of the Inquisition**, which set up shop in Palma in 1484 determined to impose orthodoxy on all of the island's citizenry. The Inquisitors bore down on the Jews, most of whom either left or chose the course of least resistance and converted to Christianity, though a small percentage were burnt to death. As late as the 1970s, the descendants of these converts still formed a distinct group of Palma gold- and silversmiths, but no such enclave exists today.

backwater – even more so when, following Columbus's reaching the Americas in 1492, the focus of European trade moved from the Mediterranean to the Atlantic seaboard almost at a stroke. The last commercial straw was the royal decree that forbade Catalunya and the Balearics from trading with the New World. By the start of the sixteenth century, the Balearics were starved of foreign currency and the islands' merchants had begun to leave, signalling a period of long-term economic decline.

Sixteenth-century decline

Political and economic difficulties destabilized the islands' social structures throughout the sixteenth century. The **Jews**, as useful scapegoats, focused some of the swirling antagonisms that perturbed the islands, but there were many other signs of discontent. The aristocracy was divided into warring factions, the country districts were set against the towns, and perhaps most destabilizing of all were high taxes and an unreliable grain supply. In Mallorca, this turbulence coalesced in an **armed uprising** of peasants and artisans in 1521. Organized in a **Germania**, or armed brotherhood, the insurrectionists seized control of Palma, whose nobles beat a hasty retreat to the safety of either Palma's Castell de Bellver or the Alcúdia citadel – those who didn't move fast enough were slaughtered in the streets. The rebels soon captured the Bellver, and polished off the blue-bloods who had sought protection there, but Alcúdia held out until relieved. It was a long wait: only in 1523 did the forces of authority return under the command of **Emperor Charles V**, king of Spain, Habsburg Holy Roman Emperor and the grandson of Fernando and Isabella. Charles negotiated generous terms for the surrender of Palma, but once in possession of the city, promptly broke the agreement and ordered the execution of five hundred rebels, who were duly hung, drawn and quartered.

The Balearics witnessed other sixteenth-century horrors with the renewal of large-scale **naval raids** from North Africa. This upsurge of piratical activity was partly stimulated by the final expulsion of the Moors from Spain in 1492, and partly by the emergence of the Ottoman Turks as a Mediterranean superpower. Amongst many attacks, Muslim raiders ransacked Pollença (1531 and 1550),

Alcúdia (1551), Valldemossa (1552), Andratx (1553) and Sóller (1561), whilst **Hizir Barbarossa** ravaged Menorca's Maó after a three-day siege in 1535. Hundreds of Menorcans were enslaved and carted off, prompting Charles V to construct the fort of Sant Felip to guard Maó harbour. Two decades later, the Turks returned and sacked Ciutadella, taking a further three thousand prisoners – about eighty percent of the city's population. Muslim incursions continued until the seventeenth century, but declined in frequency and intensity after a combined Italian and Spanish force destroyed the Turkish fleet at **Lepanto** in 1571.

The arrival of the British

The Balearics' woes continued throughout the **seventeenth century**. Trade remained stagnant and the population declined, a sorry state of affairs that was exacerbated by continued internal tensions. Palma, in particular, was plagued by **vendettas** between its aristocratic families, with the Canavall and Canavant factions regularly involved in street battles and assassinations, whilst the (often absentee) landowners failed to invest in their estates. By the 1630s the population problem had become so critical that Philip IV exempted the islands from the levies that raised men for Spain's armies, though this gain was offset by the loss of 15,000 Mallorcans to the **plague** in 1652.

A new development was the regular appearance of **British** vessels in the Mediterranean, a corollary of Britain's increasing share of the region's seaborne trade and the Royal Navy's commitment to protect its merchantmen from Algerian pirates. The British didn't have much use for Mallorca, and largely ignored it, but they were impressed by **Maó's splendid harbour**, a secure and sheltered deep-water anchorage where they first put in to take on water in 1621. Forty years later, Charles II of England formalized matters by instructing his ambassador to Spain to "request immediate permission for British ships to use Balearic ports and particularly Port Mahon". The Spanish king granted the request, and the advantages were noted by a poetic British seaman, a certain John Baltharpe:

Good this same is upon Minork
For shipping very useful 'gainst the Turk.
The King of Spain doth to our King it lend,
As in the line above to that same end.

For a time the British were simply content to "borrow" Maó, but their expanding commercial interests prompted a yearning for a more permanent arrangement. It was the dynastic **War of the Spanish Succession** (1701–14), fought over the vacant throne of Spain, which gave them their opportunity. A British force invaded Menorca in 1708 and, meeting tepid resistance, captured the island in a fortnight. Apart from the benefits of Maó harbour, Menorca was also an ideal spot from which to blockade the French naval base at Toulon, thereby preventing the union of the French Atlantic and Mediterranean fleets. In fact, Menorca was so useful to the British that they negotiated its retention at the **Treaty of Utrecht**, which both rounded off the war and formalized the island's **first period of British occupation**, which was to last from 1708 to 1756.

The British occupation of Menorca

Sir Richard Kane, Menorca's first significant British governor, was an energetic and capable man who strengthened the island as a military base and worked hard at improving its administration, civilian facilities and economy. He built the first **road** across the island from Maó to Ciutadella and introduced improved strains of seed and livestock. Indeed, such were the benefits of British rule that during the first forty years of the occupation the production of wine, vegetables and chickens increased by five hundred percent. Relations between the occupying power and the islanders were generally good – though the Catholic clergy no doubt found it difficult to stomach the instruction to "pray for His Britannic Majesty".

The first phase of British domination ended when the **French** captured Menorca in 1756 at the start of the **Seven Years War**. Admiral Byng was dispatched to assist the beleaguered British garrison, but, after a lacklustre encounter with a French squadron, he withdrew, leaving the British force with no option but to surrender. Byng's indifferent performance cost him his life: he was court-martialled and executed for cowardice, prompting Voltaire's famous aphorism that the English shoot their admirals "pour encourager les autres". The new French governor built the township of **Sant Lluís** (see p.237) to house his Breton sailors and, once again, the Menorcans adjusted to the occupying power without too much difficulty. In 1763, Britain regained Menorca in exchange for the Philippines and Cuba, which it had captured from France during the Seven Years War.

The **second period of British occupation** (1763–82) proved far less successful than the first. None of the governors proved as adept as Kane and their tendency to ignore the islanders undermined the Menorcans' trust in the British. The crunch came in 1781, when, with Britain at war with both Spain and France, the Duc de Crillon landed on the island with eight thousand soldiers. In command of a much smaller force, the British governor, John Murray, withdrew to Fort Sant Felip, where he was promptly besieged. Crucially, the Menorcans decided to succour Crillon's Franco–Spanish army and, with this material support, they were able to starve the British into submission after eight long months; thereafter, Menorca temporarily reverted to Spain.

The **third and final period of British rule over Menorca** ran from 1798 to 1802, when the island was occupied for its value as a naval base in the Napoleonic Wars. Landing at Port d'Addaia, the British took just nine days – and suffered no casualties – in recapturing the island, helped in no small measure by the foolhardy destruction of Fort Sant Felip by the Spaniards in the mid-1780s. It seems that the Spanish high command did not believe they could defend the fortress, so they simply flattened it, thereby denying it to any colonial power – and, of course, making the island vulnerable in the process. The British finally relinquished all claims to Menorca in favour of Spain under the terms of the Treaty of Amiens in 1802.

Eighteenth-century Mallorca

Meanwhile **Mallorca**, lacking a harbour of any strategic significance, was having a much quieter time, though the islanders did choose the wrong side in the War of the Spanish Succession (1701–14). Most of Spain favoured the French candidate, Philip of Anjou, but Catalunya and Mallorca preferred the Austrian Habsburg Charles III, who was supported by Britain and the Netherlands. Philip won, and promptly proceeded to strip the island of its title of kingdom and remove many of its historic rights. Otherwise, Mallorca was left pretty much untouched by the European conflicts that rippled around it, but even so it did not prosper. Instead it turned in on itself, becoming a caste- and priest-ridden backwater preoccupied with its own internal feuds. By the 1740s, however, this reactionary introspection was ruffled by more progressive elements, who, influenced by the **Enlightenment**, introduced liberal and rationalist ideas into island society. Oddly enough, the ideological conflict between Conservatives and Liberals focused on Ramón Llull (see p.75), with the former keen to have him beatified, the latter eager to denigrate his complex mysticism. The traditionalists won, but the bitterness of the dispute combined with its length (1749–77) divided the middle class into hostile camps.

One other major change was Madrid's edict pronouncing **Castilian** as the official language of the Balearics in place of the local dialect of Catalan.

The nineteenth century

For both Mallorca and Menorca, the **nineteenth century** brought difficult times. Neglected and impoverished outposts, they were subject to droughts, famines and epidemics of cholera, bubonic plague and yellow fever. Consequently, the islanders became preoccupied with the art of survival rather than politics, and generally stayed out of the **Carlist** wars that raged between the Liberals and the Conservatives on the Spanish mainland. Nevertheless, the islanders were obliged to implement a Liberal decree of 1836, which suppressed all of Spain's larger convents and monasteries – hence George Sand and Frédéric Chopin's extended stay in a monk-free Valldemossa monastery. The leading political figure of the period was the historian **Josep Quadrado**, who led the reactionary Catholic Union, which bombarded Madrid with petitions and greeted every Conservative success with enthusiastic demonstrations. Otherwise, many islanders emigrated, some to Algeria after it was acquired by the French in 1830, others to Florida and California.

Matters began to improve towards the end of the nineteenth century, when **agriculture**, particularly almond cultivation, revived. Modern services, like gas and electricity, began to be installed and a regular steam-packet link was established between Mallorca and the mainland. Menorca also developed a thriving export industry in footwear thanks to the entrepreneurial Don Jeronimo Cabrisas, a Menorcan who had made his fortune in Cuba and later supplied many of the boots worn by the troops in World War I. Around this time too, a **revival of Catalan culture**, led by the middle classes of Barcelona, stirred the Balearic bourgeoisie. In Palma in particular, Catalunyan novelists and poets were lauded, Catalan political groupings were formed, and the town was adorned with a series of splendid *Modernista* buildings.

Much less positively, Balearic politics became polarized between Conservative and Liberal groupings. This failure to create a political discourse between rival factions mirrored developments in the rest of Spain, and both here and on the mainland chronic instability was to be the harbinger of the military coup that ushered in the right-wing dictatorship of General Primo de Rivera in 1923.

The Spanish Civil War

During the **Spanish Civil War** (1936–39), Mallorca and Menorca supported opposing sides. General Goded made Mallorca an important base for the Fascists, but when General Bosch attempted to do the same on Menorca, his NCOs and men mutinied and, with the support of the civilian population, declared their support for the Republic. In the event – apart from a few bombing raids and an attempted Republican landing at Porto Cristo (see p.198) – the Balearics saw very little fighting. Nevertheless, the Menorcans were dangerously exposed towards the end of the war, when they were marooned as the last Republican stronghold. A peaceful conclusion was reached largely through the intervention of the British, who brokered the surrender of the island aboard *HMS Devonshire*. Franco's troops occupied Menorca in April 1939 and the *Devonshire* left with 450 Menorcan refugees.

1945 to 1995

The rich and famous discovered Mallorca's charms in the late nineteenth century – Jules Vernes, for one, liked to visit and both Edward VII and the German Kaiser regularly cruised its waters. The high-water mark of this elitist tourist trade was reached in the 1930s when a wealthy Argentinian, Adan Diehl, opened the *Hotel Formentor* (see p.162). Never knowingly outdone, Diehl advertised the hotel in lights on the Eiffel Tower and attracted guests such as Edward VIII, the Aga Khan and Winston Churchill – no mean guest list by any standard.

From such small and privileged beginnings, the Balearics' **tourist industry** mushroomed at an extraordinary rate after World War II. In 1950, Mallorca had just one hundred registered hotels and boarding houses, but by 1972 the total had risen to over 1600, and similarly the number of visitors to Menorca rose from 1500 in 1961 to half a million in 1973. It was an extraordinary phenomenon and the prodigious pace of development accelerated after the **death of Franco** in 1975, thereby further strengthening the local economy. One twist, however, was the relative price of real estate: traditionally, island landowners with coastal estates had given their younger children the poorer agricultural land near the seashore, but it was this land the developers wanted – and so younger siblings found their prospects transformed almost at a stroke. In more general terms, the burgeoning tourist economy pumped huge quantities of money into the Balearics and, by the 1990s, the archipelago had one of the highest per capita incomes in Spain, four times that of Extremadura for instance, and well above the EU average. There was also the small matter of **sex**: the Franco regime had reinforced a strict moral code in which Spanish girls kept their bodies to themselves until they were married. Many of the arriving tourists had no such inhibitions – much to the delight of a legion of local men – and it took a couple of decades for Spanish women to re-focus their sights – and their mores.

The Autonomous Communities

The Balearics also benefited from the political restructuring of Spain following the death of Franco. In 1978, the Spanish parliament, the Cortes, passed a new **constitution**, which reorganized the country on a federal basis and allowed for the establishment of regional Autonomous Communities. In practice, the demarcation of responsibilities between central and regional governments has proved immensely problematic, leading to intense wrangling that continues unabated to this day, not least because the Madrid government has often been reliant for its majority in the Cortes on the support of the regionalists (primarily the Basques and the Catalans). Nonetheless, the Balearics, constituted as the **Comunidad Autónoma de las Islas Baleares** in 1983, have used their new-found independence to assert the primacy of their native Catalan language – now the main language of education – and to exercise a tighter local control of their economy.

1996 to 2003

In 1996, after fourteen years in power, the Socialist **PSOE** was defeated in the Spanish **general election**, but although the new Conservative regime – led by the **Partido Popular (PP)** – had strong centralizing credentials, it was also

A Spanish chronology

c.11th–5th BC Phoenicians, Greeks and Celts invade Spain and intermingle with the native (Iberian) population.

c.3rd BC Carthaginians conquer southeast Spain.

c.3rd–2nd BC Carthage and Rome wrestle for control of the Iberian Peninsula in three Punic Wars. Rome wins the lot and Spain is incorporated within the Roman Empire.

c.1st AD Christianity makes rapid progress across Roman Spain.

c.5th AD The Roman Empire collapses and the Visigoths become Spain's dominant military force.

711 Islamic Moors (Arabs and Berbers from North Africa) conquer the Visigoths' kingdom in a whirlwind campaign that lasts just seven years. However, a Christian victory at the battle of Covadonga (722) halts the Moorish advance and leads to the creation of the kingdom of Asturias – a solitary Christian toehold on the northwest corner of the Iberian peninsula.

756 Abd ar-Rahman I proclaims the Emirate of Córdoba, confirming Moorish control over almost all of Spain.

c.9th The Christian kingdoms of Catalunya and Navarra are founded.

c.10th–early 11th The Emirate of Córdoba flourishes, its capital becoming the most prosperous and civilized city in Europe. Abd ar-Rahman III breaks with Baghdad to declare himself caliph of an independent western Islamic empire.

c.11th The caliphate disintegrates into squabbling *taifas*, or petty fiefdoms.

1037 Fernando I unites the Christian kingdoms of Castile and León-Asturias.

1162 Alfonso II unites the Christian kingdoms of Aragón and Catalunya.

c.13th The pace of the Christian Reconquista accelerates; the Moors lose control of the Balearics.

1479 Castile and Aragón, the two pre-eminent Christian kingdoms, are united under Isabella I and Fernando V, the so-called Catholic Monarchs (*Los Reyes Católicos*). Spain subsequently emerges as a single political entity, with the Inquisition acting as a unifying force.

1492 The fall of Granada, the last Moorish kingdom. Columbus reaches the Americas.

1494 At the Treaty of Tordesillas, drawn up under the approving eye of the pope, Spain and Portugal divide the New World between them. Portugal gets Brazil and Spain takes the rest of modern-day Latin America.

1519 Cortés lands in Mexico, seizing its capital two years later.

1532 Pizarro "discovers" Peru, capturing Cuzco the following year.

1556 Felipe II (Philip II), becomes king of Spain and its colonies, Naples, Milan and the Low Countries. His brother, Ferdinand I, becomes Holy Roman Emperor, ruling Germany and Austria. An ardent and autocratic Catholic, Felipe wages war against Europe's Protestants. He funds his campaigns with the gold and silver bullion that is pouring into Spain from the New World, where Spanish adventurers have now colonized and exploited a vast new empire.

1567 The Protestants of the Low Countries rise against Felipe II, beginning a protracted conflict that will drain Spanish resources.

1571 Spain wins control of the Mediterranean after defeating the Turkish fleet at Lepanto.

1588 The English defeat Felipe II's Armada, eliminating Spain as a major sea power.

1598 Felipe II dies. His legacy is an enormous but bankrupt empire: Spain's great wealth, so ruthlessly extracted from its colonies, has been squandered in over seventy years of continuous warfare.

c.17th Spain enters a period of precipitate military, economic and political decline. Cervantes publishes *Don Quixote* in 1605.

1701–14 Europe's nation states slug it out in the War of the Spanish Succession. The Bourbon (French) claimant – as opposed to that of the Holy Roman Emperor – wins out to become Felipe V. The British pick up Gibraltar and Menorca. As Spain declines further, so it moves into the French sphere of influence.

1804 Napoleon crowned Emperor of France. Spain assists him in his war against England.

1805 The British navy, under Nelson, destroys the Franco-Spanish fleet at the Battle of Trafalgar.

1808 Napoleon arrests the Spanish king and replaces him with his brother, Joseph. This starts the War of Independence (otherwise known as the Peninsular War) in which the Spaniards fight the French army of occupation with the help of their new-found allies, the British.

1811 onwards The South American colonies take advantage of the situation to assert their independence, detaching themselves from Spain one by one.

1815 The end of the Napoleonic Wars.

c.19th Further Spanish decline. The nineteenth century is dominated by the struggle between the forces of monarchist reaction and those of liberal constitutional reform. The progressives finally triumph in the 1870s, but the new government's authority is brittle and Spanish society remains deeply divided. Elsewhere, Puerto Rico, the Philippines and Cuba shake off Spanish control with the help of the USA. Spain's American empire is at an end.

1900–31 Liberals and Conservatives fail to reach a secure constitutional consensus, keeping the country on a knife edge. Working-class political movements – of anarchist, Marxist and socialist inclination – grow in strength and stir industrial and political discontent. Spain stays neutral in World War I, but the success of the Russian Bolsheviks terrifies King Alfonso XIII and the bourgeoisie, who support the right-wing military coup engineered by General Primo de Rivera in 1923. Rivera dies in 1930 and the king abdicates in 1931 when anti-monarchist parties win the municipal elections.

1932–36 The new Republican government introduces radical left-of-centre reforms, but separatists, revolutionaries and rightists undermine its authority. Spain polarizes to the political left and right. Chaos and confusion prevail.

1936–39 The Spanish Civil War. General Francisco Franco leads a right-wing military rebellion against the Republican government. His Nationalists receive substantial support from Hitler and Mussolini. The Republicans get sporadic help from the Soviet Union and attract thousands of volunteers, organized in the International Brigades. The Civil War is vicious and bloody, ending in 1939 with a Fascist victory. Franco becomes head of state and bloody reprisals follow. Pope Pius XII congratulates the dictator on his "Catholic victory".

1939–75 Franco establishes a one-party state, backed up by stringent censorship and a vigorous secret police. By staying neutral during World War II, he survives the fall of Nazi Germany. In 1969, Franco nominates the grandson of Alfonso XIII, Juan Carlos, as his successor, but retains his vice-like grip on the country until his death in 1975.

1976–82 Juan Carlos recognizes the need for political reform and helps steer the country towards a parliamentary system. He reinforces his democratic credentials by opposing the attempted coup of 1981, when Colonel Tejero leads a group of Guardia Civil officers loyal to Franco's memory in the storming of the Cortes (parliament). The coup fails.

(contd...)

1982–96 In 1982, Felipe González's Socialist Workers' Party – the PSOE – is elected to office with the votes of nearly ten million Spaniards. It's an electoral landslide and the PSOE promises change and progress. Spain's economy grows dramatically, the country becomes a respected member of the EU, and the PSOE attempts to deal with Spain's deep-seated separatist tendencies by permitting a large degree of regional autonomy. No effort is made to hunt down Franco's thugs – part of an accommodation between left and right designed to stop Spain from degenerating into a cycle of political revenge.

1996–2000 At the 1996 general election, the Conservative Popular Party, the PP, becomes the largest party in the Cortes, but does not get an overall majority. The PP enlists the support of Catalan and Basque nationalist deputies to form an administration. The price is more powers to the regions.

2000–2003 The PP wins the general election of 2000 and this time they have an overall majority in the Cortes. Nonetheless, the PP leadership emphasizes the need for consensus not confrontation.

The 2004 election At the start of 2004, the opinion polls show solid public support for the PP administration, suggesting that the general election scheduled for March will return them to office. Then, on March 11, three days before polling day, a series of bombs explode on Madrid's commuter trains, killing 192 people and injuring almost two thousand more. Rashly, the PP leadership immediately blames the Basque terrorist/separatist group ETA for the explosions, believing, so it would seem, that this false accusation will deflect attention away from the real reason for the attack – Spain's support for the Iraq war (ninety percent of Spaniards had been against it) – just long enough for the votes to be counted. It doesn't wash and by the time the polls open, many have come to believe – as was subsequently proved to be the case – that Islamic terrorists had blown up the trains. The voters vent their political spleen against the PP, giving the PSOE an unexpected victory; the new regime's first act is to announce the immediate withdrawal of Spanish troops from Iraq.

2004 to today After the 2004 election, the PSOE pursues a liberal social agenda – authorizing fast-track divorces, for example – and adopts competent if unspectacular economic policies. The government fails, however, to reach an accommodation with ETA, the Basque separatist group, after high-level negotiations flounder, and ETA resumes, albeit intermittently, its bombing campaign. The PSOE remains popular enough to win the next general election in March 2008 despite the country feeling the first effects of the worldwide recession. In the event, Spain is particularly badly hit by the slow-down: the country's housing market takes a nose dive and at time of writing unemployment stands at an unbearable seventeen percent. The PSOE's ability to deal with the crisis as it unfolds and unravels will undoubtedly define its immediate political future.

reliant on the regionalists. Consequently, the trend towards **decentralization** continued with most government expenditure now coming under the control of the Autonomous Communities. In particular, the Balearic administration used these regionalized resources to upgrade a string of holiday resorts and modernize much of the archipelago's infrastructure. In part this reflected a particular concern with Ibiza and Mallorca's somewhat tacky image and was accompanied by the imposition of stricter building controls, a number of environmental schemes and the spending of millions of pesetas on refurbishing the older, historical parts of Palma. On Menorca, the money also paid for the creation of a Parc Natural protecting the wetlands of S'Albufera d'es Grau along with the adjacent coastline.

The Conservative-led Balearic administration also made moves to curb tourist development, but in this they failed to keep pace with public sentiment – as exemplified by a string of large-scale **demonstrations** held during 1998 and 1999. The demonstrations focused on four primary and inter-related concerns: the spiralling cost of real estate, foreign ownership of land (some twenty percent of Mallorca is in foreign hands), untrammelled development and loutish behaviour in the budget resorts. This failure to keep abreast of popular feeling resulted in the defeat of the Conservatives in the **1999 regional elections** and their replacement by an unwieldy alliance of regionalists, socialists and greens committed to halting further tourist development in its tracks. As one of its spokesmen expressed it: "We need to dignify the tourist sector, not promote it as the cheapest in Europe with the idea that you can come here and do whatever you like." Faced with an annual influx of around eleven million holidaymakers, few islanders disagreed, and the coalition made significant progress, though they came unstuck when the tourist industry hit (comparatively) hard times in 2002 with an eight percent drop in the number of visitors. The main reason for the decline was the economic travails of Germany, but Balearic anxieties focused on the so-called **tourist tax** imposed by the regional government in May 2002. The idea was to impose a modest tax on every visitor over twelve years of age and spend the money – potentially about thirty million euros a year – on environmental improvements. However, the tourist industry created a huge hullabaloo that undermined the Balearic administration, and the Conservatives, who had pledged to rescind the tax, were returned to office in the **regional elections of 2003**. This was a major setback for the environmentalist cause at a time when Spain's regionalists were already losing ground to Madrid – the Conservatives had won a second **general election in 2000**, but this time with an overall majority in the Cortes, thus firmly sidelining the regionalists.

2004 to the present

After their 2003 election victory, the Conservative-led Balearic administration proved remarkably gung-ho when it came to **development**, ignoring environmental concerns by embarking, for example, on a large-scale road-building programme in the belief that more roads create better motoring – never mind the disfiguring of agricultural land that this involved. They even became quite evangelical in their desire for development, most notably supporting a mass demonstration in favour of the expansion of port facilities at Ciutadella – an expansion that Menorca's PSOE-led council strongly opposed. The PP Mayor of Andratx, one Eugenio Hidalgo, joined in the development bonanza, but in his case there were shady dealings involving illegal construction permits – amongst much else – and in 2008, two years after the scandal broke, Hidalgo was sent to prison for four years. This was all very depressing, but nevertheless the PP still managed to garner more votes than any other party in the **regional elections of 2007**. The catch was that they didn't quite secure an overall majority and their opponents united to form a new ruling PSOE-led coalition. The new administration, under the leadership of Francesc Antich, put the brakes on the helter-skelter development of its predecessor, but its priorities were soon muddied and modified by the worldwide recession: in 2009, the number of tourists dropped by about ten percent, bringing many hotels to the point of bankruptcy. Antich and his colleagues were obliged to consider all sorts of stimulus packages and then, as if things weren't bad enough, ETA, the Basque separatist group, exploded a number of **bombs** on Mallorca in the summer of the same year. At time of writing, there have been just a handful of explosions – but there are fears there will be more.

Flora and fauna

Despite their reputation as overdeveloped, package-holiday hotspots, Menorca and more especially Mallorca have much to offer birders and botanists alike. Separated from the Iberian Peninsula some fifty million years ago, the Balearic archipelago has evolved (at least in part) its own **distinctive flora and fauna**, with further variations between each of the islands. Among the wildlife, it's the raptors inhabiting the mountains of northwest Mallorca – particularly the black vulture – which attract much of the attention, but there are other pleasures too, especially the migratory birds which gather on the islands' saltpans and marshes in April and May and from mid-September to early October. The islands are also justifiably famous for their fabulous range of wild flowers and flowering shrubs.

Some of the islands' most important habitats have, however, been threatened by the developers. This has spawned an influential conservation group, **GOB** (Grup Balear d'Ornitologia i Defensa de la Naturalesa; ⓦwww.gobmallorca .com), which has launched several successful campaigns in recent years. It helped save the S'Albufera wetlands from further development; played a leading role in the black vulture re-establishment programme; successfully lobbied to increase the penalties for shooting protected birds; and won its fight to protect and preserve Cabrera island.

The account below serves as a general introduction, and includes mention of several important birding sites, cross-referenced to the descriptions given throughout our *Guide*. For more specialist information, some recommended **field guides** are listed on p.303.

Habitats

The Balearic islands are a continuation of the Andalucian mountains of the Iberian Peninsula, from which they are separated by a submarine trench never less than 80km wide and up to 1500m deep. **Mallorca** comprises three distinct geographical areas with two ranges of predominantly limestone mountains/hills falling either side of a central plain, **Es Pla**. Mallorca's northwest coast is dominated by the **Serra de Tramuntana**, a slim, ninety-kilometre-long range of wooded hills and rocky peaks, which is fringed by tiny coves and precipitous sea-cliffs; it reaches its highest point at Puig Major (1447m). Also edged by sea-cliffs is the **Serres de Llevant**, a range of more modest hills that runs parallel to the island's east shore and rises to 509m at the Santuari de Sant Salvador.

Menorca has less topographical diversity, dividing into two distinct but not dramatically different zones. The **northern half** of the island comprises rolling sandstone uplands punctuated by wide, shallow valleys and occasional peaks, the highest of which is Monte Toro at 357m. To the **south** lie undulating limestone lowlands and deeper valleys. Steep sea-cliffs and scores of rocky coves trim the island's north and south shores.

Mallorca and Menorca share a temperate Mediterranean **climate**, with winter frosts a rarity, but there are significant differences between the two. The Serra de Tramuntana protects the rest of Mallorca from the prevailing winds that blow from the north and also catches most of the rain. Menorca, on the other hand, has no mountain barrier to protect it from the cold dry wind (the Tramuntana) which buffets the island from the north, giving much of the island's vegetation a wind-blown look, and obliging farmers to protect their crops with stone walls.

Mallorcan flora

The characteristic terrain of Mallorca up to around 700m is **garrigue**, partly forested open scrubland where the island's native trees – Aleppo pines, wild olives, holm oaks, carobs and dwarf palms – intermingle with imported species like ash, elm and poplar. Between 700m and 950m, the *garrigue* gives way to **maquis**, a scrubland of rosemary, laurel, myrtle and broom interspersed with swaths of bracken. Higher still is a rocky terrain that can only support the sparsest of vegetation, such as an assortment of hardy grasses and low-growth rosemary.

Across much of the island, this indigenous vegetation has been destroyed by cultivation. However, the **Aleppo pine** and the evergreen **holm oak** – which traditionally supplied acorns for pigs, wood for charcoal and bark for tanning – are still common, as is the **carob tree**, which prefers the hottest and driest parts of the island. Arguably the archipelago's most handsome tree, the carob boasts leaves of varying greenness and bears conspicuous fruits – large pods that start green, but ripen to black-brown. The **dwarf palm**, with its sharp lance-like foliage, is concentrated around Pollença, Alcúdia and Andratx. The **wild olive** is comparatively rare (and may not be indigenous), but the cultivated variety, which boasts silver-grey foliage and can grow up to 10m in height, is endemic and has long been a mainstay of the local economy. There are also **orange** and **lemon** orchards around Sóller and innumerable almond trees, whose pink and white blossoms adorn much of the island in late January and early February.

Mallorca has a wonderful variety of **flowering shrubs**. There are too many to list here in any detail, but look out for the deep blue flowers of the **rosemary**; the reddish bloom of the **lentisk** (or mastic tree); the bright yellow broom which begins blossoming in March; the many types of **tree heather**; and the autumn-flowering **strawberry tree**, found especially around Ca'n Picafort. **Rockroses** are also widely distributed, the most common members of the group being the spring-flowering, grey-leafed cistus, with its velvety leaves and pink flowers, and the narrow-leafed cistus whose bloom is white.

Wild flowers and plants

In spring and autumn the fields, verges, woods and cliffs of Mallorca brim with **wild flowers**. There are several hundred species and only in the depths of winter – from November to January – are all of them dormant. Well-known flowers include marigolds, daisies, violets, yellow primroses, gladioli, poppies, hyacinths, several kinds of cyclamen, the resinous St John's wort with its crinkled deep-green leaves and, abundant in the pine woods near the sea and in the mountains, many types of orchid. Two common mountain plants are the pampas-like grass **Ampelodesmos mauritanica**, giant clumps of which cover the hillsides, and a local variety of the sarsaparilla, **Smilax balearica**, which flourishes in limestone crevices where its sharp thorns are something of a hazard for walkers. Other common and prominent plants are the giant-sized **agave** (century plant), an imported amaryllid with huge spear-shaped, leathery leaves of blue-grey coloration, which produces a massive flower spike after ten years (just before it dies). There's also the distinctive **asphodel**, whose tall spikes sport clusters of pink or white flowers from April to June. The asphodel grows on overgrazed or infertile land and its starch-rich tubers were once used by shoemakers to make glue. Another common sight is the **prickly pear**, traditionally grown behind peasants' houses as a windbreak and toilet wall. A versatile plant, the smell of the prickly pear deflects insects (hence its use round toilets) and its fruit is easy to make into pig food or jam.

Finally, many islanders maintain splendid **gardens** and here you'll see species that flourish throughout the Mediterranean, most famously bougainvilleas, oleanders, geraniums and hibiscus.

Mallorcan birds

Mallorca's diverse **birdlife** has attracted ornithologists for decades. The island boasts a whole batch of resident Mediterranean specialists and these are supplemented by migrating flocks of North European birds that descend on the island in their thousands during the spring and autumn.

The limestone **Serra de Tramuntana** mountains crimping the northwest coast are a haven for birds of prey. The massive **black vulture** is the real star here. This rare and impressive raptor, with its near three-metre wingspan, breeds in small numbers, but its size and residency means there's a reasonable chance of a sighting. The Puig Roig area (see p.149) is an excellent place to see this vulture, but note that during late spring and summer there are sometimes access restrictions to the bird's active sea-cliff nesting areas. The booted eagle is another mountain highlight, and there's a supporting cast of ospreys, red kites, Eleonora's falcons, kestrels and peregrines.

The **Embassament de Cúber** (Cúber Reservoir; see p.146), just west of Lluc, provides a natural amphitheatre from where up to ten species of bird of prey can be seen, including ospreys and red-footed falcons hunting over the water itself. The colourful rock thrush breeds in the quarry just west of the reservoir dam and on the nearby crags. The **sea-cliffs** of the western coast are the breeding grounds of shearwaters, Mediterranean shag, storm petrels and Audouin's gulls. The most impressive seabird colonies are in the *Parc Natural de Sa Dragonera*, an island fastness off Sant Elm (see p.136), which is home to all these birds as well as several dozen pairs of Eleonora's falcons. The district's seabirds may also be viewed from **La Trapa**, a small headland nature reserve of pristine coastal *garrigue* that will soon have its own hikers' hostel (or *refugi*; see p.137). The reserve is about an hour's walk north of Sant Elm, but the going is fairly tough. A similarly good spot for seabirds is the **Cap de Formentor** (see p.162), at the other end of the island, from where a wide range of birds wander the neighbouring bays of Pollença and Alcúdia.

Scrub and wetland birds

Characteristic birds of the island's **scrubland** can also be found around the Embalse de Cúber, including a variety of warblers and small songbirds, such as nightingales, larks, pipits and colourful chats. Another area of rich scrubland is the **Vall de Bóquer** (see p.158), near Pollença. Thoughtless development has harmed the olive groves and almond orchards at the base of the valley, but the Bóquer remains a migration hotspot, its pine avenues and denser wooded slopes hosting firecrests and crossbills among more familiar woodland birds like tits and woodpigeons. If you venture to the north end of the valley, you should be rewarded with the colourful delights of Marmora's warbler and the blue rock thrush. In spring, hundreds of bee-eaters can be heard and seen in and around the valley, as these stunning birds move through to breed elsewhere in the Mediterranean.

Wetlands are a magnet for birds in the arid climate of the Mediterranean. Mallorca boasts the most important birdwatching spot in the whole of the

Balearics in the marshes of the **Parc Natural de S'Albufera** (see p.172). Here, resident species are augmented by hundreds of migrating birds, who visit to find fresh water after their long journey north or south. Amongst scores of species, the shorter grasses shelter moorhens, coots, crakes and the re-introduced purple gallinule, while the reeds hide healthy numbers of several species of heron, bittern and egret as well as the occasional flamingo. A wide variety of small wading birds visit the marsh too, including the distinctively long-legged black-winged stilt and the abundant Kentish plover. The open water is popular with ducks, while in spring large numbers of terns may be seen. In winter the variety of duck species increases and kingfishers are common. This rich diversity of birdlife attracts birds of prey and this is as good a place as any to see ospreys and marsh harriers. In addition, over one hundred Eleonora's falcons have been seen together over the marsh in spring. Among the smaller birds, the spring dusk and dawn choruses provided by wetland warblers such as Cetti's, moustached and great reed are unforgettable. Neither is the sound of birds restricted to the daytime. At night, listen for the plaintive single note of the scops owl against a backdrop of warblers, crakes and crickets. The scops owl can also be heard in the south of the island, usually preferring almond groves and olive clumps.

The birds of the saltpans and the central plain

Generally speaking, the south is not as rich in birdlife as other parts of the island, the main exception being the **saltpan** habitat of the **Salines de Llevant**, near Colònia de Sant Jordi (see p.210). Here, a wide variety of migrant wading birds, wintering duck and small flocks of wintering flamingoes and cranes can be seen. The site also has a breeding flock of over a hundred black-winged stilts in summer and the abundance of prey attracts raptors, most frequently marsh harriers, kestrels and ospreys. The pans also host terns and Audouin's gulls: this red-billed gull is a Mediterranean specialist and although favouring the southern saltpans, can be chanced upon at many coastal spots.

The country lanes that lattice Mallorca's **central plain**, Es Pla, also have their own distinctive birdlife. In spring and summer, the calls and songs of small birds like serins, corn buntings and Sardinian warblers and the ubiquitous fan-tailed warbler create a busy backdrop to hot, lazy afternoons. Nightingales seem to be everywhere and their rich song leaves a lasting impression. In the shade of the abundant olive groves, the subtly plumaged wryneck can be found all year, often sharing this ancient landscape with the striking hoopoe.

Other Mallorcan fauna

Mallorca's surviving **mammals** are an uninspiring bunch. The wild boar and red fox were eliminated early in the twentieth century, leaving a motley crew of mountain goats, wild sheep, pine martens, genets, weasels and feral cats, as well as commonplace smaller mammals such as hedgehogs, rabbits, hares and shrews.

As far as **reptiles** go, there are four types of snake – all hard to come by – and two species of gecko (or broad-toed lizard): the lowland-living wall gecko and the mountain-dwelling disc-fingered version. With any luck, you'll spot them as they heat up in the sun, but they move fast since warm gecko is a tasty morsel for many a bird. Off the south coast of Mallorca, the island of Cabrera (see p.210) has a large concentration of the rare, blue-bellied Lilford's wall lizard.

Among **amphibians**, Mallorca has a healthy frog population, concentrated in its marshlands but also surviving in its mountain pools (up to around 800m). There are also three types of toad, of which the **Mallorcan midwife toad**,

Selected birds of Mallorca and Menorca

The list below describes many of the most distinctive **birds** to be found on Mallorca and/or Menorca. We have given the English name, followed in italics by the Latin, a useful cross-reference for those without a British field guide.

Serin (*Serinus serinus*). Menorca. Winter visitor. Tiny, green-and-yellow canary-like bird of the finch family, with characteristically buoyant flight. Appears in virtually any habitat.

Fan-tailed warbler (*Cisticola juncidis*). Mallorca & Menorca. Very common breeding resident. Typical small brown bird, but with very distinctive "zit-zit-zit" song, usually uttered in flight. Prefers wetland areas.

Nightingale (*Luscinia megarhynchos*). Mallorca & Menorca. Common breeding summer visitor. Rich-brown-coloured, robin-like bird with astonishingly rich, vigorous and varied song. Prefers to sing from small bushes, often deep inside and out of sight.

Wryneck (*Jynx torquilla*). Mallorca & Menorca. Mallorca: breeding resident. Menorca: spring, autumn and winter visitor. Medium-sized bird with a complex pattern of brown, grey and lilac plumage. A member of the woodpecker family. Favours olive groves.

Hoopoe (*Upupa epops*). Mallorca & Menorca. Common breeding resident. Pigeon-sized, pinky-brown bird with black head-crest. It is named after its distinctive "upupu upupu" call. Its wings sport a complex black and white barring, creating a striking sight when in flight. Favours open areas with some trees nearby for nesting.

Black vulture (*Aegypius monachus*). Mallorca. Breeding resident only in the northern mountains. Massive, dark, powerful and solitary raptor with a wingspan approaching three metres. The most distinctive of the islands' birds. Faced extinction in the 1980s, but a concerted conservation effort has raised the population to around 125 individual birds and about 20 reproductive pairs.

Booted eagle (*Hieraaetus pennatus*). Mallorca & Menorca. Resident breeder. A small and very agile eagle, similar in size to a buzzard. Prefers the mountains, but happily hunts over scrub and grasslands.

Eleonora's falcon (*Falco eleonorae*). Mallorca & Menorca. Mallorca: fairly common breeding summer visitor. Menorca: spring and autumn migrant. Dark, slim, elegant falcon. Hunts small birds and large insects with fantastic speed and agility. Often seen hunting insects near water.

Rock thrush (*Monticola saxatilis*). Mallorca & Menorca. Mallorca: breeding summer visitor. Menorca: spring and autumn migrant. Beautifully coloured rock- and quarry-loving thrush. Males have a pale blue head and orangey-red breast and tail. Females are a less distinctive brown and cream.

Blue rock thrush (*Monticola solitarius*). Mallorca & Menorca. Common breeding resident. Blue-coloured thrush, recalling a deep-blue starling. Can be found in any rugged, rocky areas at any time of year.

Firecrest (*Regulus ignicapillus*). Mallorca & Menorca. Common breeding resident. The smallest bird on the islands. This tiny pale green bird is named after its vivid orange and yellow crown. Abundant in any woodland.

Crossbill (*Loxia curvirostra*). Mallorca. Abundant breeding resident. The vivid red males and the lemon-green females of this bulky finch have an unusual crossed bill and a distinctive parrot-like appearance. The bill is adapted to extract seeds from pine cones.

Marmora's warbler (*Sylvia sarda*). Mallorca. Common breeding resident. A small blue-ish grey warbler with a long, often-upright tail and distinctive red eye-ring. Prefers the bushy cover of the coastal lowlands.

Purple gallinule (*Porphyrio porphyrio*). Mallorca. Breeding resident only at Mallorca's S'Albufera. This purple-blue oddity was re-introduced to its marshland habitat at

S'Albufera in 1991. It is now well established. Its incredibly long feet and swollen red bill make this hen-like bird very distinctive.

Little egret (*Egretta garzetta*). Mallorca & Menorca. Mallorca: breeding resident. Menorca: spring and autumn migrant. Long-legged, elegant white wading bird. In summer has beautiful long white plumes trailing from the back of its head. Breeds at S'Albufera only. A wetland specialist, though well adapted to treetop life.

Little bittern (*Ixobrychus minutes*). Menorca. Spring and autumn visitor. Secretive wetland specialist. This is the smallest member of the heron family breeding in Europe at little more than 30cm tall. The male is an attractive pink-cream colour with contrasting black wings and cap. Males advertise themselves with a far-carrying gruff basal note, repeated regularly.

Purple heron (*Ardea purpurea*). Mallorca. Breeding summer visitor. Large, slender heron fond of reed beds. The male plumage has beautiful purple and rich-brown tones. Despite its size it can be rather elusive, hiding deep inside the reeds.

Black-winged stilt (*Himantopus himantopus*). Mallorca & Menorca. Mallorca: common breeding resident; Menorca: summer visitor. Incredibly long-legged black-and-white wader. Its medium size is somewhat extended by its long, straight, fine, red bill. Can appear anywhere there is mud, but particularly common on saltpans.

Kentish plover (*Charadrius alexandrinus*). Mallorca & Menorca. Mallorca: common breeding resident. Menorca: spring and autumn visitor. Small, delicate wader of saltpans and marshes. Its pale-brown upper body contrasts with its gleaming white head-collar and underparts.

Cetti's warbler (*Cettia cetti*). Mallorca & Menorca. Very common breeding resident. This rather nondescript, chunky, wren-like warbler prefers dense thickets close to water. It possesses an astonishingly loud explosive song: "chet-chet-chet-chetchetchet".

Great reed warbler (*Acrocephalus arundinaceus*). Mallorca & Menorca. Breeding summer visitor. This large, unstreaked, brown warbler can be found in significant numbers where there is reed and marsh vegetation. Its song is a loud and harsh mixture of unusual grating, croaking and creaking noises.

Scops owl (*Otus scops*). Mallorca & Menorca. Common breeding resident. This tiny owl (only 20cm tall) is stubbornly nocturnal. At night, its plaintive "tyoo" note is repeated every few seconds often for long (monotonous) periods. Groves, plantations, small clumps of trees, conifer woodland and even gardens can host this bird.

Greater flamingo (*Phoenicopterus ruber*). Mallorca & Menorca. Winter/spring visitor in small numbers. The unmistakable silhouette of this leggy wader with roseate wings, bill and legs can be seen on any wetland in spring. In winter, it's confined to the southern reaches of Mallorca – and especially the S'Albufera wetland.

Great white egret (*Egretta alba*). Mallorca & Menorca. Winter visitor. This marshland specialist is really just a large version of the commoner little egret – an all-white, tall, elegant heron.

Audouin's gull (*Larus audouinii*). Mallorca & Menorca. Resident breeder. This rare gull favours the rocky coastline of both islands. It's the size and light-grey colour of a typical "seagull" but boasts a rather splendid red bill. Unfortunately it takes three years for birds to reach this adult plumage and prior to this they are much less distinctive.

Bee-eater (*Merops apiaster*). Mallorca & Menorca. Mallorca: common spring visitor, rare summer breeder. Menorca: breeding summer visitor. A brightly coloured, medium-sized bird, with a slim body, long pointed wings and slightly de-curved bill. As if the iridescent green, orange, yellow and blue of this bird aren't distinctive enough, its bubbling "pruuk" call is instantly recognizable. It prefers open, relatively flat, rugged countryside.

(contd...)

Egyptian vulture (*Neophron percnopterus*). Mallorca & Menorca. Mallorca: rare migrant. Menorca: breeding resident. Medium-sized raptor with small, rather pointed protruding head and featherless face. Wings held flat when soaring.

Cattle egret (*Bubulcus ibis*). Mallorca & Menorca. Mainly winter visitor. This small heron-like wader is a regular winter visitor to the larger Balearic marshes. In winter it is white, but is distinguished from the little egret by its stubby all-yellow bill and stockier gait.

Night heron (*Nycticorax nycticorax*). Mallorca & Menorca. Mallorca: small resident population, increasing in summer with migrants. Menorca: spring and autumn migrant. Adults of this stocky, medium-sized heron are an attractive combination of black, grey and white. In contrast, younger birds up to three years old are a rather nondescript brown with cream speckling. This water bird is most active at night or dawn and dusk. By day they roost in the tree canopy or in large bushes.

Stone curlew (*Burhinus oedicnemus*). Mallorca & Menorca. Resident breeder, more common in summer. Thick-set wader that prefers dry rolling countryside to mud. Has a large, yellow, almost reptilian eye. Largely dull brown with some darker streaking, but with relatively distinctive long yellow legs. When in flight, its striking black and white wings become apparent.

Cory's shearwater (*Calonectris diomedea*). Mallorca & Menorca. Common breeder on offshore islands, but seen regularly all along the coast from March to August. Fairly large seabird. Like all the shearwaters, this bird flies close to the sea's surface with stiff outstretched wings. This pattern of flight as well as its size (nearly half a metre long with a wingspan of more than a metre) are its most distinctive features as its plumage is rather boring. At sea it appears dark-backed and dirty-white below. A close view should reveal some yellow on the bill and a white eye ring. Thousands breed on offshore islands across the Balearics and at sea they will often mix with the smaller, pale brown Mediterranean shearwater.

---

hanging on in the northern corner of the island, is the rarest. With no natural predators, its evolution involved a reduction in fecundity (it produces only a quarter of the number of eggs laid by its mainland relative) and the loss of its poison glands. This was fair enough until someone introduced the viperine snake to the island and, in the ensuing slaughter, the midwife toads were all but wiped out – only about five hundred pairs remain.

Common **insects** include grasshoppers and cicadas, whose summertime chirping is so evocative of warm Mediterranean nights, as well as over two hundred species of moth and around thirty types of **butterfly**. Some of the more striking butterflies are red admirals, which are seen in winter, and the clouded yellows and painted ladies of spring. One of the more unusual species is the two-tailed pasha, a splendidly marked gold-and-bronze butterfly that flits around the coast in spring and late summer, especially in the vicinity of strawberry trees.

Menorcan flora

Far flatter than its neighbour, Menorca's indigenous vegetation is almost all **garrigue**, though intensive cultivation has reduced the original forest cover to a fraction of its former size – nowadays only about fifteen percent of the island is wooded. Native trees are the holm oak, the dwarf palm, the carob and, commonest of all, the **Aleppo pine**, which has bright green spines, silvery twigs and ruddy-brown cones. Olive trees are endemic and illustrate the effects of the prevailing Tramuntana, with grove upon grove almost bent double under the weight of the wind.

Menorca's soils nourish a superb range of **flowering shrubs** and **wild flowers**. There is less variety than on Mallorca, but the islands have many species in common. In addition, Menorca boasts a handful of species entirely to itself, the most distinguished of them being the dwarf shrub **Daphne rodriquezii**, a purple-flowering evergreen, present on the cliffs of the northeast coast. In addition, the cliffs of much of the coast have a flora uniquely adapted to the combination of limestone yet saline soils. Here, **aromatic inula**, a shrubby perennial with clusters of yellow flowers, grows beside the **common caper**, with its red pods and purple seeds, and the **sea aster**.

Menorcan birds

The varied **birdlife** of Menorca includes birds of prey, wetland specialists, seabirds, waders and characteristic Mediterranean warblers, larks and pipits, but perhaps the most striking feature is the tameness of many of the birds – presumably because there is **less shooting** here than in almost any other part of the Mediterranean.

There are several ornithological hotspots, but wherever you are birds of prey should be evident. Of these, the Egyptian vulture is the most impressive; there are around a hundred of them, the only resident population in Europe. Red kites, booted eagles and ospreys can also be seen year round, and they are joined by marsh and hen harriers in winter. Peregrines, kestrels and, in winter, sparrow-hawks complete the more reliable raptors, although in spring and autumn several others – such as the honey buzzard and black kite – may appear. **Monte Toro** (see p.250), the highest point on Menorca, is as good a vantage point for birds of prey as any.

The island's **best birdwatching spot** is the marshland, reeds and *garrigue* (partly forested scrubland) fringing the lake of **S'Albufera**, near Es Grau (see p.239), which is itself part of the larger Parc Natural S'Albufera des Grau that extends north to Cap de Favaritx. The lake and its environs are popular with herons and egrets, the most elegant of wetland birds. Over the course of a year, little and cattle egrets, purple, grey, night and squacco herons can all be seen too. Booted eagles are also common, flying over the area, while the muddy parts of the marsh attract many smaller waders in spring and the leggy black-winged stilt in summer. The lake itself hosts several thousand ducks in winter. The nearby pine woodland, next to the beach at Es Grau, is used by night herons that rest high in the trees by day and then move onto the marsh at dusk. Also at dusk, listen out for the plaintive single note of the scops owl against a backdrop of warblers, crakes and crickets; and, most strikingly, the rich-toned song of the nightingale. The tiny firecrest is common in the woodland, and in the spring this whole area comes alive with hundreds of migrants.

Birds of Son Bou, Cala Tirant and the Cap de Cavalleria

There are smaller marshes elsewhere on the island and those at Cala Tirant in the north and Son Bou in the south are very good for birds. The wetland at **Son Bou** (see p.249) holds the island's largest reed-bed and the characteristic species of such a rich habitat are the noisy great reed warbler, moustached warbler and Cetti's warbler. The wetland at **Cala Tirant**, near Fornells, can be just as prolific and the sandy area just inland of the beach is a first-rate place to see the spectacular bee-eater, which breeds in several small colonies on the island. Nearby, the **Cap de Cavalleria** (see p.244), at the northern tip of the island, attracts the curious-looking stone curlew, several larks and pipits; and ospreys can often be seen fishing in the cape's **Port de Sanitja** (see p.245). Another special Balearic bird is the distinctive red-billed Audouin's gull, one of the world's rarest. A good place to see these is just off the coast by the lighthouse at the end of Cap de Cavalleria, where Mediterranean shags and shearwaters are also regularly seen. Audouin's gulls can also be seen in and around Maó.

Birds of the Algendar Gorge and Punta de S'Escullar

The lush vegetation in the bottom of the **Algendar Gorge**, just inland of **Cala Galdana** (see p.254), is a magnet for small birds and a perfect setting to hear nightingales and the short explosive song of Cetti's warbler. Above the gorge, booted eagles, Egyptian vultures and Alpine swifts nest. The ravine also attracts a wonderful array of butterflies.

Finally, although the barren, stony landscape of the northwest coast may seem an unpromising environment, **Punta de S'Escullar** is the site of one of the largest colonies of Cory's shearwaters in the western Mediterranean. Thousands return to their cliffside burrows in the late afternoon throughout the summer. This rugged terrain also hosts the attractive blue rock thrush and migrant chats, wheatears and black redstarts. Pallid swifts and crag martins also breed on the cliffs.

Other Menorcan fauna

Menorca's **mammals** are a low-key bunch, an undistinguished assortment of weasels, feral cats, hedgehogs, rabbits, hares, mice and shrews. The one highlight is the island's **reptiles**. Of the four species of Balearic lizard, Menorca has three. There are two types of **wall lizard** – Lilford's, a green, black and blue version, and the olive-green and black-striped Italian lizard – as well as the Moroccan rock lizard, with olive skin or reticulated blue-green coloration.

Common **insects** include grasshoppers and cicadas as well as over a hundred species of moth and around thirty types of **butterfly**. Three of the more striking butterflies are red admirals, which are seen in winter, and the clouded yellows and painted ladies, seen in spring.

Books

M ost of the books listed below are **in print and in paperback**, and those that are **out of print** (o/p) should be easy to track down either in secondhand bookshops or through Amazon's used and second-hand book service (🌐www.amazon.co.uk or www.amazon.com). That said, you may have a little more difficulty in finding those few titles we mention that are published locally either in Mallorca or Menorca, though in these cases we've given the name of the publisher. If you do have difficulty unearthing any title, one excellent specialist source of books about Spain – new, rare, used and out of print – is Paul Orssich, 2 St Stephen's Terrace, London SW8 1DH (☎020/7787 0030, 🌐www.orssich.com). Titles marked with the ⚞ symbol are especially recommended.

Travelogues

Sir John Carr *Descriptive Travels in the Southern and Eastern Parts of Spain and the Balearic Islands.* Written in 1811, and very much a period piece, Carr's detailed description of Mallorca is both well written and entertaining, though his anti-Semitism – the British consul in Palma was Jewish – is hard to bear.

Tom Crichton *Our Man in Majorca* (o/p). The American sailor, adventurer and journalist Tom Crichton was briefly a package-tour representative on Mallorca in the early 1960s. With the encouragement of Robert Graves, he published this account of a comical, disaster-filled fortnight. A book for the sunlounger.

Lucy McCauley (ed) *Spain: True Stories (Travelers' Tales).* It would be hard to better this anthology of writing on Spain, which gathers its short stories and journalism from the last twenty years. Featured authors include Gabriel García Márquez, Colm Tóibín and Louis de Bernières, whose "Seeing Red", on the tomato-throwing festival of Buñol, is worth the purchase price alone, and there's

also the striking "In a Majorcan Garden" by Jill Burberry.

George Sand *A Winter in Majorca.* Accompanied by her lover, Frédéric Chopin, Sand spent the winter of 1838–39 on Mallorca, holed up in the monastery of Valldemossa. These are her recollections, often barbed and sharp-tongued – and very critical of the islanders. Readily available in Valldemossa and Mallorca's better bookshops but otherwise o/p. Read an extract on p.129.

Gordon West *Jogging Round Majorca.* This gentle, humorous account of an extended journey round Mallorca by Gordon and Mary West in the 1920s vividly portrays the island's pre-tourist life and times. The trip had nothing to do with running, but rather "jogging" as in a leisurely progress. West's book lay forgotten for decades until a BBC radio presenter, Leonard Pearcey, stumbled across it in a secondhand bookshop and subsequently read extracts on air. The programmes were very well received, and the book was reprinted in 1994.

General background

Phil Ball *Morbo: The Story of Spanish Football.* Excellent account of the history of Spanish football from its

nineteenth-century beginnings with the British workers at the mines of Río Tinto in Huelva to the golden years of Real Madrid and the dark days of Franco. Ever-present as a backdrop is the ferocious rivalry or *morbo* – political, historical, regional and linguistic – which has driven the Spanish game since its birth. Essential reading for every football aficionado visiting (or even thinking about visiting) Spain.

Vicky Bennison *The Taste of a Place – Mallorca*. Enjoyable, well-illustrated book giving the lowdown on Mallorcan food and wine – not so much where to eat it, but more what it is like and where to buy it. Recipes too.

Anthony Bonner (ed.) *Doctor Illuminatus: A Ramon Llull Reader.* A selection from the lengthy and heavy-going treatises on mysticism and Christian zeal written by Llull, the thirteenth-century Mallorcan scholar and philosopher (see p.75). Llull's works were some of the first to be written in Catalan, but are not for the faint-hearted. A more manageable introduction to Llull is provided by Henry Carrigan (see below).

Henry Carrigan Jnr (ed.) *Romancing God: Contemplating the Beloved* (o/p). Billed as a "Christian Classic", this 120-page book serves as a useful introduction to the collected thoughts of Ramon Llull.

Barbara Catoir *Miró on Mallorca* (o/p). Lavishly illustrated, if somewhat dated book covering Miró's lengthy residence in Cala Major, just outside Palma. There's discussion of the work Miró produced in this period and of his thoughts on the island as a whole. Too hagiographical for some tastes, however.

🏃 **Brian Dendle & Shelby Thacker** *British Travellers in Mallorca in the Nineteenth Century: An Anthology of Texts.* There are perhaps no outstanding contributors in this

anthology, but the overall picture is intriguing and informative in equal measure: the engineer E.G. Bartholomew took a liking to stewed hedgehog ("dainty fat little joints") and the aristocrat Sir John Carr raved about the Jardins d'Alfàbia (see p.112) and was welcomed in style by the grandees of La Granja (see p.130).

Carrie B. Douglass *Bulls, Bullfighting and Spanish Identities* (o/p). Anthropologist Douglass delves into the symbolism of the bull in the Spanish national psyche, and then goes on to examine the bullfight's role in some of the thousands of fiestas countrywide that support it.

🏃 **Lucia Graves** *A Woman Unknown: Voices from a Spanish Life.* This moving memoir, by one of Robert Graves's children, is a succinct and thoughtful exploration of a life in between cultures – English and Mallorcan/Spanish. No-one has explored the deadening psychological weight of Franco's regime better.

Tomás Graves *Bread & Oil: Majorcan Culture's Last Stand.* Written by a son of Robert Graves, this intriguing and entertaining book explores Mallorca via its palate, with sections on what the islanders eat and how the ingredients end up where they do. Adopting a similar approach, but with music in mind, is the same author's *Tuning up at Dawn: A Memoir of Music and Majorca*.

William Graves *Wild Olives: Life in Mallorca with Robert Graves.* Another son of Robert Graves, William was born in 1940 and spent much of his childhood in Palma and Deià, sufficient inspiration for these mildly diverting accounts of his Mallorcan contemporaries. The book's real focus, however, is his troubled family life and his difficult relationship with his father.

Gijs van Hensbergen *Gaudí: the Biography*. At last, a worthy biography of one of the world's most distinctive architects. Van Hensbergen puts substantial flesh on the man while placing his work firmly in context.

John Hooper *The New Spaniards*. This excellent, authoritative portrait of post-Franco Spain was first written by *The Guardian's* former Spanish correspondent in the 1980s and published in a revised edition in 2006. It is one of the best possible introductions to contemporary Spain.

David Huelin (ed.) *Folk Tales of Mallorca*. The nineteenth-century priest and academic Mossèn Antoni Alcover spent decades collecting Mallorcan folk tales and this is a wide selection of them, running to almost 400 pages. They range from the intensely religious through to parable and proverb, but many reveal an unpleasant edge to rural island life, both vindictive and mean-spirited. Makes for intriguing background material, but unfortunately particular places on the island are never mentioned or described.

Robert Hughes *Goya*. No, there aren't any Goyas on public display in Mallorca or Menorca, but he was one of Spain's greatest painters and Hughes is arguably the world's finest writer on art – so we can't resist mentioning this book here. Hughes has written a simply fabulous biography, a gripping account of Goya's life and work, placed within the context of turbulent eighteenth- and early nineteenth-century Spain.

Arthur Koestler *Dialogue with Death* (o/p). Koestler was reporting the Civil War in 1937 when he was captured and imprisoned by Franco's troops – and this is essentially his prison diary.

Janis Mink *Miró* (o/p). Beautifully illustrated book that tracks through the artist's life and times. The text is rather ponderous, but there are lots of interesting quotations and, at 96 pages, you're not drowned in detail.

George Orwell *Homage to Catalonia*. Stirring account of Orwell's participation in, and early enthusiasm for, leftist revolution in Barcelona, followed by his growing disillusionment with the factional fighting that divided the Republican forces during the Civil War.

Jan Read *Wines of Spain* Encyclopaedic but still pocket-able guide to the classic and emerging wines of Spain by a leading authority. Includes maps, vintages and vineyards and has a chapter devoted to the Balearic and Canary islands. First published in 1983, it was last updated in 2001.

Miranda Seymour *Robert Graves: Life on the Edge*. Lengthy account of Robert Graves's personal life with lacklustre commentary on his poetry and novels. Includes much detail on Graves's residence in Deià.

Giles Tremlett *Ghosts of Spain*. Tremlett (*The Guardian's* Madrid correspondent) digs into the untold story of Spain's Civil War dead and the collective conspiracy of silence surrounding the war's terrors; he then goes on to peel away the layers of the post-Franco era to present an enthralling and often disturbing study of contemporary Spain.

History

David Abulafia *A Mediterranean Emporium: the Catalan Kingdom of Majorca*. Detailed, serious-minded study of medieval Mallorca that is

something of a specialist read. The same author's *The Western Mediterranean Kingdoms: The Struggle for Dominion 1200–1500* may be of more general appeal, though both – especially the former – are expensive.

Michael Baigent and Richard Leigh *The Inquisition*. Trenchant trawl through the history of this infamous institution from medieval beginnings to gradual collapse. Particularly good on the Inquisition's relationship with the papacy.

Antony Beevor *The Battle for Spain: The Spanish Civil War*. Long before Beevor hit the headlines with *Stalingrad*, he was ploughing an historical furrow – and this competent synopsis of the Civil War, running to just over three hundred pages, was first published in 1982.

Raymond Carr *The Spanish Tragedy: the Civil War in Perspective* and *Modern Spain 1875–1980*. Over the years, Carr has worked his way through Spain's convoluted history, producing a series of classic texts. These are two of the best, especially as both of them – unlike some of Carr's books – are relatively short and readily absorbed. Carr also edited and compiled the nine essays that comprise the much-praised *Spain: A History*.

Roger Collins *The Arab Conquest of Spain 710–97* (o/p). Much lauded, enjoyably concise study documenting the Moorish invasion of Spain and the significant influence that the conquered Visigoths had on early Muslim rule. Published in 1994, it's currently out of print but its companion title, Collins's *Visigothic Spain 409–711*, is still in print and contains an intriguing insight into what is an oft neglected corner of Spanish history. The same author's *Early Medieval Spain 400–1000* takes a broader overview of the same subjects.

🏃 **J.H. Elliott** *Imperial Spain 1469–1716*. The best introduction to Spain's "golden age" – academically respected as well as

being a gripping yarn. Also see his erudite *The Revolt of the Catalans: A Study in the Decline of Spain 1598–1640*, though this comes in at a whopping 648 pages.

Desmond Gregory *Minorca, the Illusory Prize: History of the British Occupation of Minorca between 1708 and 1802* (o/p). Exhaustive, scholarly and well-composed narrative detailing the British colonial involvement with Menorca. It's only published in hardback, however, and is therefore expensive.

🏃 **Henry Kamen** *The Spanish Inquisition: An Historical Revision*. A highly respected examination of the Inquisition and the long shadow it cast across Spanish history. Kamen's *Philip of Spain* was the first full biography of Felipe II, the ruler most closely associated with the Inquisition, and there's also his intriguing *Imagining Spain: Historical Myth and National Identity*.

Bruce Laurie *Life of Richard Kane: Britain's First Lieutenant Governor of Minorca* (o/p). Detailed (290-page) historical biography providing a fascinating insight into eighteenth-century Menorca. Only available in hardback – and consequently very pricey.

Fernando Martí *History of Menorca*. There aren't many dedicated histories of Menorca, but this is one, a curiously informal little book dotted with odd little details. Readable and of manageable length, but old hat – it was published in 1974.

🏃 **Geoffrey Parker** *The Army of Flanders and the Spanish Road (1567–1659)*. Sounds dry and academic, but this fascinating book gives a marvellous insight into the morals, manners and organization of the Spanish army, then the most feared in Europe.

Paul Preston *Franco: A Biography* and *The Spanish Civil War*. A penetrating – and monumental – biography of

Franco and his regime, which provides as clear a picture as any of how he won the Civil War and survived in power so long. The same author's *Spanish Civil War* is a compelling introduction to the subject and is also more accessible for the general reader than Hugh Thomas's work (see below). Preston's latest work is a similarly authoritative account of the life and times of the Spanish king entitled *Juan Carlos: A People's King*,

exploring in depth how Carlos helped move the country from beneath the long shadow of Franco.

Hugh Thomas *The Spanish Civil War*. Exhaustively researched, brilliantly detailed account of the war and the complex political manoeuvrings surrounding it, with a small section on Mallorca. First published in 1961, it remains the classic text on the subject.

Fiction and contemporary expat tales

Agatha Christie *Problem at Pollensa Bay*. Amongst her many attributes, Agatha Christie (1890–1976) was a pioneering world traveller, who spent long periods of time in the Middle East working on archeological digs alongside her husband Max Mallowan. Christie visited Mallorca on several occasions and the eponymous tale that gives this collection of short stories its title is redolent of the days when only the well-heeled few could visit the island.

Elena Davis *Witches, Oranges and Slingers: Half a Century on Mallorca*. Well, some expats may breeze in and out, but not Elena Davis, who first visited the island in 1955. The perspective adds an extra dimension to this 200-page memoir.

Juan Goytisolo *Marks of Identity, Count Julian, Juan the Landless*, and *Makbara*. Born in Barcelona in 1931, Goytisolo became a bitter enemy of the Franco regime and has spent most of his life in exile in Paris and Morocco. Widely acclaimed as one of Spain's leading modern novelists, his most celebrated works (the first three titles listed above) confront ambivalent ideas of Spain and Spanishness. The fourth title above (from 1980) explores the Arab culture of North Africa in sharp and perceptive style. Goytisolo has also written an autobiography, *Forbidden Territory*.

Ernest Hemingway *The Sun Also Rises* and *For Whom the Bell Tolls*. Hemingway remains a big part of the American myth of Spain – *The Sun Also Rises* contains some lyrically beautiful writing, while the latter – set in the Civil War – is a good deal more laboured. Hemingway also published two books on bullfighting, the better of which is the enthusiastic *Death in the Afternoon* (1932).

Roderic Jeffries *Sun, Sea and Murder*. Jeffries has turned out a number of murder mysteries set in Mallorca with Inspector Alvarez as his protagonist cop. The author is a Londoner by birth, but is now resident on the island. Other novels in the Alvarez series that are currently in print and in paperback include *The Ambiguity of Murder, An Artistic Way to Go* and *A Maze of Murders*.

Peter Kerr *Snowball Oranges: One Mallorcan Winter*. Scottish farmer moves to a farmhouse in Mallorca – and loves it. In fact, he loves it so much that he goes on to write *Manana, Manana: One Mallorcan Summer; Viva Mallorca! One Mallorcan Autumn*; and *A Basketful of Snowflakes: One Mallorcan Spring*.

Sian Mackay *Rafael's Wings* Mackay knows contemporary Mallorca like the back of her hand and, although the drama at the centre of the book doesn't work too well, there's all sorts of interesting stuff on the island, its customs and predicaments.

Chuck Maisel *Majorca, Paradise Not Lost: Living the Dream on a Spanish Island*. More tales of expat lives and rural idylls – this time one is a painter, the other a writer.

Javier Marias *Tomorrow in the Battle Think on Me*. There are many who rate Marias as Spain's finest contemporary novelist – and the evidence is here in this searching, psychological thriller with its study of the human capacity for concealment and confession. Several other Marias novels are also available in English translation, including *A Heart So White* and *All Souls*.

Manuel Vázquez Montalbán *Murder in the Central Committee, An Olympic Death, The Angst-ridden Executive, Off Side*. Original and wonderfully entertaining tales by the man who was, until his untimely death in 2003, Spain's most popular crime thriller writer. A long-time member of the Communist Party and Barcelona resident, Montalbán became a well-known journalist in post-Franco Spain. His great creation was the gourmand private detective Pepe Carvalho. If this quartet of titles whets your appetite, move on to *Southern Seas* and a world of disillusioned Communists, tawdry sex and nouvelle cuisine – Montalbán's trademark ingredients – but don't bother with his very disappointing *The Man of My Life*.

Anna Nicholas *A Lizard in my Lounge*. Racy tale of the author's breathless escape from PR hell in Mayfair to sun-kissed evenings in rural Mallorca. One of a trilogy – *Goats from a Small Island* and *Cat on a Hot Tiled Roof* are the other two and both plough a similar furrow. Full marks to Nicholas for getting to know the island and its inhabitants.

George Scott *The Bloody Bokhara* (o/p). Set in modern-day Mallorca, this detective thriller was the literary debut of a long-term island resident and hotel owner, the American George Scott. It's a fairly good yarn, if a bit ponderously written, and is excellent for background information – as is his second novel, *The Chewed Caucasian*.

Llorenç Villalonga *The Dolls' Room* (o/p). Subtle if somewhat laboured portrait of nobility in decline in nineteenth-century Mallorca. Villalonga (1897–1980) was Mallorca's most prominent writer for several decades, but none of his books is currently in print in English. The author's old house in Binissalem is now a museum (see p.180).

Carlos Ruiz Zafón *The Angel's Game*. The fastest selling book in Spanish publishing history, this lengthy novel is an idiosyncratic mix of supernatural thriller-chiller and murder mystery. It's set in the backstreets of Barcelona in the early twentieth century.

Specialist guidebooks

David & Rosamund Brawn The Brawns produce regularly updated hiking books and hiking maps of both islands. In the hiking books, directions are almost always easy to follow and each slim booklet comes with a 1:25,000 or 1:40,000 map;

they're inexpensive too. Current offerings include the *Menorca Tour & Trail Map* (2009); the *Mallorca North and Mountains Tour and Trail Map* (2009); the *Palma South Tour & Trail Map* (2008); the *Palma North Tour & Trail Map* (2008); *Walk! Mallorca West*

(2005); and *Walk! Menorca* (2005). Brawn publications are, however, almost impossible to find on Mallorca or Menorca, so get them beforehand from a major supplier or direct from Discovery UK (ⓦwww.walking .demon.co.uk). For recommended **hiking maps**, see Basics p.43.

Gaspar Martí *Walking Tours Around the Historical Centre of Palma* (Ajuntament de Palma, Mallorca; o/p). Detailed and enjoyable exploration of Palma's historical nooks and crannies. Quality sketches illuminate the text. Published by Palma city council and available in most leading bookshops in the city.

June Parker *Walking in Mallorca.* Refreshed in 2006, this popular hiking guide is easily the most detailed book on its subject currently on the market. Published by Cicerone – and up to their usual high standard.

Flora and fauna

Michael Eppinger *Field Guide to the Wild Flowers of Britain and Europe.* Published in 2006, this is the most recent field guide on this subject.

Christopher Grey-Wilson, et al. *Wild Flowers of the Mediterranean.* Excellent, comprehensive field guide.

Graham Hearl *A Birdwatching Guide to Mallorca* (o/p) and *A Birdwatching Guide to Menorca, Ibiza and Formentera* (o/p). First-rate descriptions of where to see what bird in every one of the Balearic islands. There is a handy bird checklist at the back of both books and the text is sprinkled with useful local maps. The sketches of various birds are, however, not very illuminating – so you'll still need a field guide – and both books could do with an update as they were published in the mid-1990s.

Lars Jonsson *Birds of Europe.* As good a field guide as the Collins guide by Mullarney et al. (see below), but more specialized.

Killian Mullarney, et al. *Collins Bird Guide: The Most Complete Field Guide to the Birds of Britain and Europe.* Excellent field guide to birds – there's nothing better on the market.

Language

Language

Language

n recent years the Balearics have attracted thousands of migrants from the rest of western Europe and today German, English, Catalan and Spanish are all widely spoken. Traditionally, the islanders are bilingual, speaking **Castilian** (Spanish) and their local dialect of the **Catalan** language – *Mallorquín* or *Menorquín* – with equal facility. *Català* (Catalan) has been the islanders' everyday language since the absorption of the Balearics into the medieval Kingdom of Aragón and Catalunya in the thirteenth century; Castilian, on the other hand, was imposed much later as the official language of government and business at the instigation of Madrid – and with special rigour by Franco. Almost inevitably, therefore, Spain's recent move towards regional autonomy has been accompanied by the islanders' re-assertion of Catalan as their official language. The most obvious sign of this has been the change of all the old Castilian town and street names into their Catalan equivalents.

On paper, **Catalan** looks like a cross between French and Spanish and is generally easy to understand if you know those two languages, although when it is spoken it has a very harsh sound and is surprisingly hard to come to grips with.

Numerous **Spanish phrasebooks and dictionaries** are available with the most user-friendly being Rough Guide's *Spanish Dictionary Phrasebook*. No **English–Catalan phrasebook** is currently in print and the pick of several **dictionaries** is published by Oxford University Press.

Introduction

When **Franco** came to power in 1939, *Català* publishing houses, bookshops and libraries were raided and their books destroyed. Furthermore, throughout his dictatorship Franco excluded Catalan from the radio, TV, daily press and, most importantly, the schools, which is why many older people cannot read or write *Català* even if they speak it all the time. More recently, the islands' linguistic jigsaw has been further complicated by the emigration of thousands of mainland Spaniards to the islands, and nowadays it's estimated that Castilian is the dominant language in around forty percent of Balearic households.

Català is a Romance language, stemming from Latin and more directly from medieval Provençal, and is spoken by over six million people in the Balearics, Catalunya, part of Aragón, most of Valencia, Andorra and parts of the French Pyrenees; it is thus much more widely used than several better-known languages such as Danish, Finnish and Norwegian. While Spaniards in the rest of the country often belittle it by saying that to get a *Català* word you just cut a Castilian one in half (which is often true), in fact the grammar is much more complicated than Castilian and there are eight vowel sounds, three more than in Castilian.

www.roughguides.com

Getting by in Mallorca and Menorca

Although Catalan is the preferred **language** of most islanders, you'll almost always get by perfectly well if you speak Castilian (Spanish), as long as you're aware of the use of Catalan in timetables and so forth. Once you get into it, Castilian is one of the easiest languages there is, the rules of pronunciation pretty straightforward and strictly observed. You'll find some basic pronunciation rules below for both Catalan and Castilian, and a selection of words and phrases in both languages. Castilian is certainly easier to pronounce, but don't be afraid to try Catalan, especially in the more out-of-the-way places – you'll generally get a good reception if you at least try communicating in the local language.

Castilian (Spanish): a few rules

Unless there's an accent, words ending in d, l, r, and z are **stressed** on the last syllable, all others on the second to last. All **vowels** are pure and short; combinations have predictable results.

A somewhere between b**a**ck and f**a**ther.

E as in g**e**t.

I as in pol**i**ce.

O as in h**o**t.

U as in r**u**le.

C is lisped before E and I, hard otherwise: cerca is pronounced "thairka".

CH is pronounced as in English.

G is a guttural H sound (like the ch in lo**ch**) before E or I, a hard G elsewhere: gigante is pronounced "higante".

H is always silent.

J is the same sound as a guttural G: jamón is pronounced "hamon".

LL sounds like an English Y: tortilla is pronounced "torteeya".

N as in English, unless it has a tilde (ñ) over it, when it becomes NY: mañana sounds like "man-yaana".

QU is pronounced like an English K.

R is rolled, RR doubly so.

V sounds more like B, vino becoming "beano".

X has an S sound before consonants, a KS sound before vowels.

Z is the same as a soft C, so cerveza is pronounced "thairvaitha".

Catalan: a few rules

With *Català*, don't be tempted to use the few rules of Castilian pronunciation you may know – in particular the soft Spanish Z and C don't apply, so unlike in the rest of Spain it's not "Barthelona" but "Barcelona", as in English.

A as in h**a**t if stressed, as in **a**lone when unstressed.

E varies, but usually as in g**e**t.

I as in pol**i**ce.

IG sounds like the "**tch**" in the English scratch: lleig (ugly) is pronounced "yeah-tch".

O varies, but usually as in h**o**t.

U lies somewhere between p**u**t and r**u**le.

Ç sounds like an English S: plaça is pronounced "plassa".

C followed by an E or I is soft; otherwise hard.

G followed by E or I is like the "zh" in Zhivago; otherwise hard.

H is always silent.

J as in the French "**J**ean".

LL sounds like an English Y or LY, like the "yuh" sound in "million".

N as in English, though before F or V it sometimes sounds like an M.

NY replaces the Castilian Ñ.

QU before E or I sounds like K; before A or O as in "quit".

R is rolled, but only at the start of a word; at the end it's often silent.

T is pronounced as in English, though sometimes it sounds like a D, as in viatge or dotze.

TX is like the English CH.

V at the start of a word sounds like B; in all other positions it's a soft F sound.

W is pronounced like a B/V.

X is like SH in most words, though in some, like exit, it sounds like an X.

Z is like the English Z.

Useful words and phrases

Basics

English	Castilian	Catalan
Yes, No, OK	Sí, No, Vale	Si, No, Val
Please, Thank you	Por favor, Gracias	Per favor, Gràcies
Where, When	Dónde, Cuándo	On, Quan
What, How much	Qué, Cuánto	Què, Quant
Here, There	Aquí, Allí, Allá	Aquí, Allí, Allà
This, That	Esto, Eso	Això, Allò
Now, Later	Ahora, Más tarde	Ara, Més tard
Open, Closed	Abierto/a, Cerrado/a	Obert, Tancat
With, Without	Con, Sin	Amb, Sense
Good, Bad	Buen(o)/a, Mal(o)/a	Bo(na), Dolent(a)
Big, Small	Gran(de), Pequeño/a	Gran, Petit(a)
Cheap, Expensive	Barato/a, Caro/a	Barat(a), Car(a)
Hot, Cold	Caliente, Frío/a	Calent(a), Fred(a)
More, Less	Más, Menos	Més, Menys
Today, Tomorrow	Hoy, Mañana	Avui, Demà
Yesterday	Ayer	Ahir
Day before yesterday	Anteayer	Abans-d'ahir
Next week	La semana que viene	La setmana que ve
Next month	El mes que viene	El mes que ve

Greetings and responses

English	Castilian	Catalan
Hello, Goodbye	Hola, Adiós	Hola, Adéu
Good morning	Buenos días	Bon dia
Good afternoon/night	Buenas tardes/noches	Bona tarda/nit
See you later	Hasta luego	Fins després
Sorry	Lo siento/discúlpeme	Ho sento
Excuse me	Con permiso/perdón	Perdoni
How are you?	¿Cómo está (usted)?	Com va?

I (don't) understand	(No) Entiendo	(No) Ho entenc
Not at all/You're welcome	De nada	De res
Do you speak English?	¿Habla (usted) inglés?	Parla anglès?
I (don't) speak	(No) Hablo Español	(No) Parlo Català
My name is...	Me llamo...	Em dic...
What's your name?	¿Cómo se llama usted?	Com es diu?
I am English	Soy inglés/esa	Sóc anglès/esa
Scottish	escocés/esa	escocès/esa
Australian	australiano/a	australià/ana
Canadian	canadiense/a	canadenc(a)
American	americano/a	americà/ana
Irish	irlandés/esa	irlandès/esa
Welsh	galés/esa	gallès/esa

Hotels and transport

English	Castilian	Catalan
I want	Quiero	Vull (pronounced "fwee")
I'd like	Quisiera	Voldria
Do you know...?	¿Sabe...?	Vostès saben...?
I don't know	No sé	No sé
There is (is there?)	(¿)Hay(?)	Hi ha(?)
Give me...	Deme...	Doneu-me...
Do you have...?	¿Tiene...?	Té...?
...the time	...la hora	...l'hora
...a room	...una habitación	...alguna habitació
...with two beds/	...con dos camas/	...amb dos llits/
double bed	cama matrimonial	llit per dues persones
...with shower/bath	...con ducha/baño	...amb dutxa/bany
for one person	para una persona	per a una persona
(two people)	(dos personas)	(dues persones)
for one night	para una noche	per una nit
(one week)	(una semana)	(una setmana)
It's fine, how much is it?	Está bien, ¿cuánto es?	Esta bé, quant és?
It's too expensive	Es demasiado caro	És massa car
Don't you have anything cheaper?	¿No tiene algo más barato?	En té de més bon preu?
Can one...?	¿Se puede...?	Es pot...?
...camp (near) here?	¿...acampar aquí (cerca)?	...acampar a la vora?
Is there a hostel nearby?	¿Hay un hostal aquí cerca?	Hi ha un hostal a la vora?
It's not very far	No es muy lejos	No és gaire lluny
How do I get to...?	¿Por dónde se va a...?	Per anar a...?
Left, right, straight on	Izquierda, derecha, todo recto	A l'esquerra, a la dreta,tot recte
Where is...?	¿Dónde está...?	On és...?

...the bus station	...la estación de autobuses	...l'estació de autobuses
...the bus stop	...la parada	...la parada
...the railway station	...la estación de ferrocarril	...l'estació
...the nearest bank	...el banco más cercano	...el banc més a prop
...the post office	...el correo/ la oficina de correos	...l'oficina de correus
...the toilet	...el baño/aseo/servicio	...la toaleta
Where does the bus to... leave from?	¿De dónde sale el autobús para...?	De on surt el auto bús a…?
Is this the train for Barcelona?	¿Es este el tren para Barcelona?	Aquest tren va a Barcelona?
I'd like a (return) ticket to...	Quisiera un billete (de ida y vuelta) para...	Voldria un bitllet (d'anar i tornar) a...
What time does it leave (arrive in...)?	¿A qué hora sale (llega a...)?	A quina hora surt (arriba a...)?
What is there to eat?	¿Qué hay para comer?	Què hi ha per menjar?
What's that?	¿Qué es eso?	Què és això?

Days of the week

English	Castilian	Catalan
Monday	lunes	dilluns
Tuesday	martes	dimarts
Wednesday	miércoles	dimecres
Thursday	jueves	dijous
Friday	viernes	divendres
Saturday	sábado	dissabte
Sunday	domingo	diumenge

Months of the year

English	Castilian	Catalan
January	enero	gener
February	febrero	febrer
March	marzo	març
April	abril	abril
May	mayo	maig
June	junio	juny
July	julio	juliol
August	agosto	agost
September	septiembre	setembre
October	octubre	octubre
November	noviembre	novembre
December	diciembre	desembre

Numbers

English	Castilian	Catalan
1	un/uno/una	un(a)
2	dos	dos (dues)
3	tres	tres
4	cuatro	quatre
5	cinco	cinc
6	seis	sis
7	siete	set
8	ocho	vuit
9	nueve	nou
10	diez	deu
11	once	onze
12	doce	dotze
13	trece	tretze
14	catorce	catorze
15	quince	quinze
16	dieciséis	setze
17	diecisiete	disset
18	dieciocho	divuit
19	diecinueve	dinou
20	veinte	vint
21	veintiuno	vint-i-un
30	treinta	trenta
40	cuarenta	quaranta
50	cincuenta	cinquanta
60	sesenta	seixanta
70	setenta	setanta
80	ochenta	vuitanta
90	noventa	novanta
100	cien(to)	cent
101	ciento uno	cent un
102	ciento dos	cent dos (dues)
200	doscientos	dos-cents (dues-centes)
500	quinientos	cinc-cents
1000	mil	mil
2000	dos mil	dos mil

Food and drink

Although we've provided a reasonably extensive **Castilian and Catalan menu reader** below, most restaurants, cafés and bars have **multilingual menus**, with English, Catalan and Castilian almost always three of the options. The main exceptions are out in the countryside, where there may only be a Catalan menu or maybe no menu at all, in which case the waiter will rattle off the day's dishes in Catalan or sometimes Castilian.

Basics

English	Castilian	Catalan
Bread	Pan	Pa
Butter	Mantequilla	Mantega
Cheese	Queso	Formatge
Eggs	Huevos	Ous
Fruit	Fruta	Fruita
Garlic	Ajo	All
Oil	Aceite	Oli
Pepper	Pimienta	Pebre
Rice	Arroz	Arròs
Salt	Sal	Sal
Sugar	Azúcar	Sucre
Vinegar	Vinagre	Vinagre
Vegetables	Verduras/Legumbres	Verdures/Llegumes
To have breakfast	Desayunar	Esmorzar
To have lunch	Almorzar	Dinar
To have dinner	Sopar	Cenar
Menu	Carta	Menú
Bottle	Botella	Ampolla
Glass	Vaso	Got
Fork	Tenedor	Forquilla
Knife	Cuchillo	Ganivet
Spoon	Cuchara	Cullera
Table	Mesa	Taula
The bill/check	La cuenta	El compte
Grilled	A la brasa	A la planxa
Fried	Frit	Fregit
Stuffed/rolled	Relleno	Farcit
Casserole	Guisado	Guisat
Roast	Asado	Rostit

Fruit (fruita) and vegetables (verdures/llegumes)

English	Castilian	Catalan
Apple	Manzana	Poma
Asparagus	Espárragos	Espàrrecs
Aubergine/eggplant	Berenjenas	Albergínies
Banana	Plátano	Plàtan
Carrots	Zanahorias	Pastanagues
Cucumber	Pepino	Concombre
Grapes	Uvas	Raïm
Melon	Melón	Meló

Mushrooms	Champiñones	Xampinyons (also bolets, setes)
Onions	Cebollas	Cebes
Orange	Naranja	Taronja
Peach	Melocotón	Préssec
Pear	Pera	Pera
Peas	Arvejas	Pèsols
Pineapple	Piña	Pinya
Potatoes	Patatas	Patates
Strawberries	Fresas	Maduixes
Tomatoes	Tomates	Tomàquets

Bocadillos fillings

English	Castilian	Catalan
Catalan sausage	Butifarra	Butifarra
Cheese	Queso	Formatge
Cooked ham	Jamón York	Cuixot dolç
Cured ham	Jamón serrano	Pernil salat
Loin of pork	Lomo	Llom
Omelette	Tortilla	Truita
Salami	Salami	Salami
Sausage	Salchichón	Salxitxó
Spicy sausage	Chorizo	Xoriç
Tuna	Atún	Tonyina

Tapas and racions

English	Castilian	Catalan
Anchovies	Boquerones	Anxoves
Stew	Cocido	Bollit
Squid, usually deep-fried in rings	Calamares	Calamars
Squid in ink	Calamares en su tinta	Calamars amb tinta
Snails, often served in a spicy/curry sauce	Caracoles	Cargols
Cockles (shellfish)	Berberechos	Cargols de mar
Whole baby squid	Chipirones	Calamarins
Meat in tomato sauce	Carne en salsa	Carn amb salsa
Fish or chicken croquette	Croqueta	Croqueta
Fish or meat pasty	Empanadilla	Empanada petita
Russian salad (diced vegetables in mayonnaise)	Ensaladilla	Ensalada russa
Aubergine (eggplant) and pepper salad	Escalibada	Escalibada

Broad beans	Habas	Faves
Beans with ham	Habas con jamón	Faves amb cuixot
Liver	Hígado	Fetge
Prawns	Gambas	Gambes
Mussels (either steamed, or served with diced tomatoes and onion)	Mejillones	Musclos
Razor clams	Navajas	Navallas
Olives	Aceitunas	Olives
Hard-boiled egg	Huevo cocido	Ou bollit
Bread, rubbed with tomato and oil	Pan con tomate	Pa amb tomàquet
Potatoes in garlic mayonnaise	Patatas alioli	Patates amb all i oli
Fried potato cubes with spicy sauce and mayonnaise	Patatas bravas	Patates cohentes
Meatballs, usually in sauce	Albóndigas	Pilotes
Kebab	Pincho moruno	Pinxo
Octopus	Pulpo	Pop
Sweet (bell) peppers	Pimientos	Prebes
Kidneys in sherry	Riñones al jerez	Ronyons amb xeres
Sardines	Sardinas	Sardines
Cuttlefish	Sepia	Sípia
Tripe	Callos	Tripa
Potato omelette	Tortilla española	Truita espanyola
Plain omelette	Tortilla francesa	Truita francesa
Pepper, potato, pumpkin and aubergine (eggplant) stew with tomato purée	Tumbet	Tumbet
Mushrooms, usually fried in garlic	Champiñones	Xampinyons
Spicy sausage	Chorizo	Xoriç

Selected Balearic dishes and specialities

Many of the **specialities** that follow come from the Balearics' shared history with Catalunya. The more elaborate fish and meat dishes are usually limited to the fancier restaurants.

Sauces	
Salsa mahonesa	Mayonnaise
Allioli	Garlic mayonnaise
Salsa romesco	Spicy tomato and wine sauce to accompany fish (from Tarragona)

Soups (sopa), starters and salads (amanida)	
Amanida catalana	Salad with sliced meat and cheese
Carn d'olla	Mixed meat soup
Entremesos	Starter of mixed meat and cheese

Escalivada	Aubergine/eggplant, pepper and onion salad
Escudella	Mixed vegetable soup
Espinacs a la Catalana	Spinach with raisins and pine nuts
Esqueixada	Dried cod salad with peppers, tomatoes, onions and olives
Fideus a la cassola	Baked vermicelli with meat
Llenties guisades	Stewed lentils
Pa amb oli	Bread rubbed with olive oil, eaten with ham, cheese or fruit
Samfaina	Ratatouille-like stew of onions, peppers, aubergine/eggplant and tomato
Sopa d'all	Garlic soup
Sopas mallorquínas	Vegetable soup, sometimes with meat and chickpeas (garbanzos)
Truita (d'alls tendres; de xampinyons; de patates)	Omelette/tortilla (with garlic; with mushrooms; with potato). Be sure you're ordering omelette (tortilla), not trout (truita).

Rice dishes

Arròs a banda	Rice with seafood, the rice served separately
Arròs a la marinera	Paella: rice with seafood and saffron
Arròs negre	"Black rice", cooked with squid ink
Paella a la Catalana	Mixed meat and seafood paella, sometimes distinguished from a seafood paella by being called Paella a Valencia

Meat (carn)

Albergínies en es forn	Aubergines/eggplants stuffed with grilled meat

Botifarra amb mongetes	Spicy blood sausage with white beans
Conill (all i oli)	Rabbit (with garlic mayonnaise)
Escaldum	Chicken and potato stew in an almond sauce
Estofat de vedella	Veal stew
Fetge	Liver
Fricandó	Veal casserole
Frito mallorquín	Pigs' offal, potatoes and onions cooked with oil
Mandonguilles	Meatballs, usually in a sauce with peas
Perdius a la vinagreta	Partridge in vinegar gravy
Pollastre (farcit; amb gambas; al cava)	Chicken (stuffed; with prawns; cooked in sparkling wine)
Porc (rostit)	Pork (roast)
Sobrasada	Finely minced pork sausage, flavoured with paprika

Fish (peix) and shellfish (marisc)

Bacallà (amb samfaina)	Dried cod (with ratatouille)
Caldereta de llagosta	Lobster stew
Cloïsses	Clams, often steamed
Espinagada de Sa Pobla	Turnover filled with spinach and eel
Greixonera de peix	Menorcan fish stew, cooked in an earthenware casserole
Guisat de peix	Fish and shellfish stew
Llagosta (amb pollastre)	Lobster (with chicken in a rich sauce)
Lluç	Hake, either fried or grilled
Musclos al vapor	Steamed mussels
Pop	Octopus
Rap a l'all cremat	Monkfish with creamed garlic sauce
Sarsuela	Fish and shellfish stew
Suquet	Fish casserole
Truita	Trout (sometimes stuffed with ham, a la Navarre)

Desserts (postres) and pastries (pastas)

Cocaroll	Pastry containing vegetables and fish
Crema Catalana	Crème caramel, with caramelized sugar topping
Ensaimada	Flaky spiral pastry, often with fillings such as cabello de
	ángel (sweetened citron rind)
Mel i mató	Curd cheese and honey
Postres de músic	Cake of dried fruit and nuts
Turrón	Almond fudge
Xurros	Deep-fried doughnut sticks (served with hot chocolate)

Drinking

English	Castilian	Catalan
Water	Agua	Aigua
Mineral water	Agua mineral	Aigua mineral
(sparkling)	(con gas)	(amb gas)
(still)	(sin gas)	(sense gas)
Milk	Leche	Llet
Juice	Zumo	Suc
Tiger nut drink	Horchata	Orxata
Coffee	Café	Café
Espresso	Café solo	Café sol
White coffee	Café con leche	Café amb llet
Decaf	Descafeinado	Descafeinat
Tea	Té	Te
Drinking chocolate	Chocolate	Xocolata
Beer	Cerveza	Cervesa
Wine	Vino	Vi
Champagne/ Sparkling wine	Champán/Cava	Xampan/Cava

Glossary

Glossary of Catalan terms

Ajuntament Town Hall

Albufera Lagoon (and surrounding wetlands)

Altar major High altar

Aparcament Parking

Avinguda (Avgda) Avenue

Badía Bay

Barranc Ravine

Barroc Baroque

Basílica Catholic church with honorific privileges

Cala Small bay, cove

Camí Way or road

Ca'n At the house of (contraction of casa and en)

Capella Chapel

Carrer (c/) Street

Carretera Road, highway

Castell Castle

Celler Cellar, or a bar in a cellar

Claustre Cloister

Coll Col, mountain pass

Convent Convent, nunnery or monastery

Correu Post office

Coves Caves

Església Church

Estany Small lake

Festa Festival

Finca Estate or farmhouse

Font Water fountain or spring

Gòtic Gothic

Illa Island

Jardí Garden

Llac Lake

Mercat Market

Mirador Watchtower or viewpoint

Modernisme Literally "modernism", the Catalan form of Art Nouveau, whose most famous exponent was Antoni Gaudí; adjective "*Modernista*".

Monestir Monastery

Mozarabe A Christian subject of a medieval Moorish ruler; hence **Mozarabic**, a colourful building style that reveals both Christian and Moorish influences.

Mudéjar A Moorish subject of a medieval Christian ruler. Also a style of architecture developed by Moorish craftsmen working for Christians, characterized by painted woodwork with strong colours and complex geometrical patterns; revived between the 1890s and 1930s and blended with Art Nouveau.

Museu Museum

Nostra Senyora The Virgin Mary ("Our Lady")

Oficina d'Informació Turistica Tourist office

Palau Palace, mansion or manor house

Parc Park

Passeig Boulevard; the evening stroll along it

Pic Summit

Plaça Square

Platja Beach

Pont Bridge

Port Harbour, port

Porta Door, gate

Puig Hill, mountain

Rambla Avenue or boulevard

Reconquista The Christian Reconquest of Spain from the Moors beginning in the ninth century and culminating in the capture of Granada in 1492.

Rei King

Reial Royal

Reina Queen

Reixa Iron screen or grille, usually in front of a window

Renaixença Rebirth, often used to describe the Catalan cultural revival at the end of the nineteenth and beginning of the twentieth centuries. Architecturally, this was expressed as Modernisme.

Retaule Retable or reredos, a wooden ornamental panel behind an altar

Riu River

Romeria Pilgrimage or gathering at a shrine

Salinas Saltpans

Santuari Sanctuary

Sant/a Saint

Serra Mountain range

Talayot Cone-shaped prehistoric tower

Taula T-shaped prehistoric megalithic structure

Torrent Stream or river (usually dry in summer)

Urbanització Modern estate development

Vall Valley

LANGUAGE

Glossary

Glossary of English art and architectural terms

Ambulatory Interior covered passage around the outer edge of the choir in the chancel of a church.

Apse Semicircular protrusion (usually) at the east end of a church.

Art Deco Geometrical style of art and architecture popular in the 1930s.

Art Nouveau Style of art, architecture and design based on highly stylised vegetal forms. Popular in the early part of the twentieth century.

Balustrade An ornamental rail, running, almost invariably, along the top of a building.

Baroque The art and architecture of the Counter-Reformation, dating from around 1600 onwards. Distinguished by its ornate exuberance and (at its best) complex but harmonious spatial arrangement of interiors. Some elements – particularly its gaudiness – remained popular in the Balearics well into the twentieth century.

Caryatid A sculptured female figure used as a column.

Chancel The eastern part of a church, often separated from the nave by a screen; contains the choir and ambulatory.

Churrigueresque Fancifully ornate form of Baroque named after its leading exponents, the Spaniard José Churriguera (1650–1723) and his extended family.

Classical Architectural style incorporating Greek and Roman elements – pillars, domes,

colonnades, and so on – at its height in the seventeenth century and revived, as Neoclassical, in the nineteenth.

Clerestory Upper storey of a church, incorporating the windows.

Cyclopean Prehistoric style of dry-stone masonry comprising boulders of irregular form.

Fresco wall painting – durable through application to wet plaster.

Gothic Architectural style of the thirteenth to sixteenth centuries, characterized by pointed arches, rib vaulting, flying buttresses and a general emphasis on verticality.

Majolica See p.149.

Nave Main body of a church.

Neoclassical Architectural style derived from Greek and Roman elements – pillars, domes, colonnades, and so on – that was popular in the nineteenth century.

Plateresque Elaborately decorative Renaissance architectural style, named for its resemblance to silversmiths' work (platería).

Renaissance That period of European history – beginning in Italy in the fourteenth century – that marks the end of the medieval and the beginning of the early modern era. It is defined, amongst many criteria, by an increase in classical scholarship, geographical discovery, the rise of secular values and the growth of individualism; the term is also applied to the art and architecture of the period.

www.roughguides.com

319

Retable Altarpiece.

Romanesque Early medieval architecture distinguished by squat forms, rounded arches and naive sculpture.

Rood screen Decorative screen separating the nave from the chancel; a rood loft is the gallery (or space) on top of it.

Stucco Marble-based plaster used to embellish ceilings, etc.

Transept Arms of a cross-shaped church, placed at ninety degrees to nave and chancel.

Triptych Carved or painted work on three panels.

Tympanum Sculpted, usually recessed, panel above a door.

Vault An arched ceiling or roof.

Es Molí
HOTEL
★★★★

Ctra. Valldemossa - Deià, s/n - 07179 DEIÀ - MALLORCA
Tel.: +34 971 63 90 00 - Fax: +34 971 63 93 33
reservas@esmoli.com

www.esmoli.com

Small print and
Index

A Rough Guide to Rough Guides

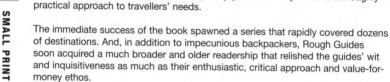
Published in 1982, the first Rough Guide – to Greece – was a student scheme that became a publishing phenomenon. Mark Ellingham, a recent graduate in English from Bristol University, had been travelling in Greece the previous summer and couldn't find the right guidebook. With a small group of friends he wrote his own guide, combining a highly contemporary, journalistic style with a thoroughly practical approach to travellers' needs.

The immediate success of the book spawned a series that rapidly covered dozens of destinations. And, in addition to impecunious backpackers, Rough Guides soon acquired a much broader and older readership that relished the guides' wit and inquisitiveness as much as their enthusiastic, critical approach and value-for-money ethos.

These days, Rough Guides include recommendations from shoestring to luxury and cover more than 200 destinations around the globe, including almost every country in the Americas and Europe, more than half of Africa and most of Asia and Australasia. Our ever-growing team of authors and photographers is spread all over the world, particularly in Europe, the US and Australia.

In the early 1990s, Rough Guides branched out of travel, with the publication of Rough Guides to World Music, Classical Music and the Internet. All three have become benchmark titles in their fields, spearheading the publication of a wide range of books under the Rough Guide name.

Including the travel series, Rough Guides now number more than 350 titles, covering: phrasebooks, waterproof maps, music guides from Opera to Heavy Metal, reference works as diverse as Conspiracy Theories and Shakespeare, and popular culture books from iPods to Poker. Rough Guides also produce a series of more than 120 World Music CDs in partnership with World Music Network.

Visit www.roughguides.com to see our latest publications.

Rough Guide travel images are available for commercial licensing at www.roughguidespictures.com

Rough Guide credits

Text editor: Brendon Griffin
Layout: Pradeep Thapliyal
Cartography: Maxine Repath
Picture editor: Emily Taylor
Production: Rebecca Short
Proofreader: Margaret Doyle
Cover design: Dan May, Chloë Roberts
Photographer: Simon Bracken, Suzanne Porter
Editorial: Ruth Blackmore, Andy Turner, Keith
Drew, Edward Aves, Alice Park, Lucy White,
Jo Kirby, James Smart, Natasha Foges, Róisín
Cameron, James Rice, Emma Traynor, Emma
Gibbs, Kathryn Lane, Monica Woods, Mani
Ramaswamy, Harry Wilson, Lucy Cowie, Alison
Roberts, Joe Staines, Peter Buckley, Matthew
Milton, Tracy Hopkins, Ruth Tidball; **Delhi**
Madhavi Singh, Karen D'Souza, Lubna Shaheen
Design & Pictures: **London** Scott Stickland,
Dan May, Diana Jarvis, Mark Thomas, Nicole
Newman, Sarah Cummins; **Delhi** Umesh
Aggarwal, Ajay Verma, Jessica Subramanian,
Ankur Guha, Sachin Tanwar, Anita Singh, Nikhil
Agarwal, Sachin Gupta.

Production: Liz Cherry
Cartography: **London** Ed Wright, Katie Lloyd-
Jones; **Delhi** Rajesh Chhibber, Ashutosh Bharti,
Rajesh Mishra, Animesh Pathak, Jasbir Sandhu,
Karobi Gogoi, Alakananda Bhattacharya, Swati
Handoo, Deshpal Dabas
Online: **London** Faye Hellon, Jeanette Angell,
Fergus Day, Justine Bright, Clare Bryson, Aine
Fearon, Adrian Low, Ezgi Celebi; **Delhi** Amit
Verma, Rahul Kumar, Narender Kumar, Ravi
Yadav, Debojit Borah, Rakesh Kumar, Ganesh
Sharma, Shisir Basumatari
Marketing & Publicity: **London** Liz Statham,
Louise Maher, Jess Carter, Vanessa Godden,
Vivienne Watton, Anna Paynton, Rachel
Sprackett, Laura Vipond; **New York** Katy Ball,
Judi Powers; **Delhi** Ragini Govind
Reference Director: Andrew Lockett
Operations Assistant: Becky Doyle
Operations Manager: Helen Atkinson
Publishing Director (Travel): Clare Currie
Commercial Manager: Gino Magnotta
Managing Director: John Duhigg

Publishing information

This fifth edition published April 2010 by
Rough Guides Ltd,
80 Strand, London WC2R 0RL
14 Local Shopping Centre, Panchsheel Park,
New Delhi 110017, India
Distributed by the Penguin Group
Penguin Books Ltd,
80 Strand, London WC2R 0RL
Penguin Group (USA)
375 Hudson Street, NY 10014, USA
Penguin Group (Australia)
250 Camberwell Road, Camberwell,
Victoria 3124, Australia
Penguin Group (Canada)
195 Harry Walker Parkway N, Newmarket, ON,
L3Y 7B3 Canada
Penguin Group (NZ)
67 Apollo Drive, Mairangi Bay, Auckland 1310,
New Zealand
Cover concept by Peter Dyer.

Typeset in Bembo and Helvetica to an original
design by Henry Iles.

Printed in Singapore

© Phil Lee, 2010

Maps © Rough Guides

No part of this book may be reproduced in any
form without permission from the publisher except
for the quotation of brief passages in reviews.

336pp includes index

A catalogue record for this book is available from
the British Library

ISBN: 978-1-84836-473-8

The publishers and authors have done their best
to ensure the accuracy and currency of all the
information in **The Rough Guide to Mallorca
and Menorca**, however, they can accept no
responsibility for any loss, injury, or inconvenience
sustained by any traveller as a result of
information or advice contained in the guide.

1   3   5   7   9   8   6   4   2

Help us update

We've gone to a lot of effort to ensure that
the fifth edition of **The Rough Guide to
Mallorca and Menorca** is accurate and up-to-
date. However, things change – places get
"discovered", opening hours are notoriously
fickle, restaurants and rooms raise prices or lower
standards. If you feel we've got it wrong or left
something out, we'd like to know, and if you can
remember the address, the price, the hours, the
phone number, so much the better.

Please send your comments with the subject
line "**Rough Guide Mallorca and Menorca
Update**" to ✉mail@roughguides.com. We'll credit
all contributions and send a copy of the next
edition (or any other Rough Guide if you prefer)
for the very best emails.
   Have your questions answered and tell others
about your trip at ✆www.roughguides.com

Acknowledgements

Phil Lee would like to thank his editor, Brendon Griffin, for his thorough and efficient attention to detail during the preparation of this new edition of Mallorca and Menorca. Special thanks also to Maria Peterson and Richard Strutt for their help with all sorts of queries; Rosie Davies for the restaurant reviews; George Scott as always; James Hiscock for the chance to eat a hedgehog; Ilse Bock; and the author Anna Nicholas for pointing me in the right direction in Sóller.

SMALL PRINT

Readers' letters

Thanks to all the readers who have taken the time to write in with comments and suggestions (and apologies if we've inadvertently omitted or misspelt anyone's name):

Javier Berastain; Roger Berkley; Peter Bettess; Christopher Bowers; Derek Brampton; Philip Burnard; Tom Coley; S.M.Cooper; Jane Crawford-Baker; William J Drake; Rob Duckett; Hugo & Sue Dunknley; Nina Holmes; Nadia Hull; Carl Jackson; Coloma Jaume; Hugh Josty; Carmela Lo Presti; M.J.D. Mackenzie; Judy Mallett; S.F.A. Martin; Andy Mitter; Clive Paul; Mandy Revel; Cherie Rogers; Eric & Sally Rowland; Carol Saddington; David Taylor; Ronald Turnbull; Judith Weller; Paul Westlake.

www.roughguides.com

Photo credits

All photos © Rough Guides except the following:

Title page
Palma Cathedral © Fantuz Olimpio/SIME/
  4 Corners

Full page
Cala Fornells, Mallorca © Canali Pietro/
  SIME/4 Corners

Introduction
Locals in Alcudia © Kaos02/SIME/4 Corners
Serra de Tramuntana, Mallorca © Siepmann
  Siepmann/Photolibrary

Things not to miss
02 Valldemossa, Mallorca © www.flickr.com/
  photos/hywell/1200772841/
04 Cabrera Island © Pictures Colour Library

Great places to stay colour section
Holiday *finca* in Mallorca © Andreas Prott/
  iStock
Gran Hotel Soller © Mark Dyball/Alamy

Island hiking colour section
Serra de Tramuntana, near Valldemossa
  © Siepmann Siepmann/Photolibrary
Dry-stone walls in Menorca © www.flickr
  .com/photos/enbodenumer/3276343545
Hiking in Sant Elm © FAN Travel Stock/
  Alamy Black European Vulture (*Aegypius
  monachus*) © Richard Kolar/Photolibrary
Hiking in Serra de Tramuntana
  © imagebroker/Alamy
Hiking from Deia to Port de Soller
  © www.flickr.com/photos/
  enbodenumer/3276351077

Black and whites
p.50 Palma Cathedral © www.flickr.com/photos/
  beastman/2489400011
p.143 Cap Formentor, Mallorca © www.flickr
  .com/photos/gheeke/2774286826/
p.225 Mao, Menorca © Bartomeu Amengual/
  Photolibrary
p.263 Ciutadella harbour in Menorca © Andrew
  Hill/iStock

Index

Map entries are in colour.

Map symbols

maps are listed in the full index using coloured text ·

– – –	Chapter divisions boundary		🕯	Lighthouse
▬▬▬	Motorway		⬇	Viewpoint
═══	Main road		⋀	Spring
═══	Minor road		🏛	Stately home
───	Unpaved road		🌳	Gardens
▓▓▓	Pedestrianized road		⌒	Arch
- - - -	Footpath		𝝠	Campsite
⊞⊞⊞	Steps		◉	Accommodation
▬·▬	Railway		▣	Restaurant
⊢⊢⊢⊢	Tram line		ⓘ	Information office
— —	Ferry route		⊠	Post office
───	Waterway		@	Internet access
───	Wall		✈	Airport
♦	Point of interest		★	Bus stop/taxi stand
⸶	Church/cathedral (regional maps)		🅿	Parking
⋔	Monastery		⊞	Hospital
♛	Castle		▬	Building
▆	Tower		⊞	Church (town maps)
∴	Ruin		▨	Park
⌓	Cave		▨	Beach
▲	Mountain peak		▨	Saltpan
⌇	Cliff		⊞	Restricted area

So now we've told you about the things not to miss, the best places to stay, the top restaurants, the liveliest bars and the most spectacular sights, it only seems fair to tell you about the best travel insurance around

WorldNomads.com
keep travelling safely

Recommended by Rough Guides

www.roughguides.com
MAKE THE MOST OF YOUR TIME ON EARTH

ROUGH
GUIDES